Scott, Foresman
Language

Authors
Ronald L. Cramer
James Beers
DeWayne Triplett
Norman Najimy
Linda Ward Beech
Chris Welles Feder
Tara McCarthy

Educational Consultants
Marcia L. Anker
Robert Davis

Reader Consultants
Irene Boschken
Teri Coburn

Scott, Foresman and Company
Editorial Offices:
Glenview, Illinois

Regional Offices:
Sunnyvale, California
Tucker, Georgia
Glenview, Illinois
Oakland, New Jersey
Dallas, Texas

Acknowledgments

Text

All dictionary entries and pronunciation symbols have been reprinted from the *Scott, Foresman Advanced Dictionary*. E. L. Thorndike and Clarence L. Barnhart. Copyright © 1988, Scott, Foresman and Company. All thesaurus entries have been reprinted from *In Other Words: A Junior Thesaurus*. Andrew Schiller and William A. Jenkins. Copyright © 1987, Scott, Foresman and Company.

p. 14: Harold Krents, *To Race the Wind*. New York: G. P. Putnam's Sons and International Creative Management, 1972, pp. 84–85: **p. 16:** From *The Red Pony* by John Steinbeck. Copyright 1933, 1937, 1938 by John Steinbeck. Copyright renewed © 1961, 1965, 1966 by John Steinbeck. Reprinted by permission of Viking Penguin Inc. and William Heinemann Ltd.; **p. 18:** Excerpt from *Phoebe and the General* by Judith Berry Griffin, text copyright © 1977 by Judith Berry Griffin. Reprinted by permission of Coward, McCann & Geoghegan, Inc.; **p. 19:** Cynthia Voight, *Dicey's Song*. New York: Atheneum, 1982; **p. 24:** Marjorie Kinnan Rawlings, *The Yearling*. New York: Charles Scribner's Sons, 1938; **p. 26:** Rosa Guy, *Paris, Pee Wee, and Big Dog*. New York: Delacorte Press, 1984, p. 84; **p. 26:** From "The Circuit" by Francisco Jiménez. Reprinted by permission of the author; **pp. 50–54, 62:** "Lucas and Jake" and an excerpt from pp. 106–107 from *I Thought You Were a Unicorn and Other Stories* by Paul Darcy Boles. Copyright © 1963 by Paul Darcy Boles. First appeared in *Seventeen* Magazine. Reprinted by permission of Little, Brown and Company and

ISBN 0-673-27508-6
Copyright © 1989
Scott, Foresman and Company, Glenview, Illinois.
All Rights Reserved.
Printed in the United States of America.

1234567890-KPH-979695949392919089 88

Russell & Volkening, Inc. as agents for the author; **pp. 90–93:** Lincoln Colcord, "Rölvaag the Fisherman Shook His Fist at Fate." *American Magazine*, 1928, pp. 36–37; **p. 130:** Samuel Scoville, Jr., "The Reef." *St. Nicholas Magazine*, 1923; **p. 136:** From *The Hobbit* by J.R.R. Tolkien. Copyright © 1966 by J.R.R. Tolkien. Reprinted by permission of Houghton Mifflin Company and Urwin Hyman Ltd. **p. 141:** N. Scott Momaday, *The Names*. New York: Harper & Row, Publishers, Inc., 1976, pp. 5–6; **p. 142:** Winifred Madison, *Maria Luisa*. New York: J. B. Lippincott Company, 1971, p. 41; **p. 144:** Nicholasa Mohr, *El Bronx Remembered*. New York: Harper & Row, Publishers, Inc., 1975, pp. 48–49; **p. 172:** "Fog" from *Chicago Poems* by Carl Sandburg, copyright 1916 by Holt, Rinehart and Winston, Inc.; renewed 1944 by Carl Sandburg. Reprinted by permission of Harcourt Brace Jovanovich, Inc.; **p. 172:** "Morning Mood" by M. Panegoosho in *I Breathe a New Song, Poems of the Eskimo* edited by Richard Lewis. Copyright © 1971 by Richard Lewis. Reprinted by permission of Richard Lewis; **p. 173:** "Women" from *Revolutionary Petunias and Other Poems*, copyright © 1973 by Alice Walker. Reprinted by permission of Harcourt Brace Jovanovich, Inc. and David Higham Associates Ltd.; **p. 178:** Excerpted from "The Seal" by William Jay Smith from *Laughing Time: Nonsense Poems* by William Jay Smith, published in 1980 by Delacorte Press, copyright © 1957, 1980 by William Jay Smith. Reprinted by permission; **pp. 208–211:** From *Flavio* by Gordon Parks. Copyright © 1978 by Gordon Parks. Reprinted by permission. **p. 254:** From *How Things Work* by Michael Pollard. Copyright © 1978 by Ward Lock Limited. Reprinted by permission of Ward Lock Limited; **p. 257:** From *All About Horses* by Marguerite Henry. Copyright © 1962 by Marguerite Henry. Reprinted by permission of Random House, Inc.; **p. 264:** From "One Smart Bird" by Katherine Hauth. Appeared in *Cricket*, November 1983. Reprinted by permission of the author; **pp. 286–287:** Excerpt from *Fifth Chinese Daughter* by Jade Snow Wong. Copyright 1945, 1948, 1950 by Jade Snow Wong. Reprinted by permission of Harper & Row, Publishers, Inc. and Curtis Brown Ltd.; **pp. 322–324:** "Rhythmic Gymnastics" by Herma Silverstein. Copyright © 1986 *Highlights*

(Acknowledgments cont. p. 610)

Warm-up Time

Narrative Writing
Theme: The Power of Words

SECTION

2

SECTION

3

Narrative Writing
Theme: Breakthroughs

88

Descriptive Writing
Theme: The Seas Around Us   128

Descriptive Writing
Theme: Encounters **206**

SECTION 6

ix

x

Explanatory Writing
Theme: Americans All   284

Persuasive Writing
Theme: Spare Time

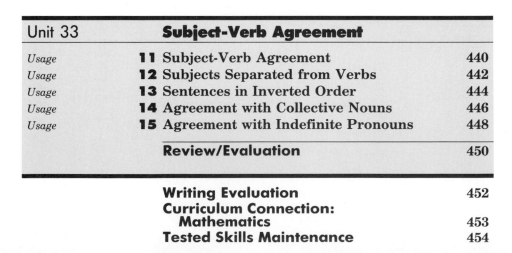

Persuasive/Analytical Writing
Theme: A Far Other Time   **456**

Handbooks

Skills Summary

Tested Skills

1. Drawing Conclusions
2. Paragraphs: Main Idea
3. Writing a Narrative Paragraph
4. Writing a Friendly Letter
5. Kinds of Sentences
6. Subjects and Predicates
7. Correcting Sentence Fragments
8. Correcting Run-on Sentences
9. Writing a Short Story
10. Plural Nouns
11. Identifying Kinds of Pronouns
12. Writing a Personal Experience Narrative
13. Distinguishing Action/Linking Verbs
14. Principal Parts of Verbs
15. Perfect Tenses
16. Comparison and Contrast
17. Paragraphs: Topic Sentences
18. Writing a Descriptive Paragraph
19. Writing a Comparison/Contrast Description
20. Functions of Adverbs
21. Comparative Forms
22. Using *good, well, bad,* and *badly*
23. Writing a Poem
24. Kinds of Prepositional Phrases
25. Identifying Conjunctions
26. Writing a Character Study
27. Commas in Writing
28. Quotation Marks
29. Capitalization: Nouns, Adjectives, Titles
30. Cause and Effect
31. Making Analogies
32. Writing an Explanatory Paragraph
33. Writing a Cause/Effect Paragraph
34. Writing a Business Letter
35. Appositives
36. Combining Subjects/Predicates
37. Direct Objects and Subject Complements
38. Indirect Objects
39. Writing a How-to Report
40. Possessive Nouns
41. Pronoun Homophones
42. Using Reflexive, Intensive, and Indefinite Pronouns

Tested Skills (cont.)

Grammar, Usage, Mechanics Skills

Sentences

Nouns and Pronouns

Grammar, Usage, Mechanics Skills (cont.)

Grammar, Usage, Mechanics Skills (cont.)

Warm-up Time

A new school year is just beginning. It's time to get ready to learn. The warm-up activities that follow contain tips, tools, skills, and strategies to help you become a better listener, speaker, reader, and writer. When you complete these activities, you'll be on the right track for success all through the year.

Parts of a Book

You don't have to eat all the meals served in a restaurant to be able to judge its food. You also don't have to read a whole book to find out what kind of information it contains. Just as restaurants have menus, books have parts that tell what's inside.

Table of Contents This is similar to a menu. From beginning to end, the table of contents tells the chapter titles, or titles of stories and articles, and the page on which each begins. You can tell a lot about what's in a book by its table of contents.

Index This is similar to a list of ingredients. Topics and subtopics are listed alphabetically, giving all the pages where you will find them in the book. Use the index to learn quickly whether the book mentions the specific topic you want.

Preface This introduces many nonfiction books and some fiction books. It may provide a general outline of the book, or it may give the author's reasons for writing the book. Some restaurant menus have similar paragraphs from the owners or chefs.

Title and Copyright Pages The title page names the book's title, the author, and the publisher. The copyright page, on the back side of the title page, could be compared to the date on a carton of milk. It includes a publication date that tells you how new or old the product is. It also gives some details, such as the publisher's complete address and how many printings the book has had.

Glossary Some books have a glossary, which gives the meanings of some words in the book. You could liken a glossary to a menu that gives explanations of the dishes in a foreign-food restaurant.

Appendix At the ends of some books, appendices provide additional information, special charts and graphs, or guides to further information. A restaurant often has a dessert menu for the "appendix" to your dinner.

Activity Find several books on one main topic and explore their various features. Ask yourself some questions about the topic and look for clues to the answers in the tables of contents and indexes. Divide the books into three piles: (1) could really use for a report; (2) might be useful; (3) no way.

Study Conditions and Habits

Have you ever watched a real pro make pizza? Plop! goes the dough on the floured counter. Punch! go the hands to flatten out the dough. In a flash the dough is thin enough to toss into the air, spinning itself even thinner. With a flick of the wrist, the pizza maker spreads sauce and casually tosses on mushrooms, onions, peppers, and cheese. Within minutes the pizza is in the oven.

What does this have to do with studying? The pizza maker has two things to teach us: a **system** and **practice.** Every gesture is planned. Every gesture was practiced and repeated over and over. The result is that the pizza maker turns out dozens of pizzas in the time it might take you to make just one. With a system and a little practice, you can turn out more homework and better homework than ever before.

Here is a brief summary of a system that will help you study more effectively. As you read, notice the order of steps in the system.

The LEARNER Study System

> **LEARNER** stands for
> *L*isten, *E*xamine, *A*sk, *R*ead, *N*ote, *E*ase away, and *R*eview.

Listen to class discussions and for details about assignments.
Examine your materials before you read them. Look for charts, pictures, summaries, glossaries, and so on that help you understand the materials.
Ask questions. As you skim the materials, form questions about who, what, where, when, why, and how.
Read the materials carefully to answer the questions and to discover new facts.
Note the facts you learn. Write careful notes. Make charts, construct time lines, draw pictures or diagrams.
Ease away from the materials. Take a break. Reward yourself before going on to another subject.
Review your notes often to keep your memory fresh. Summarize the facts on paper. Use a colored pencil to underline important terms, names, dates, and statistics that you need to remember.

Once you have a system for studying, you also need to make sure that "all conditions are go" for getting enough practice. Here are two areas that will help you get the practice you need.

Study Conditions   You can create conditions that make studying satisfying and effective. Make sure you have a regular time for study. Don't try to fit it in between TV and bedtime! You may find it best to study in two shorter periods of time rather than all at once each day.

Find a quiet place that, at least during your study time, you can call your own. Assemble all the equipment you need: pencils, erasers, notebooks, textbooks, and so on. If your study space is shared or used for other activities, keep your supplies in a box you can carry with you. Make sure the place is comfortable and well lighted.

Habits   Few people can remember lots of facts without taking notes. As you read, and as you listen in class, you should get in the habit of writing down the important facts. You might want to use one of the following methods to help organize your facts.

- Make a comparison-contrast chart relating one set of facts to another.
- Make a time line showing how events are related.
- Make flash cards for vocabulary words, math problems, grammar facts, important dates.

Make your own "educational toys" so that at least some of your studying becomes a game.

Activity A.   Copy the labels of the LEARNER system (*Listen, Examine, Ask,* etc.) onto a card or piece of paper. Keep it with your study materials, or put it on the wall in your study space as a constant reminder. Follow the steps as often as you can.

Activity B.   During the next two weeks, try various note-taking methods. Make at least one chart, one time line, and one set of flash cards for appropriate subjects. Invent one "educational game" you can play, with a partner or by yourself, to help you remember what you are studying.

Kinds of Tests

By now, you have had some experience in taking tests. If you know how tests are made, then you can concentrate on the subjects of the tests. Here are some reminders about how to prepare for and take tests.

General   Keep up with your studies. If you have made studying a habit, and if you have used a system like the LEARNER Study System, you will feel quite confident going into a test.

Read through the entire test first. This will give you a chance to plan your time. Decide how much time you will devote to each section of the test.

Do the easy items first. Answering them will give you confidence, and the answers may even give you clues to the other, harder questions.

True-False Items   Make sure a statement is completely true before you mark it as true. Beware of words like *always* and *never*.

Completion Items   Your answer must make sense in the sentence that it completes. Don't write a noun where a verb is required.

Multiple-Choice Items   Cross out the obviously incorrect answer choices. Then it will be easier to find the right answer.

Match Items   Do the easy matches first, and cross them out as you go. Then the remaining items won't be as confusing.

Short-Answer Items   Make sure each answer makes sense in terms of the question asked. Check your spelling.

Essay Items   Prepare an essay answer the same way you would do a homework essay. Read the question carefully, and underline key words. On scrap paper or in your head, make notes about what you want to put in the answer. Write a strong beginning sentence, which may be a rewrite of the question. Then write one or more sentences for each note you made. End with a strong summary. More information on essay tests appears in the Study Skills Handbook.

Activity   Work with two classmates. Choose a subject you all have been studying. Write two of each kind of test item and exchange papers. Take each other's tests and compare results.

Spelling Power

Good news! You already know how to spell thousands of words. You can write them without thinking too much about them. You should be having trouble with only a few "old enemies" and some new words as you come across them. (Will I ever stop writing *bicycle* as *bicicle?* Where does the **y** go, anyway?)

There's a sign in a country store that says, "There are no strangers . . . only friends we haven't met." New words may seem strange at first, and you may think you'll never learn how to spell them. With a little time and practice, however, you will become familiar enough with them to spell them with confidence and then use them in your writing.

Here is a plan for learning how to spell a word.

A Study Plan for Spelling

1. Look at the word. Say it and listen to its sounds.
2. Say the letters in order.
3. Close your eyes and recall the letters.
4. Write the word while looking at it.
5. Cover the word and write it. Check to see if you spelled it correctly. If not, repeat the steps.
6. Write the word correctly two more times.

You should use the six steps on any new word you see. For now, here are twenty words for you to use the plan on.

accept	difference	personal	receive
affect	excellence	piece	recommend
already	government	prejudice	similar
article	library	principal	their
course	pastime	principle	there

Word Pruning

Some long words look impossible to learn. They have five or six syllables, and they seem to have dozens of vowels. The longer you look at such words, the more it seems that the letters are swimming around, changing places. How can you master these monster words? Prune them!

Many long words are made up of smaller units of meaning. Just separate the meaningful parts and learn them in isolation from each other. Take a word like *photosynthesis,* which is the word for the process by which the cells of green plants make carbohydrates by combining carbon dioxide and water in the presence of light. It is made up of two word parts: *photo* (light) and *synthesis* (combination of parts). Since you already know how to spell *photo,* you can concentrate on *synthesis.* The word *predisposition* has three meaningful parts: The prefix *pre-,* the root *dispose,* and the noun-forming ending *-tion.*

Hard-Word List

One way to keep track of the words you need to learn is to list them in a place where you will see them often. You could list your spelling "demons" on a sheet of paper and tape it to the inside cover of a notebook, for instance. When you master one list, replace it with another.

Activity A.   Use the six-step plan to learn the spellings of the twenty words listed in this lesson. If you don't know the meaning of a word, look it up in the dictionary. Then choose one of the following challenges.

- Choose ten of the words, list them in alphabetical order, and write a story using the words in that order.
- Have a contest with a few of your classmates. Choose one of the words and then see who can make up the most smaller or different words using only the letters in the spelling word. Give extra credit to anyone who uses *all* the letters of the original word in the new word.
- Choose other words from the list and follow the same procedure for each one.

Activity B. Find five words that you can prune, and write down their separate parts. Use a dictionary that shows word origins.

Developing a Writer's Notebook

The notebooks of many great scientists are filled with "failures." The files of many successful writers are full of rejection slips from publishers. Engineers and architects often have to "go back to the drawing board." Are these people failures? Definitely not! They have found ways to succeed by keeping track of their work and learning from their mistakes.

All writing is experimental. No writer knows for sure how a story or article will turn out until it has been written and, often, rewritten. If an experiment doesn't succeed, a good writer figures out what went wrong and tries again.

As you write, you will begin to develop a style. To keep track of your experiments with style, you should keep a *writer's notebook*. This is different from a journal, which is where you keep your ideas and where you practice your writing. A writer's notebook is a place to analyze your writing and to note, for future reference, how you can improve it.

As you complete writing assignments in this book, you will work to analyze and improve your writing style. During the year, you will be keeping a notebook to record your analyses. Following are suggestions for developing your writer's notebook.

Sentence Variety   If all your sentences are the same length and have the same structure, you may put your readers to sleep. In this section of your notebook, you can analyze your work to make sure your sentences are not all the same.

Powerful Verbs   You can pack more action into every story and article you write simply by using verbs that capture your readers' imaginations. As you revise your work to replace dull or overused verbs, you can record the results in your notebook. Later, you can come back to the notebook for fresh ideas.

Creating Vivid Images   Have you ever read a story in which you could almost hear the characters talking, see the scenery, feel the emotions, even smell the air? In this section of your notebook, you can record your progress in appealing to your readers' senses through carefully chosen words and phrases.

Wordiness   We have all been guilty of this. We say or write "the place in which" instead of "where." We write "The dog gave a howl" instead of "The dog howled." Government officials are likely to say "at this point in time" instead of "at this time" or "now." In this section of your notebook, you can record your wordy sentences and how you fixed them.

Precise Words   Do you want to say *tool* or *wrench? car* or *limousine? sad* or *miserable?* Your first drafts may contain some vague or lifeless words simply becaue they're so familiar and easy to write. In this section of your notebook, you can record your attempts to find just the right words.

Context Clues   Writers usually don't try to confuse their readers. If you use special terms, you must provide definitions of them. Often you can provide enough information in the words surrounding the special terms so that the readers can figure out their meanings. Your notebook is the place to record the results of your experiments with context clues.

Specific Details   "Can't you be more specific?" Your ideas may be great, but they will be hard to believe unless you can support them with specific details. In this section of your notebook, you can show how you have improved your paragraphs to make them more convincing.

Sentence Combining   You can make your writing style smoother and clearer by combining shorter sentences of related ideas. Sentences like "It snowed all night. School will not open today" can be combined in this manner: "Since it snowed all night, schools will not open today." Not only have you replaced two choppy sentences with one smoother one, but you have also shown the relationship between the events. You will want to fix sentences like these and record the various techniques you used in your writer's notebook.

Activity Get or make up a loose-leaf notebook with eight dividers. Label the dividers with the section titles given on these two pages. Keep your notebook with you when you write or revise. Throughout this textbook, you can write in your notebook the things you learn about your own writing style.

Narrative Writing

Theme: Family Matters

What does the word *family* make you think of? You may associate the word with particular people, certain occasions, or special feelings. Whatever the associations, **family matters** are a recurring theme in literature, as you will see in many of the excerpts in this section. As you complete the writing assignments in Unit 2, consider narrating a family experience or corresponding with a family member.

1 Literature: Narrative Writing

Because families share so much, one person's problem can become a family matter. Harold Krents, the author of the passage below, learns at age nine that he is going to lose his sight. This news affects both him and his parents. Read the excerpt to learn what Harold decides to do. Notice how the author narrates, or tells, what happens.

from **To Race the Wind** *by Harold Krents*

That night I lay there and argued the pros and cons of a life of dependence on others or a life of independence. Of course, the argument was handled at a nine-year-old level, but the problem was wrestled with nonetheless.

"It would be kind of nice to have people always doing things for me," I thought. "People would feel very sorry for me, and so I'd get a lot of attention."

However, the argument on the other side was just as strong.

"You like running around, and if you let everybody do things for you, you'll just sit. Besides, who really wants everybody to feel sorry for you."

It was very, very late when I finally determined that I wanted to be independent.

I went into my parents' room and found them still awake.

"I want to try to fight," I said. "I don't want everybody to feel sorry for me just because I can't see. I want to pick up again like nothing has happened and make it here—right here."

"Harold, it isn't going to be easy, I don't honestly know how or where we're going to be able to do it now . . . how you're going to read, how we can work it out. But I promise you we're going to find out. If it's Braille we must learn, then we'll learn it. Only I can't promise that we'll do it here. If your chances are better of making it in blind school, then I guess it will have to be that. But one thing I can promise you, whatever we decide will be only because it will be better for you. And if we find out that we can do it right here, it will be a rough road, Hal—probably much tougher than it would be in the blind world. Will you help Mom and me to make the decision when the time comes?" Dad asked quietly.

"I've made it already. I want to stay here."

► **Discussing**

1. What did Harold decide to do?
2. Why did Harold want to be independent?
3. What arguments did Harold present to himself?
4. How did Harold's father react to his son's decision?
5. Why do you think Harold's father said it would be tougher to stay at home rather than go to blind school?
6. What kind of person do you think Harold's father is? Why?
7. What would you have done if you were Harold? Why?

► **Analyzing: Narrative Writing**

Narrative writing relates an event or story. It gives details of a particular event or a series of events. The details are usually given in the order in which they occurred. Novels, short stories, histories, and biographies are forms of narration.

The following events occurred in Harold's life. Write them in the correct order.

Harold thought about his problem.
Harold learned that he was going to be blind.
Harold talked to his father.
Harold decided that he wanted to be independent.

► **Writing**

Pretend you are one of Harold's teachers. Write a paragraph or two telling what kind of person Harold is. Also predict how you think he will cope with his handicap.

► **Extending**

Speaking and Listening   Meet with classmates in a small group to make up a story about a family matter. Think of a situation like Harold's, where what happens to one family member affects the rest of the family. If you want, you can base the story on a real experience that happened to someone in the group. Select one person in the group to tell the story to the rest of the class.

Reading   *A Summer to Die,* by Lois Lowry, is about a serious family matter. It is the story of how a thirteen-year-old girl copes with her older sister's degenerating health and eventual death.

2 Sequencing

Sequence is the arrangement of events in time order.

▶ **Focus**   As you read and write, you need to know the **sequence,** or order, in which events happen. There are many kinds of sequence, but time order, the arrangement of details in chronological order, is most often used in narrative writing. In the excerpt from *To Race the Wind* in Lesson 1, the events of Harold's life were given in time order.

Read the passage below from *The Red Pony* by John Steinbeck. The sequence of events in it also follows time order. At this point in the novel, a farmhand named Billy Buck has told a boy named Jody that he can leave his pony outside because it will not rain that day.

> Billy Buck wasn't wrong about many things. He couldn't be. But he was wrong about the weather that day, for a little after noon the clouds pushed over the hills and the rain began to pour down. Jody heard it start on the schoolhouse roof. He considered holding up one finger for permission to go to the outhouse and, once outside, running for home to put the pony in. Punishment would be prompt both at school and at home. He gave it up and took ease from Billy's assurance that rain couldn't hurt a horse. When school was finally out, he hurried home through the dark rain. The banks at the sides of the road spouted little jets of muddy water. The rain slanted and swirled under a cold and gusty wind. Jody dogtrotted home, slopping through the gravelly mud of the road.

from **The Red Pony**
by John Steinbeck

▶ **Guided Practice**   Billy Buck said it wouldn't rain. What happened after that? Discuss where to add the three events below, in sequence, to the time line at the bottom of the page.

Jody considered running home   school let out   rain began

Billy Buck said it wouldn't rain.	Jody recalled Billy's assurance that rain would not hurt a horse.	Jody dogtrotted home.

► **Practice** **A.** Continue reading Jody's story in the passage below. Then sequence the events in time order. The first and last events have been filled in for you.

From the top of the ridge he could see Gabilan standing miserably in the corral. The red coat was almost black, and streaked with water. He stood head down with his rump to the rain and wind. Jody arrived running and threw open the barn door and led the wet pony in by his forelock. Then he found a gunny sack and rubbed the soaked hair and rubbed the legs and ankles. Gabilan stood patiently, but he trembled in gusts like the wind.

Events

1. Jody saw Gabilan from ridge.   Gabilan stood with head down.
2. _____   Jody arrived running.
3. _____   He rubbed Gabilan's legs.
4. _____   Jody saw Gabilan from ridge.
5. _____   Jody found a gunny sack.
6. _____   Gabilan trembled in gusts.
7. Gabilan trembled in gusts.   Jody opened the barn door.

B. Read these additional paragraphs from *The Red Pony*. Then make a time line for the five underlined events. One of the events is presented out of time order in the paragraphs.

When he had dried the pony as well as he could, Jody went up to the house and brought hot water down to the barn and soaked the grain in it. Gabilan was not very hungry. He nibbled at the hot mash, but he was not very much interested in it, and he still shivered now and then. A little steam rose from his damp back.

It was almost dark when Billy Buck and Carl Tiflin came home. "When the rain started we put up at Ben Herche's place, and the rain never let up all afternoon," Carl Tiflin explained. Jody looked reproachfully at Billy Buck and Billy felt guilty.

"You said it wouldn't rain," Jody accused him.

► **Apply/Writing** Imagine you were shipwrecked on an island or lost somewhere in the wilderness. Tell the story of how you made it back to safety. Sequence five key events in time order.

3 Drawing Conclusions

A conclusion is a decision you make or an opinion you reach after thinking about facts or details.

▶ **Focus**   As a reader and writer you **draw conclusions** when you make decisions or form opinions based on facts or details. In the passage from *The Red Pony* in the previous lesson, the writer never states that Jody is worried. Nonetheless, you, as the reader, can draw that conclusion by using the details in the passage.

In the following paragraph, what details has the writer used to help you draw a conclusion about the kind of person Phoebe works for?

> Day after day Phoebe watched, and waited, and listened. The house was full of people all the time—officers of the army, friends, members of the bodyguard. Phoebe slipped among them silent as a shadow, as her father had taught her. Whenever she saw anyone talking softly, she stopped to poke the fire, fill their glasses, light new candles. But still she saw nothing, heard nothing.
>
> *from **Phoebe and the General***
> *by Judith Berry Griffin*

The author never states that Phoebe works for someone involved in government and/or politics. Readers can draw that conclusion, though, by using the detail "The house was full of people all the time—officers of the army, friends, members of the bodyguard." What detail helps you draw the conclusion that Phoebe wants to learn what is going on?

Help your readers draw correct conclusions about your narratives by choosing details carefully.

Guided Practice   Discuss the cartoon.

1. Why is the alarm clock so effective?
2. What does the alarm clock have that helps you draw this conclusion?

"It's our most effective alarm clock ever!"

▶ Practice   A. Study each cartoon and question below. Draw a conclusion to answer each question. Write your answer. Then write the information on which you based your conclusion.

1. What has happened?

"That's him, officer! That's the one!"

2. Did the man take his vitamins?

"Are you sure you're taking that vitamin prescription?"

B. Read the passage below. Then answer the questions that follow.

Mr. Lingerle stayed to have supper with them, stayed for music after supper, stayed even after Sammy and Maybeth had gone upstairs to bed. Dicey regretted having built a fire, when she came back into the living room to see him sitting in front of it. He leaned toward the crackling logs with a dreamy expression on his face. Gram was coming out of the kitchen with another cup of coffee for the man. She looked at Dicey and shrugged her shoulders. What did that mean? Dicey wondered.

*from **Dicey's Song**
by Cynthia Voigt*

3. How do you think Dicey feels about Mr. Lingerle's visit?
4. Why do you think Dicey regretted having built a fire?
5. What do you think Gram's shrug meant?

▶ Apply/Thinking Skills   When you write, your readers will need to draw conclusions to understand you. Keep your readers in mind. Think of three topics. For each one, list three or more details that suggest the topic but do not state it.
Example: Topic—*sleep*   Details—pajamas, yawn, weary eyes

4 Parts of a Dictionary Entry

A dictionary entry is made up of a number of parts.

▶ **Focus**   When you write, one of your basic tools should be a dictionary. The entries in a dictionary are the basic source of information about words. Each entry contains several parts.

Look carefully at the sample entries below. Then read the explanations that are keyed to the various parts of the entry.

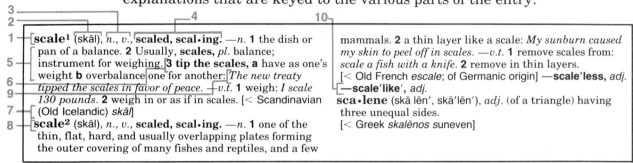

1. An **entry word** shows how a word is spelled and how it is divided if it has two or more syllables.
2. A **pronunciation** is a respelling of the entry word using letters and symbols explained in the pronunciation key.
3. **Part-of-speech labels** are abbreviations for the functions of the entry word.
4. **Inflected forms,** shown in dark type, are forms of the entry word whose spelling might give you trouble.
5. A **definition** is a meaning of a word. A word with more than one meaning has numbered definitions, one for each meaning.
6. An **idiom** can be found under its most important word. It is an expression whose meaning cannot be understood just by knowing the meaning of each word in it.
7. An **etymology,** or word history, tells the entry word's origin.
8. A **homograph** is a word that is spelled the same as another word but has a different origin and meaning. Homographs are followed by raised numbers in many dictionaries.
9. An **illustrative sentence** or phrase shows how a word can be used with one particular meaning.
10. **Run-on entries** are undefined words. Their meanings combine the meaning of the entry word with that of a suffix.

▶ **Guided Practice**   Discuss the entry *scalene.*

1. How many syllables does *scalene* have?
2. From what language does *scalene* come?
3. In how many ways can *scalene* be pronounced?

▶ **Practice**   **A.** Use the dictionary entries and explanations on the opposite page to answer these questions.

Example: How many parts of speech are shown for *scale¹*?
Answer: two

1. How many syllables are there in the inflected form *scaling*?
2. What is the second definition of the noun use of *scale²*?
3. What illustrative sentence is given for the second definition of the noun use of *scale²*?
4. What part of speech is *scale¹* when it means "weigh"?
5. What inflected forms are given for *scale²*?
6. From what language is *scale¹* derived?
7. How many meanings does the idiom "tip the scales" have?
8. What part of speech are the run-on entries *scaleless* and *scalelike*?
9. What is the illustrative phrase for the first definition of the verb use of *scale²*?
10. From what language did *scale²* come directly into English?

B. Write each word below two times. First write it as it appears. Then write it divided into syllables. Use a dictionary.
Example: laboratory   *Answer:*   laboratory   lab o ra to ry

11. sophomore	16. mischievous	21. business
12. appreciate	17. occurrence	22. cafeteria
13. accomplish	18. quantity	23. courteous
14. experience	19. recommend	24. embarrass
15. independence	20. argument	25. caterpillar

▶ **Apply/Study Skills**   Choose three of the words below. Write a brief definition for each, using your own words. Then look up the word in the dictionary and write the dictionary definition that is most like yours.

beauty   kindness   charity   truth

5 Using a Dictionary

A dictionary is an aid in spelling and pronouncing words.

a hat	**oi** oil
ā age	**ou** out
ä far	**u** cup
e let	**ù** put
ē equal	**ü** rule
ėr term	
i it	**ch** child
ī ice	**ng** long
o hot	**sh** she
ō open	**th** thin
ô order	**ᴛʜ** then
zh measure	

ə = { a in about
e in taken
i in pencil
o in lemon
u in circus

< = derived from

▶ **Focus**   Suppose you were writing a story and didn't know how to spell a certain word—for example, *heinous* (hā′ nəs), meaning "very wicked." How can you use a dictionary to look up a word you cannot spell? Use a spelling chart. Many dictionaries include such a chart, which gives examples of all possible spellings for each of the English sounds. The beginning of a spelling chart is shown at the left.

Heinous is a tricky word because the long /ā/ sound is spelled *ei*. After you have looked in a dictionary under *ha-, hay-,* and *hey-,* you may have run out of ideas as to how the word is spelled. Then use the chart. You'll find fourteen ways that the long /ā/ sound is spelled, and you can check on each possible spelling until you get to *hei-*. At this point, *heinous* will be easily recognizable.

Now take the opposite situation. Suppose you have read a word and want to know how it is pronounced. You find it in a dictionary and look at its pronunciation, but you do not remember how all the symbols are pronounced. That is when you use a **pronunciation key.**

All dictionaries have pronunciation keys. A complete key appears in the front or back of a dictionary. However, a short pronunciation key, like the one at the left, appears on every other page. This key tells what sounds the most commonly used pronunciation symbols stand for. Suppose you look up *queue* (kyü) and cannot remember how /ü/ is pronounced. Look for /ü/ in the short pronunciation key. Next to it is the word *rule*. The /ü/ in *queue* is pronounced the same as the /ü/ in *rule*.

▶ **Guided Practice**   Discuss these questions.

1. How many ways can the sound /ä/ be spelled?
2. Which example word on the chart has letters that spell the sound /ā/ the same way that *parquet* (pär kā′) does?
3. Which pronunciation-key word has the o in *osprey* (os′ prē)?

▶ **Practice**   **A.** Pronounce each word, using the pronunciation in Column 1. Then choose the word from Column 2 or 3 and write it. Before writing the word, look at it carefully and say it again. Then check your dictionary to make sure you have spelled it correctly.

Example: (lī′brer′ē) liberty   library
Answer: library

	1	**2**	**3**
1.	(prob′ə bəl)	probable	probably
2.	(kon′shəns)	conscious	conscience
3.	(bel′ō)	below	bellow
4.	(nō′tə blē)	notable	notably
5.	(lē′tər)	litter	liter
6.	(pā′shəns)	patience	patient
7.	(ek sklām′)	exclaim	explain
8.	(mə säzh′)	message	massage
9.	(môr′gij)	mortgage	marriage
10.	(kon′stənt)	consent	constant

B. Rewrite the paragraph. Write the correct spelling of each word in parentheses. Use a dictionary if you need help.

Example: Jan ate two fried eggs for (brek′fəst).
Answer: Jan ate two fried eggs for breakfast.

(1) Have you ever invented a (sand′wich)? (2) You can probably (krē āt′) several different sandwiches. (3) Simply look in your (ri frij′ə rā′tər) and see what's there. (4) My brother Tony invented a sandwich for (lunch). (5) He put (tü′nə) salad, Swiss (chēz), and tomato slices on an onion (rōl). (6) It sounded like a (strānj) sandwich to me, but Tony said it was (di lish′ əs).

(7) The next (dā) my Uncle Pete made a sandwich of chopped (liv′ər), crisp (bā′kən), shredded lettuce, and (un′yən). (8) He put it all (bi twēn′) two thick slices of (bred).

▶ **Apply/Writing**   Write a note to a classmate. Instead of words, use pronunciations. Exchange messages with your friend and decode each other's sentences. Be sure to consult a dictionary when you write your note and when you decipher your classmate's.

6 Main Idea in a Paragraph

A paragraph is a group of sentences that develops one main idea. In a narrative paragraph the main idea is usually not directly stated.

▶ **Focus**   Most paragraphs focus on one **main idea,** the one idea that the paragraph is about. A narrative paragraph tells about something that happened; its main idea is not usually directly stated. The reader may have to draw a conclusion as to what the main idea is by examining the details in the paragraph.

Read the paragraph below from the novel *The Yearling,* set about a century ago in Florida. Jody Baxter has raised a fawn named Flag for nearly a year. One day his mother is preparing dinner; Jody has brought the young deer into the house and leaves it alone for a moment. Use your ability to draw conclusions to decide what the main idea of the paragraph is.

> She set the dish of shelled dried peas on the table and went to the hearth. Jody went to his room to look for a piece of rawhide. There was a clatter and commotion and then Ma Baxter's storm of fury. Flag had leaped onto the table, seized a mouthful of the peas and sent the pan sprawling, the peas scattered from one end of the kitchen to the other. Jody came running. His mother threw the door open and drove Flag out with the broom. He seemed to enjoy the fracas. He kicked up his heels, flicked his white flag of a tail, shook his head as though threatening to attack with imaginary antlers, sailed over the fence and galloped away to the woods.
>
> *from* **The Yearling**
> *by Marjorie Kinnan Rawlings*

The unstated main idea of the paragraph is that Flag is now too wild and big to be allowed in the house any longer.

▶ **Guided Practice**   Answer these questions about the paragraph.
1. If the main idea of the paragraph were to be stated, where do you think it would fit best—at the beginning, in the middle somewhere, or at the end?
2. What details support the idea that Flag is too wild and big to be allowed in the house any longer?

▶ **Practice   A.** Read this later paragraph from *The Yearling* and answer the questions. Jody has just discovered that Flag can jump the fence he built and has been eating the farm's corn plants.

Jody clung to the fence. He was numb. He could neither feel nor think. Flag scented him, lifted his head, and came bounding to him. Jody climbed down into the yard. He did not want to see him. As he stood, Flag cleared, as lightly as a mockingbird in flight, the high fence on which he had labored. Jody turned his back on him and went into the house. He went to his room and threw himself on his bed and buried his face in his pillow.

1. Which of these three statements expresses the main idea?
   a. Jody decided immediately to get rid of Flag.
   b. Jody was shocked and upset by Flag's behavior.
   c. Jody was too young to understand what was happening.
2. Add a third detail, labeled **c,** that supports the main idea.
   a. Jody buried his face in his pillow.
   b. Jody turned his back on Flag.
   c.

B. Write out the main idea and three supporting details for each of these paragraphs. One main idea is unstated.

3. Melissa wanted to prove that she could do her share on the camping trip with her dad. She rushed to unpack the tent and camping gear while her dad removed stones from their site. She helped put up the tent and set out the necessary items for dinner. Melissa then insisted that she do all the cooking as well as build the fire. After sunset she even contributed a number of scary stories as they sat by the dying fire.
4. Beth and Luisa first met in kindergarten. During fourth grade they joined Girl Scouts and did projects together. In the fifth grade, they both started guitar lessons. Last year they had fun in the park-district softball program. Now, in seventh grade, they are taking swimming lessons together.

▶ **Apply/Prewriting**   Think of an idea for a narrative paragraph based on a family outing. Write a statement of your main idea. Then write two sentences as supporting details.

7 Writing a Narrative Paragraph

Write a narrative paragraph when you want to tell a story about events that have happened over a period of time.

▶ **Focus** A **narrative paragraph** tells a story or part of a story. The person telling the story is the narrator and can be someone in the story or an outside observer. A narrative paragraph presents a series of events in time order and often uses words and phrases such as *first, then,* and *after that* to make the order clearer. Such words and phrases are called **transition words and phrases.**

Read the narrative paragraphs below. Notice the transition words and phrases. In the first paragraph, the narrator is an outside observer. Three friends—Paris, Pee Wee, and Big Dog—are walking near a river when Big Dog falls in. As Paris leans out to help Big Dog, Pee Wee holds on to Paris's legs.

Transition Words and Phrases
after
at first
eventually
finally
later
meanwhile
next
second
soon
then

> "Tread water," Paris called. "Tread the water like I showed you last summer." Big Dog started treading the water. "Your hand," Paris called out. Big Dog reached up. At first Paris couldn't catch it. Then he did. He pulled. But instead of Big Dog coming up, Big Dog started pulling him over. He felt himself slipping through Pee Wee's little arms.
>
> *from **Paris, Pee Wee, and Big Dog** by Rosa Guy*

In this second paragraph, the narrator is a character. He and his family move often because they are migrant workers. They are in the process of moving again.

> Papá parked the car out in front and left the motor running. "Ready," he yelled. Without saying a word, Roberto and I began to carry the boxes out to the car. Roberto carried the two big boxes and I carried the two smaller ones. Papá then threw the mattress on top of the car roof and tied it with ropes to the front and rear bumpers.
>
> *from **"The Circuit"** by Francisco Jimenez*

▶ **Guided Practice** Answer these questions about the paragraphs.

1. What transition words and phrases are used in the first paragraph?
2. Draw a conclusion to tell the main idea of the second paragraph.

▶ **Practice** **A.** Copy the narrative paragraph below, filling in each blank with a transition word or phrase that makes the sequence of events clear. Use the words in the box on page 26.

Noni grabbed his warmest boots and sealskin hat. _____ he put on his heaviest coat, because the trip ahead would be a long one. Outside his two faithful dogs, Nikki and Rikki, greeted him. The dogs were _____ hitched to the sled and they all set off. However, _____ traveling only a short distance, the sled overturned on a steep slope. Noni tumbled down the snowy slope and was shaken but not hurt. _____ he wanted to continue the trip, but _____ he decided to put it off a day. _____ the dogs barked loudly, wanting to be unhooked from the sled. _____ they were freed and ran on ahead of Noni back to home, happy the journey was over so soon.

B. Read the sentences below. Then rearrange them in time order. Use the transition words and phrases and other clues to help you. Finally, rewrite the sentences as a narrative paragraph.

1. Immediately he rushed past the dogs and stormed into the cabin.
2. Then, as Noni came close to the cabin, he panicked.
3. At last, he rushed out the front door with them, flinging them into the snow.
4. After a while, Noni neared home, dragging the sled.
5. Smoke was coming from a side window near the stove.
6. Even before he arrived, he could hear the sled dogs barking.
7. Then he ripped flaming curtains from the wall.

▶ **Apply/Writing** Write a narrative paragraph. Use your idea from Lesson 6 or one listed below. Use an outside narrator or, if you want, narrate the events yourself. When you have finished, use the Narrative Paragraph Revision Checklist to improve your work.

- being lost in a crowd
- the most exciting day
- the most courageous person
- a hospital or dental emergency

Narrative Paragraph Revision Checklist
✔ Does my paragraph have a main idea?
✔ Does my paragraph tell a story, with emphasis on events?
✔ Have I told the actions in order, first to last?
✔ Have I used words that clearly show the sequence of events?
✔ Have I avoided sentence fragments and run-ons?

8 Writing a Friendly Letter

A friendly letter is a way to communicate with people.

▶ **Focus**   A **friendly letter** often contains narrative paragraphs that tell about an experience or event. Some friendly letters have a specific purpose. For example, **notes of regret** or **acceptance** are responses to invitations. Read the letter and envelope below.

Heading

> 2074 Franklin Road
> Mt. Cloud, MI 40012
> May 20, 1988

Greeting

> Dear Pat,

Body

> I have exciting news to share! My family spent a week with Grandpa Joe in New York during school break. We climbed the Statue of Liberty and saw a Broadway show. We are going again in July. Maybe you could come with us. It would be fun to have my favorite cousin along! What have you been doing? Write back soon.

Closing

Signature

> With love,
> Ellen

▶ **Guided Practice**   Answer these questions.

1. What are the five parts of a friendly letter?
2. Which words are capitalized in the heading? the greeting? the closing?

► **Practice** **A.** The following note of regret is not correct. Rewrite the note, using correct punctuation and capitalization.

120 Lake street
foster city, CA 94404

dear Dianne

    Thank you for inviting me to your Labor Day party. I'm sorry but I won't be able to attend. I will be out of town that day. Thank you for thinking of me. I'll give you a call after the holiday.

your friend
Joseph

B. Imagine a person from List I has invited you to an event in List II. Write a letter of acceptance or regret.

I	II
a friend from another town	a community walkathon
your grandparents	a barbecue
a friend's parents	opening night of a play
an aunt or uncle	a weekend in the country
a cousin	a football game

C. Imagine you attended one of the events in List II. Write a friendly letter that tells about the event to one of the people in List I. Label the five parts of the letter.

► **Apply/Writing** Think of someone you would like to write a letter to. Write a friendly letter to that person, telling about something that happened to you or what you have been doing lately. Be sure that you put events in the correct order.

Friendly Letter Revision Checklist
- ✔ Have I included all parts of a letter and punctuated them correctly?
- ✔ Have I used words and phrases that express my thoughts clearly and completely to my reader?
- ✔ Have I presented events in the proper order?
- ✔ Have I proofread my letter for any spelling or punctuation errors?

Revising and Editing Workshop

Connecting Writing and Grammar

- In Unit 1 you read an example of narrative writing.
- In Unit 2 you wrote a narrative paragraph and a friendly letter.

Now it's time to use your skill as an editor to improve another writer's first draft. Read this narrative carefully. As you read, ask yourself these questions.

✔ Are the actions told in order, first to last?
✔ Do all sentences end with the correct punctuation?
✔ Are there any sentence fragments or run-ons?

(1) Gramps and his dog Murph came to live with us last year. (2) Mom was happy to have Gramps, but she had second thaughts about Murph. (3) Murph is the kind of dog who likes rolling in dirt but doesn't like having baths?

(4) Gramps left to answer the phone. (5) One day after Gramps had put Murph in the bathtub, the telephone rang. (6) Guess what happened next? (7) Murph grabbed a towel in his mouth, jumped out of the tub, and raced down the stairs. (8) He went out the back door. (9) Do you know what Murph did then! (10) He found a patch of dirt—Mom's favorite flower bed—and rolled around in it. (11) Crushing all of the flowers. (12) He dug a huge hole in the middle of the lawn. (13) He lay down on the towel he had dragged outside. (14) Making it dirtier than it already was.

(15) Mom has summoned us together she said we have an important family matter to discuss. (16) Murph isn't the only one in the doghouse now!

▶ Revising the Draft

1. The writer never tells how Murph got out the back door. Draw a conclusion about how Murph did it. Add this information to the draft.
2. Find two sentences in the second paragraph that are not in the correct sequence. Rewrite them correctly.
3. Make the sequence of events clearer in the second paragraph by adding transition words and phrases.
4. Add, delete, or rearrange any other information you think would improve the draft.

▶ Editing the Draft

5. Find three sentences that do not have the correct end punctuation. Correct these sentences.
6. Find a misspelled word in the first paragraph. Use a dictionary to check the correct spelling. Write the sentence, spelling the word correctly.
7. Find two sentence fragments in the second paragraph. Correct the fragments by attaching them to the sentences they belong with.
8. One sentence in the last paragraph is a run-on sentence. Rewrite it correctly.

▶ Working Together on the Draft

Meet with a group of your classmates. Discuss the changes you made in the draft. Listen to the changes your classmates made. Then rewrite the draft on page 30. Include all the revisions you think are important.

▶ Evaluating Your Own Writing

Now review your own writing. Look over the narrative paragraph you wrote in this unit and any other written work you have. Did you have any problems writing and correctly punctuating the four kinds of sentences? Did your writing contain sentence fragments or run-ons? The lessons that follow will help you with these writing problems.

9 Kinds of Sentences

A sentence may be declarative, interrogative, exclamatory, or imperative.

▶ **Focus**   A sentence begins with a capital letter, expresses a complete thought, and ends with a punctuation mark. There are four kinds of sentences. The paragraph below has an example of each.

> Firecrackers banged! What was going on? A family in the sleepy town of Rich Square, North Carolina, was battling some pesky birds. Read on to find out more about this problem.

The first sentence is an **exclamatory sentence.** It is a statement or command that expresses surprise or strong feeling. The next sentence is an **interrogative sentence.** It asks a question. The third sentence is a **declarative sentence.** It is a statement that tells something. The last sentence is an **imperative sentence.** It is a command or request in which the subject *you* is understood.

Now study the chart below.

Kind	Purpose	Example	Punctuation
declarative	telling	The family had troubles.	period
interrogative	asking	Can they solve the problem?	question mark
exclamatory	showing strong emotion	Birds love their town!	exclamation mark
imperative	ordering or requesting	Don't do that! Think about it.	exclamation mark or period

▶ **Guided Practice**   Decide on the purpose of each sentence below. Then tell what kind of sentence it is.

> Imagine thousands of birds invading your home. That's what took place in Rich Square. It was incredible! What happened?

▶ **Practice**   **A.** Read these sentences and write what kind each one is.
Example: Families face many challenges.
Answer: Declarative

1. Listen to this story.
2. It's fantastic!
3. One family had a problem.
4. They lived in a small town.
5. It is filled with birds.
6. The birds roost all over.
7. Would you like to live there?
8. Think of the problems!
9. First, the family just complained.
10. Matters got worse.
11. More families began to worry.
12. Could they scare the birds?
13. No, but they tried!
14. They set off firecrackers.
15. They banged pots and pans.
16. They even set off flares.
17. Nothing worked.
18. What else could they do?
19. The birds weren't scared.
20. Think of a possible solution.

B. Write what kind each sentence is. Then copy the sentence, adding the correct end punctuation.
Example: What a problem these birds were
Answer: Exclamatory—What a problem these birds were!

21. Soon the town asked for help from outside
22. Please send helicopters right away
23. Do you suppose that worked
24. The birds scattered at first but returned again
25. Whew, were the townspeople disappointed
26. The whole town was awakening at sunrise with the birds
27. What did the people try next
28. Didn't experts arrive with special loudspeakers
29. They aimed loud, high-pitched sounds at the birds
30. How frustrated the people were by yet another failure
31. Guess what happened next
32. Someone tried rock and roll on the loudspeakers
33. It took a while, but it actually worked
34. What a happy day it was when the birds left

▶ **Apply/Writing**   Can you imagine what it would be like to live in this town? Write a paragraph about the situation there. Use each kind of sentence at least once. Capitalize and punctuate correctly.

10 Subjects and Predicates

A sentence has a simple and complete subject and predicate.

▶ **Focus** Every sentence has two parts—the **complete subject** and the **complete predicate.**

> Many colorful tulips | are grown in Holland.

In the sentence above the complete subject is *Many colorful tulips.* The complete subject tells whom or what the sentence is about. The complete predicate is *are grown in Holland.* The complete predicate tells what the subject is or does.

The most important word in the complete subject is the **simple subject.** It names whom or what the sentence is about. The simple subject can be a noun or a pronoun.

> My brother **Ed** | visited Holland early last May.
> **He** | was a tourist in a group of tulip lovers.
> Several **passengers** on his flight | are going on other tours.

The simple subject can be the same as the complete subject, as in the second example. The simple subject may also have various modifiers, such as prepositional phrases. Note that in the third example *passengers,* not *flight,* is the simple subject.

The most important word in the complete predicate is the **simple predicate,** usually called the **verb.** The verb tells what the subject does or is. It may be a one-word verb or a verb phrase. What are the verbs in the three example sentences above?

In a sentence the subject, predicate, or both may be compound. A **compound subject** is made up of two or more subjects, usually joined by *and* or *or.* A **compound predicate** is two or more predicates joined by *and, but,* or *or.* (For help in diagraming all kinds of sentences, see the handbook on pages 550–557.)

> **Ed** and his **wife** | **flew** to Amsterdam but **took** trains after that.

▶ **Guided Practice** Name the simple and complete subjects and predicates.

1. My mother and I plant many tulips in the fall.
2. Red flowers of any kind are our favorites.

▶ **Practice** **A.** Copy these sentences. Draw a vertical line between the complete subject and the complete predicate.

Example: The motorcycle was invented by Gottlieb Daimler in 1885.
Answer: The motorcycle | was invented by Gottlieb Daimler in 1885.

1. It was made of wood and traveled at only twelve miles per hour.
2. The first double-decker buses appeared in London in the 1850s.
3. Horses of great size pulled them on tracks.
4. The first true submarine was used in 1776.
5. No American President rode in one until Harry Truman.
6. Alexander Graham Bell invented the telephone in 1876 yet had originally intended a hearing aid for the deaf.
7. Telephone service from coast to coast began in 1914.
8. The invention of the radio by Marconi in 1895 revolutionized communications almost overnight.
9. Boats at sea could send messages and distress signals.

B. Divide your paper into two columns. Label the first column *Simple Subject* and the second column *Verb*. Write the simple subjects and verbs of the sentences below in the correct columns. Some sentences may have compound subjects or predicates.

Example: Either a Greek or an Egyptian invented the first pipe organ.
Answer: **Simple Subject**　**Verb**
　　　　Greek, Egyptian | invented

10. Both Greece and Egypt claim credit for its invention.
11. A man from Greece became the first organist.
12. Egyptian inventors developed the instrument further.
13. Their instrument had a keyboard and ran on water power.
14. Historians and researchers have studied the origins of the first pipe organ and have discovered these ancient models.
15. Someone built and played a wind-powered organ in the tenth century.
16. Innovators and musicians produced later improvements.
17. Handel and Bach were great organ composers.
18. Gottfried Silbermann improved the organ's sound and added more voices.

▶ **Apply/Writing** Write a paragraph about an instrument or a sport that you play. Use compound subjects and predicates.

6 More practice on page 503.

11 Sentences with Modifiers

The subject or predicate in a sentence may contain other words that modify, or add to, the meaning.

▶ **Focus**   The sentence *Families moved* has only two words—a subject and a predicate. Few sentences are that short. Usually writers add a few well-chosen words to the subject and the predicate to make the sentence clearer. Study these examples.

Families	moved.
Several families	moved.
Several old families	quietly moved.
Several old families from our town	quietly moved into the city.

The first sentence has only a subject—*Families*—and a verb—*moved*. In the second sentence, the adjective *Several* was added. It modifies *families* by telling how many families moved.

In the third sentence, the adjective *old* was added. It tells what kind of families moved. The adverb *quietly* was also added, before the verb. It tells how they moved. Adjective and adverb modifiers may come before or after the words they modify.

In the last sentence, the prepositional phrases *from our town* and *into the city* were added. *From our town* modifies the noun *families* by telling which families—families from our town. Prepositional phrases that modify nouns always come after the nouns they modify. *Into the city* modifies the verb *moved* by telling where the families moved. Prepositional phrases modifying verbs may come anywhere in a sentence.

Remember that most sentences contain modifiers. They give more exact meaning to simple subjects and predicates.

▶ **Guided Practice**   Tell which words modify each subject and predicate. Do not count *a, an,* or *the.*

1. Two nervous teams headed for the baseball field.
2. The wooden bleachers filled quickly with noisy fans.
3. The first batter from our team swung violently at the softball.
4. The ball burst apart from the impact.
5. People in the bleachers immediately laughed.

► **Practice**   **A.** Divide a sheet of paper into two columns. In the first column, write the simple subject of each sentence below. In the second column, write the adjectives or prepositional phrases that modify each subject. Do not count *a, an,* or *the*.
Example: A severe snowstorm from Canada hit our city.
Answer: snowstorm—severe, from Canada

 1. A small wooden house on our street was afire.
 2. The electric heater in the living room had exploded.
 3. Some flimsy lace curtains had caught fire.
 4. An alert neighbor called the police.
 5. Ten firefighters from various stations answered the alarm.
 6. Deep, blowing snow hindered their job.
 7. A large family from that house was saved.
 8. Many residents in adjoining houses fled to safety.
 9. The terrible fire could have cost many lives.
10. The brave firefighters should receive medals.

B. Divide your paper into two columns. In the first, write the verb in each sentence. In the second, write the adverbs or prepositional phrases that modify it. One sentence has a compound predicate.
Example: Spring moved gradually into the area.
Answer: moved—gradually, into the area

11. The dirty wet snow melted slowly.
12. Birds chirped noisily in the budding trees.
13. The sun rose earlier on each new morning.
14. People often smiled now.
15. The grass grew quickly in people's yards.
16. Storms sometimes blew from the west.
17. Trees bent in the heavy rains.
18. Telephone lines sometimes broke.
19. Schools closed occasionally.
20. Children ran out into the warmth and played excitedly.

► **Apply/Writing**   Add adjectives, adverbs, and prepositional phrases to each sentence base below. Then use the sentences in a paragraph.

Fires spread.	Timber is destroyed.	Forests rebuild.
Animals are killed.	Campers blamed.	Time passes.

12 Inverted Order in Sentences

In some sentences, the complete subject does not come before the complete predicate.

▶ **Focus**   In most sentences the subject comes before the predicate. Sometimes, as in interrogative sentences, part or all of the verb comes before the subject. This kind of sentence is said to be in **inverted order.** Study these examples.

> Has the detective solved the case?
> Is he an employee of the store?

One helpful way to find the subject in sentences like these is to turn the question into a statement.

> The **detective** *has solved* the case.
> **He** *is* an employee of the store.

Other kinds of inverted sentences begin with the complete predicate and end with the complete subject. These sentences can also be put into natural order to find their subjects.

> On a shelf above my desk are several models.
> Several **models** *are* on a shelf above my desk.

> Nearby is my dictionary.
> My **dictionary** *is* nearby.

Sentences that begin with *Here* or *There* are often in inverted order. To find the subject, first find the verb. Then ask who or what is doing the action.

> Here comes my train. (What comes? train)
> There goes my allowance for the next month. (What goes? allowance)

▶ **Guided Practice**   Name the simple subject in each sentence.

1. Near the stream in our pasture stands a huge tree.
2. Have you noticed its golden branches in the springtime?
3. There was mud all around it after the recent heavy rains.
4. Was Tom in the basement during that last storm?

▶ **Practice** **A.** Write the following sentences. Underline the subject and draw two lines under the verb or verb phrase.
Example: <u>Did</u> <u>you</u> <u>see</u> today's assignment?

1. Is your homework on the desk?
2. Did you get the assignment from Dan?
3. Is it difficult work?
4. Will you help me?
5. Do you want a snack?
6. Are the apples sweet and juicy?
7. Are they studying hard?
8. Can you discuss the assignment?
9. Have you finished already?
10. Have the others left?

B. Divide a sheet of paper into two columns. In the first column, write the subject. In the second column, write the verb.
Example: There are my grandparents.
Answer: grandparents   are

11. Here is Uncle Chet in his sports car.
12. Here is a birthday present.
13. There are many other great gifts as well.
14. Here is my favorite one.
15. There is my second choice.
16. Here is my new glove from Mom and Dad.
17. There is the baseball.
18. Here is the camera.
19. There are several pictures of the guests.
20. Here is the best one.

C. Underline the subject and draw two lines under the verb.
Example: Into the hole <u>jumped</u> the <u>rabbit</u>.

21. Into the hall went my two cousins with their dog.
22. Under the shade trees sat my aunts and uncles.
23. Above them floated fat, puffy clouds.
24. Beyond the tree flowed the river.
25. Over the rocks gushed cool, clear water.

▶ **Apply/Writing** Make up and write three questions with subjects and predicates in inverted order, similar to the sentences below. Then label the subject in each sentence with *S* as shown.

      S   S
Did you see the musical?   *Are those my tickets?*

13 Sentence Fragments

A group of words punctuated like a sentence but not expressing a complete thought is called a sentence fragment.

▶ **Focus**   You have already learned that a sentence contains a subject and a predicate and expresses a complete thought. A **sentence fragment** is a group of words punctuated like a sentence but not expressing a complete thought.

> **Sentence:**   The outfielder ran to the fence.
> **Fragment:**   Caught the ball with ease.

Some fragments can be corrected by adding words. Remember that a complete sentence must have a subject and a verb.

> **Fragment:**   Early this morning.
> **Corrected:**   Early this morning, the builder arrived.

Some fragments are parts broken off from complete sentences. To correct these, attach them to the sentences they belong with. Notice you must change capitalization and punctuation.

> **Sentence and fragment:**   Luis felt energized. After his workout.
> **Corrected:**   Luis felt energized after his workout.

Some fragments are more difficult to spot because they do contain a subject and verb. Fragments like these must also be corrected by attaching them to the sentences they belong with.

> **Sentence and fragment:**   Emma received the vase. That Hal sent.
> **Corrected:**   Emma received the vase that Hal sent.

▶ **Guided Practice**   For each item, identify the sentence fragment and tell how to correct it.

1. Left the tools out at the end of the day.
2. No one touched the electrical tools. Because they had warned us not to.
3. Work on the kitchen went fast. Once the cabinets arrived.
4. Carpenters measure things carefully. To avoid mistakes.
5. Will be done by the end of next week.

▶ **Practice**   **A.** Correct the sentence fragments below. Attach each one to the sentence next to it. Change capitalization and punctuation as necessary.

Example: Tigers have a bad reputation. For fierceness.
Answer: Tigers have a bad reputation for fierceness.

1. They are often feared. Because they attack people.
2. Most tigers are really shy. And avoid contact with people if possible.
3. Tigers sometimes attack people. After being cornered.
4. They live in Indian forests. As well as Manchurian ones.
5. Tigers can live anywhere. Needing only food and water to survive.
6. They do not run well. For long distances.
7. Nowadays tigers are no longer captured for zoos. Since enough are born in captivity.
8. Some zoos have special areas. That are magnificent.
9. These areas are quite large. And similar to the animals' natural home.
10. People can see tigers in the open now. Instead of seeing them in cages with metal bars.

B. Correct each item by using one of the methods you have learned. If an item is correct, write *Correct.*
11. My dad often has scraps of wood lying around the basement.
12. My sister, who knows carpentry.
13. She built my brother a bookshelf for his room.
14. For her next project for her class at school.
15. And required precise measuring and cutting.
16. Her project kept the family awake all night long.
17. She called us. And warned us not to come down.
18. Just a secret surprise for Mom and Dad!
19. By morning, all of the noise.
20. The family will be surprised. By the creation.

▶ **Apply/Revising**   Find the groups of words in Practice B above that can be corrected by adding words. Rewrite them, adding any necessary sentence parts, such as subjects and predicates, in order to make them complete sentences.

7   More practice on page 504.   **41**

14 Run-on Sentences

A run-on sentence contains two or more sentences written together without the proper punctuation between them.

▶ **Focus** Sometimes you may be in a hurry to put your thoughts down on paper. Be sure not to write two or more sentences and improperly join them with no punctuation or with just a comma. Sentences that run together without the proper punctuation between them are called **run-on sentences.** Read this pair of example sentences.

> Juan writes music he does not write stories.
> Kelly is a mechanic, she repairs her own car.

The first example has no punctuation between the two sentences. The second example has only a comma. Both are run-on sentences. The chart below shows three ways to correct run-on sentences.

Guidelines for Correcting Run-on Sentences

1. Separate the two sentences in a run-on with a period. Use a capital letter to begin the second sentence.

> Juan writes music. He does not write stories.
> Kelly is a mechanic. She repairs her own car.

2. If two ideas in a run-on sentence are closely related, join them with a comma and a conjunction such as *and, but, or,* or *so*.

> Juan writes music, but he does not write stories.
> Kelly is a mechanic, so she repairs her own car.

3. Join two closely related ideas with a semicolon.

> Juan writes music; he does not write stories.
> Kelly is a mechanic; she repairs her own car.

▶ **Guided Practice** Tell three ways to correct the following run-on sentence.

Jean is an artist she paints children's portraits.

► **Practice**   **A.** Use one of the guidelines on the previous page to correct each of the seven run-on sentences in the exercise below. For the three correct items, write *Correct*.

Example: Karen writes music she is a fine pianist.
Answer: Karen writes music. She is a fine pianist.

1. Wolfgang Amadeus Mozart was born in Austria his father was a musician.
2. At age three Mozart showed musical talent, he was composing music at the age of five.
3. Mozart never attended school his father gave him a musical education himself.
4. By age fourteen Mozart had composed many musical works.
5. Mozart played the piano, he gave many public performances.
6. He wrote several operas and forty-one symphonies almost all of his works are still performed today.
7. Mozart had severe hardships and disappointments his music is cheerful and vigorous.
8. Mozart had a sense of humor, he enjoyed making puns and practical jokes.
9. During his lifetime Mozart's works were well-known.
10. He died in poverty at the age of thirty-five.

B. Rewrite the paragraph below, correcting all run-on sentences. Your paragraph should have between seven and ten sentences.

   (**11**) Rock 'n' roll is a form of contemporary music, it is especially popular among young people.   (**12**) This music grew out of the blues it also has its roots in gospel music.   (**13**) Chuck Berry is often considered a founder of rock music, he is a composer and a performer.   (**14**) Rock songs often speak about current problems some people consider rock to be a way people communicate with each other.   (**15**) There are many rock 'n' roll performers, Elvis Presley is regarded by some people as the most popular artist ever.

► **Apply/Writing**   Write about your favorite kind of music or about your favorite musical performer. Then have a partner check your paper to make sure there are no run-on sentences. You may wish to write these sentences in your journal.

8   More practice on page 505.

Review/Evaluation

For more review,
see Tested Skills Practice,
pages 502–549

⑤ Kinds of Sentences Write the letter of the answer that names each sentence and gives the correct end punctuation.
- **a.** Declarative (.)
- **c.** Imperative (. or !)
- **b.** Interrogative (?)
- **d.** Exclamatory (!)

1. Have you read about the boy pharaoh of ancient Egypt
2. A pharaoh was both the king and chief priest of Egypt
3. The pharaoh was also considered a god by the Egyptian people
4. Imagine what it would be like to be both a king and a god
5. What wealth and power you would have
6. After a ten-year search, Howard Carter discovered the tomb of the boy pharaoh
7. His name was Tutankhamun, or Tut for short
8. Call him King Tut
9. His tomb contained gold chairs and other precious things
10. Would you be as patient as Howard Carter

⑥ Subjects and Predicates Write the letter of the answer that names the underlined sentence part or parts.
- **a.** Simple subject
- **c.** Simple predicate
- **b.** Complete subject
- **d.** Complete predicate

11. <u>The tomb of King Tut</u> was underground.
12. <u>It</u> had false doors and secret passages.
13. Carter <u>found</u> four rooms in the boy pharaoh's tomb.
14. One <u>room</u> contained the mummy of Tutankhamun.
15. The mummy of the pharaoh <u>was buried</u> inside eight coffins.
16. The innermost <u>coffin</u> was made of solid gold.
17. The wise <u>Mr. Carter</u> discovered treasures in three rooms.
18. The ancient Egyptians <u>believed in an afterlife</u>.
19. His <u>people</u> provided King Tut with things for his next life.
20. <u>Furniture, jewels, and fine clothes</u> were placed in the tomb.
21. The rare <u>treasures</u> are now owned by the Egyptian government.
22. Visitors to Egypt <u>can see</u> them at the museum in Cairo.
23. <u>Carter and his partner</u> did not die of the mummy's curse.
24. The famous King Tut's curse <u>was only an old legend</u>.
25. You <u>can read and enjoy</u> many books about King Tut's treasures.

7 **Correcting Sentence Fragments** Write **a** if the word groups are two sentences. Write **b** if they are a sentence and a fragment.

26. There was a legend about a curse. Which protected Tut's tomb.
27. Robbers had once entered Tut's tomb. But had taken little.
28. They may have become afraid. If they harmed the tomb, they might die.
29. Carter entered the underground tomb. Cautiously and somewhat fearfully.
30. He went in. With his partner and several workers.
31. Carter was the first person. To enter the burial chamber.
32. The others followed him. And stared in silent amazement.
33. They saw two life-sized statues of Tut. They were guarding a sealed door.
34. Later they found the ebony and ivory throne. It had come from central Africa.
35. There is some mystery. Surrounding the death of Tutankhamun.

8 **Correcting Run-on Sentences** Write **a** if the sentence is a run-on sentence. Write **b** if the sentence is correctly punctuated.

36. The Hawaiian Islands are volcanic peaks they erupted from the ocean floor.
37. The first Hawaiians reached the islands in canoes approximately 1,600 years ago.
38. The men caught fish, and they grew a starchy root called taro.
39. They cooked the taro roots on hot stones, they pounded it and made pudding.
40. Women soaked and pounded the inner bark of trees they made it into cloth.
41. Women wove leaves into sails and mats; they wove cord into fish nets.
42. Rulers wore helmets, these helmets were covered with feathers.
43. A worker plucked a few feathers from a bird, then he let the bird fly away.
44. Early Hawaiians rode the waves on surfboards; each island had its champion.
45. Volcanoes still erupt on one island, new islands may rise from the sea in the future.

Thinking/Writing Evaluation

1. **Drawing Conclusions** Read the paragraph and answer the questions.

It was after ten o'clock when the telephone rang. Dr. Dean listened for a few minutes and then said, "Don't let her put any weight on that back leg. She's a strong horse; she'll be OK. I'll be there soon." Dr. Dean hung up the phone, grabbed his black case, and then got into his van. Soon he would be with his patient.

1. What do you conclude is Dr. Dean's occupation?
   a. a dentist   **b.** a veterinarian   **c.** a bus driver
2. What did the horse hurt?   **a.** her head   **b.** her front foot
   c. her back leg

2. **Narrative Paragraphs**   **A.** Read the paragraph and answer the
3. questions.

(1) Jamie had looked everywhere.   (2) First, he searched all of his pockets.   (3) The eyeglasses weren't in his desk, so he then felt under his bed.   (4) The second place he looked was inside his messy desk drawers.   (5) Eyeglasses are very expensive!   (6) He pulled his closet apart, but the glasses weren't there.   (7) Finally, Debby came into his room and said smugly, "Excuse me, brother dear.   (8) If you're looking for your glasses, you might try the top of your head."

3. What is the main idea?   **a.** Jamie's glasses   **b.** Debby and Jamie   **c.** Jamie's search for his glasses
4. Which sentence does not support the main idea?   **a.** sentence 2
   b. sentence 5   **c.** sentence 8
5. Which transition word tells you that sentence 4 is not in sequence?   **a.** inside   **b.** messy   **c.** second
6. Which transition word could be used to begin sentence 6?
   a. Next   **b.** Before   **c.** Meanwhile
7. What conclusion can you draw about Jamie?   **a.** He is worried.   **b.** He lost his glasses yesterday.   **c.** He needs his glasses for reading.

3. **B.** Write a narrative paragraph on one of the topics below.

- the best afternoon I ever spent   • a close call
- the morning the dog came to the library

Curriculum Connection: A Learning Log

At the end of each section in this book, you will be asked to connect what you have learned with another subject that you are studying in school. In this section, you will be asked to make an entry in a learning log.

A **learning log** is a record of what you learn each day in school. As you record this information, you might apply the thinking skills you learn in this book. For example, as you record information learned in your literature or reading class, you might jot down conclusions you draw about characters and situations in stories.

▶ **Think**   What kinds of people do you read about in literature? Does the author explain their motives and personalities, or are you expected to draw conclusions based on the details provided? How do the actions and dialogue of characters help reveal their personalities?

▶ **Discuss**   Get together with a small group of classmates to discuss the characters you have recently read about in school. Make a list of characters you have studied. Under the name of each character, record descriptions that reveal what kind of person he or she is.

▶ **Find Out**   Check your group's list. Use the books on which your lists are based so that you can check the descriptions or references to dialogue for accuracy.

▶ **React: Start Your Log**   Label a notebook *Learning Log*. Begin each entry with the date and the subject. Start your log by recording clues from the book along with conclusions you have drawn. Below is an entry made by a student who read *The Red Pony* in its entirety.

> Literature   October 12, 1988
> Jody—10 years old with "shy, polite gray eyes" and a mouth "that worked when he thought." He views life with "a feeling of change and of loss." Conclusion—Jody is thoughtful, shy, and in the process of growing up.

Narrative Writing

Theme: The Power of Words

Words are powerful tools. They can start disputes and settle them. They can add beauty or excitement to life. In this section you will learn how writers use the **power of words** to create exciting stories. You will also learn about words that name things and help you to express yourself clearly.

1 Literature: Short Story

*Writers can take you on a jungle safari, put you in the middle of a desert, or bring you into someone's home—all through the power of words. In the following short story, "**Lucas and Jake**," the author, Paul Darcy Boles, takes you to a zoo.*

*In a short story, much happens in a few pages. Characters are introduced, they become involved in some sort of conflict, and their situation is brought to a close. As events unfold, it is fun to imagine characters, settings, and what will happen next. As you read "**Lucas and Jake**," pay attention to the words that Boles uses to create the characters in the story.*

from **Lucas and Jake**
by Paul Darcy Boles

It was the time when he could relax a little, letting go in all the clean sun that showered down on this part of the zoo.

So Lucas, who would be sixty-five next Tuesday, July sixteenth, was sitting on a box beside Jake's cage down on one of the side paths where not many sightseers came. He was eating a winesap apple, a fine specimen of its kind. He took distinct pleasure in biting into it with teeth that were largely his own.

All morning he'd been thinking back to when he'd been a boy and, on a day like this, would have been footloose and free as a big bird. He'd always liked zoo work, even if it didn't give you much status with friends and fellow men. Yet a man needed somebody to look up to him. An admirer, maybe a relative. Lucas didn't have one ring-tailed relative, admiring or not, on earth.

He finished his apple, flipped its core into a trash can and leaned back, hugging his knees and cutting an eye at Jake.

Jake lay quiet, cinnamon-colored body shadowed, just a few flecks of sunlight picking out bits of his mane, one splash of light in his left eye. The eye, large and golden, resembled some strange pirate coin. Jake possessed awful patience. He could watch an inconsequential bug on the cage floor hours on end, not even his tail twitching, its very tuft motionless.

Lucas sat up as two boys came around the lilac bush and moved toward Jake's cage. And Lucas's mustache bristled a bit. His eyes got the stern cool look of a TV Westerner's—a town marshal, summing up transients.

The older boy, about twelve, padded along on sneakers soundless as a brace of leopards. The younger, eight or nine, with a thatch of sheep-doggish hair, was fiddling with a Yo-Yo. It reeled out smartly enough, but when he tried to flip it back it nearly banged his nose.

Both stopped at the cage and looked in at Jake. Lucas waited for their first smidge of smart talk. But the bigger boy's voice sounded thoughtful, not smart talking at all. "Wonder how come they keep him here, Paddy? Not back with all the others?"

The smaller boy shrugged. He went on making his Yo-Yo climb up and roll down. "Maybe he *likes* it here."

That was as good an answer as Lucas had ever heard from a layman who couldn't know anything solid about lions. Most people thought they were lion experts.

The bigger boy's eyes widened toward Lucas. "Sir, how come he's here? Not messing around with the other lions up at the moat?"

Paddy let his Yo-Yo spin to a stop. He wanted to know too.

Lucas cleared his throat. But before he could say word one, information fountained out of the taller boy: "My name's Ridefield Tarrant. This is Patrick McGoll. Call him Paddy, sir. We came out on the bus. We each had two bits for Saturday. I didn't like the baboons; they make me nervous barking. But I sure like the lions and the tigers. Especially lions." He drew fresh breath. "We could have gone seen *Dancers in the Dark Night of Time*, adults only, we know how to sneak in. But it felt like a better day for animals."

When he was sure Ridefield had finished, Lucas nodded. "You can't miss, with animals." He waited; the word coast still seemed clear. "You asked about this lion. His name's Jake. They keep Jake all by himself for"—Jake coughed—"for certain secret reasons."

Ridefield's face lighted all over. He owned very black hair and eyes like a bold Indian's. He was polite, but in a flash Lucas could tell nobody was ever going to break his inquiring spirit. The knowledge made Lucas happy about something in the universe no man ever really had a name for: glory, ecstasy; he wouldn't know.

With a glance at his own bronzed knuckles, hard as oak roots soaking up sunlight, Lucas nodded again. "Going to tell you boys the secret. Because you look like you want to know. Listen real close."

Ridefield Tarrant was leaning toward Lucas like an arrow set on the bowstring, and the mouth of Paddy McGoll had come a trifle open like that of a young bird expecting food.

Lucas narrowed his eyes. "Ever hear of a Cape lion?"

Their heads shook.

"Well"—Lucas shook his head—"only the kings of the whole lion breed. That's all they are, gents. Never in your life see a Cape lion doing push-ups on a barrel in a circus. No, sir! Wouldn't catch him dead in such a place." Almost casually, Lucas added, "Jake's a Cape lion."

"Yike," murmured Ridefield.

Lucas folded his arms. "Yep. Took from his mother when he was a young brave. Fought all the way. Killed . . . more'n you could count. Notice the bars of this here now cage." He pointed. "Put Jake in a cage with *lighter* bars, why, he'd be right out among you with a baseball bat. Put him up at the moat with the rest, he'd eat 'em like cornflakes. Cornflakes." Lucas touched his mustache reflectively. "He's my sole and particular charge. Jake's my special talent."

At this moment Jake twitched his left ear to discourage a bluebottle fly. Paddy McGoll stiffened like a little post with hair all over the top of it. Ridges and valleys leaped into the leather of Lucas's forehead. They vanished into the tufts of white hair which made him resemble a tough Santa Claus. "Now, I hope I did right to tell you, gents. Most people, you tell 'em about Jake, they'd write to editors about him, stir up trouble. I'd hate for the zoo to have to shoot him."

Ridefield said, "I won't say a thing! Neither will Paddy."

Paddy nodded. "I don't write so good, anyhow. In penmanship I use my fingers instead of my wrists. I wouldn't *tell* anybody."

"Good." Lucas stood. He felt his joints creak, but the looseness of the sun was warming him too. "Well, I got to be going. I won't be far off—but I hate to leave you here alone with him—"

Ridefield spoke rather swiftly. "We'll be going; we haven't seen the birds yet."

Lucas snorted. "Birds. They're all right, but a lion like Jake—now, he teaches you something. Well, c'mon."

The three started off. Lucas noted that Ridefield and Paddy were walking backward, taking one last look.

And it was just then that Paddy did the foolish thing. It happened because his Yo-Yo finger was too small for the string's loop. Suddenly, there went the whole Yo-Yo, string and all, sailing between the cage bars and coming to rest with a clack eight inches in front of Jake's nose.

"*Yike,*" breathed Ridefield.

Lucas could feel all the radiance of the day pour itself into his veins as though he himself were about twelve again, or even nine, tough as nails, but desperately searching for a key to the whole world and all the whirling planets. Low-voiced, he said, "Don't move an inch."

Ridefield's nostrils were white. Paddy stood as if whacked to the spot with spikes. Lucas walked back to Jake's cage.

He could hear the soda water fizz of Jake's breath through great nostrils. The gold coins of the eyes—sometimes pale green, at other times so full of sun they, too, were like suns—were tightly covered. Jake's chin lay on the backs of his paws.

Lucas put his right arm between the bars. The arm moved very

slowly. Then his fingers were touching the Yo-Yo, his arm actually brushing Jake's whiskers. Lucas drew his arm out, stepped back to the boys, said, "Here y'ar," and put the Yo-Yo in Paddy's fingers.

Ridefield tried to speak, and couldn't. He stuck his right hand up to Lucas, and Lucas shook it. Then Paddy, dropping the Yo-Yo into a pocket, stuck his hand out, and he and Lucas shook. Then Ridefield and Paddy moved off. It was as if they held something so tremendous they might burst. Strength and wonder and greatness, all understood, all there . . . .

They were out of sight around the lilac bush before Lucas smiled. It was the smile of a man who'd earned something: more than status. And after a moment Lucas strolled back to Jake's cage. He thrust his arm in, took hold of the mane, which felt like rope fibers, and gave it a minor tug.

All at once Jake came awake, the eyes staring at Lucas with green-gold enigmatic quiet. Jake was no Cape lion. But he might have been. *All* animals of this kind were brave and glorious. If they got old and preferred to sleep, if they couldn't really be terrible any longer, or even roar much, that was their business. In some definite way Lucas felt he'd done something for Jake today, for the whole kingdom of lions.

He couldn't have put a finger on it. He tousled the dark mane, felt of the veinous surface behind the left ear—soft as a velvet mouse—and drew his arm back out of the cage. He turned away; there was plenty to do, and he didn't want to get chewed out for not doing it. He walked off.

Behind him, alone again to sleep out his years quietly, Jake kept his eyes open for a few more seconds. Then the eyelids trembled. The eyes shut. The body lay unmoving, powerful, in the huge green afternoon.

► **Discussing**
1. Who are the characters in the story? Describe each one.
2. In what part of the zoo is Jake's cage?
3. What happens to Paddy's Yo-Yo? What does Lucas do?
4. How do Paddy and Ridefield react to what Lucas does?
5. How would you have acted and felt if you were with Ridefield and Paddy?

► **Analyzing: Drawing Conclusions**
   You will recall that when you draw a conclusion you make a decision or form an opinion based on facts or details. Answer these questions by drawing conclusions.

1. Why did Lucas say what he did about Jake?
2. Why do the boys decide to leave? Do you think they are actually going to see the birds?
3. Do Ridefield and Paddy believe Lucas's story? How can you tell?
4. Why does Lucas say that the story about Jake is a secret?
5. What does Lucas think he has done for Jake?

► **Writing**
   Pretend you are either Ridefield or Paddy. You want to tell someone about your experience with Lucas and Jake, but you have promised not to. Write about your experience in your diary or journal.

► **Extending**
   Speaking and Listening   Meet with a small group of classmates to discuss the theme of this section, The Power of Words. Talk about how words can affect the way you feel or act. For example, a teacher's words of encouragement may have the power to motivate you to work even harder in school. Try to think of as many ways as possible that the power of words affects you.
   Reading   *Words from the Myths,* by Isaac Asimov, contains retellings of myths and a discussion of how many words in English are rooted in mythology. Readers can take a new look at myths by recognizing the power of these words.

2 Listening for Details

Listening for details requires paying careful attention to the speaker. Good listeners think as they listen.

▶ **Focus**   In "Lucas and Jake," Paddy and Ridefield listen carefully to what Lucas says about Jake because they want to learn about the lion. You, too, need to listen carefully at times for details. Listening can help you do assignments correctly, deliver messages, study for tests, or retell stories. Remember these guidelines.

Guidelines for Good Listening

1. Look at the speaker, watching for gestures that emphasize important details.
2. Listen for information that answers the questions *who, what, where, when* and *how.*
3. Listen for transition words such as *first, next, before,* and *after.*
4. Listen for changes in the speaker's voice.
5. Identify techniques a speaker uses to emphasize details, such as repeating information.
6. To remember important details, repeat the details silently to yourself; take short notes; rewrite your notes later; discuss details of what you heard with another person.

▶ **Practice**   Listen for details as your teacher reads an excerpt from *Barrio Boy* by Ernesto Galarza. Then answer the questions below.

1. Where was the narrator sitting?
2. What was the trunk covered with?
3. What held the trunk together?
4. What was put into the trunk?
5. Who took the trunk away?

▶ **Apply/Social Studies**   Think of someone you know who remembers a historical event, such as the first landing of astronauts on the moon. Ask the person to describe the event in detail. Listen carefully to the description, taking notes if necessary. Then share what you learned with your classmates.

3 Synonyms and Antonyms

**Synonyms are words whose meanings are nearly the same.
Antonyms are words whose meanings are nearly opposite.**

▶**Focus**   For emphasis, writers often use **synonyms,** words with
similar meanings, and **antonyms,** words with opposite meanings.
In "Lucas and Jake," Lucas says of Jake "He's my sole and
particular charge." Lucas emphasizes how special Jake is by using
two synonyms, *sole* and *particular.*

---

sole[1] (sōl), *adj.* **1** one and only; single: *the sole heir.* **2** only: *We
three were the sole survivors.* **3** of or for only one person or group
and not others; exclusive: *the sole right of use.*
par tic u lar (pər tik′yə lər), *adj.* **1** considered by itself or apart
from others; taken separately; single: *That particular chair is
already sold.* **2** belonging to some one person, thing, group,
occasion, etc.: *A particular characteristic of a skunk is its smell.*
3 different from others; unusual; special: *a particular friend.*

The following sentence about Jake appears in another part of the
story "He could watch an inconsequential bug on the cage floor
hours on end, not even his tail twitching, its very tuft motionless.
Twitching and *motionless* are antonyms. *Twitching* means "move
with a quick jerk." *Motionless* means "not moving."

Learning synonyms and antonyms can be valuable to you as a
writer. They can help increase your vocabulary. They can also give
emphasis or variety to your writing.

▶**Guided Practice**   Discuss answers for each of these questions.

1. What is a synonym for each word below?

   liberty   idea   shout

2. What is an antonym for each word below?

   boring   moist   smooth

3. What is a synonym for *ran* in the sentence below?

   My aunt *ran* a grocery store and earned a good living.

4. Using its antonym as a clue, what does *din* mean in the sentence
   below?

   The *din* of low-flying jets broke the quiet of the afternoon.

▶ **Practice**   **A.** Choose a synonym from the Word Bank to replace each underlined word. Rewrite the sentence, using the synonym. Use a dictionary if you need help.

Word Bank
applauded
crackled
stumbling
cajoled
groaned
debated

Example: The audience *cheered* enthusiastically.
Answer: The audience applauded enthusiastically.

1. The conductor <u>coaxed</u> the musicians.
2. They <u>discussed</u> the issue for hours.
3. The roaring fire <u>popped</u>.
4. The injured player <u>moaned</u> loudly.
5. You're acting like a <u>bumbling</u> fool!

B. Read each sentence noting the word in italics. Choose the *antonym* for the word in italics. Use a dictionary if you need help.

Example: We learned not to trust *hypocritical* people.
                         sincere   critical   hypnotized
Answer: sincere

6. The *tumult* of the thunder and wind scared the puppy.
          uproar   fear   peacefulness
7. The *avarice* of King Midas made him hide all of his money.
          wealth   generosity   intelligence
8. While we were painting the house, the rooms looked *chaotic*.
          changed   pleasant   orderly
9. The Sons of Liberty expressed their *opposition* to the tax.
          uncertainty   agreement   thankfulness
10. My *pessimistic* friend always says something will go wrong.
          hopeful   purposeful   dutiful

▶ **Apply/Science**   Create a list of words to describe lions. Afterwards, for each word, write either a synonym or antonym and identify which it is. Compare your list with a classmate's.
Examples: wild—domesticated (antonym)
                      ferocious—fierce (synonym)

Our Living Language

Introduction

> New circumstances . . . call for new words,
> new phrases, and the transfer of old words
> to new objects.
> —*Thomas Jefferson*

Just as the clothes people wear and the houses they live in change over the centuries, so does the language they use. New inventions and interactions with other countries affect the words we use to communicate what we know. As you will see, the English language has undergone many changes.

In "Our Living Language" throughout this book, you'll go on a voyage. You'll travel through time as you read the history of the English language from the year A.D. 500 to the present.

Your first stop is England between the years 500 and 1100. Here you'll meet the Anglo-Saxons who spoke the language we call Old English. Will you understand Old English? Wait and **sehwan!**

Next, you'll visit England after it was conquered by French-speaking Normans in 1066. You'll **witnesse** the impact of French on our language. Between 1100 and 1500, English borrowed many French words and became what we call Middle English.

How did Greek and Latin words enter our vocabulary? You'll find out as your travels take you to the year 1500, when Modern English began. You'll also learn how words were invented or borrowed from foreign languages. In the end, you'll understand why English grows, changes, and remains a "living language."

Word Play Think of some inventions that required new words.

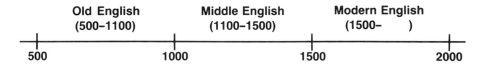

Old English (500–1100)   Middle English (1100–1500)   Modern English (1500–)

500   1000   1500   2000

4 Conflict in Story Plots

A story's plot is a series of events creating a conflict that is eventually resolved.

▶ **Focus**   Most good stories follow a similar pattern. In the beginning, characters are introduced. Soon these characters become involved in events that center on a problem, or **conflict.** The conflict may be between one character and another, between a character and some outside force, or between a character and himself or herself. As the characters deal with more events, often tension rises. The conflict reaches a critical level, or **climax.** At this point, the course of events changes. The conflict is resolved in some way, and the story comes to an end, or **resolution.** In some stories, the resolution is not directly stated and the reader must draw a conclusion about it.

The diagram below shows the usual pattern of a story's plot line.

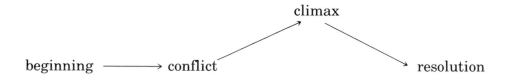

Read the following summary of the plot of "The Circuit." Try to fit the summary to the plot pattern shown in the diagram.

> Francisco hates the idea of moving again. He and his family are migrant workers and move often. This time they find work in a vineyard and move into an old garage with no windows and a dirt floor. Francisco works long and hard. His muscles ache after a day's work. When the grape season ends in November, Francisco goes to school. He is very nervous the first day. Everyone has books and friends; Francisco has neither and has trouble remembering English. When asked to read in class, he becomes dizzy. Francisco asks his teacher for help, and for a month the two work on English during lunch. One day Francisco's teacher offers to teach him how to play the trumpet. When Francisco comes home from school, excited about his teacher's offer, he finds everything is packed up in cardboard boxes.

▶ **Guided Practice**   Use the plot summary of "The Circuit" to discuss these questions.

1. What conflict or problem is evident early in the story?
2. Give three details from the summary that contribute to the conflict.
3. What type of conflict does the summary present?
4. What is the story's climax?
5. What information is given to help you draw a conclusion about the resolution?
6. What is the resolution?

▶ **Practice**   A. Write a plot summary of one of the following items. Identify the plot's conflict, climax, and resolution. Then state whether you think the resolution could have been predicted and whether it was believable.

1. "Lucas and Jake" (pages 50–54 of your text)
2. a movie or play you have seen recently
3. a short story you have read recently

B. Divide into groups of four or five. Read the following beginning of a plot summary and discuss possible developments, climax, and resolution. When group members agree on how to finish the plot summary, have a volunteer write it down to present to the class. As you work, consider questions like these: What three things might Tom do to accomplish his goal? How might others respond to his actions? Does he accomplish what he sets out to do?

Tom is a class leader. A new student, Jerry, arrives. Jerry is a talented athlete and math student. His good nature wins friends quickly. Tom is unhappy because he is no longer the center of attention. He schemes to regain his role as class leader.

▶ **Apply/Prewriting**   Think of a conflict for a short story. It may be a problem you have experienced or one you imagine. Check work from earlier lessons for ideas you may have written down.

Then write a plot summary based on the conflict you have chosen. Include two main characters, a climax, and a resolution. Save your summary for possible use when you write your own short story later in this unit.

5 Characters and Dialogue

Dialogue helps make story characters come alive.

▶ **Focus**   Readers get to know characters in a story in a number of ways. One way is through the narrator's description of their appearance, actions, and feelings. Another way is through **dialogue,** the exact words of characters. In the following excerpt from "Lucas and Jake," the author uses all of these methods. Pay attention to things you learn about the characters.

> Lucas waited for their first smidge of smart talk. But the bigger boy's voice sounded thoughtful, not smart talking at all. "Wonder how come they keep him here, Paddy? Not back with all the others?"
> The smaller boy shrugged. He went on making his Yo-Yo climb up and roll down. "Maybe he *likes* it here."
> That was as good an answer as Lucas had ever heard from a layman who couldn't know anything solid about lions. Most people thought they were lion experts.
> The bigger boy's eyes widened toward Lucas. "Sir, how come he's here? Not messing around with the other lions up at the moat?"
> Paddy let his Yo-Yo spin to a stop. He wanted to know too.
> Lucas cleared his throat. But before he could say word one, information fountained out of the taller boy: "My name's Ridefield Tarrant. This is Patrick McGoll. Call him Paddy, sir. We came out on the bus. We each had two bits for Saturday. I didn't like the baboons; they make me nervous barking. But I sure like the lions and the tigers. Especially lions." He drew fresh breath. "We could have gone seen *Dancers in the Dark Night of Time,* adults only, we know how to sneak in. But it felt like a better day for animals."

Before you begin writing dialogue, decide how you want your characters to come across. If you want to portray a character as confident, curious, or angry, create dialogue that is appropriate for this type of person. For example, if Paul Darcy Boles wanted to portray Lucas as an angry person, he might have written dialogue like this: "You boys just get away from here. Don't bother me. And don't go near that lion!" However, if he wanted Lucas to come across as curious, he might have written dialogue like this: "What are you boys doing here? Are you lost? Have you been to this zoo before?"

Guidelines for Writing and Punctuating Dialogue

1. Enclose a speaker's exact words in quotation marks.
2. Begin a new paragraph each time the speaker changes.
3. Begin a direct quotation with a capital letter.
4. Set off a direct quotation with a comma when it is preceded or followed by a phrase such as *he said* or *she replied*.
5. Avoid overusing the word *said*. The Work Bank contains examples of more descriptive words.

▶ **Guided Practice**   Answer these questions about the excerpt.

1. When the boys first stop at Jake's cage, how is Ridefield's voice described? What does this tell you about him?
2. Paddy stops playing with his Yo-Yo to hear Lucas's answer to Ridefield's question. What does this action tell you about Paddy?
3. What details of Ridefield's long speech to Lucas suggest that he is friendly, adventuresome, and interested in animals?

▶ **Practice**   **A.** Write two sentences that tell more about each character that is described below. In one, tell something he or she says. In the other, describe something he or she does.

1. Josita was happy when she won the swimming event.
2. Morgan became curious about a strange shadow in the hall.
3. Allison was upset when she learned Pam was moving.
4. David was surprised to see a deer in the yard.

B. Choose one of the following situations and write a brief dialogue between the two characters involved. You may add other characters and descriptions if you wish.

5. two scientists first discovering a way to become invisible
6. a salesperson trying to sell someone a carrot peeler
7. two people in a spaceship approaching an unknown planet

▶ **Apply/Prewriting**   Look at one of the plot summaries you wrote in the preceding lesson. Write some dialogue that might take place between characters in the summary. Jot down any ideas about the characters' personalities that occur to you. Save them for later use.

6 Setting

The setting in a story adds convincing physical details.

▶ **Focus**   When and where a story takes place is the story's setting. The setting may be in the past, the present, or the future. The place may be real or imaginary. It may be general, like the zoo in "Lucas and Jake," or specific, like the San Diego Zoo. Time may also be general, such as a summer sometime in the future, or specific, such as July of 1997. To make your setting come alive, provide details that appeal to your readers' senses of sight, sound, touch, taste, and smell. Observe how details in this passage appeal to your senses.

> The night was not calm. The irregular blasting of nearby cannons kept Cal well aware of the danger of his position. Frequently he dodged little circles of silvery light that spilled from the full moon through trees as he sneaked deeper behind Union lines. Cal thought he must be miles north of Maryland, in Pennsylvania. He resisted breathing deeply, trying to avoid coughing out the smoke from enemy campfires. A charcoal taste coated the inside of his mouth. His greatest discomfort came from his too-tight Confederate army boots, which were now clammy from the wet ground. What a way to spend the Christmas of 1861.

▶ **Guided Practice**   Discuss these questions about the passage.
1. Where and when does the action take place?
2. What details appeal to the senses? Identify the particular sense in each.

▶ **Practice**   Below are some possible settings for stories. For each, write one sentence that indicates when the action is taking place and another sentence that appeals to one of the five senses.

1. an abandoned house
2. the middle of a traffic jam on a very hot day
3. a classroom while a test is being given

▶ **Apply/Prewriting**   Look again at your plot summary. Be sure to indicate something about time and place. Make a list of details about the setting that will appeal to your readers' senses.

7 Writing a Short Story

A short story has a beginning, a conflict, a climax, and a resolution.

In Lesson 1 of this section you read a short story. Now you will write one of your own. Keep in mind the importance of clearly sequencing the events in a narrative. Construct your plot carefully so that it has a beginning, a conflict, a climax, and a resolution. Provide vivid descriptions, dialogue, and a setting.

As you think about how to use the power of words to create a story, think, too, about your **purpose** and **audience.** Imagine you are submitting a story for your school's story writing contest.

1. Prewriting

▶ **Choose a Topic**   If you do not use your prewriting work from the preceding lessons, you will need to choose a topic. To choose a topic, try **brainstorming.** Using the headings *Conflict, Characters,* and *Setting,* jot down as many people, places, and problems as come to mind. Model your lists after these samples.

Conflict	Characters	Setting
writing a novel	speech writer	bookstore
battling stage fright	teenage athlete	newsroom
surviving an earthquake	spelling bee champ	the year 2050

Remember you might also look in your journal for possible story ideas. For more ideas on prewriting and other steps in the writing process, see The Writer at Work, pages 558–569.

▶ **Develop Ideas**   Once you decide on characters, setting, and conflict, **use the thinking skill of sequencing** to plan the events in the story's plot. Figure out your story's climax and end. Write an opening sentence; you may want to establish relationships or setting right from the beginning.

Next, think of a title for your story. Organize all these sketchy ideas on a planning chart like the one on the next page.

Finally, make a word bank. Consider using the words at the right.

Word Bank
leisurely
flimsy
awkward
confidently
carelessly
forceful
clever

Story Plan

Title: "The Winner"

Setting: A cross-country track meet

Opening Sentence: "You sure are a good runner, Meg," Amy panted.

Characters: Meg, the fastest runner on the team; easygoing Amy, a good runner; friends with Meg

Conflict: Amy wants to beat Meg and win the race to prove she can be a champion.

Events:

1. Amy and Meg run together.
2. Amy thinks about the upcoming race.
3. Meg and Amy race against Rendale School.
4. Meg twists her ankle.
5. Meg encourages Amy to win.
6. Amy wins the race.

2. Writing

▶ **Study the Draft** Before you begin to write, read the following first draft of "The Winner." Notice how the writer has expanded on the story plan with description and dialogue. Remember that the first draft is not a final product. The writer has made spelling and grammatical errors and has changed the wording in some places.

The Winner

"You sure are a good runner. Meg."
Amy panted. The two took grabbed
towels to dry off their bodys.

"You're not bad yourself." laughed Meg.
who curly dark hair was soaked.

Meg was the fastest runner on the
Claymoor School team. Amy. though.
was hopping to give Meg a challenge
in the meet with Rendale School on
saturday during the weekend. She had
been training and working out for weeks.

"If only I can finish first." thought
Amy. As she towel-dried her blonde
hair. "I could also show I'm a
champion too."

The next afternoon provided perfect
running weather. Peoples from both of
the schools lined the route.

"Good luck!" shouted Meg and Amy
to each other just as the gun went off.

A Rendale runner was first in the
lead. Meg was a close second. and Amy
was just behind her.

Suddenly. Meg stopped running and
limped over to some bushs she had
twisted her ankle.

"C'mon. Amy." Meg yelled. "Pass

Rendale! You can do it! You have to be our champion."

The power of those words did something to Amy. Like a greyhound freed from a chain, Amy confidently sped past the rendale runner to the finish line.

Later, Meg congratulated Amy. "I have you to thank," Amy told Meg. "It was your forceful words that pushed me across the finish line."

▶ **Write a Draft**   Now write your first draft. You can correct mistakes later.

3. Revising

▶ **Read and Confer**   Reread your first draft. Have a partner read your story. Use the following questions.

Conference Questions
1. Are events presented in a logical sequence?
2. Are the characters and setting clearly pictured?
3. Is the dialogue natural sounding?
4. Does the story reach a climax and have a resolution?
5. Should any information be added or deleted?

▶ **Make Changes**   Use your conference suggestions and the strategy below. Record various strategies in your writer's notebook. See page 8 for more ideas about developing a writer's notebook.

STRATEGY: Use a red pencil to make changes when you revise. To delete words, mark them with a (   ). To add words, use a (∧). To move words around, use an arrow (→). Notice how the writer of "The Winner" eliminated words that repeat the same idea.

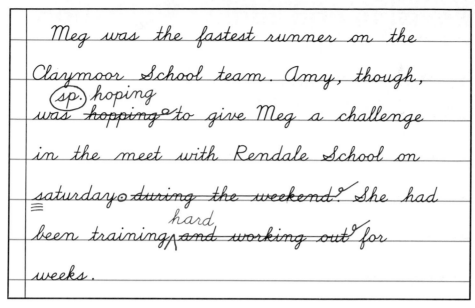

Proofreader's
Marks

Make a capital.

Make a small letter.

Add a period.

Add a comma.

Add quotation
marks.

Add something.

Take out something.

Move something.

New paragraph.

Correct spelling.

▶ **Proofread and Edit**   Check your draft for errors in spelling, punctuation, and grammar. Use proofreader's marks and the following questions.

Proofreading Questions
1. Did I capitalize and punctuate each sentence correctly?
2. Did I correct sentence fragments and run-on sentences?
3. Did I capitalize all proper nouns?
4. Did I use pronouns correctly?
5. Did I spell noun plurals and all other words correctly?

▶ **Make a Final Copy**   Now make a final draft of your short story. Be sure to include all of the changes you made during the revising step. Don't forget to give your story a title.

4. Presenting

You might read your story and hear those that your classmates have written in a class story festival. Then put copies in a notebook.

Revising and Editing Workshop

Connecting Writing and Grammar

- In Unit 4 you read a short story.
- In Unit 5 you wrote a short story.

Now it's time to use your skill as an editor to improve another writer's first draft. Read this short story carefully. As you read, ask yourself these questions.

✔ Does the story have a climax and a resolution?
✔ Are plural nouns spelled correctly?
✔ Are all proper nouns capitalized?

(1) Jim and Lena watched in horror as their miniature car crashed into a tree. (2) Lena ran to pick it up.

(3) Jim asked if the car was OK. (4) Lena said that it wasn't. (5) She explained that a part was cracked and it was the last one in stock. (6) She didn't think they had a chance in friday's race. (7) Of all crisis that could have occurred, this was the worst!

(8) The next morning Jim tried without success to fix the broken part. (9) He felt depressed and pouted all morning. (10) Eventually his mood changed. (11) "Only babys pout," he thought to himself. (12) "I'll think of something."

(13) Later, Jim met Lena between classes. (14) Jim said he dreaded seeing Nancy and Brian, that built last year's winning car. (15) Sure enough, as they entered carpentry class, Nancy and Brian taunted Lena and he. (16) Them said they had heard rumors about *someone* having car troubles. (17) They said that soon they would have two trophys. (18) The carpentry teacher was demonstrating how to attach table legs with a small, metal disk. (19) Jim started getting an idea. (20) Mr. erb began discussing a new project, a short table.

(21) "Will this really work?" Lena later asked jim.

(22) Even though Lena was uncertain, Jim felt differently. (23) "We'll shock the racing world," Jim said with a smile.

(24) After a tense hour of tapping and bending the metal disk from carpentry class, the two of them attached it to the car. (25) Lena took the remote-control box. (26) The car sped forward.

(27) "Now we'll see who car will win the race!" Jim said.

▶ Revising the Draft

1. The second paragraph would be more interesting if it was written as dialogue between Jim and Lena. Rewrite the sentences as dialogue.

2. The sentences in the fourth paragraph are not in a logical sequence. Rewrite them correctly.

3. You don't know where Jim and Lena work on the car because the writer does not provide a setting. Add this information to the draft.

4. Find a sentence about Lena's and Jim's feelings that incorrectly uses an adverb instead of an adjective. To give more emphasis to their feelings, rewrite the sentence so that it has an antonym. Be sure to delete the incorrect adverb.

5. Add, delete, or rearrange any other information you think would improve the draft.

▶ Editing the Draft

6. Find three plural nouns that are misspelled. Correct the sentences in which these nouns occur.

7. The writer used the pronouns *that* and *who* incorrectly. Correct the two sentences with these errors.

8. Two proper nouns are not capitalized. Correct the sentences with these errors.

9. Find two sentences that use personal pronouns incorrectly. Rewrite the sentences correctly.

▶ Working Together on the Draft

Meet with a group of your classmates. Discuss the changes you made in the draft. Listen to the changes your classmates made. Then rewrite the draft on page 70. Include all the revisions you think are important.

▶ Evaluating Your Own Writing

Now review your own writing. Look over the short story you wrote in this unit and any other written work you have. Did you have any problems using nouns and pronouns? Did you have any problems forming plural nouns? The lessons that follow will help you with these writing problems.

8 Identifying Nouns

A noun is a word that names a person, place, thing, or idea.

▶ **Focus** Words used to name people, places, things, and ideas are called **nouns.** Here are some examples. Which ones name ideas?

snow	kindness	music	apple
teacher	neighborhood	odor	grief

The following clues can help you identify nouns in sentences.

1. Many nouns in sentences are preceded by the articles *a, an,* and *the.* If you see one of these words in a sentence, you know that a noun will soon follow. One or more words may come between the article and the noun.

The fierce storm blew down **a** portion of **an** old, empty barn.

2. Most nouns have a singular and a plural form.

Singular	Plural
guard	guards
radio	radios
toy	toys
grief	griefs

3. Some nouns end with one of these suffixes: *-hood, -dom, -ment, -ance, -ness, -er, -or.* Study the examples below.

Word Root	+	Suffix	=	Noun
happy		-ness		happiness
free		-dom		freedom
amuse		-ment		amusement
insure		-ance		insurance

▶ **Guided Practice** Identify each noun in these sentences.

1. The four friends hiked into the dark woods.
2. Suddenly a boy in the group shouted in amazement.
3. His surprise was caused by a bulldozer clearing the small trees.

▶ **Practice**   **A.** Begin each group of words with *a* or *an* and then use each in a sentence. Underline each noun in your sentences.
Example: lively discussion
Answer: A <u>class</u> held a lively <u>discussion</u> about the <u>comet</u>.

1. good idea
2. firm promise
3. angry, loud voice
4. intense debates
5. sincere apology

6. evil laugh
7. offhand comment
8. brief order
9. silly, unwise remark
10. intelligent choices

B. Change the words below into nouns by adding one of these suffixes: *-hood, -dom, -ment, -ance, -ness, -er, -or.* Use a dictionary to check your spelling.
Example: advertise   *Answer:*   advertisement or advertiser

11. strange   **12.** wise   **13.** false   **14.** observe   **15.** govern

C. Copy the nouns from each sentence below.
Example: The children discussed a legend popular in their town.
Answer: children, legend, town

16. The tale explained that a pirate had his base there.
17. For years and years, people searched for his chest in the cove.
18. Searchers never found the golden coins and the bars of silver.
19. One child took a rope and a basket from his attic.
20. This boy led the group down a path to the deserted beach.
21. With great excitement, they scrambled to the end of a pier.
22. A girl tied the cord to the basket and tossed it in the water.
23. Their dreams of sunken wealth increased their anticipation.
24. They felt a weight on the end of the line and hauled it up.
25. The "treasure" was only a big crab in a bad mood.

▶ **Apply/Writing**   Imagine that you could invent any machine that you wanted. Write a description of it for a sales catalog and underline the nouns. You may use one of the following "inventions" if you wish.

1. a machine that picks up dirty clothes
2. a remote-control lawn mower
3. a robot that does homework and extra-credit assignments

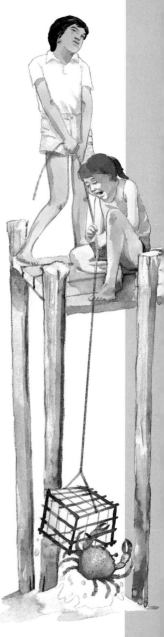

9 Kinds of Nouns

Nouns that name particular persons, places, or things are proper nouns. All other nouns are common nouns. Nouns may also be categorized as concrete or abstract.

▶ **Focus** Nouns that name something general—*person, city,* and *day*—are **common nouns.** Nouns that name particular persons, places, or things—*Roy Evans, San Diego,* and *Friday*—are **proper nouns.** A proper noun begins with a capital letter. A common noun does not, unless it begins a sentence. What are the common and proper nouns in these sentences?

> **Teresa Rojas** rode a **bicycle** from **San Francisco** to **Oakland.**
> **Artists** live in **Monterey,** a **town** in **California** near the **Pacific.**

Nouns can also be categorized as concrete or abstract. A noun is a **concrete noun** if it names someone or something that can be heard, seen, touched, smelled, or tasted.

> **Mr. James** parked his **car** in his **driveway.**

Can you see and touch Mr. James? his car? the driveway?
An **abstract noun** names an idea, quality, or state of mind. Abstract nouns often end with such suffixes as *-ty, -ism, -ment, -hood, -ness, -ion, -tion, -dom, -ance,* and *-ence.*

> Her **freedom** is of **importance** to the **government.**

Freedom, importance, and government are real, but they do not exist in the physical world. They exist in our minds as ideas. They cannot be seen or touched. These words are abstract nouns.

▶ **Guided Practice** Identify each noun as proper or common. Then tell whether it is concrete or abstract.

1. Miss Simmons asked her students to write essays or poems.
2. George Evans wrote an essay about the quality of honesty.
3. The poem that Jean Yu created expressed lovely ideas.
4. Both George and Jean wrote with confidence.
5. Their compositions were sent to a writing contest in St. Louis.
6. First prize was an eight-day trip to Hawaii.

▶ **Practice** **A.** Write each sentence. Underline the twenty-one common nouns once and the nine proper nouns twice.
Example: Mr. Leo Ferencik had his dream come true.

1. Mr. Ferencik, my neighbor, came to America from Europe.
2. This brave man wanted freedom from persecution.
3. He arrived in New York City on a freighter.
4. The Statue of Liberty appeared in the distance.
5. Tears of joy and anticipation welled up in his eyes.
6. His loneliness for his country changed to happiness.
7. Mr. Ferencik wanted the advantages of a democracy.
8. America had a tradition of liberty and justice.
9. The new immigrant would be free from unjust treatment here.
10. The Constitution guaranteed Mr. Ferencik equality.

B. Read the sentences below. Make lists of the concrete and abstract nouns.
Example: The joys and sorrows of the artist were reflected on the canvas.

Answer: **Concrete**   **Abstract**
            artist, canvas   joys, sorrows

11. An artist planned a painting of genuine value.
12. He drew his sketches from his thoughts.
13. Finally, the painter had a brilliant idea that seemed a true inspiration.
14. Using his creativity, he imagined two characters.
15. He painted them with dark colors for a mood of sadness.
16. The faces of these people were partly in shadows and darkness.
17. Their shabby clothes and bundles showed their poverty.
18. Unhappiness and despair, however, were not their only emotions.
19. His painting suggested confidence in the future too.
20. It shone with hope and belief in progress.
21. The man considered this canvas his masterpiece.

▶ **Apply/Writing** Think about something you have created (for example: a model from a kit, an object in woodworking class, or something to take home from art class). In a few sentences describe your struggles and your feelings. Try to use an equal number of concrete and abstract nouns.

10 Plural Nouns

Most plural nouns are formed by just adding -s or -es to the singular. Some nouns require a spelling change to form plurals.

▶ **Focus**   There are several ways singular nouns are made plural. Study the chart to review the most common ways. If you have a question about the spelling of a plural form, check a dictionary.

Plural Nouns

Most nouns: add -s

boat—boats; bottle—bottles

Nouns ending in **s, x, ch, z, sh, ss:** add -es.

fox—foxes; brush—brushes; lass—lasses; lunch—lunches

Nouns ending in **y:** change **y** to **i** and add -es unless a vowel precedes **y.**

diary—diaries; body—bodies; monkey—monkeys; toy—toys

Nouns ending in **f** or **fe:** change **f** to **v** and add -es for some; add just -s for others; use either form for a few. See dictionary.

loaf—loaves; wife—wives; half—halves; thief—thieves; roof—roofs; safe—safes; hoof—hoofs or hooves

Nouns ending in **ff:** add -s.

tariff—tariffs

Nouns ending in **o:** if **o** is preceded by a vowel, add -s. If **o** is preceded by a consonant, add -s for some and -es for others; add either -s or -es for a few. See dictionary.

radio—radios; zoo—zoos; solo—solos; piano—pianos; echo—echoes; tomato—tomatoes; zero—zeros or zeroes; cargo—cargoes or cargos

Compound nouns of more than one word: make only the most important word plural.

father-in-law—fathers-in-law; double play—double plays; great-grandson—great-grandsons

Nouns that change spelling.

mouse—mice; tooth—teeth; man—men; alumnus—alumni; basis—bases

Nouns that do not change.

moose—moose; species—species

► **Guided Practice**   Spell the plurals of these nouns: *maid of honor, potato, chief, branch, valley.*

► **Practice**   **A.** Write the plural of each noun below. Then choose five of the plural words and use them in sentences. Use the chart on the previous page or a dictionary if you need help.

Example: penny
Answer: pennies   Do pennies have any real value anymore?

1. book	**6.** spy	**11.** stereo	**16.** pogo stick
2. bunch	**7.** aluminum	**12.** house	**17.** dictionary
3. foot	**8.** half	**13.** bush	**18.** fisherman
4. allergy	**9.** spaghetti	**14.** story	**19.** golf course
5. thief	**10.** lunchbox	**15.** woman	**20.** sandwich

B. Copy the sentences, changing the nouns in parentheses to their plural forms.

Example: Unusual (creature) are seldom found in (city).
Answer: Unusual creatures are seldom found in cities.

21. (Zoo) give people in (city) a chance to see wild (animal).
22. (Fox) lie by their dens, and (monkey) play on (rope).
23. (Sea lion) and (seal) frolic and splash in two (pool).
24. The (wolf) pant in the shady (area) of their (cage).
25. (Rhino) and (hippo) rest in separate (enclosure).
26. (Child) and (adult) can see what (farm) are like.
27. Many have (incubator) that hatch (chick) from (egg).
28. Most have (donkey) and (horse) in their (barn) too.
29. Some keep milk (cow) and operate model (dairy).
30. Everyone enjoys watching the baby (calf) and (pony).
31. (Goat) and (deer) are gentle and allow (baby) to pet them.
32. A zoo may keep (wild fowl) like (duck) and (goose).
33. Others may have (hutch) filled with (bunny).
34. (Staff) try to make (inhabitant) happy and to avoid (crisis).

► **Apply/Study Skills**   Get in the habit of checking a dictionary for plural forms you're not sure of. Look up and write down the plural form or forms of each of the following nouns.

ox   antenna   veto   radius   Filipino   bus   torpedo

10   More practice on page 507.   **77**

11 Personal Pronouns

A personal pronoun takes the place of one or more nouns. An antecedent is the word or words to which the pronoun refers.

▶ **Focus** **Personal pronouns** take the place of nouns and other pronouns. The word (or words) a pronoun refers to is called its **antecedent.** Pronouns and their antecedents are shown below.

Juan and **Laura** ate **lunch,** but **they** thought **it** was too salty.

Below is a chart of personal pronouns arranged according to person: first person (referring to the speaker), second person (the one spoken to), and third person (the one spoken about).

Personal Pronouns		
Person	**Singular**	**Plural**
First person	I, me	we, us
Second person	you	you
Third person	he, she, it, him, her	they, them

Other personal pronouns take the place of possessive nouns. They are called **possessive pronouns**. Study the example and the chart.

If Sue has forgotten **her** sweater, will Donna lend Sue **hers**?

Possessive Forms of Personal Pronouns		
Person	**Used Before Nouns**	**Used Alone**
First person	my, our	mine, ours
Second person	your	yours
Third person	his, her, their, its	his, hers, theirs, its

▶ **Guided Practice** Make up a sentence with a possessive pronoun before a noun and one that stands alone.

► **Practice**   **A.** List the personal pronouns in each of these sentences. There are forty-one pronouns in all.

Example: I lost the pocket calculator that Julio let me borrow.
Answer: I, me

1. I asked my friends, "Have you found a calculator today?"
2. "Oh, so the strange object we found is yours?" Ben kidded me.
3. "Why isn't your name on the back?" his brother Jack said.
4. I said it was not mine; my brother Julio owned the calculator.
5. "You should feel lucky it was found by us," Mara said.
6. "Its case is ripped, but I bet your father could repair it."
7. Later, she and we boys discussed our summer plans.
8. "Are you going to try out for our community play?" Ben asked.
9. "Yes, I would like the hero's role. Are you two trying out?" I asked him and his brother.
10. They said they would rather try their luck as villains.
11. Mara complained, "Jana told me the part of the heroine was already hers and I shouldn't waste my time trying for it."
12. "We will all be lucky if they choose us," I commented.

B. Write the twenty-two personal pronouns in the following ten sentences. After each one, write in parentheses its antecedent.

Example: Denise told friends she would entertain them with magic.
Answer: she (Denise), them (friends)

13. They saw Denise do her first magic trick.
14. She started it by borrowing Carmen's straw hat.
15. "What are you going to do with my hat?" she asked.
16. Denise took off the ribbon and cut it into several pieces.
17. She told Carmen to put them into the hat and shake it.
18. "Will I get the ribbon back?" she asked.
19. Denise replied, "You can trust me, Carmen."
20. Then she told Carmen to jump up and down with her.
21. The crowd was amazed when Denise pulled the ribbon out of her hat and it was whole again.
22. They applauded her magic, and Carmen waved her hat.

► **Apply/Writing**   Imagine what Denise's second magic trick might be. Write a paragraph describing it. Underline all the pronouns.

11   More practice on page 508.

12 Interrogative and Relative Pronouns

Interrogative pronouns introduce questions. Relative pronouns introduce groups of words that act as adjectives.

▶ **Focus**   We often begin questions with pronouns. The most common of these pronouns are *who, whom, whose, which,* and *what.* They are called **interrogative pronouns.** Read the examples and notice where the interrogative pronouns are located.

> **Who** is that scientist?   **Which** is your book?
> **Whom** did the author choose?   **What** is its main idea?
> **Whose** is that book?

The pronouns *who, whom, whose,* and *which* can also be used to introduce a group of words that acts as an adjective. When used for this purpose, they are called **relative pronouns.** Another relative pronoun is the word *that.* Read these sentences.

The scientist **who** wrote the book on dinosaurs is Joan Riley.

The book, **which** is a best seller, was made into a movie.

Joan gave a talk **that** explained the great Ice Age.

In the sentences above, each relative pronoun introduces a word group that acts as an adjective. Each word group modifies a noun. In the first sentence, *who wrote the book on dinosaurs* modifies *scientist* by telling which one. In the second sentence, *which is a best seller* modifies *book* by telling what kind. What modifies *talk* in the third sentence?

▶ **Guided Practice**   Tell which underlined pronouns are interrogative and which are relative.

1. <u>Which</u> of the North Shore suburbs will hold the Tour of Homes?
2. It will be in Evanston, <u>which</u> has many fine old houses.
3. Some <u>that</u> we will see contain beautiful antique furniture.
4. <u>Who</u> will be the leader of this year's tour?
5. Mary Phillips, <u>who</u> is an expert on architecture, is the leader.

▶ **Practice**   **A.** Write the sentences below. Then underline the interrogative pronoun in each.
Example: <u>Which</u> is the horse you bought?

1. Who owned the horse?
2. What is the horse's name?
3. Which is the best saddle?
4. Whom did you ask?
5. What is the price of the harness?

6. Whose are these boots?
7. Whom did you pay?
8. Which of the trails is best?
9. What is calf roping?
10. Which is Gail's farm?

B. Copy each sentence. Underline the relative pronoun.
Example: The principal thanked the photographers, <u>who</u> are students.

11. One photographer whom she congratulated won first prize.
12. Each photo that was selected pictured a person or landscape.
13. One man who was photographed wore overalls.
14. The man whom Harvey photographed was a veteran.
15. The photographer who won second prize is a good friend of mine.
16. She lives in Golden Gate Park, which is nearby.
17. The photograph that won third prize was taken on a boat.
18. The best photo, which took fourth prize, was of a farm.
19. A barn that is very old can be quite lovely.
20. One photographer, whom I don't know, is on the school paper.

C. Tell whether the underlined pronouns in the following sentences are interrogative or relative.
Example: <u>Who</u> is the youngest senator in Congress?
Answer: Interrogative

21. The bill, <u>which</u> you supported, did not pass.
22. <u>Who</u> are the female senators in Congress now?
23. <u>What</u> is the best day to tour the Senate Office Building?
24. The tour, <u>which</u> is given at noon, is quite informative.
25. The senator <u>whom</u> the President applauded is from Iowa.

▶ **Apply/Writing**   Think of a famous person you would like to meet. Write questions that you would ask this person. Try using a variety of interrogative pronouns at the beginnings of your questions.

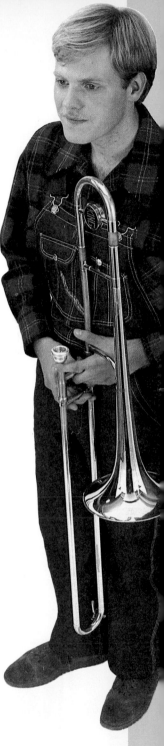

Review/Evaluation

For more review, see Tested Skills Practice, pages 507–509.

[10] **Plural Nouns**   Write the letter of the answer that describes the underlined word in each sentence.
a. Singular noun   **b.** Correct plural   **c.** Incorrect plural

 1. Three enormous <u>moose</u> came charging out of the burning forest.
 2. Each of the queen's <u>great-grandchildren</u> became a ruler.
 3. Mr. Murray grew plump, red, juicy <u>tomatos</u> in his yard.
 4. Loretta gave a woolen <u>scarf</u> to her brother.
 5. The planets and stars are heavenly <u>bodies.</u>
 6. The dog chased a <u>sheep</u> away from the pond.
 7. Janet has at least one hundred old <u>radioes</u> in her collection.
 8. Never pet or feed any of the many <u>deer</u> in our national parks.
 9. We sat around the campfire and told each other scary <u>stories.</u>
10. Did you know that wheat is a <u>species</u> of grass?
11. I read a story about a band of forty <u>thiefs</u> who robbed the rich and gave the money to the poor.
12. Suddenly the <u>monkies</u> stopped their chattering, and it became very quiet and still.
13. The performers practiced their guitar <u>soloes</u> all afternoon.
14. The queen's <u>ladys-in-waiting</u> picked bouquets of flowers to decorate the hall.
15. At sunset, thousands of <u>mouses</u> gathered on the river banks.
16. We sat on the grass in the park and ate our <u>lunches</u>.
17. Several <u>rooves</u> in our neighborhood were blown off.
18. Mandy and Len are always going through <u>crisises</u>.

[11] **Identifying Kinds of Pronouns**   **A.** Write the letter of the answer that identifies the underlined word in each sentence.
a. Possessive form   **b.** Other personal pronoun   **c.** Not a pronoun

19. <u>Our</u> astronomy club is not very large at all.
20. In fact, <u>it</u> has only five members.
21. <u>We</u> want to learn about the solar system.
22. The moons of Uranus really fascinate <u>us</u>.
23. We want to learn everything about <u>them</u>.
24. The members of our club use <u>Jim's</u> telescope.
25. Walt and Lil's is not as powerful as <u>his</u>.

26. Sheila attaches <u>her</u> camera to Jim's telescope and takes pictures.
27. Walt and Lil develop the pictures in <u>their</u> new darkroom.
28. <u>They</u> give everyone in the club copies of the photographs.
29. The club held <u>its</u> election last week.
30. Sheila was willing to be president, and now the job is <u>hers</u>.
31. <u>She</u> will work hard to interest others in the club.
32. The job of helping Sheila recruit new members will be <u>mine</u>.
33. Jim mentioned that <u>his</u> telescope needed minor adjustments.
34. Walt and Lil offered to help <u>him</u> make the adjustments.
35. <u>He</u> said help would be appreciated.
36. Walt and Lil then said to Sheila, "These are <u>yours</u>."
37. Walt and Lil had brought along <u>Sheila's</u> developed pictures.
38. <u>We</u> all thought the pictures were great.

11 **B.** Write the letter of the answer that identifies each underlined word.

a. Interrogative pronoun   **b.** Relative pronoun   **c.** Not a pronoun

39. <u>Who</u> was invited to see the new pictures of Uranus?
40. Uranus, <u>which</u> has nine rings around it, is very difficult to photograph.
41. Whose is that telescope over <u>there</u> on the balcony?
42. <u>Whose</u> is that other telescope?
43. Jim, <u>whom</u> you just met, owns the terrific telescope we use.
44. The pictures for the show were selected by Sheila, <u>who</u> is the club's photographer.
45. <u>Who</u> developed and printed these photographs?
46. The darkroom <u>that</u> Walt and Lil used must be very modern.
47. Look <u>here</u> at that lumpy-looking moon circling Saturn.
48. The moon, <u>which</u> has been named Miranda, was discovered only recently.
49. <u>Which</u> of the planets in our solar system has only one moon?
50. Sheila, <u>whose</u> pictures you are admiring, is our president.
51. <u>What</u> do you like most about the pictures?
52. <u>Which</u> of them might win an award?
53. Are there any more pictures <u>that</u> we might see?
54. <u>Whom</u> do we thank for the show?
55. Jim is the one <u>whom</u> you should thank.

Writing Evaluation

9   This is a picture of conflict, of people seeking a way to convince each other about something through the power of words. Write a short story of at least five paragraphs based on this picture. Include some dialogue that reveals what these characters are like and what they are arguing about.

1. Brainstorm ideas and list them under the headings *conflict,* *characters,* and *setting*. Then sketch out a story plan.
2. Write your short story, using these questions as guidelines.
   ✔ Are all the essential story elements included?
   ✔ Can a reader clearly picture the characters and setting?
   ✔ Are the conflict and the dialogue believable?
   ✔ Will the opening sentence attract a reader's attention?
3. When you have finished writing, spend a few minutes checking and revising your story.
   ✔ Can you answer "yes" to all the questions above?
   ✔ Have you used the correct forms of pronouns?
   ✔ Have you spelled noun plurals correctly?

Curriculum Connection:
Reading/Literature

Every short story contains a conflict of some kind. It is the conflict that makes a story interesting, for you want to see how it turns out. You learned that in some stories, the conflict is between one character and another, as in a story in which a young woman's desire to be a doctor is opposed by her father. In other stories, the conflict is between a character and some outside force, as in a story in which people in a lifeboat fight against the elements of nature to survive. In still other stories, the conflict is between a character and himself or herself. This is the conflict in "Lucas and Jake." Lucas wants to be admired and respected. He invents a story about the ferocity of Jake, who is really a tired old lion. When he retrieves the Yo-Yo from the "vicious" lion, the boys are impressed, and Lucas has earned their respect. In addition, Lucas feels that "he'd done something for Jake today, for the whole kingdom of lions."

▶ **Think**   Recall a number of short stories that you have read in your literature or reading textbook. Identify the major conflict in each. Review how the conflict was resolved.

▶ **Discuss**   Meet with a group of classmates to discuss short stories that you have read recently. Identify and explain the conflict in each story. In each case, how was the conflict resolved?

▶ **Find Out**   Read a short story or review one that you have read on your own. Choose a story that your classmates are unlikely to have read. Decide whether the conflict is between characters, within one character, or between a character and an outside force. Then use the plot diagram on page 60 to briefly outline the beginning, conflict, climax, and resolution of the story.

▶ **React: Summarize**   Now use your outline to write a summary of the story. Draw a line in your summary between the point at which you have mentioned the conflict and the rest of the summary, where you mention the climax and resolution. Read your summary aloud to your classmates, stopping where you have drawn the line. Ask classmates to guess the climax and resolution of the story. Then, read the rest of your summary. Have classmates compare the actual climax and resolution with those that they have proposed.

Tested Skills Maintenance

5 **Kinds of Sentences**   Copy the sentences, adding appropriate end punctuation. Tell what kind of sentence each is.

1. Look in the bottom drawer of that chest
2. What will I find there
3. It's a present for you and your sister
4. What a pleasant surprise this is
5. Do the two of you like hand-embroidered knee socks

6 **Subjects and Predicates**   Copy the sentences. Draw a vertical line between the complete subject and complete predicate. Underline the simple subject once and the verb twice.

6. My cousin broke his left leg last Saturday.
7. He was playing touch football at Larry Glazer's house.
8. Several of the players slipped on the damp grass.
9. A doctor in the emergency room put a cast on Ted's leg.
10. Larry's parents called Ted's parents from the hospital.

7 **Correcting Sentence Fragments**   Rewrite the sentences below to correct the sentence fragments.

11. Sue and I really enjoyed the tennis tournament. In spite of the occasional showers.
12. Sue missed the first game. Because her bus was late.
13. We've been taking lessons. And practicing every day.
14. Arnie Loudent played a good match. But didn't win.
15. Maybe I can play in a tournament. If my game improves.

8 **Correcting Run-on Sentences**   Correct each run-on sentence below. Use a period and a capital letter to make it two sentences or make it a compound sentence, using a conjunction and comma or a semicolon. Use each way at least once.

16. Carlo's ambition is to be a writer he writes daily.
17. Carlo comes by his talent naturally, his mother is a writer.
18. He reads many novels he doesn't really want to write one.
19. An art council published a poem of his, it later won an award.
20. Everyone congratulated Carlo he didn't say much about it.

1. **Drawing Conclusions**   Write a sentence that tells what is happening in the following paragraph.

(21) The ring was loud and clear. It woke Lucy up. She rubbed an eye with one hand while she searched for the source of the sound with the other. She picked up the receiver and sleepily said hello.

2. **Paragraphs: Main Idea**   Read the paragraph and decide what the main idea is. Write a sentence stating that main idea. Then write the numbers of the two sentences that give details that most directly support the main idea.

(22) John's parents told him that he was small for his age. (23) He couldn't run very fast either. (24) His knees were weak they said. (25) They were afraid he could get injured if he played football. (26) Furthermore, football practice would take time away from his studies.

3. **Writing a Narrative Paragraph**   Read the following paragraph, which begins with the main idea. Then write a sentence, adding one more supporting detail. Use a transition word to begin the sentence.

(27) Kay did everything she could think of to delay writing the letter. First, she found her nails needed polishing. Next, her room needed straightening. Then she had to read a magazine article.

4. **Writing a Friendly Letter**   Copy the friendly letter below, using the correct form. Capitalize and punctuate correctly. When you are finished, label the parts of the letter: *Heading, Greeting, Body, Closing,* and *Signature.*

(28) It was fun visiting you. Since I've been home. I've been listening to the cassettes you gave me. They're great. I've also been reading a book that you would like it's about artists. I miss you.

February 22 1988
145 S. barry street
Oklahoma City, Oklahoma 73112

love
Shirley   dear Grandma

Narrative Writing

Theme: Breakthroughs

Have you ever faced an obstacle that you felt you couldn't overcome? Perhaps you made a **breakthrough** and figured out a way to surmount this obstacle. In Unit 7 you will read about a breakthrough an immigrant from Norway makes when he comes to America. Then you will have a chance to write your own personal narrative and tell about a breakthrough you have made.

Unit 7 Thinking About Literature: Personal Narrative

Unit 8 Writing Personal Narratives

Unit 9 Verbs

1 Literature: Personal Narrative

America has been called a nation of immigrants. One such immigrant, Ole Edvart Rölvaag (ō'lə ed'värt rōl'väg), came from Norway in 1896. Rölvaag was not prepared for his early experiences in America. When he arrived in New York he felt lost and helpless. This was an important breakthrough for Rölvaag because now he understood what it was to be an immigrant.

The following personal narrative gives a nonfiction account of Rölvaag's life in America. A **personal narrative** *tells the story of a person's life. In the following excerpt Rölvaag narrates his own story to the author Lincoln Colcord. As you read, try to see America through the eyes of a newcomer.*

from "Rölvaag the Fisherman Shook His Fist at Fate"
by Lincoln Colcord

All of my people for generations had followed the sea, and at fifteen I had taken my place in the fisheries. It was a hard life, and I went at it hard. There was nothing else to do. I had been a failure at school, while my older brother had been a brilliant success. When my father took me out of school at the age of fourteen, he had told me bitterly that education was not for me. And I had believed it; the iron had sunk deep into my soul. I had to prove that I was worth something in other directions.

I am proud to say that I became a good fisherman and an expert seaman. But I wasn't satisfied. There was something else I wanted in life, yet I couldn't put my finger on it. In 1893, the twenty-fifth of January to be exact, I remember the whole fishing fleet was caught out in a terrible storm. Many of my friends were lost that day. The man I sailed with was an old Viking, the finest seaman I have ever known. He brought us through the storm by superhuman efforts. How I loved and admired him for this and other feats.

Yet, thinking the experience over afterwards, it struck me that my way of living was awfully futile. In fact, that storm changed my nature. As the seas broke over us and I believed that death was inescapable, I felt a resentment against Destiny. Why was my life to be snuffed out just as it was about to begin? I was going to die without a chance to express my real self, to show what was in me. It seemed such utter nonsense!

But I had to keep with the fishing to earn my living; and two more years went by. At last I wrote to my uncle, who had emigrated to South Dakota. I asked him if he could send me a ticket to America. I said that I would pay him back after I arrived. One day the next summer the ticket came.

Annually, a great market was held at the little town of Björn, about twenty English miles from my home. There was much merrymaking and dancing. I sailed over with my master, the old sea king who had saved my life two years before. On the way I told him my plans—that I was going to quit the fishing and emigrate to America. He objected fiercely. As soon as we got ashore, he said, "Come here. I want to show you something."

He led me down among the new boats exposed for sale, the first fishing craft of their kind on the coast of Norway. We looked them all over. At last he picked out the best boat of the lot, a brand-new hull built to carry a crew of five men. I had never seen such a handsome craft.

"As you know, I am fairly well-to-do," he said. "I like you, and you like me. You are making a great mistake. If you will send back that ticket to your uncle, I will buy this boat for you."

Well, you can imagine! Here was success, material success, along with the backing of the man I respected above all others. I can honestly say that I have never felt such a surge of pride. Yes; it made me proud and happy—and very, very sad. His generous offer only complicated everything in a way that tore my heart.

"Thank you, sir," I said shortly. "I will have to think it over. Give me till tonight."

Then I turned and left the row of new boats, walked through the town, and climbed the hill behind it. Somewhere up on the hillside I sat down. I sat there all afternoon.

It was a fine clear day. I sat there gazing off across the fiord. What ought I to do? How could I refuse such a splendid offer?

Down below in the town they were having a jolly time. The sound of it came up to me. I might have been the gayest of the lot; but now I felt entirely cut off from the others. I had to decide something; life had made me tragic. Would my heart stop aching as I set sail, as I paid for the boat and grew prosperous as the years went by?

On the other hand, what was my heart aching for? I honestly didn't know. I just felt that I wasn't fulfilling myself. I wanted to go

away, find out what the world was like, and see if I didn't fit in somewhere else. But how could I explain that to sensible, practical people? To their minds, I'd simply be acting like a fool. . . .

I finally did manage to make up my mind that afternoon, though it meant a heartbreaking struggle. I came down into the town at last and hunted up my master, the old Viking. I marched straight up to him and looked him in the eye, a deep, piercing eye it was, too.

"I'm sorry, sir," I said, "but I cannot accept your offer. I have decided to go to America."

"You're a fool!" he said and turned away.

I went to a port down the coast and took ship for the New World. I was nothing but a boy from the provinces, ignorant of travel. You'll have an idea of the extent of my wardrobe when I tell you that I wore one shirt from Norway to South Dakota; it had its last washing the day before we arrived in New York. The ocean voyage was only a pleasure for me. The sea was my home. Meals were furnished with my ticket, there were plenty of Norwegians to talk to, and I had nothing to worry about except to wonder what would happen when I got ashore.

But when I landed in New York things were very different. The vast harbor, the teeming city, and the alien language threw me into a terrible confusion. I couldn't speak or understand a word of English. It wasn't until I got on board the train that I discovered meals weren't furnished with my railroad ticket. By that time I was down to ten cents in American money and a copper pocket piece from Norway. I went without food for three days and three nights, all the way from New York to South Dakota.

I left the train at a little station on the Dakota prairie. Looking around, I saw nothing but level land, like the sea. My uncle was to have met me but had made a mistake in the day of my arrival. I tried to ask my way, but no one at the station spoke Norwegian. At last a Swede who worked on the railroad came along, and I was able to communicate with him. He thought he knew approximately where my uncle lived, and gave me some direction; I had a twelve-mile walk ahead of me. When he found that I hadn't eaten for three days, he gave me what remained in his dinner pail—one sandwich and some coffee.

By this time the sun was going down. I struck out on foot, soon lost my way, and walked far into the night. It was one of those still prairie nights, breathless with heat. I've learned to love them since, but then I was worn out and discouraged. I felt as if I had been dropped down in the midst of nowhere. At last I came upon something in the darkness, a man driving a horse hitched to a wagon. The man was a Norwegian, and he took me to the farm where my uncle was employed. I stumbled into the house more dead than alive.

In that experience I learned the first lesson of the immigrant. It was the first and perhaps the greatest lesson: a feeling of utter helplessness, as if life had betrayed me. It comes from a sense of being lost in a vast strange land. In this case it was largely physical; but I soon met the spiritual phase of the same thing: the sense of being lost in a strange culture, the sense of being thrust somewhere outside the charmed circle of life. If you couldn't conquer that feeling you were lost indeed. Many couldn't and didn't and many were lost thereby.

► **Discussing**

1. How does Rölvaag feel after he arrives in New York? What are some of the things that cause him to feel this way?
2. What two reasons does Rölvaag give for becoming a fisherman?
3. Why is he both happy and sad at the seaman's offer of a boat?
4. Do you think that young people today have the same chance to prove themselves as Rölvaag did a century ago? Why or why not?

► **Analyzing Characterization**

The methods an author uses to develop the personality of a character is called **characterization.** Rölvaag's character is revealed through descriptions of his speech, behavior, and feelings. Read the passages below and explain what each reveals about Rölvaag's character.

1. "When my father took me out of school at the age of fourteen, he had told me that education was not for me. And I had believed it; the iron had sunk deep into my soul. I had to prove that I was worth something in other directions."
2. "I was going to die without a chance to express my real self, to show what was in me. It seemed such utter nonsense!"
3. "I wanted to go away, find out what the world was like, and see if I didn't fit in somewhere else."

► **Writing**

If you were Rölvaag, would you have come to America? What factors would have influenced the decision? What questions would you ask yourself? Write a paragraph to explain your decision.

► **Extending**

Speaking and Listening Meet with a small group of classmates. Think about and discuss the kind of breakthroughs Rölvaag probably made when he settled in America. For example, learning to speak English would be an important breakthrough. Compare your group's breakthroughs with the other groups' breakthroughs.

Reading *Breakthrough: Women in Aviation,* by Elizabeth Simpson Smith, is about nine women who made breakthroughs in aviation by pursuing careers in this field. Their jobs range from a cargo pilot to an astronaut.

2 Speaking About a Personal Experience

Narrate a personal experience so that your audience understands what it meant to you.

▶ **Focus**   Television reporter Charles Kuralt often relates personal experiences from his travels around the world. Listen as your teacher reads Kuralt's narrative titled "Unlikely Heroes."

After you have listened to Kuralt's narrative, answer this question: Why does Kuralt consider the rancher an unlikely hero?

You will often have occasion to tell about your own experiences. Choose an experience that your classmates would enjoy hearing about. You may wish to describe something that has made you proud, fearful, embarrassed, angry, or puzzled. Think of how you would relate this experience in a three-minute talk. Use the following guidelines to help prepare for and deliver your talk.

Guidelines for Speaking

1. Consider your **purpose.**
   What is the purpose of your talk? Is it to share a message? to entertain? Is it to make a conclusion, as Kuralt does? Do you want to discuss a breakthrough, as Rölvaag does in his narrative? Once you have a purpose, you will know what to emphasize.
2. Decide who your **audience** will be.
   Ask yourself who your listeners are. Focus on your audience to make your narrative more interesting for them.
3. Use **chronological order** to relate the events.
   Use sentences like Kuralt's that sequence events as they happened.
4. Include **details** to make your experience vivid.
   Help your audience feel they are sharing your experience.
5. Use your **voice** to get your message across.
   Adjust the **pitch,** or tone, of your voice to match your feelings. Adjust the **volume** of your voice to match the size of the place in which you are speaking. **Stress,** or emphasize, important words or phrases in your story.
6. **Look** at your audience as you speak.

▶ **Practice** **A.** Pretend you are O. E. Rölvaag. Give a three-minute talk about your first weeks in America. Use information from the last four paragraphs of Rölvaag's narrative. (This passage begins, "But when I landed. . . ." page 93). Follow the guidelines on page 95.

B. Prepare a personal-experience talk of your own by filling out a chart. Your audience will be your class. Your purpose will be to entertain. The results may resemble the chart below. Charts will vary.

Topic: The day I ate 3 pounds of jellybeans
Purpose: to entertain
Audience: class
Order of Events: save $4.25 recycling cans
   buy 3 pounds of licorice jellybeans
   eat them all on front porch
   brother finds out
   I get sick
Details: black teeth give me away
   terrible stomachache
   brother calls me "Jelly Belly"
Feelings: embarrassment
Phrases to stress: hot July afternoon
   I was 7
   always loved licorice jellybeans
   have never eaten one since

▶ **Apply/Oral Language** Relate your personal experience to the class. Use the chart you filled out in Practice B to help you. Keep in mind the speaking guidelines that appear in this lesson.

3 Using Context Clues

Context clues can help you determine the meaning of a word.

▶ **Focus**   You may be able to understand an unfamiliar word or a familiar word used in a new way by examining **context clues**—the words, phrases, and sentences surrounding the word. Look for clues to the meaning of *hull* in this sentence from "Rölvaag the Fisherman Shook His Fist at Fate."

> At last he picked out the best boat of the lot, a brand-new **hull** built to carry a crew of five men.

The word *boat* is a context clue. It tells you what a hull is.

In another sentence from the same selection, the word *utter* is used. Utter can mean "complete; total; absolute," or it can mean "speak." Which meaning is correct here?

> It was the first and perhaps the greatest lesson: a feeling of **utter** helplessness, as if life had betrayed me.

Four kinds of context clues are illustrated in the sentences in the chart below.

Clue	Context Sentence	Using the Clue
synonym	Bob was *reminiscing*, remembering his boyhood.	What two words have the same meaning?
antonym	It took no important figure but only an *inconsequential* bug to get Ruth's attention.	The word *but* points out opposites. What words are opposites?
definition	Some *transients*, people only passing by, asked questions about her.	What phrase defines *transients?*
example	Millie grew *indolent:* she slept late and never exercised.	What do examples of *indolent* suggest the word means?

▶ **Guided Practice**   In this sentence, find examples that help explain the meaning of *engrossed*. Then define *engrossed*.

The computer's problem so *engrossed* me that I thought of nothing else and tried twelve times to make it work.

▶ **Practice**   Study each italicized word in context. Use context clues to choose the correct meaning of the word.

1. We analyzed the computer problem, making a *check* on every bit of data and watching each step of its operation.
    a. restaurant ticket   **b.** examination   **c.** pattern of squares
2. A specialist examined the computer's *vitals*—all the chips, cables, and keys that are essential to its operation.
    a. necessary parts   **b.** instructions   **c.** faulty parts
3. Well-known *technologists* who know most about computer science were asked to solve the problem.
    a. scientific experts   **b.** salespeople   **c.** students
4. We refused to give in to *despondency* and remained hopeful of solving the problem.
    a. cheerfulness   **b.** hopelessness   **c.** confidence
5. The solution required some *innovative* thinking, for we had tried all the old ideas and they had not worked.
    a. not important   **b.** quiet   **c.** new
6. Suddenly, as if I had *peered* into the computer's heart and had seen its emotions, I discovered the cause of the problem.
    a. gazed   **b.** spoken   **c.** smashed
7. Thinking itself a person, the computer would not *operate* correctly until someone gave it a human name.
    a. perform surgery   **b.** manage   **c.** work
8. The computer was looking for *compassion*, a feeling of appreciation, from its operators that would show that it was highly thought of.
    a. talent   **b.** sympathy   **c.** strength

▶ **Apply/Vocabulary**   Choose five unfamiliar words in a story. Find a synonym, antonym, example, or definition for each word. Then use each in a sentence with context clues. Ask a partner to read your sentences and give meanings for the unfamiliar words.

Our Living Language

Old English

Gif man ōþerne mid fȳste in naso slæhð, III scillinga.

What language do you think the above sentence represents? You may be surprised to know that this is English, as it was spoken over 1,000 years ago. Scholars who study language call it Old English. The sentence was one of the laws proclaimed in the sixth century in England. Loosely translated into Modern English, it means, "If a man hits another in the nose with his fist, three shillings." How many of these words did you recognize in Old English?

Old English was the language of Germanic tribes from northern Europe. These tribes were called the Angles, the Saxons, and the Jutes. When they invaded England in the late fifth century, they brought their language, *Englisc. Englisc,* or Old English, was more like German than the English that you speak.

Later, missionaries from Rome introduced Latin words into the language of the Angles, the Saxons, and the Jutes. Vikings from northern Europe added Scandinavian words.

Although only scholars can really understand the original Old English, many Old English words survive today, with some spelling changes. *Day, night, mother, father, a, the, and, of,* and *that* are only a few such words.

Word Play These Old English words look very much like Modern English. Try to translate them.

1. sunne   **2.** dor   **3.** mann   **4.** fisc   **5.** cild

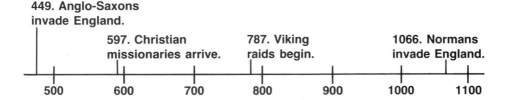

449. Anglo-Saxons invade England.
597. Christian missionaries arrive.
787. Viking raids begin.
1066. Normans invade England.

500   600   700   800   900   1000   1100

4 Writing a Personal Narrative

A personal narrative can tell a story about a breakthrough in your life.

In this unit you will write a narrative like the ones that appeared in Unit 7. The first narrative was an account of O. E. Rölvaag coming to America as a young immigrant. The second narrative was Charles Kuralt's story about meeting a kindly rancher in Wyoming. In both accounts the writers tell about the breakthroughs they had during these experiences.

Think about a breakthrough you have experienced. As you think about this, think about your **purpose** and **audience.** You will want to tell your readers about events that may have caused special feelings, changed your plans, or made you see something with fresh eyes.

1. Prewriting

▶ **Choose a Topic** Make a list of events in your life that were breakthroughs for you, such as learning something new about someone. To select a topic, you might start looking through your journal. Here is a journal entry that one writer used as a topic for a personal narrative.

> One important lesson I learned was when I was nine years old. Mom made me invite my sister Laura to my birthday party. I didn't want Laura to come because I didn't want a pest ruining my party. Laura did something though that made me change my mind about her.

Review the items on your list and choose one to write about. Make sure the topic you choose is not too broad. You should be able to recount your story in a few paragraphs.

▶ **Develop Ideas** Questioning can help you focus on information you need for your narrative. Where and when did this event occur? Who was involved? What were the major actions that took place? Your answers to these questions will provide a list of details.

As you write your list, **use the thinking skill of sequencing** to put events in proper order. Do not include events that are not important. Read the list below. Notice that the writers eliminated an irrelevant detail.

Where: at the Magicians's Palace
When: my ninth birthday
Who: magician, my sister Laura, me
Actions: 1. We watch the magic show.
2. The magician calls on me.
3. The magician begins the trick.
4. Laura runs on stage to save me.
5. ~~The magician leaves the party.~~

You might also make a details list like the one below. Jot down details to describe the people or the main actions in your story.

Detail List for Laura
age four   sturdy legs, white tights
yellow party dress   determined

Next, create a Word Bank. Think of words to describe your experience. Check the Word Bank on this page for additional ideas.

2. Writing

▶ **Study the Draft**   Before you begin writing, read the first draft that follows. Note how each paragraph tells a different part of the story in sequence. The last paragraph tells how the writer felt about the experience. Note, too, that the writer has made some errors and that some words have been added or crossed out.

No Magic for Laura

For my ninth birthday, my mother had took my sister Laura, me, and some ~~freinds~~ friends to the Magician's Palace. I was happy because I ~~was very keen on~~ like magic. I wasn't happy about Laura being there though. I thought she ruin my party because she's such a pest.

We took our places and sat on the edge of our seats. I has heard that the birthday child was asked up on stage. To help the magician. We all watched with wide eyes as the magician fooled us time and time again. My big moment come, and the magician called me up on stage.

She explain that this trick involved her magic saw. To prove how good the saw was, she chopped some ~~potatos~~ potatoes in half. With a flurish, she

produce the ~~potatos~~ potatoes whole again.
Then she ~~will ask~~ asked me to put
my head under the saw blade. As I
put my head down, I heard a big
comotion.

Laura ran up to the stage as fast
as her sturdy little legs in their
white tights could carry her. She
pulled me away from the saw and
said that no one was going to cut
her brother in half! The magician
wasn't the only one who was amazed
at this determined little girl in her
yellow party dress, I was too! The
magician resolved the situation by
completing the trick with another
volunteer.

Latter on, someone asked me if Laura
had embarrassed me. I told them that
she hadn't and that even though she
be a pest, she was the best sister a
guy could have.

▶ **Write a Draft**   Now write your first draft. Write on every other line so you have room to make changes. Follow your prewriting notes. Don't worry about making mistakes. You can make corrections when you revise your work.

3. Revising

▶ **Read and Confer**   Put your draft away for a while. Then reread it and decide if it says what you want it to say. Now read your draft to a partner or a group of classmates. Discuss these questions.

Conference Questions

1. Are events told in sequence? Could more transition words and phrases be used to make the order of events clearer?
2. Are powerful verbs used?
3. Has the writer used vivid details to describe the setting and characters?
4. Is all the information important enough to include? Should anything be deleted?
5. Has the writer expressed his or her feelings about this experience?
6. Has the writer explained his or her breakthrough?

▶ **Make Changes**   Consider suggestions made by your partner or classmates. Make any changes necessary in your draft with a red pencil. Following is one strategy to strengthen your writing.

STRATEGY: Use powerful verbs instead of dull or overused ones. Notice how the following sentences have been improved in this way.

> Laura, ~~ran up~~ *scampered* to the stage as fast as her sturdy little legs in their white tights would carry her. She ~~pulled~~ *yanked* me away from the saw and said that no one was going to ~~cut~~ *chop* her brother in half!

Now examine your own writing. Circle the verbs that are dull or weak and replace them with powerful ones. In your writer's notebook, list the dull verbs and their substitutions.

▶ **Proofread and Edit** Now check your work for mistakes in spelling, capitalization, and punctuation. Use the proofreading questions and the proofreader's marks to help you.

Proofreading Questions
1. Did I capitalize and punctuate each sentence correctly?
2. Did I use verbs correctly?
3. Did I keep my verb tenses consistent?
4. Did I form plural nouns correctly?
5. Are all words spelled correctly?

Make a capital.

Make a small letter.

⊙ Add a period.

⋏ Add a comma.

Add quotation marks.

⋀ Add something.

Take out something.

Move something.

New paragraph.

Correct spelling.

▶ **Make a Final Copy** Now make a final draft of your personal narrative, using your revision changes. Don't forget to give your work a title.

4. Presenting

Now that your personal narrative is finished, you will want to share it. You might read it aloud to your class. You might also consider putting your narrative in a class book with your classmates' stories. For suggestions on how to make a class book, see The Writer at Work, page 569.

Revising and Editing Workshop

Connecting Writing and Grammar

- In Unit 7 you read and listened to the personal-experience narratives of two writers.
- In Unit 8 you wrote a personal narrative.

Now it's time to use your skill as an editor to improve another writer's first draft. Read this personal narrative carefully. As you read, ask yourself these questions.

✔ Are events told in sequence?
✔ Are the verb tenses consistent?
✔ Are all verb forms spelled correctly?

(1) I often like to think about things that happened to me long ago. (2) Sometimes when I look back, I smile at my particular beliefs. (3) At other times, I grimaced. (4) For instance, I will think perfectionists are really off base. (5) The experience that made me feel this way occured when I was in grade school. (6) I went to Clay School. (7) What could been a demoralizing episode turned out to be an important breakthrough for me.

(8) I was then, as now, an eager but tone-deaf singer. (9) Each morning I would come to attention. (10) To sing the national anthem. (11) The echoes of my enthusiastic notes sounded perfect to my ears and my classmates accepted my squawks. (12) My patriotism was loud and firm, so no one ever said anything. (13) I truely liked my classmates' silence.

(14) A new girl joined our class. (15) I tryed to think of something to say, but I couldn't answer her. (16) Christina came up to me and said, "Couldn't you just mouth the words?" (17) I didn't feel much like singing.

(18) I have concluded that Christina was a perfectionist of the saddest kind. (19) Her had missed the point about patriotism entirely. (20) Christina's missing the point was worse than all the notes I had missed each morning.

► Revising the Draft

1. The sequence of events in the third paragraph is not clear. One sentence is out of order and transition words and phrases are not used. Rewrite the paragraph, putting the sentences in a logical sequence and using transition words and phrases.
2. Some sentences in the second paragraph would be improved if they contained more powerful verbs. Revise the sentences, substituting more powerful verbs.
3. The writer does not give much information about Christina. Add vivid details that tell about her being a perfectionist.
4. One sentence in the first paragraph is not important enough to include. Delete the sentence.
5. Add, delete, or rearrange any other information you think would improve the draft.

► Editing the Draft

6. One sentence in the first paragraph is missing an auxiliary verb. Rewrite this sentence correctly.
7. There are unnecessary tense changes in the first paragraph. Correct the verb tenses to make them consistent.
8. Find two misspelled verbs and a misspelled adverb. Spell the words correctly.
9. One sentence in the last paragraph uses a pronoun incorrectly. Rewrite the sentence, using the correct pronoun.
10. Find and correct a sentence fragment in the second paragraph.

► Working Together on the Draft

Meet with a group of your classmates. Discuss the changes you made in the draft. Listen to the changes your classmates made. Then rewrite the draft on page 106. Include all the revisions you think are important.

► Evaluating Your Own Writing

Now review your own writing. Look over the personal narrative you wrote in this unit and any other written work you have. Did you have any problems using consistent verb tenses? Did you have any problems using auxiliary verbs? The lessons that follow will help you with these writing problems.

5 Identifying Verbs

Some verbs express action. Other verbs link the subject with a word or words in the predicate.

▶ **Focus** The most important word in the predicate is the verb. A verb that expresses action, or tells what action is taking place, is called an **action verb.** Some action verbs show physical action. Other action verbs show mental action.

> Sara **ran** in the marathon in Springfield last year.
> She **believed** in herself and in her ability.

Both *ran* and *believed* are action verbs. The verb *ran* expresses physical action, and the verb *believed* expresses mental action.

Another kind of verb, called a **linking verb,** joins the subject with a word or words in the predicate that describe or name the subject. Linking verbs express no action. Some of the most common linking verbs are forms of *be,* including *is, am, are, was,* and *were.*

> The runners in the race **were** competitive.
> The first prize **was** a huge, gold-plated trophy.

In the first sentence, the linking verb *were* joins the subject with the word *competitive. Competitive* describes the subject *runners.* In the second sentence, what is the linking verb? What word in the predicate tells what the prize was?

The verbs *seem, appear, become, feel, look, taste, sound,* and *smell* can also be linking verbs. Read the examples below.

> The joggers **seem** eager.   These socks **feel** wet.
> That runner **appears** weary.   The snack **tastes** salty.

▶ **Guided Practice** Tell which verbs are action verbs and which are linking verbs.

1. Sara wore new running shoes.
2. She felt really good.
3. She finished tenth in last year's race.
4. She won many shorter races.
5. Sara is the best runner in her age group.

▶ **Practice**   **A.** Complete each sentence with an action verb.
Example: Jason _____ quite rapidly.
Answer: Jason runs quite rapidly.

1. Runners _____ daily.
2. Exercise _____ your health.
3. The athletes _____ records.
4. Two contestants _____.
5. Fans _____ the track meet.

6. I _____ the water.
7. The water _____ everywhere.
8. Soon the meet _____.
9. Everyone _____ for home.
10. The athletes _____ well.

B. Complete each sentence with a linking verb. Use a variety of verbs.
Example: A new goal _____ ahead.
Answer: A new goal was ahead.

11. My performance _____ best.
12. Her time _____ the fastest.
13. My lunch _____ good.
14. The day _____ too short.
15. Everything _____ so easy.

16. The attendance _____ higher.
17. The crowd _____ noisy.
18. That _____ a good sign.
19. The runners _____ happy.
20. Track meets _____ wonderful.

C. Write the verb in each sentence and tell whether it is an action or a linking verb.
Example: Bill and I bicycled to the lakefront.
Answer: bicycled — Action verb

21. The athletes all traveled to New Orleans.
22. New Orleans is the largest city in Louisiana.
23. The Mississippi River flows past New Orleans.
24. The trip was my first one ever outside Missouri.
25. The best restaurants seemed rather expensive.
26. Many of the buildings in New Orleans are old.
27. Tourists walk through the French Quarter every day.
28. Many of them buy *beignets* at the French Market.
29. These pastries taste warm and sweet.
30. Some tourists purchase antiques in fancy shops.
31. People in New Orleans celebrate Mardi Gras each year.
32. The citizens of the city appeared friendly and courteous to us.

▶ **Apply/Social Studies**   Write six sentences about an American city. Use action verbs in three sentences and linking verbs in three.

6 Action or Linking Verb

Some verbs can be either action verbs or linking verbs.

▶ **Focus**   Some verbs may be used as either action verbs or linking verbs. These verbs include *appear, become, feel, grow, look, remain, smell, sound,* and *taste.* How a verb is used in a sentence determines whether it is an action verb or a linking verb. Study these examples.

Ben **smelled** the soup.	Hope **felt** the confining walls.
The soup **smelled** delicious.	She **felt** panicky.
I **grow** dates on those trees.	Ann **looked** at the dresses.
I **grow** anxious to taste them.	None **looked** right for her.

In the first sentence in each pair, the subject is performing an action. In the second sentence, no action is performed. Instead, the verb links the subject to a word in the predicate.

The easiest way to tell whether a verb is used as an action verb or a linking verb is to try to replace it with a form of the verb *be.* Look at these sentences.

Ernie **looks** happy with his new library books.
Michael **looks** out the window in boredom.

In the first sentence, *looks* is a linking verb. It may be replaced with the verb *is* without changing the meaning of the sentence. In the second sentence, however, *looks* cannot be replaced with *is.* The meaning of the sentence would be completely different. In this sentence, *looks* is an action verb. Try this test on the sentence pairs above.

▶ **Guided Practice**   Tell whether each sentence contains an action verb or a linking verb.

1. Something in the kitchen smelled wonderful.
2. Suddenly Mother appeared with bread from the oven.
3. The brown, crispy loaf looked delicious.
4. Kim became very hungry.
5. She eagerly tasted the bread.
6. She remained in the kitchen for another slice.

▶ **Practice** **A.** Copy the verbs in the sentences and write whether they are action or linking verbs.

Example: The mountain looked impossibly high.

Answer: looked—Linking verb

1. The mountaineers looked at the peak from a distance.
2. They felt hopeful and courageous.
3. Few trees or shrubs grew in the rocky soil.
4. The air smelled clean and pure.
5. The water in a nearby stream looked clear and blue.
6. The climbers felt their way up slowly.
7. The click of their crampons sounded against the rocks.
8. They became more cautious.
9. The climbers remained calm during the first hour.
10. They grew tense a little later.
11. Suddenly dark clouds appeared in the sky above the mountain.
12. Everyone felt nervous.
13. The rumble of thunder sounded fearsome.
14. The climbers remained on the mountain despite the danger.
15. At last the sky grew light again.

B. Follow the same directions as for Practice A.

16. Some people look for adventure in their lives.
17. They appear at exciting places.
18. Edmund Hillary's desire for adventure grew stronger each year.
19. As a young man, he looked after bees in New Zealand.
20. Later, he became a famous mountain climber.
21. Mt. Everest, the world's tallest mountain, remained the ultimate challenge for him.
22. Hillary and his guide remained at the top for a short time.
23. The final victory at the summit, 29,141 feet above sea level, tasted sweet to him.
24. On May 29, 1953, he looked down at the world beneath him.
25. He remained only a short time but felt the thrill of his feat.
26. He became Sir Edmund Hillary at the hand of Queen Elizabeth II.

▶ **Apply/Writing** Think of a special achievement you are proud of. Describe it in a few sentences, using both action and linking verbs.

7 Verb Phrases

A verb phrase consists of a main verb and one or more helping, or auxiliary, verbs.

▶ **Focus**   The verb, or simple predicate, may sometimes be one word. Often though, the verb consists of two or more words—a main verb and one or more helping verbs. This is called a **verb phrase.**

> Mr. Velasquez **is planting** beans and tomatoes in his garden.
> He **should have been finished** yesterday.

The **main verb** is always the final word in the verb phrase. It tells what action is happening. The **helping,** or **auxiliary, verbs** precede the main verb and help it express meaning and tense. Name the main and helping verbs in the examples above. Then study the chart.

Helping Verbs

am, are, is, was, were, be, being, been
has, have, had
do, does, did
can, could, must, may, might, shall, should, will, would

Some verbs in the chart, if used alone, can be main verbs.

Main Verbs	**Helping Verbs**
He **had** the tools.	The beans **had sprouted** quickly.
The tools **were** good ones.	Onions **were growing** well.

The helping verb or verbs usually come right before the main verb. But sometimes an adverb will come in between. In questions, the helping verb and main verb are often separated by the subject.

He **will** not **plant** corn.	He **has** always **planted** squash.
Am I **planting** the peas?	**Have** you **pulled** the weeds?

▶ **Guided Practice**   Name the verb phrases in these sentences.

1. Stan has planted a vegetable garden this year.
2. Will he be doing all the maintenance himself?

► **Practice**   **A.** Write the verb phrases in the sentences. One sentence has two verb phrases.

Example: Diane has been studying electronics.
Answer: has been studying

1. She may have been attending classes this afternoon.
2. Diane should have come home twenty minutes ago.
3. What is keeping her?
4. She probably will be arriving soon.
5. Mrs. Velasquez and Connie are teaching at Union School.
6. Did Juan run in the track meet yesterday?
7. Mr. Velasquez has been working in the garden again today.
8. Should we help him, or would we only get in the way?
9. The garden can be planted in no time at all.
10. Mr. Velasquez had already prepared the soil last week.
11. Everyone is surprised at his progress since this morning.
12. The Velasquezes have invited us to dinner tonight.

B. Copy the sentences. Draw two lines under each main verb and one line under each auxiliary verb.

Example: Carlos <u>has</u> not yet <u>finished</u> his report on tennis.

13. He had at one time studied the history of the game.
14. The game of tennis was first played in France.
15. Years ago, players would usually hit the ball with their hands.
16. Now, of course, they must always use a racket, or a foul would be called.
17. Tennis back then was also played on grass courts.
18. A variety of other surfaces are widely used now, but some famous tournaments are still played on grass.
19. Ancient tennis courts were often enclosed, and players could easily participate during any season.
20. Most people could not afford such a sport, so it was customarily enjoyed by nobles.
21. Tennis has in time become a more affordable sport.
22. Have you ever seriously played the game?

► **Apply/Writing**   Verb phrases can be used when writing about events in the distant past or future. Write a paragraph about an activity in the distant past or future. Use verb phrases.

8 Simple Tenses

Verbs have simple present, past, and future tenses.

▶ **Focus**   The **tense** of a verb can help tell the time of the action. The present, the past, and the future tense are known as the **simple tenses.**

Both action and linking verbs change form to show tense. Study the tenses of the verbs in this chart.

Present Tense	Past Tense	Future Tense
I **walk** alone.	I **walked** alone.	I **will walk** alone.
She **names** it.	She **named** it.	She **will name** it.
He **tries.**	He **tried.**	He **will try.**
I **am** sad.	I **was** sad.	I **will be** sad.
They **begin** today.	They **began** yesterday.	They **will begin** tomorrow.

When you write about events or incidents and you begin writing in the past tense, do not carelessly change to the present tense. Keep writing in the tense you began in unless you have a good reason to change. Notice the unnecessary tense changes in the following paragraph.

> Harold walked with uncertainty to the open field. Suddenly, he spots Heloise, his lost dog, rolling in some waist-high weeds. He called the dog to his side, and Heloise, after a few seconds of indecision, runs up to him. "I will never let you loose in a strange neighborhood again," Harold vows.

▶ **Guided Practice**   Tell how you would correct the paragraph above to make it consistently past tense. Which verb need not be past?

▶ **Practice**   **A.** Write the verb in each sentence and tell whether it is present, past, or future.
Example: Tim will finish his assignment on the shuttle tomorrow.
Answer: will finish—Future tense

1. In 1969, American astronauts landed on the moon.
2. The moon landing still ranks as a tremendous accomplishment.

3. The idea of space travel started long ago.
4. In 1687, Sir Isaac Newton described the laws of motion.
5. In 1865, Jules Verne wrote *From the Earth to the Moon,* the first science-fiction story about space travel.
6. In 1919, Robert Goddard explained the value of rockets.
7. He realized their possible use in space travel.
8. In 1957, the Soviet Union launched *Sputnik I* into orbit.
9. Today American space vehicles visit other planets.
10. These vehicles send back new information about space.
11. The space shuttle makes interplanetary travel possible.
12. The Space Administration will use the shuttle as a supply ship.
13. The space shuttle measures about 184 feet in length.
14. Some day shuttle crews will build a space station.
15. Before the year 2000, people will explore other planets in our solar system.
16. Centuries from now, astronauts will look back at these early efforts.

B. There are several unnecessary tense changes in the following paragraph. Change verb tenses in the following paragraph to make it smooth and consistent. Do not write the numbers.

(17) We carried our canoe to the edge of the stream.   (18) The sky is clear blue, and the morning was still cool.   (19) Slowly we lower the canoe into the water.   (20) I held it steady, and my partner climbs in.   (21) She knelt down in the stern and waits for me. (22) I push the canoe into deeper water and jumped in. (23) "This will be a great day!" I remark.   (24) We paddled into deep water.   (25) The overhanging trees formed a green tunnel over the stream.   (26) Suddenly, the channel widened, for the stream will enter a lake.   (27) The lake was absolutely empty. (28) Not a soul is in sight!   (29) Occasionally an eagle or falcon circles overhead and will land in a tree.   (30) Wild rice even grew in the shallow areas.   (31) No houses cluttered the banks, and no motorboats disturb the peacefulness of these surroundings. (32) Canoeing on that lake was truly a memorable experience.

▶ **Apply/Writing**   Write a paragraph about your travels in a time machine. Tell about what you saw in the past or the future. Make sure your verb tenses are consistent with the time you chose.

9 Principal Parts of Verbs

Verbs have four basic forms, which are called principal parts. They are used to form tenses.

▶ **Focus**   The four main forms of a verb are called its **principal parts.** They are the **present,** the **present participle,** the **past,** and the **past participle.** Study the following chart. It shows how to form the principal parts of **regular verbs,** verbs spelled alike in their past and past participle forms.

Present	Present Participle	Past	Past Participle
open	(is) opening	opened	(has, have, had) opened
like	(is) liking	liked	(has, have, had) liked
try	(is) trying	tried	(has, have, had) tried
grin	(is) grinning	grinned	(has, have, had) grinned
omit	(is) omitting	omitted	(has, have, had) omitted

The first form is the present. Next is the present participle, which is formed by adding *-ing* to the present. It is used with a form of the helping verb *be*. (Verbs like these, which show action in progress, are sometimes said to be in the **progressive tense.**)

The past and past participles are formed by adding *-ed* to the present. The past participle uses a form of the helping verb.

Follow these rules for adding endings to regular verbs.

• For verbs ending in *e*, the *e* is dropped before *-ing* or *-ed* is added.
• For verbs ending in a consonant plus *y*, the *y* changes to *i* before *-ed* is added.
• For one-syllable verbs ending in a single vowel followed by a single consonant, the final consonant doubles before *-ing* or *-ed* is added.
• For two-syllable verbs ending in one vowel and one consonant, and having the accent on the final syllable, the final consonant also doubles.

Some verbs form their past and past participles in other ways—like *ring, ringing, rang, rung*. These are called **irregular verbs.** A dictionary shows the principal parts of these verbs. You will learn more about them later in this book.

▶ **Guided Practice**   Identify the verb in each sentence and tell which principal part it is formed from.

1. Jon is playing the lead in a musical.
2. We rehearse the dances for an hour or two every afternoon.
3. Nan and I danced in last year's musical too.
4. Jon's work has already inspired me for next year's production.

▶ **Practice**   **A.** Copy the verbs in the sentences and write what principal part each was formed from.
Example: Mighty dinosaurs had once roamed North America.
Answer: had roamed—Past participle

1. Dinosaurs lived in many parts of the world.
2. Some dinosaurs had measured over forty-five feet in length.
3. I have looked at many dinosaur skeletons in museums.
4. Every year, experts are discovering more and more about them.
5. Scientists consider a new discovery extremely important.
6. I am attending some lectures on dinosaurs this week.
7. They are helping me with my report for science.
8. Dinosaurs long ago disappeared from the face of the earth.
9. Even so, they still capture our imagination.

B. Write the four principal parts of each verb.
Example: jump
Answer: jump, is jumping, jumped, have jumped

10. climb	18. sail	26. shine	34. remain
11. prepare	19. try	27. hurry	35. trim
12. yell	20. sip	28. learn	36. place
13. float	21. like	29. believe	37. start
14. benefit	22. talk	30. hop	38. rescue
15. permit	23. wash	31. play	39. appear
16. patrol	24. ski	32. multiply	40. receive
17. smile	25. hope	33. comment	41. sound

▶ **Apply/Writing**   Think of an electronic device like a computer, video recorder, or stereo. Make a list of verbs and verb phrases to use in telling about it, like *tune, connect, is loading, have recorded.* Then use the verbs from your list in sentences. Use each principal part at least once.

14 More practice on page 511.   **117**

10 Perfect Tenses

Verbs have present, past, and future perfect tenses.

▶ **Focus** The **perfect tenses** express actions that were completed or will be completed by a certain time. The perfect tenses are made by using certain forms of *have* with the past participle of the verb.

Perfect Tenses	Time	Sample Sentences
Present	Begun in the past, continuing or completed now	I **have called** my best friends.
Past	Begun in the past, completed in the past	Earlier I **had compiled** a list of these friends.
Future	Begun in the past or present, completed in the future	By tonight, I **will have invited** everyone.

Notice in the chart that the words *called, compiled,* and *invited* are the past participle forms.

▶ **Guided Practice** Read the following sentences and then answer the questions about the verbs.

> She has listened to your every word.
> We both had sympathized with your position until quite recently.
> I will have stated my own point very soon now.

1. What helping verb is used with *listened* to form the present perfect tense? What other helping verb can form this tense?
2. What kind of action does the present perfect tense show?
3. What helping verb is used with *sympathized* to show the past perfect tense? What kind of action does this tense show?
4. What two helping verbs are used with *stated* to form the future perfect tense? What kind of action does this tense show?

► **Practice** **A.** Copy the sentences. Underline the perfect tense verbs and tell what tense they are.

Example: I have enjoyed all kinds of sports.
Answer: I <u>have enjoyed</u> all kinds of sports. Present perfect

1. I have taken swimming lessons since October.
2. By June 20, I will have attended thirty lessons.
3. My teacher has complimented me on my Australian crawl.
4. Before March I had won six races.
5. My diving also has improved.
6. I have practiced even more lately.
7. By the end of August I will have raced in several events.
8. Two of my friends have joined the swimming class.
9. Neither of them had swum before.
10. In a week each of them will have taken three lessons.
11. I hope they will have enjoyed these lessons.
12. By last May I had taken four tennis lessons.
13. Since then I have played tennis only twice.
14. Tennis has become my friend Rita's favorite sport.
15. By July I will have jogged fifty miles.

B. Rewrite the sentences, adding the suggested form of the verb.
Example: I _____ a great experiment. (*complete*, present perfect)
Answer: I have completed a great experiment.

16. I _____ about a life without friends. (*wonder*, present perfect)
17. Now I _____ it is no life at all. (*conclude*, present perfect)
18. I _____ at this conclusion by a simple experiment. (*arrive*, present perfect)
19. Until yesterday I _____ to no one for thirty days. (*talk*, past perfect)
20. I _____ no phone calls. (*answer*, past perfect)
21. I _____ no one. (*visit*, past perfect)
22. For thirty days I _____ without friends. (*live*, past perfect)
23. I finally _____ what friendship means. (*learn*, present perfect)
24. Soon my bad memories of loneliness _____. (*stop*, future perfect)

► **Apply/Science** Write a paragraph about a science experiment you want to try. Use these verbs: *has grown, had tried, will have observed, had recorded.*

15 More practice on page 512.

119

11 Transitive and Intransitive Verbs

Action verbs with direct objects are transitive. Action verbs without direct objects are intransitive, as are linking verbs.

▶ **Focus**   You will recall that some verbs are followed by **direct objects**—nouns or pronouns that complete a verb's meaning. When an action verb is used with a direct object, the verb is said to be **transitive**. Look at the following examples.

V   DO   V   DO

Kiku **played** the piano for hours.   Gene **baked** a cake yesterday.

Piano is the direct object of the verb *played,* and *cake* is the direct object of the verb *baked.* The objects receive the action expressed by the transitive verbs. To locate the object of the action, ask *what* or *who* receives the action expressed by the verb. What did Kiku play? What did Gene bake?

An action verb is called **intransitive** when it does not need an object to complete its meaning.

Kiku **played** for hours.   Gene **baked** yesterday.

The verb in the first sentence is *played.* Because there is no direct object, *played* is intransitive. What is the verb in the second sentence? Why is it intransitive?

As you can see, action verbs like *play* and *bake* can be either transitive or intransitive. It depends on whether they have a direct object.

Linking verbs are always intransitive. They never have objects.

Maynard **is** a good actor.   The play **seemed** a bit dull.

▶ **Guided Practice**   Tell whether each verb is transitive or intransitive.

1. Dino plays first base for the Scooters.
2. He is a good hitter.
3. He also runs well.
4. His team won their last three games.
5. They play the Cyclones tomorrow.

▶ **Practice** **A.** Copy the sentences. Label each verb *V* and each direct object *DO*.

       V   DO

Example: Jockeys ride thoroughbred horses.

1. Cortés first brought horses to America.
2. At first, Native Americans mistook men on horseback for gods.
3. They had never seen animals like horses before.
4. Some of the horses escaped their owners.
5. They roamed the West in wild herds.
6. Native Americans later captured these horses.
7. They built corrals for the animals.
8. In time, Native Americans tamed their horses.
9. Herds of horses represented wealth.
10. Some tribes took horses from others.
11. Native Americans of the Plains needed their ponies.
12. They rode horses on buffalo-hunting trips.
13. Besides food, the buffalo provided hides for clothing.
14. Horses gave a new way of life to Native Americans.
15. They treated their horses well.

B. Copy the verbs in the sentences and write whether they are transitive or intransitive.

Example: Texas has a proud history. *Answer:* has—Transitive

16. Today four-lane highways cross old cattle trails.
17. The state seems both old-fashioned and modern.
18. Ranch hands still herd cattle on the range.
19. Skyscrapers rise against the skylines of Dallas and Houston.
20. Tourists find numerous attractions in Texas.
21. The state continually expands its many cultural attractions.
22. The Lyndon Johnson Museum stores presidential papers.
23. Visitors flock to the Alamo in San Antonio.
24. Texas was an independent republic for almost ten years.
25. It eventually became a state in 1845.

▶ **Apply/Writing** Writers experiment with the language. Try an experiment. Write two brief paragraphs—one with only transitive verbs and the other with only intransitive verbs. You might use these verbs: *work, sing, file, prepare, read.*

Review/Evaluation

For more review, see Tested Skills Practice, pages 510–512.

13 **Distinguishing Action/Linking Verbs**   Write the letter of the answer that identifies each underlined word.

a. Action verb   **b.** Linking verb   **c.** Another kind of word

1. We <u>looked</u> at wild animals from a treetop house.
2. The animals <u>look</u> beautiful to us.
3. A pride of lions <u>seem</u> so peaceful lying in the sun.
4. They <u>appear</u> harmless.
5. Four giraffes <u>look</u> at some tall thorn trees.
6. Then they <u>taste</u> the leaves at the tops of the trees.
7. Not many trees <u>grow</u> in the African grassland.
8. Suddenly a distant elephant <u>sounds</u> a warning.
9. The alarm <u>sounds</u> loud even to us in the treetop house.
10. We <u>remain</u> motionless in the treetop.
11. All the animals <u>become</u> restless and nervous.
12. They <u>grow</u> very silent and wary.
13. However, nothing <u>looks</u> dangerous nor menacing.
14. Neither does anything <u>smell</u> unsafe or threatening.
15. The animals resume their <u>activities</u>.
16. They <u>feel</u> safe again.
17. The grassland <u>seems</u> quiet and serene once more.
18. We never <u>become</u> weary of the animals.
19. The treetop house <u>becomes</u> a cozy home.
20. We <u>remain</u> in the house for four days.

14 **Principal Parts of Verbs   A.**   Write the letter of the answer that names the principal part used to form each underlined verb.

a. Present   **c.** Past
b. Present participle   **d.** Past participle

21. The grasslands <u>stretch</u> for miles and miles around and below our treetop house.
22. We <u>have watched</u> many kinds of animals on the grasslands.
23. I <u>am sketching</u> some of the animals.
24. Jess <u>is recording</u> their sounds on a tape recorder.
25. Jess and I <u>compared</u> the African grasslands with the great American prairies.

26. A huge herd of wildebeests <u>is thundering</u> across the grasslands.
27. The herd <u>consists</u> of thousands of these oxlike creatures.
28. Three hungry lions <u>attacked</u> the herd.
29. One exhausted young wildebeest <u>had dropped</u> out.
30. The lions quickly <u>killed</u> it.

14 **B.** Write **a** if the underlined main verb is spelled correctly. Write **b** if it is spelled incorrectly.

31. A large python had <u>wraped</u> itself around a tree branch.
32. It was <u>hoping</u> for a meal to appear.
33. Suddenly, the python was <u>moveing</u> down the tree.
34. A small animal had <u>scurryed</u> past the tree.
35. Jess and I <u>observed</u> the snake nervously.
36. I <u>admited</u> that I was afraid of snakes.
37. Several chimpanzees were <u>makeing</u> excited sounds.
38. The monkeys had <u>noticed</u> something that disturbed them.
39. Jess and I <u>hurried</u> to the other side of the treetop house.
40. A dozen or more vultures were <u>circleing</u> overhead.

15 **Perfect Tenses**   Write the letter of the answer that identifies the tense of each underlined verb.
a. Present perfect   **b.** Past perfect   **c.** Future perfect

41. My friend Kris <u>has decided</u> to go on a bike trip with me.
42. Both of us <u>had hoped</u> to go on a trip last year.
43. We <u>have chosen</u> next Monday as the day to begin.
44. We <u>will have told</u> our friends about the trip by then.
45. Kris and I <u>will have completed</u> our plans too.
46. Some of our friends <u>had wanted</u> to go with us.
47. We <u>have decided</u> this is impractical.
48. My brothers <u>have made</u> the bike trip several times.
49. We <u>had asked</u> both of them for advice.
50. By tomorrow, Kris <u>will have repaired</u> her bike.
51. I <u>will have inspected</u> my bike by then too.
52. Both Kris and I <u>have plotted</u> our route on maps.
53. In preparation for the trip, Kris and I <u>have biked</u> twenty miles a day for two weeks.
54. By Monday night, we <u>had pedaled</u> a great many miles.
55. On Friday morning, Kris and I <u>will have achieved</u> our goal.

Writing Evaluation

12   This is a picture of volunteers putting finishing touches on a rather unusual playground. The picture may bring back memories of a time when you worked on a group project or built something by yourself. You may also be reminded of a playground you used as a child. Write a personal experience narrative of three or more paragraphs about one of these times.

1. Think of an experience from your life that is associated with work or play. You may want to look in your journal for ideas. List the actions that happened in time order.
2. Write your narrative, using these questions to guide you.

✔ Have you told events in sequence and used transition words?
✔ Does the narrative contain powerful verbs?
✔ Have you used vivid details to describe setting and characters?
✔ Is all the information important enough to include?
✔ Have you expressed your feelings about this experience?
3. When you have finished writing, spend a few minutes checking and revising your personal narrative.
✔ Can you answer "yes" to all the questions above?
✔ Have you spelled past tense verbs correctly?
✔ Have you used verb tenses consistently and correctly?

Curriculum Connection: Social Studies

O. E. Rölvaag's experience of immigrating to America was far from unique. In fact, it was shared by at least 35 million people who came to America between 1815 and 1915. By contrast, approximately 20,000 people arrived in Massachusetts from England between 1628 and 1640. Both groups of immigrants profoundly affected the development of the new nation. It was the incredible variety of the later wave of immigrants, however, that has given America its diverse flavor.

▶ **Think** Consider the general topic of immigration. Identify a narrower part of this topic that you could investigate. You might choose to investigate any of the following topics, or find one of your own. Learn about Ellis Island, the entry point for processing the majority of arrivals. Research the methods that the steamship companies employed to attract people to the American shores. Discover the conditions that caused certain groups of immigrants to flee their land in search of America.

▶ **Discuss** Conduct a class discussion of immigration. Try to determine additional narrow topics for investigation. Have members of the class volunteer information about the experiences of relatives who have immigrated to America.

▶ **Find Out** Each class member should choose a topic and begin to collect information. Start with your social studies text, and move from there to a good encyclopedia and other appropriate reference books. Then consult your library's card catalog for individual titles that provide information on your topic. You might read Rölvaag's *Giants in the Earth* or *The Rise of David Levinsky* by Abraham Cahan. Do not overlook the possibility of investigating individual family records and talking to family members who might have personal knowledge of immigration. Consult a local historical society if there is one nearby.

▶ **React: Write a Summary** Each class member should summarize the information he or she has gathered. Each written summary should be at least three paragraphs and should have a title. Summaries can be collected and compiled into a class booklet.

Quarterly Test

Sentences

5 **A.** Write the letter that identifies each sentence.

a. Declarative   **c.** Imperative
b. Interrogative   **d.** Exclamatory

1. Oh, look at all the stampeding elephants!
2. How many elephants have calves with them?
3. The fire is still spreading across the grassland.

6 **B.** Write the letter that identifies the underlined word or words in each sentence.

a. Simple subject   **c.** Simple predicate
b. Complete subject   **d.** Complete predicate

4. The terrified giraffes are galloping away from the fire.
5. Clouds of smoke blacken the sky.
6. The animals know the fire's danger and run for safety.

7
8 **C.** Write **a** if the item is a correct sentence, **b** if it is a sentence and a fragment, and **c** if it is a run-on sentence.

7. The girls had to shout. Because the wind howled furiously.
8. When the storm ended, Diane and Kristine left the cabin.
9. The two girls put on snowshoes, they trudged across the snow.

Nouns and Pronouns

10 **D.** Write the letter of the correct plural noun in each pair.

10. **a.** knifes   **b.** wives   13. **a.** spys   **b.** stories
11. **a.** buses   **b.** brushs   14. **a.** echoes   **b.** potatos
12. **a.** mice   **b.** tooths   15. **a.** rooves   **b.** thieves

11 **E.** Write the letter of the pronoun that makes each sentence correct.

16. (**a.** Who, **b.** Whom) did Mom scold this morning?
17. Mom scolded Jim because (**a.** his, **b.** him) closet is a mess.
18. Jim promised (**a.** he, **b.** him) would clean the closet at once.
19. The twins, (**a.** who, **b.** whom) are never untidy, got praise.

Verbs

13
F. Write the letter that identifies each underlined word.

a. Action verb　　**b.** Linking verb　　**c.** Another kind of word

20. At noon Stacy <u>became</u> very hungry.
21. She <u>looked</u> at the different fruits in the refrigerator.
22. The apples and pears <u>looked</u> especially delicious.

14
G. Write the letter of the principal part used to form each verb.
a. Present　　**b.** Present participle　　**c.** Past
d. Past participle

23. is calling　　**24.** changed　　**25.** have listed　　**26.** studies

15
H. Write the letter of the tense of each verb.
a. Present perfect　　**b.** Past perfect　　**c.** Future perfect

27. will have jogged　　**28.** had used
29. have fried　　**30.** has won

Thinking Skills

I. Write the letter of the answer that tells what is happening.
a. a test　　**b.** a vacation　　**c.** a party

1
31.　Carl walked into the room filled with people. He took a seat next to someone he knew. He saw his teacher on the other side of the room. Suddenly the band started playing and people started dancing. Carl decided to get some punch.

Paragraphs

2
3
J. Read the main idea of a narrative paragraph. Then write the letter of the word that signals the sequence of each event.

a. later　　**b.** eventually　　**c.** first　　**d.** now

Main idea: The earthquake was a frightening experience.

32. The ＿＿ tremor hit just as I got out of bed.
33. Another large shock came a few seconds ＿＿.
34. The rumbling stopped ＿＿, but not the thumping of my heart.
35. Buildings all over town are ＿＿ piles of rubble.

Descriptive Writing

Theme: The Seas Around Us

The sea has always suggested mystery and adventure, beauty and freedom. For centuries, writers have tried to capture the sea's magic, comparing and contrasting its various moods. As you read the lessons in this section, be on the lookout for the many themes and creatures associated with the sea. How many adjectives can you think of to describe **the seas around us?**

1 Literature: Descriptive Writing

There are many prizes to be found in the seas around us. There are many dangers too. Jim Tom brings his grandson Jimmy Tom to the reef so that Jimmy can search for hidden treasure. The following passage is a series of descriptions. Read it to find out what Jimmy and his grandfather see as they near the reef.

from **The Reef**
by Samuel Scoville, Jr.

Lune-green and amber, a strip of fading sky glowed across the trail of the vanished sun. Far below, the opal sea paled to mother-of-pearl. Then, over sea and sky, strode the sudden dark of the tropics and in an instant the southern stars flamed and flared through the violet night. A long, tense moment, with sea and sky waiting, and a rim of raw gold thrust itself above the horizon as the full moon of midsummer climbed toward the zenith. Rising, its light made a broad causeway across the sea clear to the dark reef which lurked in the shimmering water.

Suddenly, inked black against the moonpath, showed the lean shape of a canoe. All the way from Carib Island, a day and a night away, Jim Tom, who in his day had been a famous sponge diver, had brought his grandson Jimmy Tom for a first visit to the reef. Both had the cinnamon-red skins of the Red Caribs, who once had ruled mightily the whole Caribbean. Jim Tom's hair was cut to an even edge all the way around his neck; his small, deep-set eyes were like glittering crumbs of black glass, and ever since a day when he dived below the twenty-five-fathom mark both of his legs had been paralyzed.

Swiftly the little craft neared the reef, and only the plash of the paddles broke the stillness. Then in an instant the molten gold of the water was shattered by a figure like a vast bat, with black wings which measured all of thirty feet from tip to tip, a spiked tail, and long antennae streaming out beyond a huge, hooked mouth. Like a vampire from the pit, it rose into the air, blotting out the moon with its monstrous bulk, and then dropped back with a crash, raising a wave which nearly swamped the canoe. As it disappeared beneath the water, Jimmy Tom turned and looked questioningly at the old man. The latter laughed silently.

▶ **Discussing**

1. Describe what Jimmy and his grandfather saw as they neared the reef.
2. Where did Jimmy and his grandfather come from? How long did it take them to get to the reef?
3. What had happened to Jim Tom's legs?
4. How do Jimmy and his grandfather seem to feel about the sea?
5. Describe something you have seen or found in the sea or at the beach.

▶ **Analyzing: Descriptive Writing**

Descriptive writing is a way of painting pictures with words. You include details in your descriptions that bring the subject to life. Your choice of words helps to create the picture that you want the reader to see.

In the excerpt from "The Reef" you read descriptions of the sunset, the people, and the figure coming out of the water. Write a list of words and phrases from the passage that describe one of these things. Ask a classmate to do the same. Exchange lists and identify what your classmate described.

▶ **Writing**

Imagine you are a TV reporter. Your assignment is to cover the events at the reef. Write a news story about what is happening there. Remember, the excerpt does not tell you what the figure is. Therefore, you will need to use descriptive words and phrases to convey your story.

▶ **Extending**

Speaking and Listening   You can often learn new things through discussions. Meet with a small group of classmates to learn more about the seas around us. Discuss the pleasures and dangers of oceans and lakes. Base the discussion on personal experiences as well as information obtained through reading. Ask questions if someone talks about something with which you are unfamiliar.

Reading   *The Sea Around Us,* by Rachel L. Carson, provides a wide range of information about the seas around us. In this book, you can learn about such things as hidden lands in the sea, tides and currents, and volcanic islands.

2 Classifying

To classify information, arrange it into similar groups.

▶ **Focus**   When you gather information, you need to organize it so that it makes sense. You must **classify** your information, which means you arrange it into similar groups. As you prepare to write a composition, you can classify details.

Suppose you were planning to write a description of the Fourth of July celebration in your town. You would think of all the things that people will be doing to celebrate the Fourth of July. You might make a list of descriptive details. Then put these details into categories. The following chart classifies details according to the senses of sound, taste, and sight.

Sound	Taste	Sight
bangs and whistles of fireworks	grilled chicken	sparkling fireworks
oohs and ahs of viewers	sweet lemonade	crowds of people
sizzling hamburgers	buttery corn on the cob	smoke from grills
laughter	juicy watermelon	picnic tables
cheers at baseball game	creamy coleslaw	someone napping under tree

There are many other ways to classify details. The details in the chart above, for example, might be organized with categories such as these: **People, Food, Fireworks.** As you write down details in prewriting, think of categories that will help you organize your material.

▶ **Guided Practice**   Discuss the following questions, based on the chart on the opposite page, with your classmates.

1. Under what classification do you find *smoke from grills?*
2. Under which headings might you add *whining children? apple pie? red, white, and blue banners?*
3. What other detail can you think of for each classification?
4. What other senses could be added to the chart? Give two details for each.

▶ **Practice**   **A.** The words below are grouped according to something they have in common. Write the word that does not fit the classification. You may need to use a dictionary.
Example: woe, despair, joy, gloom
Answer: joy

1. orange, broccoli, apple, banana
2. Detroit, Miami, Utah, Chicago
3. poverty, early, late, middle
4. hammer, saw, tulip, chisel
5. quiet, honest, glasses, shy
6. eel, whale, cat, clam
7. mad, angry, furious, calm
8. talk, walk, speak, shout
9. dress, shirt, teeth, shoe
10. break, repair, fix, mend

B.   Each of the following groups has one or more characteristics in common. Write the common characteristic or characteristics that make each group a class.
Example: dime, nickel, quarter
Answer: American coins; round

11. fear, glee, sorrow
12. French, German, Latin
13. clank, ring, roar
14. finger, knuckle, nail
15. sticky, furry, slimy
16. lake, river, creek
17. sour, bitter, sweet
18. poem, novel, essay
19. comet, meteor, star
20. sent, tent, went

▶ **Apply/Health**   The following words and phrases describe elements that contribute to good health. Classify them by arranging each under one of the three headings Exercise, Diet, or Relaxation: *protein, bicycling, walking, deep breaths, calcium, swimming, sleep, good posture, vitamins, tennis.*

3 Comparing and Contrasting

To compare means to identify likenesses among things. To contrast means to identify differences.

▶ **Focus**   You have learned that when you **classify** you group things into similar categories. Comparing and contrasting takes two such groups and looks at their similarities or differences. When you see how something is like something else, you are **comparing**. When you see how two objects are different, you are **contrasting**. When you compare or contrast two things, you use words and phrases like the following.

For Comparisons	For Contrasts
both . . . and	but
the same as	unlike
just as	however

Sometimes, you can even compare and contrast things with themselves. Puffer fishes, for example, inflate themselves with air or water to scare off attackers. This causes spines on their bodies to stand straight up. Look at the photograph below. You can compare and contrast the appearance of a puffer on the defense (left) and a puffer at rest (right).

▶ **Guided Practice** Discuss answers for each of these questions.

1. What is the puffer's shape when it is on the defense?
2. Would the color of the puffer fish at rest and on the defense be a feature for comparison or contrast?
3. When does the puffer look frightening?

▶ **Practice** **A.** One way to make comparisons and contrasts is to create a chart. The items compared and contrasted are written in the left column, and points to compare and contrast are written at the top. Copy the chart on this page. Then fill in all of the blank boxes in the chart. Note the comparisons and contrasts.

	Shape	Color	Position of Spines	Appearance
Defending puffer		brown and white		frightening
Resting puffer	short oval		flat against body	

B. For each pair of items below, write a sentence that compares the items and a sentence that contrasts them. Use words and phrases that signal comparisons and contrasts.
Example: puffer on the defense, puffer at rest
Answers: The defending puffer's color is the same as the resting puffer's color. When the puffer fish is on the defense it looks frightening, but when it is at rest it looks harmless.

1. aquarium, zoo
2. encyclopedia, dictionary
3. television, radio
4. Hawaii, Alaska
5. volleyball, soccer
6. couch, chair

▶ **Apply/Science** Observe or read about two kinds of birds, reptiles, or other animals. Make five or more columns on a sheet of paper. List the items to be compared and contrasted in the left column; head the remaining columns with points to compare and contrast. Fill in the chart.

4 Visualizing

Visualizing is the ability to create mental images from words. Visualize details to help you understand what you read.

▶ **Focus**   In descriptions, an author gives many exact details that help the reader create a mental picture of what is described. It is this attention to detail that helps a piece of writing come alive. As you read or listen to a description, try to **visualize**—or see in your mind's eye—what is described. In some stories, you can almost feel as if you are present as the characters talk and act.

Read the following passage about Bilbo Baggins who, using a glowing sword, finds his way around a dark tunnel. Pay special attention to the details that help you picture what you read.

> Suddenly without any warning he trotted splash into water! Ugh! It was icy cold. That pulled him up sharp and short. He did not know whether it was just a pool in the path, or the edge of an underground stream that crossed the passage, or the brink of a deep, dark subterranean lake. The sword was hardly shining at all. He stopped, and he could hear, when he listened hard, drops drip-drip-dripping from an unseen roof into the water below; but there seemed to be no other sort of sound.
>
> "So it is a pool or a lake, and not an underground river," he thought. Still he did not dare to wade out into the darkness. He could not swim; and he thought, too, of nasty slimy things, with big bulging blind eyes, wriggling in the water. There are strange things living in the pools and lakes in the hearts of mountains: fish whose fathers swam in, goodness only knows how many years ago, and never swam out again, while their eyes grew bigger and bigger and bigger from trying to see in the blackness; also there are other things more slimy than fish.
>
> *from* **The Hobbit**
> *by J. R. R. Tolkien*

▶ **Guided Practice**   Discuss answers for the questions below.

1. Describe what happens to Bilbo Baggins.
2. What things does the author help you visualize?
3. What words help you feel and hear what is described?

► **Practice**   **A.** Find the words in each sentence that help you visualize what is described.

1. As we entered the house I heard the oven timer's shrill ring.
2. The warm, yeasty aroma of baking bread filled the entryway.
3. I felt the hot, smoothly textured loaves with awe.
4. The crunchy banana tasted delicious.
5. The house by the sea had been painted a glossy yellow.
6. Inside the cupboard were some tart apples.

B.   Read the following description of a mysterious figure walking on a lonely beach. Try to visualize the scene. Then copy the description, filling in the blanks with words that help a reader visualize the scene shown below. Compare your description with those of your classmates.

The ____ figure strolled ____ up and down the ____ beach. The ____ gulls and ducks circled ____ in the sky, honking and hooting. As we ____ approached, the figure became clearer. It was a ____ woman, wearing a ____ cloak with a ____ hood. She turned around and greeted us ____.

► **Apply/Prewriting**   Imagine you are in a crowded or a lonely place such as a big city or a deserted beach. List at least five phrases that would help someone else visualize your scene. Try to describe the water, the people, the smells, and so on. Be sure to use specific details in your phrases.

5 Using a Thesaurus

A thesaurus is a reference book of synonyms and related words.

▶ **Focus**   A **thesaurus** lists words in groups according to the idea or concept they have in common. A writer uses a thesaurus as an aid in finding words that express the exact meaning he or she wants to convey. If you are writing about a boat sailing on a sunny day on shining ocean water, for example, you might wish to describe the water more precisely. A thesaurus is a good source for finding numerous words meaning "shining."

In many thesauruses the entry words in dark type are arranged alphabetically, just as they are in a dictionary. Then the words in italic type that are nearly synonymous with the entry word follow it in their own alphabetical order. Often simple sentences make clear the slight differences in meaning among the group of words.

Study the thesaurus entries for *shining* below.

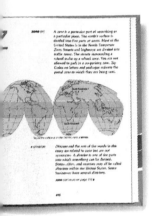

Shining describes something that gives off or reflects light. A *shining* object has a bright appearance, like the *shining* sea in the sunlight.

Lustrous can be used to describe a shining and glossy surface. A wood table can be kept *lustrous* by dusting and polishing.

Radiant means glowing brightly. The sky was *radiant* as the sun rose above the hills. Someone who looks very happy can be called *radiant*. Abe smiled *radiantly* when he won the spelling bee.

Shimmering means shining faintly and softly. The sailboat glided across the *shimmering*, moonlit waters.

Twinkling describes an unsteady light. A *twinkling* light seems to flash on and off. On a clear night you can see many *twinkling* stars.

Other thesauruses are organized according to a number system based on related meanings. To use this kind of thesaurus, you would locate a word in the index at the back and find the page or reference number for that word's synonyms.

The thesaurus in this book begins on page 584.

▶ **Guided Practice**   Use the thesaurus entries to answer these questions.

1. What is the difference between *shining* and *shimmering?*
2. What word might you use to describe a spotlight? necklace seen on a dancing woman?
3. Which of the following words might also be grouped with *shining* in a thesaurus: *ruby, humid, glimmering, bright?*

▶ **Practice**   **A.** Choose the appropriate synonym to complete each sentence. Write the sentences on your paper.

Example: Last night thousands of (twinkling, lustrous) stars filled the sky.

Answer: Last night thousands of twinkling stars filled the sky.

1. On this clear day, the hot, (shining, lustrous) sun beat down.
2. Yesterday, Alice brushed her puppy's coat until it was (lustrous, twinkling).
3. The (lustrous, twinkling) cabin lights shone in the forest.
4. As the dragonfly flew by at midnight, we could barely see its delicate, (shimmering, radiant) wings.
5. The happy graduates posed with (twinkling, radiant) faces.

B.   Replace the word *moist* in each sentence with a more precise word from the list of synonyms at the right. Then rewrite the sentences with the new word. Use each word in the list only once.

Example: We always carry umbrellas on *moist* days.
Answer: We always carry umbrellas on *rainy* days.

6. I used a *moist* cloth to clean the table.
7. Before it rains, the air here is hot, sticky, and *moist.*
8. Because of her hay fever, Ellen's eyes were *moist.*
9. That is certainly a *moist* orange.
10. A *moist* day spoiled our picnic plans and our softball game.

damp
watery
rainy
humid
juicy

▶ **Apply/Prewriting**   Choose two of the following adjectives: *great, odd, sad, happy, beautiful.* List at least three synonyms for each word you choose. Use the thesaurus at the back of this book.

6 Topic Sentences

A topic sentence is a statement of the main idea of a paragraph.

▶ **Focus**   You have already learned about the main idea in a paragraph. Often this main idea is stated in a single sentence. A **topic** is what a paragraph is all about. A sentence that tells what a paragraph is about is called a **topic sentence.** The other sentences in the paragraph support the topic sentence by providing additional details.

When a topic sentence is used, it usually appears first in the paragraph. However, a writer may choose to put the topic sentence at the end of a paragraph, or in the middle.

Read the following descriptive paragraphs. Note that the descriptive details in each support the topic sentence.

- Not all sharks have the streamlined shapes we usually visualize when we hear the word *shark*. One common kind of shark, for example, has a head shaped like a double hammer. This strange horizontal head is about three feet long. The carpet, or woebegone, shark is a squat fish with a round head. From around its mouth dangle seaweed-like tassels of skin, which look like a mustache.

- For a long stretch, dark grey rocks with sharp edges protruded out of the green water. White-headed waves rolled slowly toward the land, gathered speed, and then crashed violently against the jagged rocks. Ribbons of water shot erratically into the air and then disappeared with a splash into the sea. There was something restlessly beautiful about this side of the island.

- Red, pink, and white coral dot the white ocean floor. A school of small silver fish swim behind a red-speckled rock. A dazzling orange-striped fish is swimming near the dark green seaweed. The seas around us are filled with wonderful colors. Here comes a bright yellow fish. Look at that unusual purple plant.

▶ **Guided Practice**   Answer the following questions.

1. Which paragraph starts with a topic sentence?
2. Which paragraph has its topic sentence in the middle?
3. Which paragraph ends with a topic sentence?

▶ **Practice**　**A.** In each group of sentences find and copy the topic sentence.

Example:　Small children dug with new shovels into the damp sand.
The seashore that day was a bustle of activity.
Swimmers crowded into the water.

Answer:　The seashore that day was a bustle of activity.

1. Herons circled the marsh to search out nesting places.
The ducks began to establish their territories as well.
In spring, the marsh echoed with the cries of wild birds.

2. On that misty morning, the lake was quiet.
Two men were fishing silently from an old wooden rowboat.
The ducks floated noiselessly around the bank.

3. Just beneath the surface, tadpoles wiggled and darted.
Odd, winged creatures skimmed the surface.
The pond seemed empty of life until we looked closely.

B. Read the following descriptive paragraph.

Some of my earliest memories are of the storms, the hot rain lashing down and lightning running on the sky—and the storm cellar into which my mother and I descended so many times when I was very young. For me that little room in the earth is an unforgettable place. Across the years I see my mother reading there on the low, narrow bench, the lamplight flickering on her face and on the earthen walls; I smell the dank odor of that room; and I hear the great weather raging at the door.

from **The Names**
by N. Scott Momaday

4. Where does the topic sentence occur in the paragraph?
5. In the other sentences, what supporting details refer to sight, smell, and sound?

▶ **Apply/Prewriting**　Examine your notes from Lesson 4. Write a topic sentence that expresses your main idea about the place you are describing. Then cross out all the details on your list that do not support that topic sentence. Add other supporting details if you wish. Write at least three sentences, using the remaining details. Save your notes.

7 Arranging Details in Spatial Order

You can use spatial order to help readers visualize details.

▶ **Focus**   When you write you can use **spatial order** to describe what you want your readers to see. For example, you use spatial order when you describe a room from top to bottom or from right to left. Spatial order helps your readers visualize the scene accurately. Be sure to stick to whatever spatial order you select so that your readers' mental image moves smoothly along with your words.

The chart on the left contains some words that can help you express spatial relationships. You can also use phrases such as *off to the side* or *as far as the eye can see* to give your readers a sense of direction and distance.

The passage below describes what twelve-year-old Maria Luisa and her cousin Mike experience while on a walk. Note the words and phrases that indicate spatial order.

Spatial Order

above	near
away	over
back	right
down	left
up	beyond
toward	through
far	bottom
in	distance
under	closer
ahead	farther

> They stopped to watch the waves. Every now and then an enormous one would roll up to a huge crest as far along the coast as the eye could see, and then would burst into a long line of churning white foam which grew smaller and gentler as it came toward the shore. Little flocks of sandpipers walked rapidly up and down the edge of the water in hopes of finding food in each wave. In the distance another wave began to rise to a huge green crest.
>
> *from* **Maria Luisa**
> *by Winifred Madison*

▶ **Guided Practice**   Answer the following questions about the paragraph above.

1. Which phrase helps you see how large the beach is?
2. What other words and phrases indicating spatial order are used in this paragraph?
3. Reread the first three sentences of the description. What kind of spatial order is used in these sentences—left to right, far to near, or top to bottom?

▶ **Practice** **A.** Read the paragraph below and answer the questions.

Sarah and Bob were excited as they adjusted their air tanks and then jumped into the water. Each kick sent them closer to the ocean floor. A large school of brightly colored fish swam a few feet below Sarah. The two divers kicked harder and headed farther down into the darkening water, hoping to locate the submerged coral reef they thought was straight ahead.

1. What words and phrases indicating spatial order are used?
2. Are details presented from far to near, left to right, or top to bottom?
3. Which words help tell you direction? distance?

B. Study the painting below. Imagine that you are the woman in it. Write three sentences that describe details from her viewpoint, using spatial-order words.

▶ **Apply/Prewriting** Imagine yourself in a helicopter flying over a crowded beach, park, or some other area that is familiar to you. Describe the objects and people in this place as you see them from the helicopter. Use some of the spatial order words from the chart on the opposite page. Remember to stick to the order you select— top to bottom, near to far, left to right.

8 Writing a Descriptive Paragraph

A descriptive paragraph creates a vivid image of a person, thing, or place.

▶ **Focus**   A **descriptive paragraph** paints pictures with words. In a good description, the reader will be able to do more than see the scene, however. He or she will be able to hear, taste, smell, and touch as well. Your choice of words helps create the picture that you want the reader to visualize. That is why it is important to use a thesaurus and to classify your details so that they can be presented in an organized way. Good descriptive paragraphs create very vivid impressions but do not try to describe too much in one paragraph.

Notice the way Nicholasa Mohr paints a picture of Mr. Mendelsohn. Her choice of words helps you visualize this character. Pay special attention to the spatial order presented in the paragraph and to the adjectives that appeal to the senses.

"Good morning to you all!" He had just shaved and trimmed his large black mustache. As he smiled broadly, one could see that most of his teeth were missing. His large bald head was partially covered by his small black skullcap. Thick dark grey hair grew in abundance at the lower back of his head, coming around the front above his ears into short sideburns. He wore a clean white shirt, frayed at the cuffs. His worn-out pinstripe trousers were held up by a pair of dark suspenders. Mr. Mendelsohn leaned on his brown skiny cane and carried a small brown paper bag.

from **Mr. Mendelsohn**
by Nicholasa Mohr

▶ **Guided Practice**   Discuss answers to these questions.

1. To what sense do the details in the paragraph about Mr. Mendelsohn appeal?
2. What are some words used by Nicholasa Mohr that help you to visualize Mr. Mendelsohn?
3. What spatial order is used to describe Mr. Mendelsohn?

▶ **Practice**   **A.** List six or seven details that describe a place. Include details that appeal to at least three senses. Some of the details should also reflect your feelings about the place. Use the notes you have prepared for the last several lessons or choose one of the subjects below.

1. a swimming pool
2. a room in a house
3. a landscape through which you have traveled by plane, car, train, or boat
4. a place associated with a holiday
5. an imaginary place you would like to visit
6. a park in wintertime
7. the inside of a closet

B. Complete the following activities as preparation for writing a descriptive paragraph. Use the place you chose in Practice A.

8. Classify the details so that you will be able to present them in a clear and organized way.
9. Add appropriate adjectives and adverbs to your details.
10. Write down your feelings about this place. Try to reflect these feelings with vivid adverbs and adjectives.
11. Write two possible topic sentences that could be supported by your details.
12. Decide on a spatial order for your description. For example, will you order your details from near to far? outside to inside? left to right?

▶ **Apply/Writing**   Use the work you have done in this lesson and in the previous lessons to write a descriptive paragraph. Review the following checklist.

Descriptive Paragraph Revision Checklist
✔ Have I classified my details in groups that make sense?
✔ Have I used words and phrases to help readers visualize my description?
✔ Have I written a topic sentence?
✔ Have I used the same spatial order throughout my description?
✔ Have I included precise adjectives?
✔ Have I formed correctly adjectives and adverbs that compare?

9 Writing a Comparison/ Contrast Description

A paragraph of comparison and contrast explains how two things are alike and how they are different.

▶ **Focus** In Unit 10 you learned about comparing and contrasting. This skill can be used when you write descriptions. You may want to describe things or make a point by showing how objects are alike and how they differ. This technique is called **comparison and contrast.** In the following description, the writer compares and contrasts ballet dancers and football players.

> Ballet dancers and football players differ in physical size and appearance. Yet both are highly trained athletes. Classical ballet and pro football both demand years of training, great strength, and agility. It takes endurance and speed to run for a touchdown. Likewise, these same qualities are used by a ballerina performing a series of turns in *Swan Lake*. As the football player practices plays, the dancer rehearses steps.
>
> Physical skills, however, are used quite differently on a ballet stage and on a football field. Football players must react quickly to moves by their opponents. Ballet dancers, in contrast, follow precise steps designed by choreographers. Planned movements do not change during a ballet the way plays change during a football game. While football players use strength to overpower opponents, dancers express emotions or tell a story by using graceful movements.

Here are some ways to develop comparison/contrast descriptions:

- Clearly identify the two items being compared and contrasted.
- Give examples of how the two items are alike and different.
- Classify the characteristics being compared into clear patterns. Decide whether you will discuss each item fully in a separate paragraph or compare both items point by point within the same sentences or paragraph.
- Use words and phrases such as *both* and *just as* to indicate comparisons. Use words and phrases such as *however, differ,* and *on the other hand* to signal contrasts. (See the list on the next page.)
- Summarize or restate the point of the description for the reader.

▶ **Guided Practice**   Discuss these questions with your class.

1. What two items are compared and contrasted in the description?
2. What are the points of comparison and contrast?
3. What words or phrases indicate comparisons and contrasts?
4. What pattern of comparisons and contrasts does the writer use?

▶ **Practice**   **A.** Old-fashioned porches and new-styled decks on houses both offer places for people to sit outside in good weather. Yet porches often are found at the front door, while decks most often are built in the backyard. Read the descriptive details below. Write each one under the category, *Deck* or *Porch.* Some details may fit under both headings.

- has porch roof to block sun
- lets you see front sidewalk
- private place in backyard
- family gathering place

- place to sit and talk
- no porch roof to block sun
- lets you see backyard
- attached to or near house

B. Choose one of the following pairs of items—or two items of your own—to compare and contrast. List at least six similarities and/or differences between the two items.

1. snakes and birds
2. pencils and pens
3. movies and TV shows

4. hockey and soccer
5. photographers and painters
6. singers and dancers

▶ **Apply/Writing**   Write a description comparing and contrasting the two items that you considered in Practice B, or two other items. Use what you have learned in this section so far to develop clear and vivid comparisons and contrasts. Review the checklist below.

Comparison/Contrast Description Revision Checklist
✔ Have I clearly identified the two items being compared and contrasted?
✔ Have I included examples of how the two items are alike and different?
✔ Have I used comparison and contrast words and phrases?
✔ Have I summarized the point of the description?
✔ Have I included precise adverbs?

Comparison or Contrast Words and Phrases

as
both
just as
like
likewise
similarly
the same as

differ
different
however
in contrast
on the other hand
unlike

Revising and Editing Workshop

Connecting Writing and Grammar

- In Unit 10 you read an example of descriptive writing.
- In Unit 11 you wrote a descriptive paragraph and a comparison/contrast paragraph.

Now it's time to use your skill as an editor to improve another writer's first draft. Read this descriptive paragraph carefully. As you read, ask yourself these questions.

✔ Have I used words and phrases to help readers visualize what I am describing?
✔ Have I used comparative forms of adjectives and adverbs correctly?
✔ Have I used *good, well, bad,* and *badly* correctly?

(1) The ocean was calm. (2) The Parker family had just finished eating a dinner of lobster, salad, and corn. (3) There were more fewer people on the beach now than there had been during the day. (4) The girls, who were energetic in the morning, were tired as evening drew to a close. (5) They had swam and played all day long. (6) Lori, who was a bad swimmer, was telling everyone how good she had done in her swimming lesson. (7) She thought that the french swimming instructor was wonderful. (8) Sarah was exhausted than the others. (9) She needed rest bad. (10) In the distance on the horizon, there appeared the outline of a sailboat against the sun. (11) The sand felt cool and gritty under the Parkers' feet. (12) Other sailboats drifted back to the dock that was to the right down the beach. (13) A beautiful greek ship was docked there for the night. (14) A boy swam away from the boat toward the shoreline. (15) The calm, peaceful, blue ocean rippled farther out as a child on the beach happily and joyfully threw pebbles out toward the dock. (16) Aunt Mildred thought the sunset was the most prettiest she had ever seen.

▶ Revising the Draft

1. The spatial order used to describe what the Parkers see is from far to near. Find one sentence in the draft that does not stick to this order and put it in the correct place.
2. Find two sentences at the beginning of the draft that could be more descriptive. Rewrite these sentences, adding adjectives and adverbs. You may want to consult a thesaurus.
3. The draft does not have a topic sentence. Add a topic sentence that clearly tells what the paragraph is about.
4. Add, delete, or rearrange any other information you think would improve the draft.

▶ Editing the Draft

5. The writer used adjectives that compare incorrectly. Correct the three sentences in which this kind of error was made.
6. The draft contains errors in the use of *good, well, bad,* and *badly.* Correct the sentences with these errors.
7. Rewrite one sentence that has unneeded words in it.
8. Two proper adjectives should be capitalized. Correct the sentences with these errors.

▶ Working Together on the Draft

Meet with a group of your classmates. Discuss the changes you made in the draft. Listen to the changes your classmates made. Then rewrite the draft on page 148. Include all the revisions you think are important.

▶ Evaluating Your Own Writing

Now review your own writing. Look over the descriptive paragraph and the comparison/contrast paragraph you wrote in this unit and any other written work you have. Did you have any problems using adverbs? Did you have any problems using comparative forms of adjectives? The lessons that follow will help you with these writing problems.

10 Identifying Adjectives

An adjective modifies a noun or a pronoun.

▶ **Focus** **Adjectives** modify nouns and pronouns and make their meaning more exact. Usually an adjective precedes the word it modifies, but sometimes it follows it. Study these examples.

> A **large** sailboat capsized on the **stormy** lake at **this** spot.
> It was **unusable,** but at least the **four** sailors were **safe.**

In the first example, the adjectives come just before the nouns they modify. The second example is different. *Unusable* modifies the pronoun *It,* and *safe* modifies *sailors.*

Adjectives modify nouns and pronouns by telling what kind, which one, or how many.

> **What kind:** **black** flag, **powerful** crew, **heavy** sails, **large** mast
> **Which one:** **this** ship, **that** radio, **these** boats, **those** hatches
> **How many:** **two** oars, **few** passengers, **many** miles, **several** storms

Adjectives can be formed from some words by adding the suffixes *-ful, -able, -less,* or *-ish* to the words.

> color + ful = colorful   comfort + able = comfortable
> price + less = priceless   child + ish = childish

An adjective formed from a proper noun is called a **proper adjective** and is capitalized. Sometimes a proper adjective contains more than one word. Proper nouns may also be used as proper adjectives.

Proper Noun	**Proper Adjective**
Spain	Spanish flag
South America	South American politics
New York	New York parks

A, an, and *the* are special kinds of adjectives. You will recall that these are called **articles.** They appear before many nouns.

▶ **Guided Practice** Name the adjectives. Tell which are proper.

1. one tall ship   2. English sailors   3. that old tug

▶ **Practice**   **A.** Write an adjective before each noun. Then use each group of words in a sentence.

Example: _____ winds
Answer: gusty winds   The gusty winds filled the sails.

1. _____ waves 5. _____ afternoon 9. _____ island
2. _____ sun   6. _____ evening   10. _____ pirates
3. _____ clouds 7. _____ breeze   11. _____ submarine
4. _____ sea   8. _____ maps   12. _____ whales

B. Copy the adjectives from each sentence. Beside each adjective, write the word it modifies. Keep a separate list of the proper adjectives, as in the example. Do not copy the articles.

Example: Did the American tourists like spicy food in Mexico?
Answer: <u>Adjectives</u>   <u>Proper Adjectives</u>
            spicy—food   American—tourists

13. Uncle Henry told me about a recent trip to various countries.
14. He flew in a supersonic jet to the Amsterdam airport.
15. Then he took a small plane to an Egyptian city.
16. These photographs are beautiful, and he took them with that old camera.
17. He has several photos of this ancient temple.
18. He also visited many European museums.
19. These three recipes are from famous French restaurants.
20. Uncle amused us with several legends about a German castle.
21. He took lengthy tours of a few gardens in the English countryside.
22. The trip also included a brief stop in the Austrian mountains.
23. Uncle Henry spent eight days on a luxury ship too.
24. Aunt Meg joined him for two weeks on the islands of Hawaii.
25. I love those spectacular photos of Polynesian dancers.
26. Uncle Henry talked about the best part of the long trip.
27. He saw wonderful things, but now he is happy in America.

▶ **Apply/Writing**   Make a list of three places or things. Under each one, list several adjectives that describe it. Use each noun and some of the adjectives describing it in a sentence.

Example: groundhog—furry, plump, smart, lazy
             The plump, furry groundhog was too lazy to move.

11 Identifying Adverbs

An adverb can modify a verb, an adjective, or another adverb. Adverbs modify verbs by telling how, when, or where.

▶ **Focus**   An adverb can modify a verb in three different ways. It can tell how, when, or where an action takes place. Note in these examples what each adverb tells about the verb it modifies.

>Nick thought **carefully** about the plan. (how)
>He answered the letter **immediately.** (when)
>The bell rang **outside.** (where)

Adverbs can come before or after the verbs they modify. An adverb can also appear in the middle of a verb phrase.

>**Now** my assistant and I will perform the trick.
>My assistant and I will perform the trick **now.**
>My assistant and I will **now** perform the trick.

What is the verb that the adverb *now* modifies? What does *now* tell about that verb?

Some adverbs are formed by adding the suffix *-ly* to adjectives: *accurately, slowly, recently, humorously.* Not all adverbs end in *-ly*, however. Some of the most common ones do not. These include words like *maybe, here, never, still, also, now, then, today,* and *later.*

Do not assume that all words that end in *-ly* are adverbs. Some, such as *kindly* and *lovely,* can be adjectives. To identify an adverb, see how the word is used in a sentence.

>**Adjective:** The **kindly** gentleman opened the door for me.
>**Adverb:** He spoke **kindly** to me as he did so.

▶ **Guided Practice**   Explain what each adverb tells about the verb it modifies.

1. Yesterday Rita excitedly chose material for her prom dress.
2. First she pinned the pattern carefully to the material.
3. Then she quickly cut the various pieces.
4. She will soon start the skirt of the dress.
5. Now she is putting everything away.

▶ **Practice**   **A.** Write the sentences below. Use an adverb from the Adverb Box to complete each sentence. Each adverb should be used once.
Example: The boats glided _____ through the water.
Answer: The boats glided gracefully through the water.

1. Because of the rain, the sailboat race began _____.
2. The large crowd sat _____ on the sandy beach.
3. They had waited _____ all morning.
4. _____ the race began.
5. The boats maneuvered _____ around some obstacles.
6. _____ the wind switched to the east.
7. The gusts of wind blew _____.
8. The sailboats sped _____ over the waves.
9. Their billowing sails filled _____ with wind.
10. The crowd cheered _____ at the closeness of the race.
11. Many stood _____ for a better view.
12. The leading boat came _____ to the finish line.
13. Its crew leaned _____ out of the boat for balance.
14. They _____ smiled happily as they passed.
15. The second-place winners _____ grinned victoriously.
16. The crowd had _____ seen such an exciting race.

B. Write the adverb and the word it modifies in each sentence.
Example: The crowd applauded wildly.   *Answer:*   wildly—applauded

17. Today we watched an exciting sailboat race on the lake.
18. Many crews enthusiastically competed for first prize.
19. The clear blue water glistened brightly in the sun.
20. Colorful pennants flapped loudly in the strong wind.
21. The crews scurried around to their captains' sharp commands.
22. Often the waves drenched the prows of the sailboats.
23. They sped rapidly toward the finish line.
24. The colored sails contrasted sharply with each other.
25. Our favorite, the *Mackinaw,* pulled ahead of the rest.
26. Now they can keep the trophy until next year's race.

▶ **Apply/Writing**   List three movies or TV programs you have seen recently. Write three sentences about each. Use adverbs to tell *where* and *when* you saw it, and *how* it went.

Adverb Box
also
carefully
certainly
close
completely
down
far
finally
gracefully
late
loudly
never
patiently
smoothly
strongly
suddenly
up

12 Functions of Adverbs

Adverbs modifying verbs can function, or act, as adverbs of time, place, or manner. Adverbs modifying adjectives or other adverbs function as intensifiers.

▶ **Focus**   You know that adverbs can modify verbs by telling when, where, or how. An adverb that tells *when* is called an **adverb of time.** An adverb that tells *where* is called an **adverb of place.** An adverb that tells *how* is called an **adverb of manner** and generally ends in *-ly*. As what kind of adverb does the adverb in each of these sentences function?

TIME

> A cold front will arrive **today.**
> Sleet and freezing rain are expected **here.**
> The wind will **ferociously** blow the icy tree branches.

Adverbs can also modify adjectives and other adverbs. When adverbs are used this way, they function as **intensifiers.** An intensifier is used to increase or decrease the intensity of the adjective or adverb it modifies. It just comes before the word it modifies, and it tells *how much* or *to what extent.*

PLACE

> It was a **partly** cloudy afternoon.
> Then it rained **very** lightly.
> We were **so** happy when it stopped.

In the first example, the intensifier *partly* modifies the adjective *cloudy.* It tells how cloudy. The intensifier *very* in the second example modifies the adverb *lightly,* telling how lightly. What word does *so* modify in the third example?

MANNER

Adverbs that are often used as intensifiers include the following: *so, very, too, quite, hardly, barely, really, rather, especially, extremely, slightly, almost, nearly, somewhat.* To decide if a word is an intensifier, see how it is used in the sentence.

▶ **Guided Practice**   Tell how each adverb functions.

1. Today the races were run here.
2. Colin put in a very fast time.
3. The crowd cheered the winners quite loudly.

► **Practice** **A.** Write each sentence below. Add the kind of adverb that is indicated in parentheses.

Example: _____ I bought a pair of deck shoes. (time)
Answer: Yesterday I bought a pair of deck shoes.

1. My sister is _____ planning my birthday party. (manner)
2. Yoshi wanted to have the party _____. (place)
3. She wrapped my gift in a _____ beautiful box. (intensifier)
4. She wanted everything to go _____ smoothly. (intensifier)
5. Yoshi even called the weather forecaster _____. (time)
6. Would the weather be _____ good in two weeks? (intensifier)
7. The forecaster said it was _____ early to tell. (intensifier)
8. He told her to call him _____. (time)
9. He said it would be _____ sunny. (intensifier)
10. The day of the party it rained _____. (manner)
11. We had to have the party _____ instead. (place)
12. I thanked Yoshi for a _____ wonderful party. (intensifier)
13. I _____ told her that the weather didn't spoil it. (manner)
14. _____ I will think of a good way to show my appreciation. (time)

B. List the adverbs in the sentences. Then tell what the function of each is.

Example: Today I worked quietly in my room.
Answer: Today—Adverb of time   quietly—Adverb of manner

15. Our family held a very joyous reunion.
16. I was really anxious to see all my relatives, but I was especially happy to see my cousins.
17. My favorite aunt quite often told jokes.
18. We laughed constantly at her extremely funny stories.
19. Later we had an exceedingly large feast outside.
20. We had a very good time, but the end came quickly.
21. Some relatives packed rather speedily.
22. My aunt was nearly late for the train.
23. I tearfully waved as the train slowly departed.

► **Apply/Writing** Think of a job that you do around your home. Write several sentences describing the job. Make your description lively by using adverbs that tell when, where, and how you perform the job.

13 Comparative Forms

Most adjectives and adverbs have a positive, a comparative, and a superlative form.

▶ **Focus**   Both adjectives and adverbs have three forms to show comparison. They are the **positive form,** the **comparative form,** and the **superlative form.** Notice the endings or words that are used in building each of these forms. Also note that *more* and *most* are used with adjectives that are long words and with all adverbs that end in *-ly*. What spelling changes occur when endings are added to *big* and *speedy?*

	Positive	Comparative	Superlative
Adjectives:	big	bigger	biggest
	speedy	speedier	speediest
	beautiful	more beautiful	most beautiful
Adverbs:	soon	sooner	soonest
	seriously	more seriously	most seriously

Some adjectives and adverbs do not follow the usual rules. Their comparative and superlative forms are made differently.

	Positive	Comparative	Superlative
Adjectives:	good	better	best
	bad	worse	worst
	much	more	most
	little	less	least
	far	farther	farthest
Adverbs:	well	better	best
	badly	worse	worst
	much	more	most

▶ **Guided Practice**   Tell the form of each item.

1. happy   2. worst   3. more expensive

▶ **Practice**　**A.** Write each adjective or adverb below. Beside it, write its comparative and superlative forms.
Example: husky　*Answer:* husky, huskier, huskiest

1. quickly	**11.** spicy	**21.** low
2. cold	**12.** pretty	**22.** woolly
3. tall	**13.** happy	**23.** heavily
4. bright	**14.** coolly	**24.** flatly
5. grumpily	**15.** funny	**25.** small
6. steadily	**16.** near	**26.** colorfully
7. tan	**17.** likely	**27.** slowly
8. gracefully	**18.** sad	**28.** peacefully
9. young	**19.** practical	**29.** long
10. carefully	**20.** reasonably	**30.** dim

B. Write the sentences, using the form of the adjective or adverb indicated in parentheses.
Example:　The (early) Olympic Games had chariot races. (superlative)
Answer:　The earliest Olympic Games had chariot races.

31. The (old) Greek legend celebrated chariot racing. (superlative)
32. A king loved one of his daughters (much) of all. (superlative)
33. Each young suitor was (worthy) than the last. (comparative)
34. Still he forbade even the (noble) man her hand. (superlative)
35. The (good) one must prove himself in a race. (superlative)
36. Could any of them be a (skillful) driver than the king? (comparative)
37. He (confidently) challenged twelve to a race. (positive)
38. The king drove (good) than they. (comparative)
39. A thirteenth suitor joined the contest (late) than the others. (comparative)
40. The princess was the (beautiful) woman in the kingdom. (superlative)
41. She had fallen (deeply) in love with Pelops. (positive)
42. Pelops drove (fast) than the king. (comparative)
43. He had (little) trouble than the other suitors. (comparative)
44. He won the race and the princess (easily). (positive)

▶ **Apply/Writing**　Write a description of a race or contest. Use comparative and superlative forms of adjectives and adverbs. Try to compare one racer or contestant with another.

14 Using Comparative Forms

The comparative form is used to compare two people or things. The superlative form is used to compare three or more people or things.

▶ **Focus**   You know that most adjectives and adverbs have three forms: the positive, the comparative, and the superlative.

The **comparative form** is used to compare two people or things. The word *than* often signals the comparative form.

> One crew sailed **earlier** than the other.
> The water was **more tranquil** today than yesterday.
> Our boat moved **less speedily** through the water than your boat.

The **superlative form** is used to compare three or more.

> That crew sailed **earliest** of all.
> The water today was the **most tranquil** I've ever seen here.
> Her boat moved the **least speedily** of all the boats.

Avoid using double comparisons. Do not use both *-er* and *more* together or both *-est* and *most* together.

> **Don't write:** Tonight the sky is **more clearer** than last night's.
> **Write:** Tonight the sky is **clearer** than last night's.
> **Don't write:** Venus is the **most brilliantest** of all the planets.
> **Write:** Venus is the **most brilliant** of all the planets.

Double comparison errors are often made with irregular adjectives and adverbs. Study these examples:

> **Don't write:** The winds blew **more worser** Monday than Tuesday.
> **Write:** The winds blew **worse** Monday than Tuesday.
> **Don't write:** The winds blew **worstest** of all today.
> **Write:** The winds blew **worst** of all today.

▶ **Guided Practice**   Tell which form to use in each sentence.

1. That boat goes (faster, more faster) than this one.
2. This boat is also (less, least) easy to sail than this one.
3. The *Flying Fish* is the (fastest, most fastest) boat on the lake.
4. Its captain is the (best, bestest) I know.

▶ **Practice** **A.** Write the correct form of the adjective or adverb in parentheses.

Example: That concert is the (better, best) of the two this week.
Answer: better

1. Of the three bands, the Seven C's play (better, best).
2. Were (many, more) people at this concert than at the last?
3. The seats were (less, least) comfortable than before.
4. Of the last six concerts, this was the (less, least) exciting.
5. Our view was (worse, worst) than usual.
6. The Seven C's played (louder, loudest) than the other bands.
7. They also played (longer, longest) than the others.
8. The lights were the (brighter, brightest) we had ever seen.
9. The third encore by the group was the (more, most) thrilling.
10. We applauded (more, most) loudly than before.

B. Rewrite each sentence that contains a double comparison. If a sentence is correct, write *Correct.*

Example: Some snakes are more harder to catch than others.
Answer: Some snakes are harder to catch than others.

11. The most largest of all snakes is the anaconda.
12. The smallest snake is only six inches (15 cm) long.
13. Some people think snakes are the most creepiest of animals.
14. In some species, female snakes are more larger than males.
15. Young snakes shed their skins more frequently than older snakes.
16. A snake sheds its skin more quicklyer in warm weather.
17. Some desert snakes are more hardier than other snakes.
18. A snake's sense of smell is its most best developed sense.
19. Snakes are among the worst animals to train.
20. Are snakes less active when the weather is more colder?

▶ **Apply/Writing** Use some of the adjectives and adverbs below in a brief description of a concert, play, or show you have seen. You may also use other adjectives and adverbs. Use some positive, comparative, and superlative forms. Check your description to be sure you have avoided double comparisons.

good   interesting   slowly   rapidly   well   funny

21   More practice on page 514.

15 *Good, well, bad,* and *badly*

Good and bad are adjectives. Well and badly are adverbs.

▶ **Focus**   Do not confuse the modifiers *good* and *well* or *bad* and *badly*. *Good* is an adjective used to modify a noun or a pronoun. Do not use it to modify a verb. Use the adverb *well* to modify a verb. Look at the following examples.

> **Don't write:** Ivan swam **good** in the meet.
> **Write:** Ivan swam **well** in the meet.
> **Don't write:** He also did **good** in the diving contest.
> **Write:** He also did **well** in the diving contest.

In the first pair of sentences, the adverb *well* modifies the verb *swam*. What does the adverb *well* modify in the second pair of sentences?

Be careful also in using the modifiers *bad* and *badly*. *Bad* is an adjective. Use it to modify a noun or a pronoun. Use the adverb *badly* to modify a verb.

> **Don't write:** Ivan wanted the trophy **bad.**
> **Write:** Ivan wanted the trophy **badly.**
> **Don't write:** He took the loss **bad.**
> **Write:** He took the loss **badly.**

In the first pair of sentences, the adverb *badly* modifies the verb *wanted*. What does the adverb *badly* modify in the second pair of sentences?

▶ **Guided Practice**   Read each sentence. Tell how to correct any mistakes with *good, well, bad,* and *badly*.

1. Does Ivan play water polo good?
2. He says he doesn't play it too bad.
3. I think Ivan can do good at almost any water sport.
4. One of his sisters is a good swimmer too.
5. But she swam bad in the last meet.
6. I guess she just had a bad day.
7. She'll probably do good in the next meet.

▶ **Practice**   **A.** Write each sentence, using the correct modifier in parentheses.

Example: Their family members do many things (good, well).

Answer: Their family members do many things well.

1. Ivan's mother paints (good, well).
2. Her last exhibit went very (good, well).
3. An older sister did not do (bad, badly) in school last year.
4. This year she is doing particularly (good, well).
5. She wants to get a scholarship to college (bad, badly).
6. A younger brother did (good, well) in the state piano contest.
7. We knew he would because he always plays (good, well).
8. Does anyone in the family do anything (bad, badly)?
9. Mr. Zek burned the fish (bad, badly) at our last fish fry.
10. I was surprised because he doesn't often cook (bad, badly).

B. Copy the sentences, substituting an appropriate modifier—*good, well, bad, badly*—for the blank.

Example: Ivan wanted a part in the musical ____.

Answer: Ivan wanted a part in the musical badly.

11. At the tryouts he sang too ____ to get a leading role.
12. He sang ____ enough to get into the chorus, however.
13. Rehearsals went ____ at first because people didn't know their parts.
14. After a week of rehearsals, things finally began to go ____.
15. The chorus line still needed more practice ____, though.
16. The leading actors knew their parts ____.
17. The pianist played ____ because he hadn't practiced.
18. Even so, the singers sang ____.
19. The director said it had been a ____ rehearsal despite everything.
20. The chorus line performed ____ at an extra practice session.
21. The pianist had a ____ practice too.
22. Everything went ____ on opening night.

▶ **Apply/Writing**   Write a brief dialogue in which two people discuss their performances in a game, a show, a contest, or something similar. Use the modifiers *good, well, bad,* and *badly* in your dialogue, and be sure to use them correctly.

16 Expanding Sentences with Modifiers

Adjectives, adverbs, and phrases can make sentences more specific and descriptive.

▶ **Focus**   Often you may need to add words to a sentence to make it more descriptive. A sentence may sound dull or too plain to you. Notice how the basic sentence below becomes more informative and descriptive when adjectives and adverbs are added.

> Monkeys chattered. (basic sentence)
> **Two young** monkeys chattered. (adjectives added)
> Two young monkeys chattered **noisily.** (adverb added)

Prepositional phrases can also help make a sentence more descriptive and specific.

> Two young monkeys chattered noisily **in a tree.**
> Two young monkeys chattered noisily **in a tree near the garden.**

Now the sentence contains specific information. It answers such questions as these: How many monkeys are there? How old are they? How are they acting? Where are the monkeys?

Expand sentences only when the words you add provide useful, descriptive information. Avoid adding unneeded words. What do the words in dark type add to the sentence below?

> Two **little bitty** young monkeys chattered **very** noisily.

Little, bitty, and *very* expand the sentence, but they do not make it more descriptive or specific. The words and phrases you add to sentences should be useful to the reader. Unneeded words only clutter a sentence.

▶ **Guided Practice**   Suggest adjectives, adverbs, and prepositional phrases to insert in the places shown in parentheses.

1. The (adjective) car went (adverb) (phrase).
2. Its (adjective) engine filled the air (phrase).
3. (Adjective) animals scurried (adverb) (phrase).
4. The car stopped (adverb) (phrase).
5. (Adjective) people jumped (adverb) and ran (phrase).

▶ **Practice**   **A.** Write the sentences. Add an adjective, adverb, or a prepositional phrase in the places shown in parentheses.
Example: Nellie shut the (adjective) door and started (phrase).
Answer: Nellie shut the green door and started down the street.

1. She walked (adverb) toward the (adjective) store.
2. She was thinking about her (adjective) brother.
3. Nellie loved Benny even though he was a (adjective) boy.
4. Benny often brought some (adjective) animal (phrase).
5. Last week it was a (adjective) and (adjective) dog.
6. The dog howled all night (phrase).
7. It wouldn't have surprised Nellie if he had brought a (adjective) elephant (phrase).
8. "What a (adjective) brother I have!" Nellie said (adverb) (phrase).
9. "Does Benny think he has a (adjective) sister?" Nellie asked.
10. Nellie (adverb) rejected the idea as she (adverb) strolled (phrase).
11. She saw Benny running (adverb) toward her.
12. "Come on! I've got a surprise (phrase)!" he said.
13. Nellie (adverb) followed Benny (phrase).
14. There she saw a (adjective) alligator!
15. "Do you think Dad will let me keep it?" he asked (adverb).

B. Add adjectives, adverbs, and prepositional phrases to the sentences below. Underline the word or words you add.
Example: Children swam.
Answer: <u>Happy</u> children swam <u>rapidly</u> <u>in the pool.</u>

16. An eagle soared.
17. A child wept.
18. Students laughed.
19. Soldiers marched.
20. A pilot landed.
21. Campers complained.
22. The gymnasts trained.
23. A train rumbled.
24. A robin sang.
25. Teachers worked.

▶ **Apply/Writing**   Write a list of short sentences that do not have descriptive words and phrases, such as those in Practice B. Exchange papers with a partner. Have your partner expand your sentences to make them more descriptive while you work on your partner's paper. Then compare papers.

Review/Evaluation

For more review,
see Tested Skills Practice,
pages 513–515.

20 **Functions of Adverbs**   Write the letter of the answer that
identifies each underlined word.

  a. Adverb of time   **c.** Adverb of manner
  b. Adverb of place   **d.** Intensifier

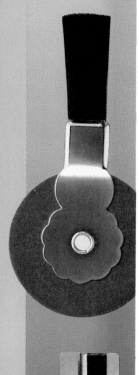

  1. Tuesday was a <u>very</u> horrible day in my life.
  2. I slept <u>too</u> late that terrible morning.
  3. I dressed very <u>quickly</u> and gulped my breakfast.
  4. I rushed <u>outside</u> to catch the bus.
  5. The bus was just driving <u>away</u> from the corner.
  6. Mom <u>immediately</u> offered me a ride to school.
  7. At school, I dashed <u>inside</u> and hurried to my locker.
  8. I was <u>almost</u> there by the nine o'clock bell.
  9. <u>Soon</u> I walked into my first class.
 10. Things did not go <u>extremely</u> well there, either.
 11. <u>Stupidly</u>, I had left my homework in Mom's car.
 12. I walked to my gym class <u>eagerly</u>.
 13. <u>Today</u> we were presenting our new gymnastics program for
     some of the faculty.
 14. I performed <u>clumsily</u> during the class.
 15. I fell <u>down</u> and scraped my knees.
 16. <u>Later</u>, I embarrassed myself in the cafeteria.
 17. <u>Quite</u> carelessly, I had brought the wrong bag to lunch.
 18. The bag contained my <u>rather</u> dirty tennis sneakers.
 19. Quickly I pushed them <u>back</u> into the bag.
 20. My friends laughed <u>loudly</u>.

21 **Comparative Form**   **A.** Write the letter of the answer that
identifies the form of each underlined adjective or adverb.

  a. Positive form   **b.** Comparative form   **c.** Superlative form

 21. Carnival day is the <u>most wonderful</u> day in the year.
 22. My friend Sam and I were much <u>happier</u> than usual that day.
 23. The Ferris wheel was the <u>biggest</u> in the world.
 24. It was really <u>huge</u>!
 25. The tickets were the <u>most expensive</u> at the carnival.
 26. Sam ran <u>faster</u> than I to the ticket booth.

27. <u>More</u> tickets were sold for that ride than for any other.
28. At first, the huge metal wheel turned <u>more slowly</u> than we expected.
29. As it speeded up, Sam yelled <u>loudest</u> of all the riders.
30. He also turned <u>paler</u> than I had ever seen him.

21 **B.** Write the letter of the adjective or adverb that completes each sentence.

31. The kids on our street had the ____ backyard games of all.
    a. great **b.** greater **c.** greatest **d.** most greatest
32. Lupe raced ____ than anyone else in the games.
    a. faster **b.** more faster **c.** fastest **d.** fast
33. In the long jump, Alan was the ____ of all the competitors.
    a. good **b.** better **c.** best **d.** bestest
34. He has the ____ legs of all the kids.
    a. long **b.** longest **c.** most longest **d.** longestest
35. All the athletes performed ____ this year than last.
    a. more better **b.** better **c.** best **d.** bester

22 **Using *good, well, bad, badly*** Write **a** if the underlined word is used correctly. Write **b** if it is not used correctly.

36. Tim Belton always treated his pet lizards <u>well</u>.
37. She didn't sing <u>bad</u>, for someone with a sore throat.
38. Bill doesn't play the guitar as <u>good</u> as he used to.
39. Our baseball team needed a new left-handed pitcher <u>badly</u>.
40. Don't you agree that Marian always dresses <u>well</u>?
41. I think they have a <u>good</u> chance to win.
42. After that, things didn't go <u>good</u> for Jake.
43. We wanted a win <u>bad</u>.
44. The ship is leaking <u>bad</u>; we will have to abandon it.
45. If a play begins <u>badly</u>, the actors become discouraged.
46. They don't dance <u>good</u>, but at least they try.
47. If I cooked as <u>bad</u> as Pat, I wouldn't enter the barbecuing contest either.
48. Her car will run <u>good</u>, once it gets a tune-up.
49. That pink shirt would go <u>well</u> with your gray slacks.
50. How <u>bad</u> do you want a new bike?

Thinking/Writing Evaluation

16 **Comparison and Contrast** Read the paragraph and answer the questions.

   (1) Both novels and short stories are popular forms of fiction. (2) Novels, of course, require more time on the part of the reader; short stories, on the other hand, can often be read in a single sitting. (3) A novel is perfect for a cold winter evening in front of the fire, but it probably wouldn't be the book to take for a short wait in a doctor's office.

1. Which sentence states a comparison between novels and short stories? **a.** sentence 1 **b.** sentence 2 **c.** sentence 3
2. Which sentence states a contrast between novels and short stories? **a.** sentence 1 **b.** sentence 2 **c.** sentence 3
3. Which sentence shows two contrasting aspects of the novel? **a.** sentence 1 **b.** sentence 2 **c.** sentence 3

17
18 **Descriptive Paragraphs** **A.** Read the two paragraphs and answer the questions.
19

   (1) The top of the mountain was ugly. (2) On every side, patches of dirty snow lay in crevices of gray rock. (3) Cold winds bent the shrubs into grotesque shapes. (4) Nothing else grew there.
   (5) Halfway down, however, the mountain was lovely. (6) Grass grew all around like a thick carpet. (7) Rainbows of wildflowers burst out everywhere, and their sweet scent rode the winds.

4. Which paragraph begins with a topic sentence? **a.** first paragraph **b.** second paragraph **c.** both paragraphs
5. Which sentences provide supporting details? **a.** sentences 1, 3, 5 **b.** sentences 2, 6, 7 **c.** sentences 1, 4, 5
6. Which word completes this sentence? The second paragraph _____ the middle of the mountain with the top. **a.** compares **b.** shows **c.** contrasts

18 **B.** Write a descriptive paragraph on one of the topics below. Apply what you have learned about descriptive paragraphs.

   • a skyscraper   • a busy highway   • a flower shop

Curriculum Connection: Science

You have learned in this section that when you classify, you sort information or things into categories. All sciences make use of classification. Life scientists, for example, have classified the birds of North America into approximately 650 species or categories. No matter where you live, at least 50 species of birds probably live around you. Get to know the birds of your area by recording in your **learning log,** the different types that you see.

▶ **Think**   How can you learn to identify the different kinds of birds in your area? To do this well, you will have to become a close observer of birds. Notice their size, their shape, how they act, how they fly, the colors of their feathers, the sounds they make, and when and where you see them.

▶ **Discuss**   Meet with your classmates. Have each person name and describe birds that they are already familiar with. Identify the features of common birds that you see all the time.

▶ **Find Out**   Look in an encyclopedia for basic information about birds. Find a handbook or study guide about birds in your library and concentrate upon the birds that are native to the part of the country in which you live.

▶ **React: Learning Log**   Record in your science learning log information about the birds you observe. Enter the name of each new bird you spot, along with the date, location, and time of the sighting. Provide a description of the bird's appearance and habits. Leave space to add to the description when you see it again and are able to record more details. Below is a sample entry.

> Science   December 12, 1988
> 8 A.M. Bob-white ate sunflower seeds
> at feeder. Dark body, white stripes
> on head, short tail, walks like a
> chicken. This bird's call sounds like
> "bob white."

Tested Skills Maintenance

10 **Plural Nouns**   Write the correct plural form of each noun.

1. berry	**6.** spy	**11.** sheriff	**16.** commander in chief
2. thief	**7.** deer	**12.** goose	**17.** tack
3. stereo	**8.** box	**13.** church	**18.** moose
4. brush	**9.** chair	**14.** baby	**19.** son-in-law
5. child	**10.** key	**15.** piano	**20.** monkey

11 **Kinds of Pronouns**   Write the pronouns in each sentence and after each write whether it is a personal, interrogative, or relative pronoun.

21. Who gave you the tape recorder?

22. My aunt was the person who gave it to me.

23. Is she the aunt that I like so much?

24. Yes, she and her new husband, whom we like a lot too, have just visited us.

25. What is their last name?

9 **Writing a Short Story**   Rewrite the following dialogue, adding appropriate capitalization, punctuation, and indention.

26. I'm not going said Harry

27. why not asked Arby

28. I don't like museums   who needs dinosaurs

29. what a grump you are   the museum has more than dinosaur skeletons

30. name something else Harry demanded

31. there's a great new space exhibit Arby replied with a movie that makes you feel as though you're blasting off and going into orbit

32. well, I'll think about it   maybe I'll change my mind

13 **Distinguishing Action/Linking Verbs**   Write the verb in each sentence. Then write whether it is an action or a linking verb.

33. Lon looked at the scoreboard.

34. His team's chances of winning looked poor.

35. Defeat seemed almost certain.

36. The coach sounded worried.

37. Lon felt the ball with sweaty palms.

38. The cheering of the crowd grew louder.

39. Then the buzzer sounded the end of the game.

14 **Principal Parts of Verbs**   Copy the verb in each sentence. After it, write what principal part it is formed from.

40. Inez attends art class on Saturdays.

41. Several times this year her class has visited the Art Institute.

42. Inez has looked especially closely at portraits.

43. She is painting a portrait of her great-grandmother.

44. She has studied photographs of her subject.

45. Her teacher had suggested the portrait.

46. Inez sketched a preliminary picture.

47. She selected her colors carefully.

48. Now she is putting the finishing touches on.

15 **Perfect Tenses**   Rewrite the sentences, adding the suggested form of the verb.

49. I _____ French for two years. (*study*, present perfect)

50. My sister _____ French too. (*learn*, present perfect)

51. We _____ to visit France this year. (*plan*, past perfect)

52. We _____ our plans. (*change*, present perfect)

53. By this time next year we _____ France. (*visit*, future perfect)

54. We _____ two weeks with a French family. (*stay*, future perfect)

55. Our French pen pals, George and Renee, _____ us. (*invite*, present perfect)

12 **Writing a Personal Experience Narrative**   Improve this narrative paragraph by eliminating events that are not important.

   (**56**) When I was five years old, I learned to listen to my grandfather. (**57**) Gramps had turned sixty the week before. (**58**) Every summer my family made a yearly visit to my gandparents' farm. (**59**) Gramps usually had something new to show us and this time it was a flock of geese. (**60**) He told us not to go near them. (**61**) He had just finished reading a book about geese. (**62**) I was very curious about why the geese should be left alone and that's how I learned my lesson.

Descriptive Writing

Theme: From Here to There

A poem can be about anything—people, places, events, emotions, imaginary things. It can tell a story, a secret, or a joke. A poem can put you in the past or throw you into the future. It can make you feel at home or estranged in a different land. It can transport you all over the world. A poem can take you anyplace, anytime—it can take you **from here to there.** As you read the poems in this section, think about where they take you. Then think about where you want to take your readers when you write a poem of your own.

1 Literature: Poetry

A poem can be about anything or anyplace. It can take you **from here to there** with just a few words.

Poets arrange their words in lines or groups of lines called **stanzas** rather than in sentences and paragraphs. They choose their words carefully for their sounds as well as for their meanings. The words poets choose help us picture in a new way what is being described.

Poetry can best be enjoyed when it is heard. Read the four poems in this lesson aloud or listen while someone else reads them. Think about the places they take you to in your imagination.

Fog

The fog comes
on little cat feet.

It sits looking
over harbor and city
on silent haunches
and then moves on.

—*Carl Sandburg*

Morning Mood

I wake with morning yawning in my mouth,
With laughter, see a teakettle spout steaming.
I wake with hunger in my belly
And I lie still, so beautiful it is, it leaves me dazed,
5 The timelessness of the light.

Grandma cares for me, and our family needs nothing more.
They share each other for pleasure
As mother knows, who learns of happiness
From her own actions
10 They did not even try to be beautiful, only true,
But beauty is here, it is a custom.

This place of unbroken joy,
Giving out its light today—only today—not tomorrow.

—*M. Panegoosho*

Women

They were women then
My mama's generation
Husky of voice—Stout of
Step
5   With fists as well as
Hands
How they battered down
Doors
And ironed
10   Starched white
Shirts
How they led
Armies
Headragged Generals
15   Across mined
Fields
Booby-trapped
Ditches
To discover books
20   Desks
A place for us
How they knew what we
Must know
Without knowing a page
25   Of it
Themselves.

I shall write of the old men I knew
And the young men
I loved
30   And of the gold toothed women
Mighty of arm
Who dragged us all
To church.

—*Alice Walker*

The title of the following poem by Edgar Allan Poe is the name of a legendary city or region supposed to be full of gold and other treasure. Sixteenth-century Spanish explorers in America traveled from here to there searching for Eldorado, or El Dorado (el də rä′ dō). *Eldorado* comes from the Spanish, meaning "the one that appears golden."

Eldorado

Gaily bedight,
A gallant knight,
In sunshine and in shadow,
Had journeyed long,
5   Singing a song,
In search of Eldorado.

But he grew old—
This knight so bold—
And o'er his heart a shadow
10   Fell as he found
No spot of ground
That looked like Eldorado.

And, as his strength
Failed him at length,
15 He met a pilgrim shadow—
"Shadow," said he,
"Where can it be—
This land of Eldorado?"

"Over the Mountains
20   Of the Moon,
Down the Valley of the Shadow,
Ride, boldly ride,"
The shade replied,—
"If you seek for Eldorado."

—*Edgar Allan Poe*

▶ **Discussing**
1. What picture does each poem create for you?
2. To what does Carl Sandburg compare the fog?
3. What is the mood of "Morning Mood"?
4. What does Alice Walker say that the women in the poem "Women" wanted for their children?
5. How does the knight change in "Eldorado"?
6. Which poem reminds you of someone you know or of a personal experience you have had? Explain.
7. Do you think each poem takes you from here to there? If so, how?

▶ **Analyzing: Figurative Language**
Literal language uses words according to their ordinary meanings. In **figurative language,** however, words are used apart from their ordinary meanings to add beauty and force.

For each literal statement below, find in the poems you read the same idea expressed in figurative language.

1. The fog appears.
2. The long-searching knight became discouraged.
3. I wake up tired.

▶ **Writing**
Be a poetry reviewer. In a few sentences tell what each poem in this lesson is about. Then give your opinion of the poem. Tell whether or not you liked the poem. Give reasons for your opinion.

▶ **Extending**
Speaking and Listening   Meet with a small group of classmates to discuss which of the poems in this lesson best fits the section theme, *From Here to There*. Then present the poem to the class. Your group might recite the poem in chorus, dramatize it, or pantomine it to appropriate music—whichever method seems to convey the theme best.

Reading   *You Come Too,* by Robert Frost, is a collection of Frost's poems that will take you on a voyage of discovery from here to there. The collection was compiled with young people in mind and contains poems about trees, flowers, birds, animals, and people.

2 Listening for Imagery

Poets use imagery to create vivid descriptions.

▶ **Focus**   Pretend that you have just read a description of a friend's old family dog. In the description you are told that the dog is large, with smooth black fur, a shrill bark, and wobbly legs. The pictures you create of this dog in your mind are called **images.** Writers create images, or **imagery,** by using words that appeal to the senses. Through these images, readers can picture in their minds how something looks, sounds, smells, tastes, and feels.

▶ **Practice**   Listen while your teacher reads the poem "The Flower-Fed Buffaloes" by Vachel Lindsay. First, just listen to what is going on in the poem. When your teacher reads the poem a second time, listen for images that appeal to particular senses. Then answer the following questions.

1. To what sense does the poet appeal when he describes the locomotive?
2. Three words, each appealing to a different sense, are used to describe the grass that has been replaced by the wheat. Write any one of the words.
3. What sound is the repetition of the word *wheels* meant to imitate?
4. Near the end of the poem, the buffaloes are said to no longer "gore," "bellow," or "trundle." With what earlier image of the buffaloes is this image of their power contrasted?
5. Name any one of the three things in the poem described as "lying low."

▶ **Apply/Oral Language**   Think of a topic or choose one of these: a heavy snowfall; an athletic event; a pet; a family outing; a fall day. List the five senses in a column. Describe your topic with at least one image that appeals to each sense. Then trade papers with a partner and read the descriptions. Tell each other how you picture the topic described, based on the images used. Save your work to use in the next unit.

3 Alliteration and Sound Words

Poets use alliteration and sound words, or onomatopoeia, to emphasize the sounds and rhythms of a poem.

▶ **Focus**   In poetry, the sounds as well as the meanings of words are important. The sounds of words can create special effects.
Alliteration is the repetition of consonant sounds occurring at the beginning of words or within words. Here is a well-known example of alliteration.

> Peter Piper picked a peck of pickled peppers.

In the example, the initial *p* is repeated. If you change the beginning sounds, the special effect of alliteration is lost.

> Ed Jones picked a bushel of green cucumbers.

Without alliteration, it is an ordinary sentence. But with alliteration, the sentence has a musical quality.
Onomatopoeia is the use of words that sound like their meanings. The word *sizzle,* for example, sounds like something cooking in a frying pan. Here are some onomatopoetic words.

Onomatopoetic Words				
pop	purr	crack	buzz	boom
whine	whoosh	jingle	clang	fizz
hiss	ding-dong	screech	growl	smack
tingle	chug	swoosh	bang	zip

Onomatopoeia can add freshness to a sentence or a line of poetry. It highlights a sound and makes it seem real.

▶ **Guided Practice**   Complete each sentence with an onomatopoetic word.

1. The alarm clock awoke me with a ____.
2. The air ____ as it escaped from the tire.
3. I heard a loud ____ as the box exploded.
4. The old gate closed with a ____.

▶ **Practice**   Find examples of alliteration and onomatopoeia in these poem excerpts. Some excerpts illustrate both poetic devices.

1. I bubble into addying bays,
    I babble on the pebbles. . . .

   from **The Brook** *by Alfred, Lord Tennyson*

2. Like trains of cars on tracks of plush
    I hear the level bee. . . .

   from **The Bee** *by Emily Dickinson*

3. In the greenest growth of the Maytime,
    I rode where the woods were wet,
Between the dawn and the daytime;
    The spring was glad that we met. . . .

   from **An Interlude** *by Algernon Charles Swinburne*

4. I sift the snow on the mountains below,
    And their great pines groan aghast. . . .

   from **The Cloud** *by Percy Bysshe Shelley*

5. Back up he swims,
   Past sting-ray and shark,
    Out with a zoom.
    A whoop, a bark.

   from **Seal** *by William Jay Smith*

6. For the moon never beams without bringing me dreams
    Of the beautiful Annabel Lee. . . .

   from **Annabel Lee** *by Edgar Allan Poe*

▶ **Apply/Oral Language**   Find some lines of poetry that contain alliteration and onomatopoeia, or write some examples yourself. You might use these devices to describe the topic you chose at the end of the last lesson. Read your examples of alliteration and onomatopoeia to a partner, and ask which effect is illustrated. Then switch roles. Save your work for use in the next unit.

Our Living Language

▶ **Middle English**

> In Middle English, it's *cū*
> That's "cow" to you.
> But it turned into *boef*
> In a Norman stew.

> An English *schep* will bleet
> And a *pigge* will squeal,
> But they're *mouton* and *porc*
> In a Norman meal.

In 1066, a French-speaking people called the Normans conquered England. They ruled for the next three centuries. French became the official language of government, law, and the ruling classes. As a result, many words in our English language are of French origin. The French words in the poem above—*boef, porc,* and *mouton*—later became *beef, pork,* and *mutton* in English.

English was spoken by Anglo-Saxon peasants and serfs, while the ruling classes spoke French. The serf who tended the cow called it "cū," but Norman lords who ate the cow called it "boef."

In the language we call Middle English, many Old English words were replaced by French words. Anglo-Saxons gave the language basic everyday terms like *eat, drink, work,* and *speak.* French words that entered the English language named things that did not exist among the simple Anglo-Saxons. A few examples are *fashion, gown, diamond, painting,* and *leisure.*

During the Middle English period, words came into English from other languages such as Latin, Dutch, Flemish, and German. It began to more closely resemble the language we speak today.

Word Play For each Middle English word related to eating, write the modern one: *meel   dinen   forke   coppe   sawce.*

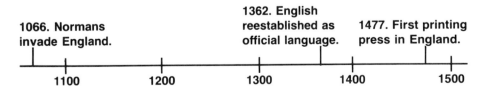

1066. Normans invade England.

1362. English reestablished as official language.

1477. First printing press in England.

1100   1200   1300   1400   1500

4 Creating Similes and Metaphors

Similes and metaphors are comparisons writers use to describe things in a fresh, vivid way.

▶ **Focus**   One way writers try to create vivid images is by using similes and metaphors, comparisons of one thing to another. Such comparisons are called **figures of speech** because words are used out of their ordinary or literal meanings.

> The world is like a theater playing twenty-four hours a day.
> The world is as fragile as a bubble.

The world is, of course, not very much like a theater or a bubble, but it is like them in some respects. **Similes** like the ones above compare two things, using *like* or *as*.

You can also make comparisons without using the words *like* or *as*. This kind of comparison is called a **metaphor.** The metaphors below further suggest what the world may be.

> The world's a spoiled child.
> The modern world is a merry-go-round of surprises.

▶ **Guided Practice**   Discuss the answer to each question.

1. What is the similarity between the world and a spoiled child?
2. How does the world remind you of a merry-go-round full of surprises?

▶ **Practice**   Complete sentences 1–5 to make similes. Complete sentences 6–10 to make metaphors.

1. The idea was like _____.
2. That forest was as _____.
3. My room was as _____.
4. A heart is as _____.
5. The sky was as _____.

6. The soldiers were _____.
7. The speech was _____.
8. My desk is _____.
9. These children are _____.
10. The trucks were _____.

▶ **Apply/Prewriting**   Warm up for the poem you will write in the next lesson. Make a list of five of your own experiences. Then compare each one, or an item in each one, to something else, using similes and metaphors. Save your work.

5 Writing a Poem

You can write poetry to express your thoughts, moods, and experiences.

You read and heard various poems in Unit 13. Now you will write one of your own. Remember what you have learned about poetic devices—similes and metaphors, imagery, alliteration, and onomatopoeia—that help make a poem enjoyable. Think about your **purpose** and **audience.** Who will read your poem—friends? family? a teacher? Do you want your readers to laugh, be sympathetic, or just share your thoughts?

1. Prewriting

▶ **Choose a Topic**   The first step is to think of a subject. Perhaps you already have a subject in mind from your writer's notebook. If you do not, here are three prewriting activities that should help you come up with a topic.

Ways to Get Started
1. *Free writing* is writing freely about whatever comes into your mind. Jot down anything—words, phrases, sentences. After a while, look back over what you have written. Does one subject stand out? Is one subject repeated?
2. Look through a family photo album or magazines that contain many pictures. Is there a person in your family or someone else you know whom you could describe in a poem? Does some pictured event remind you of happy times or sad events? Does a picture of some unusual place strike you in a particular way?
3. *Listing* is another way to create writing ideas. Think of a broad topic, such as experiences, moods, or feelings. Then simply write down what you remember. What were your four most thrilling experiences? What are your three most common moods? What feelings do you experience most?

List all the subjects that result from these prewriting activities.

Your list of these subjects may look something like this:
- Memories from childhood
- Unusual pets
- Favorite season
- Imaginary places
- Being outdoors

▶ **Develop Ideas**   After you have a list of subjects, narrow it down. Choose two or three ideas to develop more fully. Then **use the thinking skill of comparing and contrasting** to develop your possible subjects. Make a chart like the one below. Use your subjects and make comparisons and contrasts of your own.

Subjects	Is like/Is not like
small-town life	relaxation / pressure
climbing trees	a circus / walking
being outdoors	freedom / homework

Word Bank
bizarre
flinch
talkative
favorite
wander
musical
unseen
magic
rainy

At this point, choose one subject and create a list of details about it. The details will help you expand the idea, so you will have enough to write about. You might also want to create a special **Word Bank** of descriptive words for your chosen subject. The Word Bank at the left may give you some ideas.

Word Bank Being Outdoors	Descriptive Words
wet grass	glistening, slippery
soft mud	cool squishy
young bud	delicate, tender

For more ideas on prewriting and on other steps in the writing process, see The Writer at Work, pages 558–569.

2. Writing

Here are a few ideas that might help you get started writing.

State your main idea.
Example: Springtime offers temptations that are hard to resist.

Start with one word or phrase about your topic.
Example: climbing trees

Follow up with a comparison.
Example: Climbing trees is like a circus act.

▶ **Study the Draft**   Before you begin writing, read the first draft of a student's poem. Note the use of imagery and figurative language. Because this is a first draft, there are some errors and changes.

> "Spring Thoughts"
>
> Climbing trees
> Is a high-wire act that I preform
> Without a net each new spring.
>
> Fresh breese ~~breeze~~
> With some magic, can ~~make~~ transform
> A plain old day into a diffrent thing
>
> New bud
> soon to be part of a bunch of flowers.
> Popped up a small bit of green.
>
> Soft mud
> Cool and slipprey after showers.
> Temps me to step in, barefoot, unseen.

> Blue skies
> Watch with white clouds above me.
> As I try out my bike-riding stunts.
>
> ~~Searching~~ Wandering eyes
> Move from books to where I should be
> Out there, in the air, tossing sticks.

▶ **Write a Draft**   Now write a first draft of your own poem. Look often at your lists of descriptive details. Get some lines down quickly and go back later to revise and improve them.

As you write, keep the following ideas in mind. The first word in each line is generally capitalized. Several lines of a poem may make up a single thought. A poet often treats this thought as a single sentence and punctuates it as such. However, these are not hard and fast rules. Poetry allows its writers certain freedoms that other forms of literature do not. The important thing for you as a poetry writer to do is to be consistent in whatever style you choose.

3. Revising

▶ **Read and Confer**   Take time to read your poem aloud to yourself. Make notes about any changes you want to make. Then, with a conference partner, discuss the following questions.

> **Conference Questions**
> 1. Has the writer used vivid imagery that appeals to the senses?
> 2. Has the writer used similes and metaphors?
> 3. Has the writer used alliteration and onomatopoeia effectively?
> 4. Are there any colorful words that can be substituted for vague or general ones?

▶ **Make Changes**   Review your notes about the poem and make any changes needed with a red pencil. On the next page is a strategy that will help you improve your writing.

STRATEGY: Ask someone to read your poem aloud to you, or read the poem yourself into a tape recorder. Note the images that come to mind. List in your writer's notebook any vague or general words and phrases that might be changed to create more vivid images. Beside each item listed, write a new word or phrase that is more colorful. Notice how colorful words have been substituted for vague and general words in these three lines from the poem "Spring Thoughts."

> *Young*
> ~~New~~ ebud
>   *an ocean*
> soon to be part of ~~a bunch~~ of flowers
>   *delicate*
> Popped up a ~~small~~ bit of green.

▶ **Proofread and Edit**   Check your poem carefully for errors. Use the proofreader's marks and questions to help you make the final corrections.

Proofreading Questions
1. Did I capitalize all words that should be capitalized?
2. Did I use verb tenses correctly and consistently?
3. Did I use appropriate punctuation?
4. Did I spell every word correctly?

▶ **Make a Final Copy**   Recopy your poem, using your best handwriting. Be sure to include all of your changes.

4. Presenting

Here are some suggestions for presenting your poem.
- Hold a poetry reading. Have students take turns reading their poems aloud in front of the class or in small groups.
- Illustrate your poem. Use magazine pictures or original drawings to make a collage around it.

Revising and Editing Workshop

Connecting Writing and Grammar

- In Unit 13 you read several poems and learned about poetic devices.
- In Unit 14 you wrote a poem.

Now it's time to use your skill as an editor to improve another writer's first draft. Read this poem carefully. As you read, ask yourself these questions.

✔ Is vivid imagery that appeals to the senses used?
✔ Are similes and metaphors used?
✔ Is capitalization used correctly?

Talking to Myself

1   Writing a poem. Encore, where do I begin?
2   Go ahead and jump. Splash! You're in.

3   But poets write poems. I'd better just read.
4   Both pencil nor paper are all you need.

5   Oh no, I don't have a subject. Should it be fancy?
6   choose what you know best; don't make things chancy.

7   All right, here goes. I'll tell about my cat.
8   That sounds well. Does he scratch, claw, and bat?

9   My cat ambrose is a blanket in my neck,
10   But when the sun shines, he goes on the deck.
11   He'll growl and snipe at the Great Dane next door;
12   Then he'll hustle and run—to hide on the floor.
13   He walks stiff-legged like a cop through a beat.
14   He curls and uncurls the toes on his feet.
15   Ambrose's fur is brown.
16   He looks so funny bouncing around.

17   But wait, don't go, or I've only begun.
18   You're a poet now; my work here is done.

Revising the Draft

1. The writer could have used more alliteration. Add alliteration by substituting three words in lines 10–12 that begin with the same letter as two or three other words in the line.
2. The writer does not tell about the kinds of sounds Ambrose makes. Add lines to the poem using onomatopoetic words that describe cat noises.
3. Find a place where the description of Ambrose could be more vivid. Add colorful words to create imagery and a simile or metaphor.
4. The writer used an inappropriate interjection. Substitute an appropriate interjection such as *wow* or *oh* for the one in the poem.
5. Add, delete, or rearrange any other information you think would improve the draft.

Editing the Draft

6. Find two prepositions that are not used correctly. Rewrite the lines, using the correct prepositions.
7. The writer forgot to capitalize two words. Rewrite the lines in which this kind of error was made.
8. Two lines use conjunctions incorrectly. Correct the lines with these errors.
9. The draft contains an error in the use of *good* and *well*. Correct the line in which this error was made.

Working Together on the Draft

Meet with a group of your classmates. Discuss the changes you made in the draft. Listen to the changes your classmates made. Then rewrite the draft on page 186. Include all the revisions you think are important.

Evaluating Your Own Writing

Now review your own writing. Look over the poem you wrote in this unit and any other written work you have. Did you have any problems using prepositions and conjunctions correctly? The lessons that follow will help you with these writing problems.

6 Prepositions and Prepositional Phrases

A preposition is a word used with a noun or a pronoun to form a prepositional phrase.

▶ **Focus**   Prepositions are words such as *in, under,* and *over.* Below is a list of prepositions. Notice that a preposition can consist of more than one word.

aboard	before	during	near	through
about	behind	except	of	throughout
above	below	for	off	till
according to	beneath	from	on	to
across	beside	in	onto	toward
after	besides	in addition to	out	under
against	between	inside	out of	underneath
along	beyond	in spite of	outside	until
among	but	instead of	over	up
around	by	into	past	with
at	down	like	since	within

A **prepositional phrase** is a group of words that begins with a preposition and ends with a noun or pronoun. Study these examples.

The actress walked **into the room.**
The orchestra sat **below the stage.**
The lights are **above it.**

The word groups *into the room, below the stage,* and *above it* are prepositional phrases. Each phrase begins with a preposition and ends with a noun or pronoun called the **object of the preposition.**
   A preposition shows a relationship between its object and another word in the sentence. In the first example sentence, *into* explains where the actress is in relation to the room. In the second example sentence, *below* tells where the orchestra is in relation to the stage. Where are the lights in relation to the stage?
   A prepositional phrase may have a compound object. Also, a prepositional phrase may contain one or more modifiers that come

between the preposition and the object. Study the following two examples.

> One actor had problems **with the lines and movements.**
> The actor **in baggy pants** plays a clown.

In the first example, the compound object is *lines and movements.* What adjective modifies the object of the preposition in the second example?

Sentences can contain more than one prepositional phrase. Look at this example.

> **Behind the curtains** a member **of the cast** walked **toward the actress in the green costume.**

Notice that prepositional phrases can come almost anywhere in a sentence. What is the prepositional phrase at the beginning of the preceding example? What two prepositional phrases come right after each other in the example?

▶ **Guided Practice**　Find the prepositional phrases in the sentences. For each, name the preposition and its object or compound object.

1. The actress with red hair held a book in her hand.
2. She stood in the very center of the huge stage.
3. She was auditioning for the director and the producer.
4. The stage manager sat inside the wings to the right.
5. Behind him stood various members of the cast.

▶ **Practice**　**A.** Write sentences using the following prepositional phrases. Put the phrases in various places in your sentences.
Example:　near the theater door
Answer:　Near the theater door were people requesting autographs.

1. before the play
2. down the shadowy street
3. about the main performers
4. among the audience
5. in the box seats
6. near the emergency door
7. in spite of the wait
8. except you and me
9. during the brief intermission
10. behind the angry hero
11. at the very end
12. throughout the performance

B. Copy the prepositional phrases in these sentences and underline each preposition. The numbers in parentheses tell how many prepositional phrases are in the sentence.

Example: Take a ride on your bike to the theater. **(2)**
Answer: <u>on</u> your bike, <u>to</u> the theater

13. I learned about the development of the modern theater. **(2)**
14. Several texts on the theater were in our library. **(2)**
15. First I looked for a recent book with information about theater history. **(3)**
16. Along the shelf were books by many authors. **(2)**
17. During my search, I examined the contents of many books. **(2)**
18. Finally I reached above my head for two more books. **(2)**
19. I tugged at one between two larger books. **(2)**
20. It tumbled off the shelf and crashed onto my head. **(2)**
21. With my hand on my head, I moaned and staggered across the room. **(3)**
22. The title of the book was *Freak Accidents*. **(1)**

C. Copy the sentences and underline the prepositional phrases. Write *P* above each preposition and *O* above the object of the preposition.

Example: The title of my play is *The Bicycle*.

                                P   **O**
Answer: The title <u>of my play</u> is *The Bicycle*.

23. The bicycle was invented near the end of a century.
24. In 1791, a Frenchman made a machine like a bicycle.
25. It consisted of two wheels with a board on top.
26. On the board was a seat for the comfort of the rider.
27. The rider moved with this bike like a child with a hobbyhorse.
28. After some time, a steering wheel was attached to the front wheels.
29. No one used pedals on bicycles until 1839.
30. In the first scene of the play, an actor explains this background.

▶ **Apply/Writing** Write two descriptions of a performance of some kind. In the first description, use no prepositional phrases. In the second, use one in each sentence. Then compare your descriptions. Ask classmates which sounds better and why.

7 Preposition or Adverb

Prepositions are often confused with adverbs and with phrases that consist of *to* plus a verb.

▶ **Focus**   Many words can perform more than one function in a sentence. For example, some words can function as either prepositions or adverbs. Look at the words in dark type in the examples below.

> The girl was nervous **before** the game.
> She had never played on this team **before.**
> Everyone kicked the ball **around** for a warm-up activity.
> The ball was quickly moved **around** the circle of players.

In the first sentence, *before* is a preposition. You can tell because it has an object, *game*. In the second sentence, *before* is used as an adverb. It has no object. How is *around* used in the third sentence? in the fourth sentence? How can you tell?

Sometimes a phrase consists of *to* plus a verb. In such instances, *to* is not a preposition but a part of a verb form. Remember that a preposition always has a noun or pronoun as an object.

> My friend wanted **to leave.** (verb)
> We walked together **to the door.** (prepositional phrase)

Why is *to leave* a verb form? Why is *to the door* a prepositional phrase? What word is the object in the prepositional phrase?

▶ **Guided Practice**   Identify each underlined word as a preposition, an adverb, or part of a verb form. Tell how you know what the word is.

1. Una walked <u>to</u> the pier yesterday afternoon.
2. The wind was whipping the waves <u>up</u>.
3. She would have liked <u>to</u> sail across the lake.
4. The wind was coming <u>on</u> too strong though.
5. Una decided <u>on</u> a walk instead.
6. She was soon walking <u>up</u> the beach.
7. It was a good day <u>to</u> walk.

▶ **Practice** **A.** Copy each underlined word. Write whether it is an adverb or a preposition.

Example: I sat <u>down</u> at the end of the pier.   *Answer:* down, Adverb

1. I looked <u>up</u> when I heard the shout from the water.
2. I noticed a sailboat that had been sailing <u>around</u>.
3. <u>Inside</u> the cockpit sat a woman with the tiller <u>in</u> her hand.
4. She shouted <u>across</u> the water, telling me to come <u>along</u>.
5. She told me to jump <u>into</u> the boat as she came <u>by</u>.
6. I nervously looked <u>down</u> at the black water <u>below</u> me.
7. <u>From</u> experience, I knew the water was cold <u>under</u> the surface.
8. I waited until the boat came <u>near</u> before I jumped <u>in</u>.
9. She guided the boat <u>by</u> the pier and slowed it <u>near</u> me.
10. I leaped <u>over</u> the water to the deck as the boat went <u>past</u>.

B. Write the headings <u>Verbs</u> and <u>Prepositional Phrases</u>. Then list under them all the verbs that begin with *to* and all the prepositional phrases. You should find twelve verbs that begin with *to* and fifteen prepositional phrases.

Example: I tried to hit the deck without injury to myself.
Answer:

Verbs	Prepositional Phrases
to hit	without injury, to myself

11. After my leap into the boat, I had to catch my breath.
12. I was surprised to find that we were no longer near the pier.
13. The boat, under full sail, tilted to the side.
14. "Do you want to steer awhile?" the woman said to me.
15. It was all I could do to keep on my feet, going to the helm.
16. "You need to keep the sails filled with wind," she said.
17. I sat by the tiller, and the wind seemed to decrease.
18. The boat seemed to want to go across the water to the north.
19. To my surprise, the tiller seemed to know I was inexperienced.
20. All I needed to do to turn the boat was to nudge the tiller, first to one side, then to the other.

▶ **Apply/Writing**   Write five sentences that include these words. Use each word as directed.

1. *under* as an adverb
2. *before* as a preposition
3. *around* as a preposition
4. *to* as part of a verb
5. *to* as part of a prepositional phrase

8 Adjective and Adverb Prepositional Phrases

A prepositional phrase can act as an adjective or as an adverb.

▶ **Focus**   Prepositional phrases modify other words in sentences. For example, a prepositional phrase can act as an adjective in a sentence by describing a noun or pronoun. Study these examples.

> Many **red-haired** children have freckles.
> Many children **with red hair** have freckles.

In the first sentence, the adjective *red-haired* describes *children.* In the second sentence, the prepositional phrase *with red hair* describes *children.* A prepositional phrase that modifies a noun or a pronoun is called an **adjective prepositional phrase.** Like an adjective, it can tell which one, what kind, or how many. Unlike an adjective, an adjective prepositional phrase always comes *after* the word that it modifies.

Adjective prepositional phrases may also come one right after the other. In such cases, the second phrase generally modifies the object of the first phrase. Study the example.

> The woman **with the flower on her hat** is my grandmother.

The adjective phrase *with the flower* modifies the noun *woman.* The phrase *on her hat* modifies *flower.* It tells which flower.

Another kind of prepositional phrase can describe a verb. This kind of phrase acts just as an adverb does. It describes the verb by telling when, how, or where. Study these examples.

> The cat awoke **at midnight.**
> She stretched **with grace.**
> Then she padded **toward her food.**

In the first example, the prepositional phrase *at midnight* describes the verb *awoke.* It tells when. A prepositional phrase that describes a verb is called an **adverb prepositional phrase.** What verbs do the adverb phrases in the other two examples modify? Do the phrases tell when, how, or where?

An adverb prepositional phrase does not always come right after the verb it describes. Notice the adverb phrases in dark type in this sentence.

In the morning the cat followed me **around the house.**

The prepositional phrase *In the morning* modifies the verb *followed*. The phrase tells when. The prepositional phrase *around the house* also describes the verb *followed*. It tells where.

▶ **Guided Practice**   Tell what word each underlined prepositional phrase modifies. Then tell whether the phrase functions as an adjective or an adverb.

1. The girl with the poster announced details of the rummage sale.
2. It will be held on the second Sunday in May.
3. Clothing from the neighborhood has been collected by volunteers.
4. The used-book table will be run by a friend of my mother.
5. Put your used books in that box behind the red chair.

▶ **Practice**   **A.** Copy each sentence. Put two lines under the word that each underlined prepositional phrase modifies. Use *N* or *V* to tell whether the word is a noun or verb.

          N   **V**
Example: The skier on the lift rode to the top.

1. The skiers on the lift went up the mountain.
2. On each side of every chair sat a skier.
3. Some skiers at the top headed for the ski jump.
4. The jumpers glided down a slide.
5. The best skiers in the group landed on their feet.
6. One skier landed on his head.
7. A few unlucky jumpers fell into the snow.
8. Some skiers flipped through the air.
9. Another skier barely missed some trees in her path.
10. The safety patrol skied near dangerous parts of the mountain.
11. They would help people in trouble.
12. Some beginners on the mountain skied to the bottom.
13. The skillful skiers sped around all obstacles.
14. Every skier on the slopes had a wonderful day.
15. They all enjoyed the warmth of the fire.

B. Copy the sentences. Then put one line under the prepositional phrase in each sentence and two lines under the word the phrase describes. Tell what kind of prepositional phrase you underlined.

Example: Many <u>areas</u> <u>of the world</u> require more energy.
        Adjective phrase

16. Windmills offer hope for a larger energy supply.
17. A windmill of great size could serve several homes.
18. In many places, steady winds blow.
19. The high cost of wind machinery is a problem.
20. Remote areas with steady winds produce electricity now.
21. Another source of power is the sun.
22. The rays of the sun can heat water.
23. Water heats at a low cost if this method is used.
24. Heat collectors operate in sunny climates.
25. The sun's heat collects in panels.

C. Complete each sentence with the kind of prepositional phrase indicated in parentheses. You may want to begin your phrases with some of these prepositions: *in, on, by, near, around, above, about,* or *from.*

Example: The scouts camped _____. (adverb phrase)
Answer: The scouts camped by the river.

26. Their fire was built _____. (adverb phrase)
27. The scouts fished _____. (adverb phrase)
28. They bathed and swam _____. (adverb phrase)
29. The beach _____ was wide. (adjective phrase)
30. Even when it rained the scouts hiked _____ near the camp. (adverb phrase)
31. The birds _____ chirped for their young. (adjective phrase)
32. Animals _____ were hidden from view. (adjective phrase)
33. At night the scouts studied the stars _____. (adjective phrase)
34. During the day they learned _____. (adverb phrase)
35. Next year the troop will travel _____. (adverb phrase)

▶ **Apply/Social Studies**   Imagine a world with no electrical energy. Write several sentences describing how different life today would be without electricity. Include some prepositional phrases.

9 Identifying Conjunctions

A conjunction joins words or groups of words. The terms *coordinating conjunction* **and** *correlative conjunction* **describe how certain conjunctions are used in sentences.**

▶ **Focus**   A **conjunction** is a word that links one part of a sentence to another. It can join words, phrases, or entire sentences.

A **coordinating conjunction** is used to join words or groups of words of equal value in a sentence. The most common coordinating conjunctions are *and, but,* and *or.*

The coordinating conjunction *and* shows the addition of one thing to another. The conjunction *but* shows contrast between one thing and another. The conjunction *or* shows choice between things. Study these examples.

> I am wearing red socks **and** a red shirt today.
> My brother is in the crowd, **but** I can't see him.
> We didn't know whether the actor was laughing **or** crying.

What items does *and* join in the first sentence? What does *but* contrast in the next sentence? What choices does *or* present in the third sentence?

Other coordinating conjunctions include *so, yet, for,* and *nor.*

> I have read that book, **so** I know the plot.
> She liked the painting, **yet** she didn't buy it.
> We should win the game, **for** we have more talented players.
> He didn't thank Lisa **nor** anyone else.

Conjunctions that are used in pairs are called **correlative conjunctions.** Some correlative conjunctions are *both . . . and, either . . . or,* and *neither . . . nor.* A pair of correlative conjunctions is always separated by a word or group of words.

> **Both** the inventor **and** her assistant were surprised.
> They went to see **either** a play **or** a musical in the city.
> **Neither** the drummer **nor** the guitarist knew "Stardust."

What words are joined by the correlative conjunctions *both . . . and? either . . . or? neither . . . nor?*

► **Guided Practice**   Tell what coordinating or correlative conjunctions you would use to complete the sentences.

1. On our trip we will travel first to Memphis ____ then on to New Orleans.
2. Sam wants to drive, ____ I don't think it's a good idea.
3. I'm sure we can get there just as easily ____ by train ____ by plane.
4. ____ Mom ____ Dad want to go to Preservation Hall.
5. Sam and I can go with them, ____ we can do something else that evening.

► **Practice**   A. Complete these sentences with coordinating or correlative conjunctions that fit the meaning of each sentence.

Example: The governor ____ the mayor spoke on television.
Answer: The governor and the mayor spoke on television.

1. I like television, ____ I don't like everything on it.
2. I watched an entire day ____ night of television once.
3. On a quiz show, the contestants kept clapping ____ jumping.
4. On a soap opera, everyone was in trouble ____ dying.
5. ____ the quiz show ____ the soap opera devoted almost as much time to commercials as they did to the programs.

B. Make a list of the fifteen coordinating conjunctions in the sentences below.

Example: The girl and boy knew the song but didn't sing it.
Answer: and, but

6. I have three brothers, four sisters, and two parents.
7. We get along well, but we do disagree about money.
8. Two of my brothers and three of my sisters have jobs.
9. I don't care much about money, nor am I careless with it.
10. I occasionally borrow money from a brother or sister.
11. I try to pay them promptly, for I know they need money.
12. A barter system would end all our disagreeing, yet I cannot convince the family of this.
13. Trading our possessions back and forth should stop or decrease our problems, for no money would be involved.

14. No one except me finds my idea interesting or acceptable.
15. My brothers and sisters laughed when I explained it, so I talked to them one at a time.
16. I convinced one parent, one brother, and two sisters, but no one else in the family will budge.

C. Make a list of the ten pairs of correlative conjunctions in the sentences below.
Example: Neither Jennifer nor Lenore had anything to trade.
Answer: Neither . . . nor

17. Both my parents and the rest of my family have given in to me.
18. The bartering will be either a success or a disaster.
19. Neither my brother Fozzie nor my sisters like bartering much.
20. Fozzie wanted both my favorite pen and my pet duck for his oldest, most worn-out hiking boots.
21. I told him the trade would be fair neither to me nor to my duck, who dislikes Fozzie intensely.
22. "Either leave out the duck or it's no deal," I said.
23. Both he and I made new offers for other trades.
24. I wanted either his backpack or his new T-shirt for my pen.
25. Neither Fozzie nor I could come to any agreement.
26. Both my family and I have decided to forget bartering.

▶ **Apply/Writing**   Add to the thoughts begun below. Use a conjunction to join your ending to each statement. Vary your conjunctions. If you can, make a few of your endings humorous, like the example in parentheses.

They say that the best things in life are free . . .
(and I would pay to learn what a few of those things are!)
What you don't know won't hurt you . . .
Everything comes to him or her who waits . . .
A penny saved is a penny earned . . .
An apple a day keeps the doctor away . . .
Every cloud has a silver lining . . .
They who laugh last, laugh best . . .
Let a smile be your umbrella . . .
Birds of a feather flock together . . .
A friend in need is a friend indeed . . .

10 Identifying Interjections

An interjection is a word or phrase used to express strong emotion.

▶ **Focus**   An interjection is an exclamation of feeling. It usually stands alone or at the beginning of a sentence. It may consist of one word, a few words, or the spelling of a certain sound. Here are some of the feelings expressed by interjections.

> **Joy:** **Yahoo!** I made the basketball team!
> **Surprise:** **Wow,** that is an amazing Halloween costume!
> **Pain:** **Ow!** That's my sore toe you just squashed!
> **Fear:** **Oh no,** a train is coming down the tracks!

Use a comma after an interjection that expresses mild emotion. Use an exclamation mark after one that expresses stronger feelings. Remember not to overuse interjections in your writing or they will lose their effectiveness.

▶ **Guided Practice**   Tell what word or words in each sentence is an interjection and what feeling it expresses.

1. Hooray! We've won.
2. Ugh! Take it away.
3. Oh, what a disappointing day it's been.

▶ **Practice**   Make up sentences, using these interjections to express the feelings described in parentheses. Use either commas or exclamation marks with your interjections.

1. goodness (surprise)
2. okay (approval)
3. ouch (pain)
4. aha (triumph)
5. well (mild surprise)
6. yippee (joy)
7. ah (pain)
8. my (surprise)
9. hey (pleasure)
10. phew (exhaustion)

▶ **Apply/Writing**   Write a short paragraph describing a painful, surprising, or scary situation. End with an interjection and a sentence that tells how the situation would make you feel.

Review/Evaluation

For more review, see Tested Skills Practice, pages 516–517.

24 **Kinds of Prepositional Phrases** Write the letter of the answer that identifies each prepositional phrase in the sentences below. Some sentences have more than one phrase.
   a. Adjective prepositional phrase
   b. Adverb prepositional phrase

   1. On Wednesday night we had a severe electrical storm.
   2. A powerful lightning bolt struck, and a transformer at the power plant on Main Street was ruined.
   3. All the lights in Grandmother's apartment flickered briefly and then simply went out.
   4. Grandmother quickly located several candles and a pair of candlesticks.
   5. In a kitchen drawer Kevin found some books of matches.
   6. Soon Grandmother's living room was dimly lit by shimmering candlelight.
   7. None of our neighbors in the apartment building had electricity either.
   8. All the apartment windows soon glowed with warm, flickering candlelight.
   9. Below, both sides of our once-bright street were left in complete darkness.
   10. The power failure had even stopped the huge clock in the old church steeple.
   11. Every building in our neighborhood was dark and silent.
   12. The electricity was not fixed until morning.

25 **Identifying Conjunctions** **A.** Write the letter of the answer that identifies each underlined word.
   a. Coordinating conjunction
   b. One in a pair of correlative conjunctions
   c. Another kind of word

   13. I went shopping, <u>but</u> I really wasn't in the mood for it.
   14. I had only enough money for either a shirt <u>or</u> a pair of jeans.
   15. Neither Mom <u>nor</u> I had any extra money.

16. I really liked <u>both</u> a red shirt and a blue one.
17. I tried on each shirt, <u>yet</u> I didn't buy either.
18. The shirts cost too much, <u>so</u> we went on looking.
19. Either Kane's <u>or</u> Lapp's might have something in our price range, we thought.
20. Kane's had a sale, <u>but</u> nothing interested me there.
21. I went to Lapp's, for they <u>also</u> had a sale.
22. Both Mom <u>and</u> I were disappointed.
23. The merchandise we saw on their bargain table was <u>both</u> poorly made and overpriced.
24. We continued our search, <u>but</u> we were bored.
25. Shopping can be extremely tiring <u>too</u>.
26. We went to Whim's <u>finally</u>, out of desperation.
27. I bought both a shirt <u>and</u> jeans at half price.
28. <u>Neither</u> Mom nor I could believe my luck.

B. Write the letter of the answer that identifies the kind of word that is missing from each sentence.
a. Coordinating conjunction
b. One in a pair of correlative conjunctions
c. Another kind of word

29. Mom _____ Dad gave me their tickets to a concert.
30. They gave me two tickets, _____ I can take a friend.
31. _____ Mike and Ed are very good friends of mine.
32. The three of _____ usually go everywhere together.
33. _____ Mike or Ed could go with me to the concert.
34. Truly, I'd like to take both of them, _____ I can't.
35. I need another ticket, _____ all of them are sold.
36. _____ my mother nor my father can help me with my problem.
37. I could take just one friend, _____ that would be unfair.
38. I have to act soon, _____ the concert is tomorrow night.
39. I could sell one ticket, _____ I don't really want to.
40. _____ Mom and Dad suggest that I look for another solution.
41. Should I choose Mike _____ Ed?
42. _____ Mike nor Ed would be hurt if I went with someone else.
43. The three of us can _____ something else.
44. Maybe I'll take my sister _____ my cousin instead.
45. _____ my sister and my cousin are eager to go.

Writing Evaluation

23   In this picture children are having fun extending themselves from here to there. Write a poem of at least five lines based on this scene.

1. Begin by following prewriting suggestions discussed in this section. List your feelings about the picture. Then develop ideas by making a comparison/contrast chart.
2. Write your poem. You might write a free-verse poem or one that rhymes, a serious poem or a humorous one, such as a limerick. Use the following questions as a guide.
   ✔ Does the poem include at least one vivid image?
   ✔ Does the poem include at least one simile or metaphor?
   ✔ Does the poem include at least one example of alliteration or one example of onomatopoeia?
3. When you have finished writing, spend a few minutes checking and revising your poem.
   ✔ Can you answer "yes" to all of the questions above?
   ✔ Have you placed and punctuated prepositions, conjunctions, and interjections correctly?

Curriculum Connection:
Reading/Literature

Poetry is best when it is read aloud. Poets choose words carefully for their sounds and arrange them into lines with a definite beat or cadence. Consequently, the full effect of a poem can be communicated only by an oral reading. Reading poetry aloud is an art that can be mastered through practice.

In preparing an oral reading of a poem, pay attention to the punctuation. There is always a temptation to hesitate or stop completely at the end of a line. This creates a halting and unsatisfactory reading. Read the poem "Fog" by Carl Sandburg on page 172. Note that the only punctuation, a period, occurs after the second and last lines. The poem should be read without hesitation except after the second line. Remember that you should pause briefly after commas and completely after colons, semicolons, and periods.

▶ **Think**   Examine the poetry that you have read so far in this book or in your reading or literature text. Choose a poem that you enjoyed because of its pleasing sounds and colorful language. Your teacher or librarian may be able to suggest a collection of poems chosen for their suitability to be read aloud. Practice reading your chosen poem aloud, paying particular attention to punctuation and the sounds of words.

▶ **Discuss**   Meet with several classmates to discuss poems that other members of your group think are particularly suitable for oral reading. Each person should read a favorite poem aloud while the others listen and later make suggestions. Has the reader paused at appropriate places and captured the mood of the poem? Has the reader spoken the words slowly enough to be understood and appreciated?

▶ **Find Out**   From the poems your group has chosen select one that is most suitable for reading aloud to the rest of the class. Choose one member of your group to give an oral reading of this poem to the class.

▶ **React: Give a Poetry Reading**   Now it's time for the reader to present the poem to the rest of the class.

Tested Skills Maintenance

20   **Functions of Adverbs**   List the adverbs in each sentence. Tell how each adverb functions, as an adverb of time, place, or manner or as an intensifier.

1. Today Ronna came into my room and sat down dejectedly.
2. "I'm quite sure," she said, "I did poorly on the test."
3. "Yesterday you thought you'd pass easily."
4. "I was too confident," she replied sadly.
5. She stood up and walked slowly downstairs.
6. Then I quickly resumed studying for my test tomorrow.

21   **Comparative Forms**   Write the correct form of the adjective or adverb in parentheses.

7. I like Iona, Salem, and Cass, but I like Iona (better, best).
8. Don't you think Cass has (better, more better) schools?
9. Which town is (nearer, nearest) Iona—Salem or Cass?
10. The parks in Salem once were the (worse, worst) in the state.
11. Could they be (worse, worst) than our town's parks?
12. In which of the three can you live (more, most) economically?

22   **Using *good, well, bad,* and *badly***   Write each sentence, using the correct modifier in parentheses.

13. The jazz band played (good, well) last night, didn't they?
14. My sister wants a tryout with them (bad, badly).
15. She doesn't play too (bad, badly) either.
16. Sitting so far away, I couldn't see too (good, well).
17. If you could hear (good, well), that's all that counts.

16   **Comparison and Contrast**   Write whether each sentence expresses a *Comparison* or a *Contrast*.

18. The male cardinal is red, but the female is brown.
19. Tom is just like his father, tall and thin.
20. Both kangaroos and wombats carry their young in pouches.
21. Jane is easy-going; however, her twin is not.
22. Whales are mammals; sharks are not.

17 **Paragraphs: Topic Sentences**   Find and copy the topic sentence in each group.

23. **a.** Farm fields were dried up and barren.
    b. The drought had taken its toll.
    c. Rows of brittle brown stalks were all that was left of vegetable gardens.
24. **a.** Before seven, hammers began pounding.
    b. The whine of an electric saw cut into sleepers' dreams at the first rays of sunlight.
    c. The town woke early that day.
25. **a.** The old house was a forlorn sight.
    b. A broken window gaped on the upper floor.
    c. Its once-white paint was bubbled and flaking.
26. **a.** A pot-bellied stove stood in one corner.
    b. Six rows of worn, uncomfortable-looking backless benches filled the center of the room.
    c. The old schoolroom was certainly different from our classroom.

18 **Writing a Descriptive Paragraph**   Write which sense is appealed to by each of the following details about a restaurant.

27. slapping of swinging door to kitchen
28. spicy aroma of cooking chili
29. red-and-white checked tablecloths
30. lukewarm air pushed around by ceiling fans
31. salty, but stale, breadsticks
32. waitress's shrill voice calling out orders
33. dingy walls and windows

19 **Writing a Comparison/Contrast Description**   Below are five details describing a restaurant. Write five details you might use in describing a restaurant that contrasts with this one.

34. glaring neon light fixtures
35. tables crowded together
36. cluttered decor
37. noisy
38. smell of frying fish

Descriptive Writing

Theme: Encounters

How many **encounters** have you had today? What were they? How did you feel? Some encounters may make you feel angry or confused while others may make you feel wonderful and result in a new learning experience. In this section you will read about a boy who has several different kinds of encounters. Then you'll have a chance to write a character study about a memorable person that you've encountered in your own life.

1 Literature: Character Study

Flavio had spent his whole life in a favela, a slum in Brazil, until Gordon Parks brought him to America. Because Flavio had asthma, Gordon took him to the Children's Asthma Research Institute and Hospital. Flavio moved into Willens, a dormitory at the Institute. The twelve-year-old boy had many encounters as he adjusted to his new home.

In the following character study, you will meet Flavio and learn about the kind of person he is. Read the excerpt to find out how Flavio behaved in class and what happened that caused him to change.

*from **Flavio** by Gordon Parks*

In September Flavio was enrolled at Cheltenham, a Denver public elementary school. Cheltenham was a huge, ancient, two-storied redbrick building located four blocks from the Institute. It was a good school and within easy walking distance of the Willens building. Flavio's first morning there was unnerving. Having misunderstood his directions, he wandered about, jostled by swarms of jabbering strangers, with a paper on which the correct room number was written clutched in his hand. Then suddenly a shrill bell sounded, and in the next few seconds the cavernous hallway was empty. He was alone and lost. A janitor found him roaming about and took him into Eleanor Massey's first-grade classroom ten minutes after class had begun. Eleanor welcomed him and introduced him to his classmates and showed him to his desk. Ignoring everyone around him, Flavio took a pencil and started drawing unrecognizable figures on a pad. Eleanor Massey watched him for a moment, considered stopping him, thought better of it, and went on teaching.

It was a big room with a twenty-foot-high ceiling. Vertical oak paneling covered the lower walls beneath the blackboards and north windows down to the polished hardwood floors. Thirty-one wooden desks with sunken inkwells accommodated the students who made up the class. In the back of the room as well as in the outer corridors, long lines of ornate brass hooks were screwed into the walls, and on these the students hung their wraps.

"I like that place. I like it but it's crazy," Flavio confided to Gwen Rackett, a house parent at Willens, when he returned to the Institute for lunch.

"What do you like about it?" Gwen had asked.

"Oh, I don't know. It's just crazy-like."

"Is it the other chidren or the teacher?"

"The teacher is okay. She's good. Those kids are too little though. Why do I have to be around kids so little?"

Gwen knew the answer but she didn't give it to him. Although he was not much bigger in size than the six-year-olds who were his classmates, he obviously felt he had little in common with them. By the end of the first week the sudden shift of authority, plus the formality of the classroom, was beginning to frustrate him, and within a fortnight Flavio had totally withdrawn from his classmates. He wouldn't speak or play with them and stayed by himself making drawings. His pencils, crayons, and paper became his treasures. He often refused to leave his desk at lunchtime. During recess he would cram the pencils and crayons into his pockets and stuff the tablet in his shirt. Off alone in one corner of the playground, he watched his classmates at play and met all their overtures toward friendship with silence. Nevertheless, the children persisted—Flavio was something of a novelty to them; they were fascinated with his drawings because his people always resembled animals. He seemed afraid to use more than one color at a time. He became increasingly compulsive and hated being interrupted, even by Eleanor Massey. If she was reading to the class and the bell rang, he would insist upon her finishing. If he had been drawing, he would become upset if he couldn't finish before going on to the next class.

Flavio took extreme pride in his work; patiently, Eleanor used this pride to combat his loneliness and inner tensions. She encouraged and praised his efforts, pushing, coaxing, and guiding him over the rough spots. In less than two months, he had mastered the letters of the vocabulary and could read and understand an astounding number of sentences.

Flavio's rebuffs eventually had an effect on the other children, and they stopped trying to talk with him or inviting him to participate in their play. Eleanor Massey sensed his loneliness but felt helpless to do anything about it. Experience told her that when Flavio tired of being a loner, it would be up to him to do something about it, and there were signs that he was tiring. One day as sides were being chosen for a ballgame he stepped up and demanded to play. It wasn't a very gracious way to ask for acceptance, but he was allowed to play and partially redeemed himself by hitting two home runs. He further improved his status one day by picking up an injured child and carrying him to the main office for treatment.

A little girl named Sonia, newly arrived from Brazil, turned out to be the agent of his major breakthrough. She had been in the classroom for just a few minutes when Flavio realized she couldn't speak English. Jumping up, he rushed over to Sonia to translate and explain Eleanor Massey's instructions. From then on he helped in many ways, explaining to Sonia what the next day's lesson would be, and acting as a general interpreter for her and Eleanor Massey. Almost immediately he became more popular and better liked by the other children. He then began sharing his pencils, crayons, and ideas about his drawings.

Emerging now from his shell, Flavio was revealing another talent. He was a comic, an outright ham. He got to the point where he could imitate almost anything or anybody in the class. He could keep the class in stitches for ten or fifteen minutes at a time. It became a game with the children to figure out who could get him to tell the funniest story.

Flavio's academic work improved along with his attitudes. He wanted his writing to be perfect, and he hated making errors; they made him unhappy and he would bang his fist on the desk as soon as he spotted one. He also loved to tease. One day he was pounding his paper with the point of his crayon, trying to make rain. Eleanor put her finger to her mouth. "Shush," she said. A short time later she was drawing a chart with a squeaky felt pen. Flavio, with a big grin on his face, put his finger to his mouth. "Shush," he repeated to Eleanor. His humor was his saving grace, and it helped his classmates to eventually accept him and love him. Now when he did something wrong or something he felt was stupid, he would laugh out loud at himself. Whereas he used to hate criticism in the beginning, he now accepted it remarkably well. Flavio was growing more handsome by the day, and all the little girls in the rhythm class liked to dance with him. He gave the class its biggest treat one afternoon by dancing the samba the way they danced it in the *favela*.

From his very first day in class, Eleanor Massey felt that Flavio had average intelligence, but this was only a guess. He was so intellectually deprived when he arrived it was difficult for her to determine. Now, though, he had done better than she had dared to hope. At the first quarter's end she graded his art, considerably improved, and his other nine subjects, ranging from arithmetic to science, satisfactory. At the bottom of the report she commented, "Flavio is a gem."

Gradually, the protectiveness Flavio had shown for his family developed in his attitudes toward the children at Willens. At nearly thirteen he was by far the oldest child in the dormitory; the others were between seven and ten. One night when everyone was asleep, Mitsu, a Japanese boy who had mentioned his dislike for Flavio, and whom Flavio had chased with a window stick, began wheezing loudly. When he grew steadily worse Flavio got up, dressed Mitsu, and carried him to the hospital. Then one day he walked up to Gwen and volunteered to be a waiter in the dining room. Suddenly it seemed that he was again carrying out a need to do things for other people. Gradually, Gwen and her husband Dick discerned an improvement in his English. "I think he understands much more than we imagined," Gwen told Dr. Falliers. "It's amazing. He is suddenly showing a wonderful sense of humor, mimicking and using American slang like the other boys."

The Racketts had an acquarium with some rather expensive fish in it. Flavio liked the forty-cent catfish best because they were more active. One night he went to their quarters with some sort of loudspeaker arrangement and began counting the fish.

"You're frightening them, Flavio," Gwen said. He looked up and smiled, and then began whispering, "One, two, three," and so on until he accounted for every fish. The Racketts then realized he was showing them how well he could count in English. Gwen was beginning to like him more each day. She noticed that he was looking much healthier, that his color was good, and that he was gaining weight; she was happy that at last she was getting through to him.

"We'll soon have a number one American boy at Willens," she told Dick later that night.

▶ **Discussing**

1. How did Flavio first act when he was in Eleanor Massey's class? What caused Flavio to change his behavior?
2. How did Flavio act after meeting Sonia?
3. How did Flavio help Mitsu?
4. If you were "the new kid" in class, what would help you feel at home in your new surroundings?
5. What are some ways in which you might become acquainted with people you don't know?

▶ **Analyzing: Classifying**

Flavio was helpful, conscientious, and funny. Listed below is information from the excerpt. **Classify** each item—that is, put it into the proper group—according to the particular trait it illustrates: Helpful, Conscientious, Funny.

1. took extreme pride in his work
2. would imitate classmates and things
3. carried a child injured playing baseball to the main office
4. volunteered to be a waiter in the dining room
5. loved to tease
6. wanted his writing to be perfect
7. translated Eleanor Massey's instructions for Sonia
8. told funny stories
9. took Mitsu to the hospital
10. hated making errors

▶ **Writing**

Write three questions you would like to ask Flavio. You might begin your questions with the words *why* or *how*. Save them to use in a later lesson.

▶ **Extending**

Speaking and Listening   Plan a skit with a small group of classmates. Divide the skit into three acts. In the first act, you encounter a new student in your class. In the second act, you become better acquainted. In the third act, you become friends.

Reading   In *The Hobbit,* by J.R.R. Tolkien, you will meet Bilbo Baggins. You will accompany this hobbit as he encounters all sorts of new and incredible situations and characters.

2 Connotation and Denotation

Denotation is the exact, literal meaning of a word. Connotation is what is suggested in addition to the literal meaning.

▶ **Focus**   Many words can suggest, in addition to their factual meanings, certain other meanings. The exact, literal meaning of a word is its **denotation.** The attitude or tone it suggests is its **connotation.** Writers can express their feelings about a subject by choosing words with positive or negative connotations.

Compare these sentences about Flavio.

> Flavio **refused** invitations to play with his classmates.
> Flavio **declined** invitations to play with his classmates.

The words *refuse* and *decline* both mean "say no to." However, *refuse* suggests a negative connotation because it implies an ungracious denial. *Decline* has a positive connotation because it implies a polite, reluctant denial.

As you read and listen, notice how word connotations affect your feelings. In your own writing, choose words that communicate a feeling as well as the literal meaning that you intend.

▶ **Guided Practice**   Discuss with your class whether each sentence in the pairs below has a positive or a negative connotation.

1. A gang of kids demanded that the council accept their plan.
   A group of students asked the council to consider their plan.
2. Mr. Trin is firm in class, but he's friendly at recess.
   Mr. Trin is harsh in class, but he's a pushover at recess.
3. She had the free-style hair and hollow cheeks of a model.
   She had the unkempt hair and gaunt cheeks of a refugee.
4. Dad sets impossible goals that he insists we achieve.
   Dad encourages us to strive toward high goals.
5. Our coach was so concerned that he gave us a pep talk.
   Our coach was so upset that he gave us a critical lecture.

▶ **Practice** **A.** Write each word in the pairs below. Next to the word, indicate whether it has a positive or a negative connotation.

Example: capable—cunning

Answer: capable—Positive   cunning—Negative

1. relaxed—exhausted
2. stubborn—firm
3. confident—arrogant
4. puny—fragile
5. cheap—inexpensive

6. brave—reckless
7. fragrance—odor
8. slender—scrawny
9. foolish—funny
10. pampered—protected

B. Rewrite the paragraph below twice. Give your first paragraph a positive tone by using words from Column A. Then rewrite the paragraph with words from Column B to give it a negative tone.

Column A	**Column B**
colorful	gaudy
self-assured	conceited
crowd	mob
eased	shoved
stepped	swaggered
sweet	loud
stood	slouched
smiled	snickered
interesting	bizarre
gazed	glared

Mimi **(11)** ____ her way through the **(12)** ____ and toward the room. She **(13)** ____ to the doorway and **(14)** ____ in the entrance. In her **(15)** ____ clothes, she appeared quite **(16)** ____. She **(17)** ____ at us with wide-open eyes. Gradually, her facial expression changed. She **(18)** ____ and said in a **(19)** ____ voice, "I've been waiting for you." That was the beginning of our **(20)** ____ encounter with Mimi.

▶ **Apply/Writing** Use any of the words in this lesson, or come up with words of your own, to write four sentences that have a positive or negative tone. Save your work for later use.

3 Interviewing

Interviewing is a way to get firsthand information about a person.

▶ **Focus**   Gordon Parks, the author of the character study you read in Lesson 1, conducted interviews with several people in order to obtain information about Flavio. Parks used the information from the interviews to write the book *Flavio*.

At the end of this lesson, you will conduct an interview. Then in Lesson 4 you will use your interview notes as the basis for writing a character study. Keep this goal in mind as you choose a person to interview. It may be someone whose job or hobby appeals to you. You may choose someone who has had a unique experience or has led an unusual life. Make sure the person you choose is available to be interviewed in person or by phone.

Planning an Interview

- Learn enough beforehand about the person you are interviewing to be able to ask appropriate questions.
- Contact the person and arrange an appointment for the interview.
- Prepare questions. Try to phrase them in a way that invites detailed responses. Avoid questions that lead to *yes-no* answers or to short factual ones.
- Classify questions in subject categories so that the interview will flow smoothly.

▶ Conducting an Interview

- Be on time. Introduce yourself and state the purpose of the interview. Have your questions, notebook, and pen handy.
- If you want to tape-record the interview, ask permission first.
- Listen carefully to responses as you write them down.
- If you want to learn more about a certain point, ask additional questions.
- Make sure you have complete information before you leave. Check your quotations. Be sure you have quoted the person accurately. After the interview, thank the person.

► **Practice**   **A.** The questions below are for an interview with a piano teacher. Which questions invite only short answers? Which invite a person to give details? Rewrite the short-answer questions so that they invite a person to give more detailed information.

1. Do you enjoy teaching music?
2. Did you take courses to prepare you for this work?
3. What made you decide to become a piano teacher?
4. What do you find most rewarding about your work?
5. Was music an influence in your childhood?
6. Are you planning to continue teaching music?
7. What advice would you give to someone interested in teaching piano?
8. Do you have many students?
9. What do you consider the most difficult part of your job?
10. How many hours a day do you practice?

B. Imagine that you are interviewing a famous rock star. Answer the following questions.

11. How would you arrange the interview? What would you say?
12. What would be a good opening question to ask?
13. How could you check to make sure you have quoted the person exactly?
14. What kind of question would you ask to find out how the entertainer felt about his or her work?
15. What additional question could you ask to find out more detailed information about how this person regards his or her work?

C. Select someone to interview. Make up at least ten questions to ask. Follow the guidelines on the preceding page for planning an interview.

► **Apply/Oral Language**   Now conduct the interview. Follow the guidelines on the preceding page for conducting an interview. Look over your notes to make sure they are complete. Save them for use when you write a character study in Lesson 4.

Our Living Language
The Birth of Modern English

> How many goodly creatures are there here!
> How beauteous mankind is! O brave new world,
> That has such people in it!
> —*William Shakespeare*

The lines above are from Shakespeare's play *The Tempest,* which he wrote in the early 1600s. If you saw the play as it was performed during Shakespeare's time, would you understand it? For the most part, you would. By 1600, English was close to the language we speak today.

The birth of Modern English dates from the year 1500, when a strange thing began to happen. By the year 1700 all the vowel sounds in English changed. Originally, the word *see* rhymed with *bay*. After the change, *see* rhymed with *tree*, as it does today. No one can explain the phenomenon known as the Great Vowel Shift.

In Shakespeare's time, Greek and Latin were the languages of learning. English was still a simple language lacking many words for ideas. Even the word *idea* didn't exist in English and was borrowed from Greek! Thousands of Greek and Latin words entered English. For example, the word *encyclopedia* comes from the Greek words *enkyklios paideia* (meaning "well-rounded education"). Many new words were formed using Greek or Latin prefixes, suffixes, or roots—a practice that continues to this day.

Word Play Write the English word borrowed from Greek or Latin.

1. modernus (Latin)
2. specificus (Latin)
3. theatron (Greek)
4. emigratum (Latin)
5. educatum (Latin)
6. pyramidos (Greek)

1500. Birth of Modern English.   1610. Shakespeare writes *The Tempest.*   1700. Great Vowel Shift completed.

1500   1600   1700   1800

4 Writing a Character Study

A character study is a description of a person's special qualities.

In Lesson 1 of this section you read a character study. In this lesson you will write one of your own. This character study will be based on the interview you conducted in Lesson 3 or on another interview.

At this time think about your **purpose** and **audience.** Imagine that your class is planning a booklet of character studies. As you write, try to think of what kind of information your classmates would enjoy learning about people.

1. Prewriting

▶ **Choose a Topic**   Look over your interview notes from Lesson 3, along with your notes from previous lessons in this section. **Circle** a word, phrase, or sentence that could provide a main idea or focus for your character study. Use the interview guidelines on page 215 and the following suggestions if you wish to conduct another interview.

- List people you encounter often, such as family members, coaches, neighbors, bus drivers, or store clerks. Do any of these people have a job, hobby, or some quality you find interesting?
- Does a certain subject, hobby, or occupation interest you? Find someone who is an expert in this area.

Once your interview notes are complete, write down any other details that occur to you. Now decide what your tone will be toward your subject. **Tone** is the author's attitude toward a subject or audience. Tone may be stated or implied. Will the tone of your character study be humorous, admiring, or respectful?

▶ **Develop Ideas**   Now **use the thinking skill of classifying** to organize your interview notes under subject headings that can provide a main idea for each paragraph. Look at the lists on the next page that one student made from interview notes with a piano teacher. Note how each heading could supply the main idea and supporting details for a different paragraph.

> Earliest Influences
> my mother   my father
> my fingers   my name
>
> Musical Stages
> age 3 – father's lap   now – teacher
> age 9 – competition   orchestra soloist

Finally, create a **Word Bank.** Think of connotative and denotative words and phrases that you might use to describe your subject. The Word Bank at the right may help you.

2. Writing

▶ **Study the Draft** Read this first draft of a character study. Notice how each paragraph presents a different aspect of the character. There are errors, as well as crossed-out items.

> A memorable melody
> "When I was born my mother
> looked at my fingers and decided I
> would be a pianoist. They named
> me melody." Mrs. Melody Mason the
> music teacher known to many
> children in Akron ohio uses her long
> tapered fingers to empasize her words.
> Mrs. Mason began playing piano at
> three. She would sit on her fathers
> lap and play pound the keys. By
> nine she was in compititions. At the

present time mrs. mason is a very
well-known musician. In addition
to teaching she plays in an
orchestra as a featured soloist playing
alone.
This creative artist graciously agred
agreed to play for me. Her fingers
moved nimbly over the keys and she
smiled as she played a classical
spanish peice.
"Music." she said. "is a gift I can
share."

▶ **Write a Draft** Now write your own first draft, following your organized notes. Don't worry about making mistakes.

3. Revising

▶ **Read and Confer** Read your first draft to see that you have described the person accurately. Then have a partner read your character study aloud as you listen. Use the following questions to discuss how your work can be improved.

Conference Questions
1. Does each paragraph have a main idea and supporting details?
2. Has a tone been established?
3. Have words with the right connotations for the writer's tone been used?
4. Are quotes accurate? Do they make sense in the context of the study?
5. Could words be added to make the character more vivid?
6. Could anything be deleted?

► **Make Changes**   Use your conference suggestions to make any changes you think will improve your character study. Here is a strategy to help you improve your writing.

STRATEGY: Check your character study for wordiness. Do the words *very* and *really* appear too frequently? Is there unnecessary repetition in phrases such as *killed fatally*? Could one word (*while*) be substituted for a phrase (*during the time that*)?

   Circle unnecessary words or phrases in your draft, and replace them with less wordy expressions. In your writer's notebook, record the wordy expressions, along with your improvements. Notice how wordiness was eliminated in "A Memorable Melody."

nine she was in competition. ~~*At the*~~ ^Now *present time* *mrs. mason is a very well-known musician. In addition to teaching,* *she plays in an*

► **Proofread and Edit**   Check your draft for errors. Use the following questions and proofreader's marks.

> **Proofreading Questions**
> 1. Did I capitalize correctly?
> 2. Have I used commas and quotation marks correctly?
> 3. Did I spell each word correctly?

► **Make a Final Copy**   When you have made all corrections and improvements, write a final draft of your character study.

4. Presenting

   Hold a class "Guest Hour" for students to read their character studies and answer questions about the people described.

Proofreader's Marks

═ Make a capital.

/ Make a small letter.

⊙ Add a period.

⋏ Add a comma.

ⱽⱽ Add quotation marks.

⋀ Add something.

ℓ Take out something.

⟶ Move something.

¶ New paragraph.

⟨ap⟩ Correct spelling.

Revising and Editing Workshop

Connecting Writing and Grammar

- In Unit 16 you read a character study. You also learned about connotations and denotations.
- In Unit 17 you wrote a character study.

Now it's time to use your skill as an editor to improve another writer's first draft. Read this character study carefully. As you read, ask yourself these questions.

✔ Are connotative words used appropriately?
✔ Is each sentence punctuated correctly?
✔ Is capitalization used correctly?

our school janitor

(1) Mr. Sembel the custodian at Grove School is an unsung hero that is not noticed. (2) He never seems to stop working. (3) When he arrives at 600 A.M., he makes sure the heat is on in every room. (4) "Can't let the children catch chill, he mutters to himself. (5) When we come to school, we track mud into the halls. (6) his afternoon jobs include the following washing tables mopping floors and straightening tables and chairs. (7) Once a week he trims and cuts and waters the plants near the school entrance. (8) Sometimes he has to fix leaky faucets stuck lockers or broken doorknobs. (9) He goes home late in the afternoon

(10) Even when he is busy, he always has time to talk and discuss things. (11) When I ask him why he is always working he puts his hand on his messy mustache. (12) Though his eyes are shaded by shaggy eyebrows, I can see them twinkle (13) "I want you students to have a clean, bright place where you can learn," he says in his weird dialect. (14) "what would my mediterranean ancestors think if I did not do my work with pride?"

► Revising the Draft

1. The writer included a detail in the first paragraph that does not support the main idea. Delete that detail and add one that does support the main idea.
2. Two words in the second paragraph have negative connotations. Rewrite the sentences that contain these words, substituting words with positive connotations.
3. Find three sentences that are wordy. Rewrite the sentences, eliminating the unnecessary words.
4. Add, delete, or rearrange any other information you think would improve the draft.

► Editing the Draft

5. The writer made some capitalization errors. Find and correct these errors.
6. Find a quote that is not punctuated correctly. Rewrite the sentence correctly.
7. Find two places where colons are missing. Correct the sentences that contain this type of error.
8. Find four sentences where commas are missing. Correct the sentences that contain this type of error.
9. End punctuation is missing from two sentences. Rewrite the sentences, adding the correct end punctuation.

► Working Together on the Draft

Meet with a group of your classmates. Discuss the changes you made in the draft. Listen to the changes your classmates made. Then rewrite the draft on page 222. Include all the revisions you think are important.

► Evaluating Your Own Writing

Now review your own writing. Look over the character study you wrote in this unit and any other written work you have. Did you have any problems with capitalization? Did you have any problems with punctuation? The lessons that follow will help you with these writing problems.

5 Punctuating the Ends of Sentences

The punctuation mark used at the end of a sentence depends on the kind of sentence.

▶ **Focus**   A sentence may end with a period, a question mark, or an exclamation mark. Study the sentences below.

Declarative: Eve visited the White House late last summer.
Interrogative: Have you ever been there?
Exclamatory: What a beautiful mansion it is!
Imperative: Notice the lovely rooms and rare paintings.
You really must take the tour next year!

Which end punctuation is used to signal an interrogative sentence? Which is used to signal a declarative sentence? Which is used to signal an exclamatory sentence?

Notice the end punctuation for the last two example sentences. An imperative sentence usually ends with a period. If the sentence expresses strong feeling, an exclamation mark is used.

End punctuation helps make the meaning of a sentence clear. How would your voice change if you read the three sentences below aloud? Pay close attention to the end punctuation in each.

The TV isn't working.
The TV isn't working?
The TV isn't working!

Which sentence shows surprise? Which sentence makes a simple statement? Which sentence asks a question?

▶ **Guided Practice**   Tell what kind of sentence each is and how you would punctuate it.

1. Is that a bear over there in the park
2. That's a black bear beyond the evergreens
3. Oh, how friendly he looks
4. Don't go near him or you may be sorry
5. He may not be so friendly up close
6. Please take a picture of him for our album

▶ **Practice** **A.** Copy these sentences from a telephone conversation. Add the appropriate punctuation mark for each kind of sentence.

Example: May I please speak with Melinda (interrogative)
Answer: May I please speak with Melinda?

1. Melinda, this is Beth (declarative)
2. What are you doing this afternoon (interrogative)
3. I'm cleaning my room and vacuuming the rug (declarative)
4. How long will it take you (interrogative)
5. It's really a mess this time (declarative)
6. Well, hurry up (imperative)
7. It may take me all afternoon (exclamatory)
8. I wanted you to go to the movies with me (declarative)
9. I'd like to, but I can't finish in time (declarative)
10. Let me come over and help you (imperative)
11. I couldn't ask you to do that (declarative)
12. I'll come right over on my bike (declarative)
13. Do you mean it (interrogative)
14. Of course I do (exclamatory)
15. I'll see you soon (declarative)

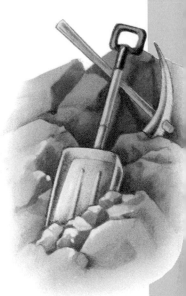

B. Rewrite the sentences below with the correct end punctuation. Then tell whether the sentence is declarative, interrogative, exclamatory, or imperative.

Example: Do you know the answer
Answer: Do you know the answer?   Interrogative

16. How does the homing pigeon find its way home
17. I read an interesting magazine article about pigeons
18. Read this article if you want to learn about them
19. Did you know that pigeons can see special light rays
20. These light rays are invisible to humans
21. Pigeons use their vision to find the sun's position
22. How remarkable that pigeons can do this
23. Imagine the world from a pigeon's-eye view
24. How different it must look

▶ **Apply/Writing**   Imagine that you are a gold miner traveling to California during the 1850s. Write a paragraph telling about a day of your journey. Use the correct end punctuation for each sentence.

6 Commas in Sentences

Use a comma to show a pause or separation between words or word groups in a sentence.

▶ **Focus**   Commas are used to indicate pauses between words and word groups in sentences. Commas are also used to make the meaning clear. Read the sentence below.

> Oh, we're having a party, and Harvey, Lee, and Glen are coming.

Which words and word groups are set off by commas? Without the commas, would you know that Harvey and Lee are two people?

Listed below and on the next page are six rules for using commas. Follow these rules as you work through the practices.

Rule 1. Use commas to separate items in a series.

> Jan, Dot, Steve, and Cory are coming to the party.
> I've called the guests, bought the food, and warned the neighbors.
> I think this will be a loud, enjoyable, and exciting party.

Use two commas when there are three items in a series. Use three commas when there are four items in a series.

Rule 2. Use a comma after introductory words and phrases.

> By the way, can you bring plates?
> Oh, I'm sure we have paper plates in the kitchen.

Rule 3. Use commas to set off nouns in direct address.

> Mike, will you come? I'd love to, Marsha.
> Remember, friends, to bring some olives.

Use one comma if a noun is the first or last word in the sentence. Use two commas if the noun is in the middle of the sentence.

Rule 4. Use commas to set off interrupting words and appositives.

> We've borrowed chairs from Mr. Wilson, our next door neighbor.
> Rosa, of course, will bring her folding table.

If the interrupting words or appositive is at the end of a sentence, use one comma. If it is in the middle, use two.

Rule 5. Use a comma after a dependent clause that begins a sentence. Do not use a comma before a dependent clause that follows the independent clause. You will learn more about these clauses in Unit 27.

> If Mr. Wilson complains, we'll invite him in for a snack.
> When he arrives, we'll ask him about his vacation.
> We'll invite Mr. Wilson in for a snack if he complains.

Rule 6. Use a comma before the conjunction in a compound sentence. Omit the comma, however, in a short compound sentence.

> Herman wanted to play charades, but no one else would play.
> The party ended and we went home.

▶ **Guided Practice**   Tell where commas are needed in each sentence. Give the number of the rule that applies.

1. Will you remember Wanda to call the twins Pat and Michelle?
2. I've bought green gold white and brown crepe paper.
3. Luis Dan will decorate two of the rooms and you can help him.
4. Henry of course will help too Luis.
5. If you finish early you can start choosing the music.

▶ **Practice**   **A.** Rewrite the following conversation. Add commas where necessary and underline each. You will add eighteen commas.

Example: Oh my filling fell out and I need to see the dentist.
Answer: Oh, my filling fell out, and I need to see the dentist.

(1) "Jerry I want to ask you something.   (2) The Encounter a new rock group is performing this afternoon.   (3) Unfortunately I can't use my ticket.   (4) I need to replace a filling and it just can't wait.   (5) If you are interested I'll sell you my ticket."

(6) "I wish I could buy it Samantha.   (7) My problem as usual is that I am broke.   (8) Of course I could borrow the money from Ivan my brother's friend.   (9) He's not here now but he should be back soon.   (10) Since I can't promise to get the money you might want to ask someone else."

(11) "If you don't mind Jerry I will.   (12) Barry Mike and June are all crazy about The Encounter.   (13) They tried to buy tickets but the concert was sold out."

B. Write each sentence, inserting commas where they are needed.

Example: Jody Harris the film critic likes horror movies.

Answer: Jody Harris, the film critic, likes horror movies.

14. If you are horror-film fans ladies and gentlemen we have some news for you.
15. Do you remember Count Dracula the stranger from Transylvania?
16. The count is the father of a terrifying daughter Draculana.
17. These terrible creatures are appearing together in *Daughter of Dracula* a new movie.
18. The count and his daughter cannot leave their lonely castle during daylight hours and no one of course comes near at night.
19. For that reason Dracula and Draculana must search for victims.
20. Dracula has his eye on Mr. Tibbs a resident of a nearby town.
21. Miss Lee meets Draculana on a dark damp and windy evening.
22. Will Draculana and her father Dracula get what they're after?
23. If you feel like screaming this movie is for you!
24. Every scene needless to say is packed with action suspense chills and thrills.
25. You won't know whether to laugh cry gasp or shiver.
26. We won't give the story away but you'll definitely be scared.
27. If you go take a friend.
28. A pillow will help to muffle your screams and a blindfold can be used to cover your eyes.
29. People in Texas Ohio and Maine really enjoyed the movie.
30. Another film *Daughter of Dracula: Part Two* is being made.
31. As usual people will wait in long lines to see it.
32. Larry Lowe by the way will play Draculana's husband.
33. If you liked *Daughter of Dracula* you'll love the new movie.

▶ **Apply/Writing** Think about your favorite monster movie or horror film. Then write a group of sentences telling about it. Try to include an example of each rule listed below.

1. Use a comma to separate words in a series.
2. Use a comma after introductory words.
3. Use a comma with a noun in direct address.
4. Use a comma with interrupting words and appositives.
5. Use a comma before the conjunction in a compound sentence.

7 Other Uses of Commas

Use commas to separate items in addresses and dates.
Also use commas in figures and in friendly letters.

▶ **Focus** In Lesson 6 you learned that commas are used in sentences to indicate natural pauses and to make meaning clear. In this lesson you will learn about some other uses of commas.

Rule 1. Use commas to separate items in a date. If a date is within a sentence, put a comma after the year.

> The art show opened on Sunday, February 2.
> The artist was born on April 15, 1950, in a small Pennsylvania
>   farmhouse.

Rule 2. Use a comma to separate items in an address. The number and street are considered one item. The state and Zip Code are also considered one item. Use a comma after the Zip Code if it is within a sentence.

> Jeremy Taylor   Ms. Julie Cohan
> 512 E. Washtenaw Avenue   1956 Beeker Street
> Joliet, IL 60411   Tulsa, OK 74129

> The letter is addressed to Sara Smith, 5019 Topanga Avenue, Los Angeles, California 98421, but was delivered to me by mistake.

Rule 3. Use a comma to separate numerals greater than three digits.

> There are 86,400 seconds in a day.
> The attendance on Monday was 15,825.
> One painting sold for $4,900.
> The new house cost $94,750.

Rule 4. Use a comma when a person's last name appears before the first name.

> Appleton, Maria   Chen, Lin
> Arden, John   Jones, Lela
> Cardozo, Victor   Torres, Isabel

Rule 5. Use a comma after the greeting in a friendly letter and after the closing in all letters.

Dear Jonah,   Yours truly,
Dear Uncle Stan,   Sincerely,

▶ **Guided Practice**   Which rule explains the punctuation in each sentence?

1. Please send a card to Cindy Perez, 3318 Plainfield Avenue, Chicago, Illinois 60634.
2. My little sister was born on January 8, 1979, in New York.
3. That building was just sold for $2,765,300.

▶ **Practice**   **A.** Copy the friendly letter below. Add commas where they are necessary. You will add fourteen commas.

> 65 River Road
> Potomac MD 20853
> March 20 1988

Dear Martha

I just got back from a family reunion in Woodstock Virginia. We celebrated my grandparents' anniversary on Saturday March 12. They were married on March 12 1930. My aunt and uncle flew in from Bangor Maine for the weekend. My cousin drove in from San Francisco California. Then he drove to see his sister in El Paso Texas. He must have driven over 10000 miles in his car during his trip!

Woodstock is a friendly town but Potomac Maryland has one big advantage. It's my home!

> Your pal
> Carrie

B. Listed below and on the next page is information about the Grand Prize Winners in the Bubble-up Soap Contest. Copy each listing and use commas where necessary.

Example: $1000000 Winner   *Answer:* $1,000,000 Winner
             Barker John   Barker, John
             248 Lerner Street   248 Lerner Street
             Niles MI 49120   Niles, MI 49120

1. $500000 Winner
2. Anderson Rodney
3. 132 Valley Terrace
4. Santa Fe CA 90670
5. Birthday: October 7 1966
6. $250000 Winner
7. Muhs Neil
8. 6 Jasper Way
9. Boston MA 01432
10. Birthday: April 26 1925
11. $100000 Winner
12. Smith Janice
13. 863-B Roper Road
14. Gaithersburg MD 20760
15. Birthday: July 17 1947
16. $50000 Winner
17. Zim Roland
18. 101 Foundry Road
19. Pecos TX 79772
20. Birthday: March 30 1958

▶ **Apply/Writing** Imagine you have been asked to edit the following letter. It will be sent to all the parents of seventh graders at Leroy Junior High School. Copy the letter and add commas where they are needed. Sign your own name at the bottom of the letter. You will use twelve commas.

November 25 1988

Dear Parents
Come and join the fun on Saturday December 3. We're holding a bazaar at Leroy Junior High School 201 Washington Street San Diego. Books clothing and baked goods will be on sale. Help us raise the $4000 we need for new library books. Our target date for purchasing the books is January 2 1989. If you can't come in person please contact Ms. Melissa Raymond. Her address is 136 Mooney Road San Diego California 92117.

Gratefully yours

8 Other Punctuation Marks

Other marks of punctuation can help make the meaning of your writing clearer.

▶ **Focus**   You have learned that a comma can have more than one use. In this lesson you will find out about the different uses that other punctuation marks can have. Study the following explanations and examples.

Colon   The colon is used after the greeting in a business letter, and it has these additional uses.
1. A colon is used after expressions that introduce a list.

> You need the following: a notebook, pencil, pen, and eraser.

2. A colon is used between the hour and minutes when you write time in numbers.

> The meetings are at 6:15, 8:30, and 10:45 A.M.

Hyphen   The hyphen is used to divide a word that breaks at the end of a line. It has two other common uses.
1. Hyphens are used to join compound words that are thought of as one.

> My older brother is a well-known favorite of the vice-president.

2. Hyphens are used in writing numbers from twenty-one to ninety-nine as words.

> The quarterback yelled, "Thirty-four, sixty-eight, hike."

Dash   The dash is used to show a sudden change in thought or to set off words that interrupt the main thought of a sentence.

> We will finish the reading—if we can—by Tuesday.
> The clumsy outfielder—he was my brother's friend—lost the final game of the season.

Parentheses Parentheses have these two uses.

1. Parentheses are used to enclose words that interrupt the thought of the sentence. The words in the parentheses usually explain or add to the sentence.

   The best answer (and the easiest answer) is no answer.

2. Parentheses are used to enclose references to page numbers, chapters, or dates.

   Mozart (1756–1791) composed music as a child (see chapter 4).

Period The period is an end mark. It also is used after titles, initials, and other abbreviations.

   Maj. Jay B. Bennington, M.D., arrived at 9:00 A.M.

Apostrophe An apostrophe is used in possessive words and in contractions. It is also used to form the plurals of letters and numbers if the plurals would be confusing without it.

   Dot your *i*'s and cross your *t*'s.

Semicolon A semicolon is used to separate the two parts of a compound sentence when they are not joined by a comma and a coordinating conjunction.

   Mary played the villain; Jack played the hero.
   Compare: Mary played the villain, and Jack played the hero.

▶ **Guided Practice** Name the punctuation needed in each sentence.

1. Dr Aldo J Ganz, PhD   wrote a biography of Lewis Carroll 1832–1898 .
2. Notice that his name is spelled with two *r*s and two *l*s.
3. Carroll his real name was Dodgson wrote books for children.
4. He was thirty two or thirty three when he wrote his first book.
5. I read the first chapter aloud Jamie read the second.
6. Her favorite chapter it is mine too is Chapter 6.
7. The following are some of the odd characters Alice meets the Queen of Hearts, the Mock Turtle, and the Cheshire cat.

▶ **Practice** **A.** Write each sentence, adding necessary punctuation.
Example: Did you read that article see pages 12–19 about Dr. Di?
Answer: Did you read that article (see pages 12–19) about Dr. Di?

1. The spelling bee starts at 830 AM
2. I signed up that was my first mistake last month.
3. Here are the names of the judges Vito Cardello, Lisa Wong, and Margaret Fenton.
4. Cara Chen always wins I'm glad she's not going to enter this year.
5. Can you I mean anyone study for a spelling bee?
6. I'd pay special attention to the medical words pages 31–42.
7. There are fifty two words on a page.
8. Your know it all attitude sometimes annoys me.
9. Are there two *m*s, *t*s, and *e*s in the word *committee?*
10. My dentist, Dr Mildred N Mann, won a spelling bee.
11. My brother in law will receive his MA in literature this June.
12. Geoffrey Chaucer 1340?–1400 was a well known teller of tales.
13. Please obtain the following a red pen, a heavy folder, and a paper.

B. Write a sentence for each item below.
Example: a colon after an expression introducing a list
Answer: Mr. Jay had the following: a dog, a cat, and a pen.

14. a colon between the hour and minutes in time
15. the number *67* written out
16. two hyphens in a compound word
17. a dash showing a sudden change in thought
18. a period in an abbreviation
19. an apostrophe with the plural of a letter or number
20. parentheses enclosing dates
21. a semicolon in a compound sentence
22. a colon after expressions that introduce a list
23. a period in an initial

▶ **Apply/Writing** Mrs. Lee is the vice-president of a video company. Her father-in-law is a doctor who has just developed a video and book about the importance of exercise. Write about how the doctor might describe his products to Mrs. Lee. Use as many of the punctuation marks discussed in this lesson as you can.

9 Quotation Marks

Quotation marks enclose a speaker's exact words.
Quotation marks are also used to enclose some titles.

▶ **Focus**   When you use someone's exact words in your writing, signal your reader with **quotation marks.** Follow these rules.

Rule 1. Enclose all quoted words within quotation marks.

Rule 2. The first word of a direct quotation begins with a capital letter. When a quotation is broken into two parts, use two sets of quotation marks. Use one capital letter if the quote is one sentence. Use two capital letters if it is two sentences.

> "Let's go home," Kate suggested, "and get some lemonade."
> "Can we leave right away?" Marta asked. "I'm really thirsty."

Rule 3. Use a comma between the words that introduce the speaker and the words that are quoted. Place the end punctuation or the comma that ends the quotation inside the quotation marks. Begin a new paragraph each time the speaker changes.

> Kate said, "There's my mom at the front door."
> "Hello," Kate's mom said. "Would you like some lemonade?"

Rule 4. Do not use quotation marks with an **indirect quotation—** that is, a quotation that does not give the speaker's exact words.

> **Indirect:** Mom told Kate that she had been waiting for her.
> **Direct:** Mom told Kate, "I've been waiting for you."

Rule 5. Quotation marks are also used to enclose the titles of songs, stories, poems, articles in newspapers and magazines, and chapters in books. They are not used to indicate book titles.

> "The Raven"   Chapter 1, "Nouns"   "Over the Rainbow"

▶ **Guided Practice**   Tell where quotation marks are needed.

1. Would you like some cornbread with your lemonade? Kate asked.
2. No thanks, answered Marta. It's too close to dinner time.
3. Kate said that she wouldn't have any either, then.

▶ **Practice   A.** Write these sentences. Add quotation marks to the direct quotations. If a sentence is correct, write *Correct*.
Example: Ky asked, What shall we do today?
Answer: Ky asked, "What shall we do today?"

1. Let's go to the beach, Ky said.
2. Would you like a picnic lunch? Pedro asked. I'm starved!
3. Why don't we invite Harriet? Ky suggested.
4. Pedro said that he didn't think she was feeling well.
5. She was out of school Thursday and Friday, he commented.
6. Ky said, Why don't you call her?
7. OK, I will, said Pedro.
8. When Harriet answered the phone, she said, What a shame!
9. I'd like to come, she explained, but I have a terrible cold.
10. She said she had been sitting around feeling sorry for herself.
11. Your call has cheered me up a little, she remarked.
12. Then she said, Maybe I could go if I took some cold capsules.
13. Pedro wondered if that was a good idea.
14. Are you sure you won't feel worse later? he asked.
15. Well, maybe you're right, Harriet said. I think I'll stay home.

B. Add quotation marks to the direct quotations and titles in the following sentences.
Example: I just read The Tell-Tale Heart, a spooky story.
Answer: I just read "The Tell-Tale Heart," a spooky story.

16. Many students were reading May Swenson's poem The Centaur.
17. Others were writing down the lyrics to America, the Beautiful.
18. Attention, class! Mrs. Gordon said. Listen carefully.
19. I'm going to put a list of stories and articles for recommended reading on the board, she said.
20. The list included the following titles: Thank You, by Alex Haley; A Haircut, by I. S. Nakata; and Drouth, by Ben Logan.
21. Should we write answers to the discussion questions? Lu asked.
22. No, the teacher replied, just read through them.

▶ **Apply/Writing**   Choose one of these ideas. Use quotation marks correctly.

1. List five stories or poems that you might read to someone.
2. Write an imaginary conversation with an eighty-five-year-old.

236   More practice on page 520.   28

10 Capitalizing First Words

Capitalize the first words in sentences, in direct quotations, and in the greetings and closings in letters.

▶ **Focus**   When you write a sentence or a direct quotation, begin the first word with a capital letter. Read the sentences that follow.

> **My** sister is interested in a radio career.
> **My** dad said, **"Y**ou could be a sports announcer."
> **"Maybe** I'd like that," she replied. **"How** do I find out about sports announcing?"
> **"There** are colleges you could write to," said Dad, "or why not try calling a local radio station for information?"

In the first example, the first word of the sentence is capitalized. In the second, the first word of the direct quotation is also capitalized. Notice that both *Maybe* and *How* are capitalized in the third example because each word begins a new sentence in the quote. In the fourth example, only *There* is capitalized. *Or* continues the quotation, but it does not start a new sentence.

When you write the greeting and closing of a letter, always begin the first word with a capital letter.

Dear Bill,	**Your** friend,
Dear Dr. Wade:	**Sincerely,**
Dear Uncle Ted,	**Very** truly yours,

Dear is capitalized in the greeting because it is the first word. *Your, Sincerely,* and *Very* are capitalized because they are the first words of the closings.

▶ **Guided Practice**   Tell what words should be capitalized in each of the following.

1. dear aunt nell,
2. thank you for the birthday present.
3. when she saw it, my mom said, "what a beautiful bracelet!"
4. "aren't you lucky," Dad kidded me, "to have a rich relative?"
5. are you coming for a visit soon?
6. gratefully yours,

▶ **Practice** **A.** Decide whether each of the following is capitalized correctly or incorrectly. Write *Correct* or *Incorrect* for each. If an item is incorrect, rewrite it correctly.

Example: dear fred,

Answer: Incorrect   Dear Fred,

1. Dear bonnie,
2. it is snowing hard here.
3. school is closed today.
4. Please write soon.
5. Sincerely,
6. dear Mona,
7. We're having a mild winter.
8. Could you send some snow?
9. thanks in advance.
10. your cousin,

11. Dear Barbara,
12. here is a surprise.
13. I know you like cats.
14. have a happy birthday!
15. Yours truly,
16. Dear Aunt Sue,
17. thank you for the book.
18. it is very interesting.
19. i love all the photos!
20. Your niece,

B. Rewrite the following, inserting capital letters where necessary. You will capitalize twenty-one words.

Example: the case was solved with the help of a letter.

Answer: The case was solved with the help of a letter.

21. we waited for the inspector. the atmosphere was tense. soon the inspector arrived.
22. he said, "the case is over. we have found the thief."
23. "it's not me," Harry said.
24. "relax, Harry," the inspector said, "because you're innocent."
25. the inspector had a note. everyone listened eagerly.
26. "dear Sir," he read. "max stole the jewels. he buried them in the yard. sincerely yours, Pat the Rat."
27. "impossible!" Kay cried. "my dog is a good dog and is not a thief. the thief wrote that!"
28. "where," the inspector asked, "does Max bury bones?"
29. "i won't tell you anything," Kay said.
30. the inspector arrested Kay. he knew she had lied.

▶ **Apply/Writing** Finish the story in Practice B. Who stole the jewels? How did the inspector know that he had found the thief? Remember to use capital letters where necessary.

11 Capitalizing Proper Nouns and Adjectives

Capitalize all proper nouns and all adjectives formed from proper nouns.

▶ **Focus**   A **proper noun** names a particular person, place, or thing. Proper nouns fall into many categories. They may name geographic areas, historic events, companies, organizations, and other persons, places, and things.

The list that follows shows the kinds of proper nouns to capitalize.

people: Jackie Robinson
initials: L. J. Bell
streets, roads: Linden Road
cities: Chicago, Madison
states: Texas, Vermont
countries: Japan, India
continents: Australia, Asia
counties: Lake County
areas, regions: South Pole, the Far East, Midwest
months, days: June, Monday
holidays: Memorial Day
schools: Sullivan High School
organizations: Board of Trade
documents: Bill of Rights

companies: Barbury Company
buildings: World Trade Center
government bodies: State Department, Congress
institutions: Booth Hospital
monuments: Lincoln Memorial
relatives: Uncle Steve
languages: English, Polish
planets: Saturn, Venus
geographical features: Gulf of Mexico, Mt. McKinley
events: World Series
periods of time: Ice Age
product names: Lemon Fizz
brand names: Washton soap

Proper nouns may consist of one word or several words. All important words in a proper noun are capitalized.

Notice the difference between product names and brand names, the last two items on the list. *Lemon Fizz* is a specific name made up and given to a product, so all the words in it are capitalized. In *Washton soap*, however, only *Washton* is the brand name, so only *Washton* is capitalized.

Here are some nouns that are not capitalized:

- the names of the seasons—*fall, winter, spring, summer*

- the words *north, south, east, west* when they refer to compass directions rather than regions of a country

A **proper adjective** is an adjective formed from a proper noun. Like a proper noun, a proper adjective begins with a capital letter. Some proper adjectives consist of more than one word. Study the following chart.

Proper Noun	Proper Adjective + Noun
Italy	**Italian** pastry
Congress	**Congressional** committee
Puerto Rico	**Puerto Rican** sunset
Midwest	**Midwestern** steak
Canada	**Canadian** mountains
Spain	**Spanish** music

You will notice that proper adjectives may have endings that differ from the noun endings. Use a dictionary to be sure that you correctly spell a proper adjective.

▶ **Guided Practice**   Tell what proper nouns and adjectives should be capitalized in the following sentences.

1. luis and delores mendez served us mexican food on labor day.
2. delores's sister, mrs. ruiz from austin, texas, was there.
3. On columbus day in october, we will serve italian food.
4. aunt rosa and uncle umberto may come from italy for a visit.

▶ **Practice**   **A.** Rewrite the sentences. Capitalize all proper nouns and initials. You will capitalize twenty-four letters.
Example: Settlers followed the oregon trail almost to the pacific.
Answer: Settlers followed the Oregon Trail almost to the Pacific.

1. Before lewis and clark, no one knew much about the west.
2. Many thought there was a great desert west of missouri.
3. oregon was still british, but yankees yearned to settle it.
4. st. joseph and independence were popular start-off cities.
5. hiram sloane joined a wagon train in early spring.
6. The plan was to cross the cascade mountains before winter.
7. The party skirted the missouri river and headed northwest.
8. It followed the valley of the platte river to the rockies.

9. It passed through areas that are now nebraska and colorado.
10. In early october, it finally got through south pass.

B. Rewrite the sentences, capitalizing all proper nouns, initials, and proper adjectives.
Example: jason went to washington, d.c., on a vacation.
Answer: Jason went to Washington, D.C., on a vacation.

11. chris johnson and I went with jason.
12. We stayed at the drake hotel near pennsylvania avenue.
13. We toured the white house on wednesday.
14. A white house guard told us to visit the jefferson memorial.
15. We met roger j. collins from the house of representatives.
16. He represents the people from a west virginia district.
17. Later we sat near ford's theatre and snacked on some granger crackers.
18. The next day chris and I went to the smithsonian institution.
19. I liked the national air and space museum the best.
20. It was april, and the japanese cherry trees near the washington monument were in bloom.

C. Follow the directions for Practice B.

21. We visited both the british and french embassies.
22. In the evening we took a boat ride on the potomac river and went through the georgetown channel.
23. There was a group of swedish tourists on our bus trip to mount vernon, george washington's home.
24. chris got acquainted with them because he knows some swedish.
25. We also went to gettysburg, pennsylvania.
26. That's where abraham lincoln made his famous address during the civil war.
27. In jamestown, virginia, we saw a replica of fort james.
28. jamestown was settled by englishmen led by john smith.
29. Before going home, we visited aunt dora in richmond.
30. aunt dora teaches at jefferson high school there.

▶ **Apply/Writing** Think of a city you would like to visit. Write a paragraph about the people and places you would like to see there. Use both proper nouns and proper adjectives.

12 Capitalizing Titles

Capitalize the first word and every important word in a title.

▶ **Focus**   When you write a title, capitalize the first word, the last word, and every word that is important. Study the following examples.

book: *The Adventures of Sherlock Holmes*

story: "A Day in May"

poem: "To a Skylark"

magazine: *Science World*

newspaper: *The Taos Post*

song: "Home on the Range"

play: *The Miracle Worker*

film: *Star Wars*

TV series: *Sesame Street*

work of art: *Mona Lisa*

article: "Rhythmic Gymnastics"

Note the book title *The Adventures of Sherlock Holmes. The* is capitalized because it is the first word of the title, but *of* is not capitalized because it is not an important word. Do not capitalize *a, an, and, of, in, on, to,* and *the* unless they are the first or last word in a title.

Notice that the titles of whole works, such as books, magazines, newspapers, plays, films, TV series, or works of art, are printed in italics. When you write one of these titles, underline it. Use quotation marks when writing the title of a story, poem, song, or article.

Begin a title with a capital letter when it is used with a person's name. Study these examples.

Ms. Ellen Murphy	**Officer** Blake	**Prince** Rainier
Dr. Maria Rivera	**Reverend** Thomas	**Captain** Cook
Mr. Henry C. Fein	**Governor** Meyers	**General** Washington

When a title is used in place of a full name, capitalize the title.

Good morning, **M**ayor.   How are you, **D**octor?

▶ **Guided Practice**   Tell what words should be capitalized.

1. "that's the way it is"
2. "on top of old smokey"
3. *a day in may*
4. *lilies of the field*
5. "escape to the city"
6. "the jay and the peacocks"

▶ **Practice**   **A.** Capitalize the following titles. You will capitalize thirty-seven letters. Remember to underline italicized titles.

Example: *giants in the earth*   **Answer:**   <u>Giants in the Earth</u>

1. "a dinner at poplar walk"
2. *julie of the wolves*
3. *oliver twist*
4. *the old curiosity shop*
5. "the three sailors"
6. "for sapphires"
7. *a christmas carol*
8. "a day in the sun"
9. *great expectations*
10. *a tale of two cities*
11. "the lady, or the tiger?"
12. "every good boy does fine"

B. Capitalize the titles of plays and the names of people. Underline italicized titles.

Example: *death of a salesman*   **Answer:**   <u>Death of a Salesman</u>

13. *the queen of hearts*
14. king leopold
15. sir isaac newton
16. president abraham lincoln
17. *land of the free*
18. mrs. mary todd lincoln
19. general robert e. lee
20. commodore oliver h. perry
21. *the pen of my aunt*
22. senator alan dixon

C. Rewrite the sentences. Capitalize the necessary words.
Example: peggy mann wrote *the street of the flower boxes.*
Answer: Peggy Mann wrote *The Street of the Flower Boxes.*

23. mayor bailey met with governor frey to discuss the bus strike.
24. officer patricia cabot was awarded a medal for bravery.
25. dr. robert conklin proved that chimpanzees can communicate.
26. *never a dull moment* is hailed as the year's best film.
27. The TV play *children of tomorrow* will be shown next week.
28. The poem "my father is a simple man" is one of my favorites.
29. Millions of people watched the weddings of prince charles and prince andrew.
30. The article "why lose weight?" is in today's *miami herald.*
31. judge wilson married ms. eva lewis to mr. rodrigues lima.
32. grandma quinn always used to recite the poem "to helen."

▶ **Apply/Writing**   Write several sentences, using a title in each. Tell about books, magazines, or newspapers you have read, TV programs or films you have seen, or songs you have heard.

29   More practice on page 521.

Review/Evaluation

For more review, see Tested Skills Practice, pages 518–522.

27 **Commas in Writing   A.** Write the letter of the word in each sentence that should be followed by a comma.

1. The <u>sergeant</u> <u>began</u> the <u>roll</u> by shouting "<u>Alvarez</u> Carmen."
         a   b   c   d

2. There <u>are</u> <u>many</u> lakes, <u>ponds</u> rivers, and <u>streams</u> in New England.
        a   b   c   d

3. <u>Hank</u> our <u>next-door</u> neighbor, just <u>returned</u> from a <u>trip</u> abroad.
     a   b   c   d

4. The <u>date</u> of the first journal <u>entry</u> was Sunday, <u>May</u> <u>1</u> 1890.
       a   b   c d

5. <u>When</u> the <u>lifeguard</u> saw the <u>shark</u> she <u>began</u> warning swimmers.
     a   b   c   d

6. Lou, of <u>course</u> <u>claimed</u> <u>that</u> he knew <u>nothing</u> about the prank.
           a   b c   d

7. One officer <u>handcuffed</u> the <u>suspect</u> and <u>two</u> others took <u>him</u> away.
             a   b   c   d

8. <u>However</u> no one <u>admits</u> <u>that</u> he was in the <u>room</u> at the time.
     a   b c   d

9. Our <u>store</u> at <u>123</u> Rose Street, Dayton, <u>Ohio</u> will <u>close</u> in May.
       a   b   c   d

27 **B.** Write **a** if the item is correct. Write **b** if it is not correct.

10. With, love	13. Detroit Michigan
11. Goldberg, Sam	14. $450,00
12. February, 22, 1948	15. Dear Peter,

28 **Quotation Marks**   Write the letter of each sentence that is capitalized and punctuated correctly.

16. **a.** Pat was reading the article Turtle soup in the newspaper.
    b. Pat was reading the article "Turtle Soup" in the newspaper.
17. **a.** "Hey, Mom!" she called. "Do you believe this?"
    b. "Hey, Mom! she called. Do you believe this?

18. **a.** "A lady, she said, "ordered turtle soup in a restaurant."
    b. "A lady," she said, "ordered turtle soup in a restaurant."
19. **a.** "She got a turtle and a bowl of hot water," she finished.
    b. "She got a turtle and a bowl of hot water." she finished.
20. **a.** Mom thought that it was a funny story too.
    b. Mom thought, "That it was a funny story too."
21. **a.** "Of course" Mom added. "It's not as funny as some."
    b. "Of course," Mom added, "it's not as funny as some."
22. **a.** "Do you know any stories, Pat asked, "funnier than that."
    b. "Do you know any stories," Pat asked, "funnier than that?"
23. **a.** "Let me see, Mom said, "Yes, I can think of one or two."
    b. "Let me see," Mom said. "Yes, I can think of one or two."

29 **Capitalization: Nouns, Adjectives, Titles A.** Write the letter of the answer that identifies the underlined noun or adjective.
a. Proper noun in which all important words need capitals
b. Proper adjective that should be capitalized
c. Noun or adjective—not proper—that should be capitalized
d. Noun or adjective that needs no capital letters

24. The Chens arrived in New York City at noon on <u>memorial day</u>.
25. <u>beautiful</u> May weather greeted them at the airport.
26. Uncle Quan would be their tour guide in the <u>city</u>.
27. They all walked to Uncle Quan's favorite cafe on <u>fifth avenue</u>.
28. The owner of the World Cafe was a young woman from <u>greece</u>.
29. The tablecloths at the cafe were made of <u>belgian</u> linen.
30. After lunch they saw the <u>statue of liberty</u> and other sights.
31. Uncle showed them his office at the <u>ling computer company</u>.
32. <u>rows</u> of computers lined the walls of Uncle Quan's big office.
33. The Chens left for <u>washington, d.c.</u>, on the following Friday.
34. Ginny Chen hoped to come back in <u>fall</u> for a longer visit.

B. Write the letter of each title that is capitalized correctly.

35. **a.** "oh, susanna"
    b. "Oh, Susanna"
36. **a.** *Anne of green Gables*
    b. *Anne of Green Gables*
37. **a.** Sir Winston Churchill
    b. sir Winston Churchill
38. **a.** *Return to the stars*
    b. *Return to the Stars*
39. **a.** "Finding a Poem"
    b. "Finding A Poem"
40. **a.** *The King and I*
    b. *The King And I*

Writing Evaluation

26 These pictures all feature whistlers as they display their talents at a national contest. Write a character study of at least three paragraphs based on one of these pictures. Adopt a tone—admiring, serious, or humorous—toward your character.

1. Before you begin writing, think of three questions that you could ask your whistler. The answers to these questions may provide main ideas for your paragraphs.
2. Write your character study. Use the following questions to guide your writing.
   ✔ Does each paragraph have a main idea?
   ✔ Do the details in each paragraph support that main idea?
   ✔ Has a tone been established?
   ✔ Is the character described with vivid details?
   ✔ Have you avoided unnecessary words and phrases?
3. When you have finished writing, spend a few minutes checking and revising your character study.
   ✔ Can you answer "yes" to all of the questions above?
   ✔ Have you punctuated any quotations properly?
   ✔ Have you capitalized all proper nouns and adjectives?

Curriculum Connection: Science

Environments can affect people in many different ways. In Unit 16 you read about Flavio, who looked at the environment from the stand-point of a twelve-year-old. Rachel Carson, a biologist and writer, looked at the environment from the standpoint of a scientist. She demonstrated that the environment is a fragile thing that must be preserved and protected. She made people aware of ecology. This is the branch of science concerned with the interrelationship of organisms and the environments in which they live.

One of Rachel Carson's most vital contributions was to make people aware of how the animals and plants in an environmental community affect each other. She showed clearly the effects of chemical insecticide sprayed on plants. The insecticide harms not only the grasshopper that eats the plants but also the bird that later eats the grasshopper and the wolf that later eats the bird.

▶ **Think** Consider the number of environmental communities with which you are familiar. You might, for example, live near a river. Think of the plants and animals that populate that community. You might live near a small wooded section of land. Think of the animals and plants that populate that community.

▶ **Discuss** Engage in a class discussion of the various environmental communities that your classmates have knowledge of. Identify in as much detail as possible the major animal and plant forms that live in that community.

▶ **Find Out** Consult your science text for information about ecological communities. Then examine an encyclopedia and more specialized books about ecology. Decide upon the community you would like to report on and visit the place. Take notes on the kinds of living things that you find there. Try to determine how the plants and animals are interrelated. Discover how the various forms of life depend upon each other for food. Your science text and other references should furnish you with this information.

▶ **React: Make a Graphic Aid** Prepare an illustrated report that describes the community you have studied. Make a graph, chart, or drawing to help present your information. Make sure your illustration is large enough to be seen by the whole audience.

Midyear Test

Sentences

5 **A.** Write the letter that identifies each sentence.
   a. Declarative   **b.** Interrogative   **c.** Imperative   **d.** Exclamatory

  1. The walls of the room are spinning around the astronaut
  2. How fast does her chair revolve on that machine
  3. What a brave person she is
  4. Would you like to try that

6 **B.** Write the letter that identifies the underlined word or words.
   a. Simple subject   **c.** Simple predicate
   b. Complete subject **d.** Complete predicate

  5. <u>Ted and Gerry</u> skied or skated every day.
  6. The <u>weather</u> had been cold, clear, and crisp for a month.
  7. They <u>sat by the fireplace and sang songs in the evening.</u>
  8. Their mother often <u>played</u> the piano for them.

7
8 **C.** Write **a** if an item is a correct sentence, **b** if it is a sentence and a fragment, and **c** if it is a run-on sentence.

   9. The lights in the house flickered and then went out.
 10. Andrea searched for candles, she couldn't find any.
 11. The house was dark. Until ten when the lights came back on.
 12. The very next day Andrea bought a box of candles.

Nouns and Pronouns

10 **D.** Write the letter of the correct plural noun in each pair.

13. a. tomatos	**b.** heroes	**16. a.** gases	**b.** watchs
14. a. diarys	**b.** berries	**17. a.** cameras	**b.** halfs
15. a. lives	**b.** thiefs	**18. a.** foxs	**b.** monkeys

11 **E.** Write the letter of the pronoun that makes each sentence correct.

 19. The man (**a.** who, **b.** whom) spoke to me is there.
 20. (**a.** Who, **b.** Whom) introduced her to the class?
 21. Did (**a.** her, **b.** she) sign the visitors' book yet?
 22. No, but she autographed (**a.** mine, **b.** my) notebook.

Verbs

13 **F.** Write **a** for each action verb and **b** for each linking verb.

23. Daniel appeared on stage in his hippo costume.
24. The costume seemed too large for him.
25. Daniel felt very awkward in the costume.

14 **G.** Write the letter of the principal part used to form each verb.
a. Present   **b.** Present participle   **c.** Past   **d.** Past participle

26. is leaping   **27.** has crawled   **28.** tries   **29.** jumped

15 **H.** Write the letter of the tense of each verb.
a. Present perfect   **b.** Past perfect   **c.** Future perfect

30. has tripped   **31.** will have replied   **32.** had scratched

Adjectives and Adverbs

20 **I.** Write the letter that describes the function of the adverb in each sentence.
a. Time   **b.** Place   **c.** Manner   **d.** Intensifier

33. The sun shines here twenty-four hours a day.
34. I am going hiking tomorrow.
35. I feel very comfortable in heavy clothing.
36. The Laplanders dress warmly in their colorful clothing.

21 **J.** Write **a** if the form of the adjective or adverb is correct. Write **b** if it is incorrect.

37. Our astronauts are better than any others.
38. They have flown more farther than other astronauts.
39. Neil Armstrong is the most famous space traveler of all.
40. No other astronaut has done more than Armstrong.

22 **K.** Write **a** if *good, well, bad,* or *badly* is used correctly in the sentences. Write **b** if it is used incorrectly.

41. Our dog Skip needs a bath bad.
42. For Skip the day will begin badly.
43. We will bathe him good.
44. His day will end well, I think.

Prepositions and Conjunctions

24 **L.** Write the letter that gives the number and kind of prepositional phrases in each sentence.
a. One adjective phrase **b.** One adverb phrase **c.** One of each kind

45. I carried Skip to the bathroom.
46. The poor dog in my arms trembled with fear.
47. He relaxed in the bathtub.
48. The cleanest-smelling dog in the neighborhood now is Skip.

25 **M.** Write the letter that identifies the kind of conjunction needed.
a. Coordinating **b.** Correlative

49. Neither Skip _____ I am happy just now.
50. The dog needs another bath _____ a severe scolding.
51. I warned Skip about skunks, _____ the dog doesn't listen.

Capitalization and Punctuation

27 **N.** Write the letter of the number of commas needed in each sentence.
a. None **b.** One **c.** Two **d.** Three

52. Larry your package finally arrived on Saturday April 23 1987.
53. His address is 111 Pine Park Pella Iowa 50211.
54. The package needless to say was a year overdue.
55. The dog biscuits were stale but the cat liked the catnip.

28 **O.** Write **a** if a sentence is correctly punctuated, **b** if it is not.

56. Larry exclaimed "That package is a year overdue".
57. Diane remarked, "It must have been sent by dogsled."
58. "The package," Larry said, "contained gifts for Diane's pets."
59. Diane said "that her pets must be pretty hungry by now."

29 **P.** Write the letter that explains why the underlined word or words in each sentence should be capitalized.
a. Proper noun **b.** Proper adjective **c.** Word(s) in a title

60. Peter is reading "<u>the</u> Rime of the Ancient Mariner."
61. The <u>british</u> poet, Samuel Coleridge, wrote the poem.
62. It first appeared in *lyrical ballads*, a book of poetry.
63. Peter is currently living in <u>cambridge</u>, England.

Thinking Skills/Paragraphs

1 **Q.** Read the paragraph. Draw conclusions to answer the questions. Write the letters of the answers.

Brenda walked into the lab. Her white uniform was spotlessly clean. "I'm here for my patient's test results," she said. "His name is Harold Schwartz and he's been in room 210 for the past two weeks. I'm hoping we'll be able to take the cast off his leg tomorrow."

64. Who is Brenda?
    a. a waitress   **b.** a doctor   **c.** a scientist
65. Where is she?
    a. a restaurant   **b.** home   **c.** a hospital
66. What is Harold Schwartz in the hospital for?
    a. tonsillectomy   **b.** blood poisoning   **c.** broken leg

2 **R.** Read the main idea of a narrative paragraph. Then write the letter of the word or words that signal the sequence of each event.
a. After that   **b.** First   **c.** Then   **d.** Eventually

Main idea: The run down the ski trail was quite eventful.

67. _____ I lost both ski poles.
68. _____ my left ski caught in a deep rut.
69. _____ my other ski veered off to the right.
70. _____ I made it safely to the bottom, but just barely.

16 **S.** Write the letter of the only sentence that contrasts something with itself.

71. **a.** The rhinoceros has two sharp and curved horns on its head.
    b. It is about five feet tall, and it weighs about two tons.
    c. A rhino looks ferocious; however, it can be very gentle.

17 **T.** Write **a** if the sentence could be used as the topic sentence of a paragraph comparing and contrasting a place. Write **b** if it could not be used in this way.

72. All around us we could see nothing but beautiful flowers.
73. I could not describe the canyon however hard I tried.
74. The canyon overwhelmed us with beauty, but it was treacherous.
75. The canyon was both serene and disquieting.

Explanatory Writing

Theme: A Sense of Direction

To get somewhere in life, people need to know where they are going. Do you have goals or **a sense of direction?** Have you ever thought of how good writing must also be directed toward a specific goal? Before you put pen to paper, think about what you are trying to accomplish. In Unit 20 you will write an explanatory paragraph, a cause-effect paragraph, and a business letter. In addition, you will learn how to use transitions to clarify your writing and give it direction.

253

1 Literature: Explanatory Writing

A parachutist, like a bird, needs to have a sense of direction. Did you know that parachutists can steer their parachutes in the direction they want? The following passage explains how a parachutist does this. Read the excerpt to find out what happens when the parachutist jumps out of the aircraft.

from **How Things Work**
by Michael Pollard

Parachutes are easy to understand. The umbrella-shaped top is called the *canopy*. When this opens out, the air trapped inside the umbrella resists the weight of the falling parachutist and so slows the parachute up. There is a small hole in the top of the canopy which allows some air to stream through from underneath. Without this, the parachute would drop too slowly and drift sideways in the wind. Suspension lines lead from the outside edge of the canopy to a harness strapped on the parachutist's back.

Before a parachutist takes off for a jump, the harness and the pack into which the parachute is folded are checked carefully. Everything must work perfectly the first time, because in parachuting there are no second chances! The parachute canopy and lines are all folded into the pack so that when the time comes everything will come out in the right order, with no snagging or twisting.

When it's time to jump, the parachutist lets himself or herself fall clear of the aircraft before opening the 'chute. If the parachutist didn't do this, the parachute might get caught in the slipstream— the air currents around the aircraft. Once clear, the parachutist pulls the ripcord on the pack, and it opens. A small parachute, called the *pilot parachute* or *drogue,* comes out first. The air opens this out, and as it opens it pulls out the main canopy and suspension lines. When the canopy is open and the suspension lines have pulled tight underneath, the parachutist feels a jerk and begins to float in the air instead of falling. The parachutist is safe—for the moment, at least.

Modern parachutes have slots in the canopy, and by pulling on the lines these can be altered in shape. In this way the parachutist can steer towards a spot that looks safe for landing.

▶ **Discussing**
1. What happens when a parachutist jumps out of a plane?
2. Why is there a small hole in the top of the canopy?
3. What is the slipstream?
4. How does the parachutist steer the parachute?
5. How do you think the author feels about parachuting? On what are you basing your opinion?

▶ **Analyzing: Explanatory Writing**

Explanatory writing is writing that explains something. It may tell the reasons for something or the way something works. In the passage from *How Things Work,* Michael Pollard explains how parachutes work.

Read the following explanation of how to study a spelling word. Then answer the questions about the explanation.

These steps are useful for studying a spelling word. First, pronounce the word and listen to its sound. Next, copy the word from your original source. Then, write the word without looking at the original. Congratulate yourself if you spell it correctly, but if you make a mistake start again with step one.

1. What topic sentence sets the stage for the explanation?
2. What transition words are used to signal connections among steps?
3. What is the order of details?

▶ **Writing**

Imagine you are teaching someone how to parachute. Based on the information in the excerpt, write a brief set of directions.

▶ **Extending**

Speaking and Listening   Test your sense of direction. Meet with a small group of classmates. Select a place in the neighborhood that everyone in the class is familiar with. Create a set of directions that explains how to get to this place from your school. Without identifying the place, present your directions to the entire class. Have your classmates tell where the directions will take them.

Reading   *Mapmaking,* by Karin N. Mango, will give you a real sense of direction as you learn about mapmaking techniques. You will also learn about map types and uses and how to read maps.

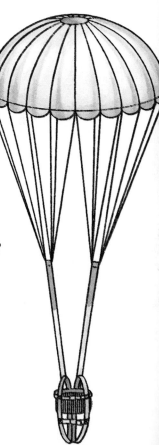

2 Cause and Effect

Understanding cause-and-effect relationships will help you improve your reading, writing, and study skills.

▶ **Focus**   In the previous lesson you learned that when a parachutist pulls the ripcord, the parachute opens. You also learned that a parachute slows down because the air trapped inside the umbrella resists the weight of the falling parachutist. These are both examples of **cause and effect.**

A **cause** is what makes something happen. An **effect** is what happens because of the cause. Pulling the ripcord causes the parachute to open; the parachute opening is the effect of pulling the ripcord. Air trapped inside the umbrella which resists the weight of the parachutist causes the parachute to slow down; the parachute slowing down is the effect of air trapped inside the umbrella which resists the weight of the parachutist. Understanding cause-and-effect relationships helps you understand what you read. Transition words such as *because* and *since* signal cause. Transition words such as *so* and *thus* signal effect.

One effect can have more than one cause, and one cause can produce more than one effect. For instance, you might have a stomachache because of two causes—overeating and the stomach flu, both at the same time. One cause—too much sun—can bring about more than one effect, as shown below.

▶ **Guided Practice**   Discuss the following questions.
1. Which diagram, A or B, illustrates a single effect? What are its causes?
2. Which diagram shows two effects? What are they?

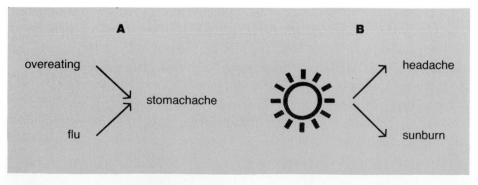

Practice   **A.** Identify the causes and effects in the following sentences.

Example: Because of the rain, our basement flooded.
Answer: Cause: rain
Effect: flooded basement

1. Jake broke his leg; therefore, he couldn't play in the game and had to use crutches to walk.
2. As a result of last night's power shortage, we ate a cold dinner by candlelight.
3. Jane forgot to put the top on the grasshopper's box; consequently, the insect escaped.
4. Since it has not rained in several days and because it has been cold, the new seedlings have died.
5. Joe's dad left his car's headlights on last night; hence the car won't start.
6. The farmland meant everything to the Hutchisons because it had been in the family for generations.
7. Rosemary overslept this morning, and as a result, she didn't have time to set breakfast and was late for work.

B. Examine the following paragraph. Then answer the questions that follow.

Yet in spite of the savagery and the ruthlessness of the Mongol conquest, some good was accomplished. Roads were built between Europe and Asia, and peoples of different cultures met each other and began to trade goods and knowledge. Oriental delicacies in foods and also fine fabrics were introduced. The Chinese areas of papermaking, woodblock printing, and painting were shared with the West.

from **All About Horses**
by Marguerite Henry

8. What caused roads to be built between Europe and Asia?
9. What other effects came about because of this?

Apply/Prewriting   Think of something you can explain that has a clear cause-effect relationship. Make notes on your idea and save them for the next unit.

3 Making Analogies

Verbal analogies are words that are related in some way to each other.

▶ **Focus**   An important thinking skill is the ability to see relationships. A **word analogy** compares the relationships of pairs of words. In the excerpt from *How Things Work,* the author mentions a safe moment for the parachutist and implies that parachuting can be dangerous. *Safe* and *dangerous* are related in the same way that *soft* and *hard* are related: they are antonyms. These two word pairs can be put together in an **antonym analogy**: safe is to dangerous as soft is to hard. You can express the analogy in the following way—safe : dangerous :: soft : hard.

When you take a word-analogy test you must figure out how a pair of words is related and then choose a second pair of words that has a similar relationship. Besides antonym analogies, tests may include the analogies shown in the chart.

Relationship	Example
Synonym	examine : study :: discuss : converse
Part/whole	finger : hand :: toe : foot
Cause and Effect	nutrition : health :: malnutrition : sickness
Type	centipede : insect :: robin : bird
Tool and Worker	paintbrush : painter :: microscope : scientist

▶ **Guided Practice**   Discuss answers to the following questions about word analogies.

1. What is the relationship between these two words: *elm : tree?*
2. Which of these pairs has the same relationship as *elm : tree?*
   leaf : branch   soil : trunk   rose : flower
3. What is the relationship between these two words: *overeating : fat?*
4. Which of these pairs has the same relationship as *overeating : fat?*
   snow : snowstorm   dieting : thin   fish : swim
5. What is the relationship between these two words: *chalk : teacher?*
6. Which of these pairs has the same relationship as *chalk : teacher?*
   wheat : bread   lead : pencil   hammer : carpenter

Practice **A.** Write the pair of words that expresses the same relationship as the words above it.

Example: noise : silence

      a. golf : sport   **b.** plum : fruit   **c.** good : bad

Answer: good : bad

1. fullback : team
   a. soldier : army   **b.** stammer : stutter **c.** hammer : drill
2. hoe : gardener
   a. florist : flower   **b.** saw : carpenter   **c.** umpire : referee
3. right : wrong
   a. lazy : idle   **b.** lost : found   **c.** word : sentence
4. present : gift
   a. tension : headache **b.** page : book   **c.** secure : confident
5. injury : pain
   a. sugar : cavities   **b.** diary : journal   **c.** wrench : plumber
6. jazz : music
   a. teeth : mouth   **b.** sunshine : light   **c.** ballet : dance
7. telescope : astronomer
   a. black : white   **b.** animals : zoos   **c.** pen : writer
8. groan : sound
   a. photo : album   **b.** water : liquid   **c.** wood : table

B. Copy each analogy, completing it with the correct word.

Example: leaf : tree :: petal : _____

Answer: flower

9. crowd : group :: solo : _____
10. carefulness : perfection :: carelessness : _____
11. calculator : accountant :: stethoscope : _____
12. sore throat : coughing :: colds : _____
13. casual : formal :: fat : _____

Apply/Math You can find relationships between pairs of numbers just as you can find relationships between words. Look at these numbers: 10 : 20. The second number is two times greater than the first. Find a similar relationship in one of the following: 1 : 18, 100 : 120, 110 : 220. The third number pair, 110 : 220, has the same relationship as 10 : 20 because 220 is two times 110. Make up other examples for classmates to solve.

4 Using Graphic Aids

Graphic aids help you organize and understand information.

▶ **Focus**   Graphic aids help clarify explanations that you read and write. **Graphic aids** include graphs, charts, diagrams, and maps.

Graphs are drawings that show how one fact is related to another. To understand a graph, read the title, the words around the graph, and any keys to symbols. Then examine the information inside the graph. The four types of graphs are **circle (or pie) graphs, bar graphs, line graphs,** and **picture graphs.**

Charts, also called tables, usually list pieces of information in columns. Read any keys that explain how the information is presented. Then look over the chart.

Diagrams allow the reader to identify each part of an object and to see how it is related to all other parts.

Maps show areas of land and water. Maps can present special information about population, climate, or geology. Always look for a map's key for symbols and abbreviations.

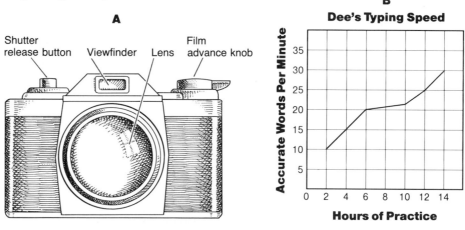

A

Shutter release button   Viewfinder   Lens   Film advance knob

B

Dee's Typing Speed

Accurate Words Per Minute

Hours of Practice

▶ **Guided Practice**   Answer the following questions about the diagram (A) and line graph (B) above.

1. What is diagramed in A?
2. In B, what do the numbers 8 and 15 refer to respectively?
3. What cause-and-effect relationship does B indicate?

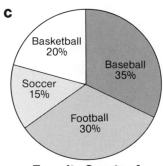

Practice   **A.** Study the pie graph (C) and bar graph (D) below. Then answer the questions.

C

Basketball 20%

Baseball 35%

Soccer 15%

Football 30%

Favorite Sports of 7th Graders at Allen School

D

Pets of Students in Lincoln School

1. What does C show?
2. What do the numbers to the left of D indicate?
3. What sport is the most popular among the seventh graders?
4. Is the total of students' dogs and cats at Lincoln School more or less than the total of all other pets?

B. Study the chart (E) and map (F) below. Then answer the questions.

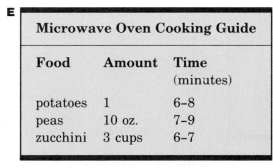

E

Microwave Oven Cooking Guide		
Food	Amount	Time (minutes)
potatoes	1	6–8
peas	10 oz.	7–9
zucchini	3 cups	6–7

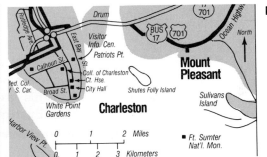

F

Charleston

5. Are equal or unequal amounts of food being compared in E?
6. On the average, which food takes the longest to cook?
7. The location of what national monument is shown in F?
8. Describe that location and its position in relation to the city of Charleston. How many miles from the city is it?

Apply/Thinking Skills   Make a graphic aid to illustrate something you know or can find out, such as the parts of a car engine or the change in high temperatures for the past month.

5 Transitions in Paragraphs

Transitions are words and phrases that show the order and relationship of ideas.

Focus   You have learned that transition words and phrases can show time order in narratives and spatial order in descriptions. Transition words are also used to show various relationships in explanatory writing. Study these charts.

Spatial	Time	Cause and Effect
above	after	as a result
behind	before	because of
below	finally	due to
far	later	for this reason
inside	meanwhile	it is evident
left	next	therefore
right	then	thus

Comparison and Contrast	Example or Classification
instead of	for example
just as	for instance
like	in fact
more than	in other words
on the one hand	in this case
similarly	to illustrate

Read the paragraph that follows. Study the underlined transition words and phrases in the sentences within the paragraph.

Jason set his goal and <u>then</u> decided how to reach it. <u>More than</u> anything, he wanted that aquarium! <u>First</u>, he was going to save his allowance. <u>Next</u>, he was going to find out everything he could about tropical fish. <u>For example</u>, he planned to spend hours in the library and in the pet shop downtown. <u>Finally</u>, he would clear a space in his bedroom to hold the aquarium. The aquarium would fit perfectly <u>next to</u> his desk. <u>Because of</u> his planning, his parents would be convinced that he was responsible enough to buy and maintain an aquarium.

▶ **Guided Practice**   Answer the following questions.

1. Which three transition words signal time relationships?
2. Which transition phrase signals a cause-effect relationship? a spatial relationship?
3. Which transition phrase signals a comparison and contrast? an example?

▶ **Practice**   Rewrite the paragraphs below. Fill in each blank with one of the transition words or phrases that are below the paragraphs.

1. The doctor looked at the X-ray and still felt uncertain about Tony's injuries. _____ his uncertainty, Tony's doctor ordered more tests and X rays. _____, severe injuries were found. _____ that Tony needed an operation.

   It was evident   Because of   As a result

2. Planning your route for a long trip is a good investment of time. _____, buy a good, up-to-date map. _____, mark your starting point and your end point. _____, with a brightly colored marker, trace the route you prefer. Whether you choose the scenic drive or the most direct route, your preparation will result in a more pleasant trip.

   Finally   Then   First

3. The road sign was a real surprise. _____ the cornfield it loomed, bright blue and tall. _____ the metal rectangular face were printed the words: Enter at your own risk. _____ the sign we saw rows of corn that extended to the horizon. Perhaps, we thought, the sign was meant to be a joke.

   Under   On   Above

▶ **Apply/Prewriting**   Think of something you can explain in a paragraph. Decide whether you want to explain your topic through definition, by telling how something works, or in some other way. Jot down your ideas and save them for later.

6 Writing an Explanatory Paragraph

An explanatory paragraph uses facts to explain something.

▶ **Focus**   You can make a topic clear to someone when you write an **explanatory paragraph.** Explanatory paragraphs define, illustrate, analyze, or explain something. You can write about what a mammal is, how to take a photograph, why one football team is better than another, or why animals hibernate. In each case, you give information that helps someone understand something.

You should always be familiar with a topic that you write about in an explanatory paragraph. You learned in Lesson 5 that transition words and phrases like *therefore, because of,* and *for example* show how ideas are connected. Use transitions when you write an explanatory paragraph to help a reader understand your ideas.

Read the following paragraph.

> Ravens are known for their intelligence as well as for their playfulness. While most other birds act mainly by instinct, ravens show curiosity, learn quickly from experience, and even use this experience to solve problems in new situations. For example, after watching its parents, a young raven puts nearly everything new into its mouth to find out if it's edible. But later it learns many different food-gathering skills. Like gulls, it drops shellfish from high in the air to break them open. A scientist observed one pair of ravens working together to take food from a cat. While one bird swooped low to make the cat drop the mouse it had caught, the second bird grabbed the dinner. This was not habit or instinct on the ravens' part—the birds had figured out how to solve a problem.
>
> *from* **"One Smart Bird"**
> *by Katherine Hauth*

▶ **Guided Practice**   Answer the following questions.

1. What topic is being explained?
2. What details does the author give you to help you understand the topic?
3. What transition words and phrases are used in the paragraph?

▶ **Practice** **A.** Read the following explanatory paragraph. List the transition words and phrases used in the paragraph.

   To most people, bees seem to fly aimlessly from place to place. However, to other bees, the pattern and speed of their flight communicates very important information. For example, to tell other bees that food is within a hundred yards of the hive, a scout bee will fly in a circle. On the other hand, if the food is farther away, the bee will move in a figure-eight formation. In addition to telling the distance to the food, the scout will cross from one loop of the figure eight to the other to indicate the direction of the food. The speed with which the bee flies also tells the distance to the food. As a result, if a bee sees another bee flying very fast in a circle, it knows that food is very close.

B. Complete the following activities as preparation for writing an explanatory paragraph.

1. Use your prewriting ideas from Lessons 2 and 5 or choose one of these suggested topics: how to cook chili, why dinosaurs are extinct, what a comet is, how a cell divides, how to play your favorite sport, how to choose and care for a pet.
2. Write a topic sentence for your paragraph.
3. List the details that you will include in your explanation.
4. List transition words and phrases that you will use.
5. Find or create a photograph or drawing that illustrates the subject you are explaining.

▶ **Apply/Writing** Use the work you have done in this lesson and in the previous lessons to write an explanatory paragraph. Use the following checklist to evaluate your paragraph.

Explanatory Paragraph Revision Checklist
✔ Have I included enough details so that the explanation is clear to the reader?
✔ Have I used transitions such as *first, behind, similarly* and *for instance* to connect the ideas in my paragraph?
✔ Have I included a graphic aid that enhances my explanation?
✔ Have I combined subjects and predicates where appropriate?

7 Writing a Cause-Effect Paragraph

A paragraph of cause and effect clearly states how one person, thing, idea, or action influences another.

▶ **Focus**   Some explanatory paragraphs tell how one action causes another or prove that a certain belief or action will lead to a certain behavior. This is a **cause-effect paragraph.** Cause-effect paragraphs rely on logical argument and clear thinking. To indicate the relationship between causes and effects you can use transition words and phrases. You learned about these in Lesson 5.

Read the following paragraphs. Note the cause (why something happened) and effects (what happened).

The decision to keep a pet can cause a major change in a family's lifestyle. Since pets require attention, family members have to be willing to give up some of their free time to care for them. Pets depend on people to keep them clean, well fed, and healthy. Therefore, families must arrange to have someone care for the animal when they go away on vacation, and, if the animal is sick, take it to the vet. If a dog is selected as a pet, time has to be set aside for walking and exercising it. Pets are fun but helpless, and consequently, are a big responsibility to a family.

Cats were not always as popular as they are today. During the Middle Ages, some people in certain parts of the world thought cats were evil. As a result, cats were feared and persecuted. Consequently, the population of rats and mice grew in the cities because there were not enough cats to hunt them. Today, cats are sometimes kept because they hunt mice, but mostly because they are good company.

▶ **Guided Practice**   Answer the following questions about the cause-effect relationships in the paragraph.

1. What is the effect of the decision to keep a pet?
2. What causes a family to arrange for pet care when they go on vacation?
3. What was the cause of cats being feared and persecuted during the Middle Ages?
4. What was the effect of not having enough cats to hunt rats and mice?

▶ **Practice A.** Read the following cause-effect paragraph. Then answer the questions.

Presenting information in a graph is an effective way to help people understand information. When, for example, you put data you have collected as part of a science project into graph form, people notice and remember what you did. A colorful, clear graph makes people pay attention and, as a result, helps them understand your research.

1. What will be the effect of a colorful, clear graph?
2. What will cause people to notice and remember what you did?

▶ **B.** Write the transition words and phrases that are in the following paragraph.

Our school needs more plants. First, plants are beautiful to look at; consequently, the school would be a more visually pleasing place. Their presence would encourage student attendance. Finally, all plants could be labeled and presented with descriptions and care instructions. As a result, they would have educational value. Plants would be appreciated by our eyes, noses, and brains.

▶ **C.** Copy the following sentences. Then fill in the blanks to complete each statement.

3. Our air conditioner is broken; as a result, _____.
4. If public transportation were cheaper, _____.
5. _____; therefore, I'm not going to the party.
6. _____; consequently, I couldn't complete my homework.
7. I fell and twisted my ankle because of _____.

▶ **Apply/Writing** Write a cause-effect paragraph. For a topic, use the prewriting notes you made in Lessons 2 and 5 or use an idea from Practice C of this lesson.

Cause-Effect Paragraph Revision Checklist
✔ Have I clearly explained the effects and the causes?
✔ Have I used transition words and phrases such as *consequently,* *because of,* and *as a result* to signal cause-effect relationships?
✔ Have I set off appositives with commas?

8 Writing a Business Letter

A business letter may explain something, request information, ask for clarification, or place an order.

▶ **Focus**   In Lesson 6 you learned to write an explanatory paragraph. You will use explanatory paragraphs in writing a **business letter.** This type of letter is written for a specific purpose, is more formal than a friendly letter, and should be clear, courteous, and brief. The form of a business letter includes an inside address and a colon after the greeting.

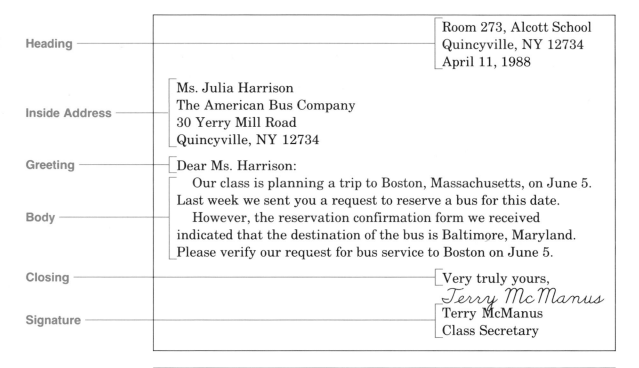

Heading	Room 273, Alcott School Quincyville, NY 12734 April 11, 1988
Inside Address	Ms. Julia Harrison The American Bus Company 30 Yerry Mill Road Quincyville, NY 12734
Greeting	Dear Ms. Harrison:
Body	Our class is planning a trip to Boston, Massachusetts, on June 5. Last week we sent you a request to reserve a bus for this date. However, the reservation confirmation form we received indicated that the destination of the bus is Baltimore, Maryland. Please verify our request for bus service to Boston on June 5.
Closing	Very truly yours, *Terry McManus*
Signature	Terry McManus Class Secretary

Terry McManus
Room 273, Alcott School
Quincyville, NY 12734

Ms. Julia Harrison
The American Bus Company
30 Yerry Mill Road
Quincyville, NY 12734

► **Guided Practice**   Answer the following questions.

1. How many parts are there to the business letter?
2. What is explained in this letter?
3. What transition word connects paragraphs one and two?

► **Practice**   **A.** Use the letter and envelope in this lesson to answer the questions below.

1. What two parts of the letter does the envelope include?
2. Does the writer's address belong in the heading or in the inside address?
3. What words are capitalized in the greeting? the closing?

B. Below is the body of a business letter. Compare and contrast the letter below with the letter on the preceding page. Rewrite the body of the letter below and make it clearer, shorter, and more courteous. Include transition words and phrases.

   I saw your pamphlets about careers advertised in the newspaper, and I really thought one might be useful, and especially I like the fact that they are cheap. I need to know if you have a booklet about what it takes to be a pilot. Do you? I really need it, because I am going to talk to my uncle this summer about how he trained to be a pilot. I want to learn too. Dad says I have to think about these things. I need to know if I should take lots of mathematics. So send a pamphlet to me immediately.

► **Apply/Writing**   Write a business letter that requests information, asks for an exchange or refund, or places an order. Include an envelope for your letter. Use the following checklist to evaluate your business letter.

Business Letter Revision Checklist
✔ Is the information presented clearly?
✔ Have you included transitions within and between paragraphs?
✔ Does the letter include an inside address?
✔ Is the greeting followed by a colon?
✔ Did you use commas in the date? after the closing? between the city and state?

Revising and Editing Workship

Connecting Writing and Grammar

- In Unit 19 you read an example of explanatory writing.
- In Unit 20 you learned about transitions and wrote an explanatory paragraph, a cause-effect paragraph, and a business letter.

Now it's time for you to use your skill as an editor to improve another writer's first draft. Read this explanation carefully. As you read, ask yourself these questions.

✔ Have transition words and phrases been used?
✔ Have appositives been set off correctly with commas?
✔ Have subjects and predicates been combined when appropriate?

(1) Alice Thomas my second cousin does well on tests. (2) Alice never worries before a test. (3) Alice never crams before a test. (4) Alice prepares well for tests. (5) She feels confident taking them. (6) She always uses as an aid in studying. (7) These strategies work whether she is studying literature or math. (8) First, Alice quickly skims on which she is going to be tested. (9) As she skims, she asks herself questions. (10) As she skims, she makes guesses about possible answers. (11) Next, she finds answers to her questions, she puts the answers in her own words. (12) She goes to bed early the night before. (13) Finally, Alice does one final review just before the test. (14) The material is still fresh in her mind when she takes the test. (15) Alice reminds me of the tortoise who wins the race in *The Hare and the Tortoise* a popular fable—she takes her time, but she always comes out ahead. (16) Alice is to tests as that fable is to the race—a winner!

▶ Revising the Draft

1. The writer gives an incorrect analogy. Rewrite the sentence that contains this error correctly.
2. The writer does not tell why Alice goes to bed early the night before the test and what effect this will have on her test performance. Add this information to the draft.
3. Two cause-effect relationships are not clear because the writer did not use transition words and phrases. Add transition words and phrases to the draft.
4. Add, delete, or rearrange any other information you think would improve the draft.

▶ Editing the Draft

5. Two sentences containing appositives are not punctuated correctly. Rewrite the sentences correctly.
6. Find two sentences that can be combined by joining their predicates. Rewrite these sentences correctly.
7. Two sentences do not make sense because each is missing a direct object. Rewrite each sentence correctly, adding a direct object.
8. Find one run-on sentence. Rewrite it correctly.

▶ Working Together on the Draft

Meet with a group of your classmates. Discuss the changes you made in the draft. Listen to the changes your classmates made. Then rewrite the draft on page 270. Include all the revisions you think are important.

▶ Evaluating Your Own Writing

Now review your own writing. Look over the explanatory paragraph, the cause-effect paragraph, and the business letter you wrote in this unit, as well as any other written work you have. Did you have any problems combining subjects and predicates and using appositives? Did you have any problems with direct and indirect objects? The lessons that follow will help you with these writing problems.

9 Appositives

An appositive is a noun or phrase that follows a noun and identifies or explains it. Appositives can be used to combine sentences.

▶ **Focus**   A noun or pronoun that follows another noun and identifies or explains it is called an **appositive.** An appositive and its modifiers make up an **appositive phrase.**

> Lea's older brother, **Gavin,** is a lawyer.
> Lea wants to be a doctor like Shawn, **her other brother.**

The appositive *Gavin* in the first sentence identifies Lea's older brother. The appositive phrase *her other brother* explains who Shawn is. Notice that the appositive in the middle of the sentence is set off by two commas. The appositive phrase at the end of the sentence is set off by only one comma.

You can use appositives to combine short, choppy sentences into longer, smoother sentences. Read the examples below.

> **Sentences:**   Chicago is the Windy City.
> We left Chicago at five o'clock.
> **Combined:**   We left Chicago, **the Windy City,** at five o'clock.
> **Sentences:**   By ten o'clock we were on Catalina.
> Catalina is a lovely island.
> **Combined:**   By ten o'clock we were on Catalina, **a lovely island.**

- What is the appositive in each of the combined sentences?
- What noun does each follow?
- Which short sentences were changed into appositives?
- What punctuation marks set each appositive off from the rest of the sentence?

▶ **Guided Practice**   Identify the sentence that has an appositive phrase. Use an appositive or appositive phrase to combine the other sentences.

My best friend is Linda. Linda always gets lost. Once I was supposed to meet her at Pages. Pages is a bookstore in our neighborhood. She was thirty minutes late because she turned onto Grover, the wrong street.

► **Practice**   **A.** Write the following sentences. Set off the appositives and appositive phrases with commas and underline them once. Underline the noun they describe twice.

Example: Chinatown a home for thousands is a lively area.

Answer: <u>Chinatown</u>, <u>a home for thousands</u>, is a lively area.

1. Chinatown a part of San Francisco has about 35,000 people.
2. Many San Franciscans visit this area a shopper's paradise.
3. Some shoppers look for porcelain a fine china.
4. Grant Avenue the main street is filled with Chinese shops.
5. The dragon a sign of good luck is a common decoration.
6. The pagoda roof an architectural style is often seen.
7. Chinatown is near Nob Hill the city's main shopping area.
8. Shoppers can ride a special trolley the cable car.
9. I often eat at Fong's a Chinese restaurant.
10. Some people like squid a common Chinese seafood.
11. I often eat with chopsticks a pair of small, slender sticks.
12. Tea a pleasantly flavored drink is usually served.
13. Much of the cooking is done in a wok a special kind of pot.
14. Visitors especially enjoy one holiday the Chinese New Year.
15. I love my home Chinatown.

B.   Use appositives to combine the following sentences. Remember to use a comma or commas to set off each appositive.

Example: I bought my cousin a tie in Chinatown. My cousin is Lee.

Answer: I bought my cousin, Lee, a tie in Chinatown.

16. Many ties are made of silk. Silk is a cloth that originated in China.
17. Lee practices Kung Fu. Kung Fu is a form of self-defense.
18. Once he tried to teach me and Ling some moves. Ling is a friend of ours.
19. Ling taught us how to make chow mein. Chow mein is a tasty dish made with fried noodles.
20. She stirred in cloud ears and soy sauce. Cloud ears are a kind of mushroom.

► **Apply/Writing**   Write five sentences about people who have interesting professions. Use an appositive or appositive phrase in each sentence to tell something about their work.

35   More practice on page 523.   **273**

10 Combining Subjects and Predicates

Sentences with the same predicate or with the same subject can often be combined into one sentence.

▶ **Focus** Sentences with the same predicate can be combined by joining the subjects to create a **compound subject.** With more than two subjects, use commas and a conjunction.

The coyote **howled all night.** The wolves **howled all night.**	The coyote and the wolves howled all night.
The bride **is in the room.** The groom **is in the room.** The best man **is in the room.**	The bride, groom, and best man are in the room.

What is the common predicate in the first group of sentences? in the second? What is the compound subject in each combined sentence?

Keep in mind when combining sentences that the verb must always agree with its subject. Notice that the verb *is* was changed to *are* to agree with the plural compound subject.

To combine sentences with the same subject, join the predicates to create a **compound predicate.** With more than two predicates, use commas and a conjunction. What is the common subject in each sentence group on the left? What is the compound predicate in each sentence on the right?

The cook tossed the salad. **The cook** stirred the soup.	The cook tossed the salad and stirred the soup.
Deer bounded across the road. **Deer** jumped over a fence. **Deer** fled into the woods.	Deer bounded across the road, jumped over a fence, and fled into the woods.

▶ **Guided Practice** Combine the sentences in each group.

1. The snake slithered through the grass. The snake paused for a moment.
2. Snakes eat flies. Frogs eat flies.
3. The rattlesnake is poisonous. The cobra is poisonous.
4. Pythons are not poisonous. Boa constrictors are not poisonous. Most garden snakes are not poisonous.

► **Practice A.** Combine the subjects in the sentences below. Be sure to make the verb agree with its subject where necessary.

Example: Angelo plays the guitar. Rita plays the guitar.
Answer: Angelo and Rita play the guitar.

1. Mr. McMann teaches music. Ms. Li teaches music.
2. The teachers want to organize a band. Their students want to organize a band.
3. Peter plays the flute. José plays the flute.
4. Cara writes music. Mitch writes music. Bo writes music.
5. Allison studies the clarinet. Monty studies the clarinet.
6. Jack reads music. Connie reads music. Richard reads music.
7. Lisa is late for practice. Barbara is late for practice.
8. Robert set up the chairs and instruments. Luis set up the chairs and instruments.
9. The violinist tunes up. The guitarist tunes up.
10. The oboe sounds lovely. The piano sounds lovely.

B. Combine the predicates in the sentences below.

Example: Gorillas travel by day. Gorillas make camp at night.
Answer: Gorillas travel by day and make camp at night.

11. These apes eat fruits. These apes also like vegetables.
12. Gorillas eat in the morning. Gorillas sleep in the afternoon.
13. Gorillas travel in groups. Gorillas never stay in the same place for more than one night.
14. Group leaders signal the time to awaken. Group leaders decide the time to rest.
15. Young adults like to wrestle with each other. Young adults enjoy playing games.
16. Gorillas do not harm people. Gorillas do not climb buildings.
17. Gorillas live in zoos. Gorillas perform in circuses.

► **Apply/Writing** Write a paragraph about your favorite animal. Use sentences that can be combined. Exchange paragraphs with a partner and combine as many sentences as possible. Make sure that the verbs agree with their subjects and that you have used commas to separate words in a series.

11 Direct Objects and Subject Complements

A direct object is a noun or pronoun that follows an action verb. A subject complement is a noun, pronoun, or adjective that follows a linking verb and refers to the subject.

▶ **Focus** A **direct object** is a noun or pronoun that follows an action verb and tells who or what receives the action of the verb. Look at these examples.

> Marvin collects baseball **cards.**
> He trades and sells **them** to his friends.
> He owns **boxes** and **boxes** of cards.

In the first sentence the direct object *cards* tells what Marvin collects. The direct object *them* in the second sentence tells what Marvin trades and sells. What is the compound direct object in the third sentence? What does it tell?

A **subject complement** is a noun, a pronoun, or an adjective that follows a linking verb and identifies or describes the subject. Study these examples.

> Louise is an **actress** in New York.
> The starring role in that play is **hers.**
> Her costume looked **regal** and **beautiful.**

In the first sentence the noun *actress* is the subject complement. It identifies the subject *Louise.* A noun used as a subject complement is called a **predicate noun.** The subject complement in the second sentence is a pronoun. What is the **predicate pronoun** in that sentence? An adjective used as a subject complement is called a **predicate adjective.** What is the compound predicate adjective in the third sentence? What do the adjectives describe?

▶ **Guided Practice** Identify the direct object or subject complement in each sentence. Tell whether the complements are predicate nouns, predicate pronouns, or predicate adjectives.

1. She played a royal princess.
2. She is a good actress.
3. The audience applauded her.
4. She appeared quite young.

▶ **Practice**   **A.** Copy the following sentences. Write *S* over each subject, *V* over each verb, and *DO* over each direct object.

                    S   **V**   **DO**

Example: Hobbies offer pleasure to many people.

1. Early baseball cards included pictures and names of players.
2. Baseball cards give many statistics about players.
3. Young hobbyists trade the cards among themselves.
4. Some people file their collections by teams.
5. One collector owned twenty thousand cards.
6. Some collections bring high prices at the time of sale.
7. Old cards bring the most money.
8. One card cost fifteen hundred dollars.
9. Mistakes on the cards increase their value tremendously.
10. Collectors love any errors in printing.

B. Copy each sentence. Write *S* over the subject and *LV* over the linking verb. Write PN, PP, or PA over the subject complement to tell what kind it is.

                     S   **LV**   **PN**

Example: Amusement parks are major locations for haunted houses at
                  Halloween.

11. Grinning vampires are popular.
12. My friend became an expert on monster costumes.
13. My friend's talent is rare.
14. His ghosts sound sorrowful.
15. His creatures grow scarier all the time.
16. His elaborate costumes look unearthly.
17. Rubber masks are the heads.
18. My friend's work appears real.
19. A successful creator is he.
20. He is helpful to people giving parties.
21. He is often the sensation of a costume party.
22. His dreadful outfits are works of art.

▶ **Apply/Writing**   Write a paragraph about an interesting collection or unusual occupation. Some of your sentences should contain direct objects and subject complements. Underline each direct object and circle each subject complement.

12 Indirect Objects

An indirect object is a noun or pronoun that tells to whom or for whom the action of the verb is done.

▶ **Focus**   Many times a sentence that contains an action verb and a direct object also contains a noun or pronoun that acts as an indirect object. An **indirect object** tells to whom or for whom the action of the verb is done. Look at the following sentences.

> The judge gave the signal.
> The judge gave **Sam** the signal.

Both sentences contain an action verb, *gave,* and a direct object, *signal.* The second sentence also contains an indirect object, *Sam.* The indirect object tells to whom the signal was given. Now look at these sentences.

> The audience made **Sam** a path.
> The audience made a path for **Sam.**

In the first sentence, the word *Sam* is an indirect object. In the second sentence, the word *Sam* is the object of the preposition *for.* An indirect object cannot be the object of a preposition. The indirect object comes before the direct object. If a word is preceded by *to* or *for,* it cannot be an indirect object.

Pronouns can also be used as indirect objects, as in the following sentences.

> The audience made **him** a path.
> The judge gave **them** ballots.

In these sentences, the pronouns *him* and *them* are indirect objects.

▶ **Guided Practice**   Identify the sentences that have indirect objects. Then identify the direct and indirect objects in those sentences.

1. Sam sang a song for us.
2. He sang us a new song.
3. Sam entered his song in a contest.
4. The judge quickly gave Sam an entry.

▶ **Practice A.**   Rewrite each sentence, changing the appropriate prepositional phrase to an indirect object.
Example: Shari gave a sheet of music to Joe.
Answer: Shari gave Joe a sheet of music.

1. The guitarist showed the music to Sam.
2. Sam whistled a few bars of an old song for him.
3. The guitarist hummed some notes for the pianist.
4. The cashiers sold tickets to newcomers.
5. Some people bought tickets for their friends.
6. Ushers found seats for people.
7. The ushers could not offer seats to some spectators.
8. Other workers gave programs to people.
9. The host handed a microphone to Sam.
10. Sam gave a nod to the leader of the band.
11. Then Sam sang his song for the audience.
12. Everyone gave their full attention to the performance.
13. The audience gave a big hand to Sam.
14. Someone gave a wreath of flowers to Sam.
15. The entertainer sent a kiss to the audience.
16. Sam sang two more songs for the crowd.

B.   Copy each sentence. Label the subject *S*, the verb *V*, the indirect object *IO*, and the direct object *DO*.

                   S   **V**   **IO**   **DO**
Example: The contest offered people some fun.

17. The whistlers gave the listeners some surprises.
18. Sweet melodies gave the crowd a thrill.
19. High notes brought fans a chill.
20. The contest gave everyone a chance.
21. Different categories offered contestants many opportunities.
22. Senior citizens taught the youngsters old tunes.
23. This unusual event brought Carson City recognition.
24. The judges promised each entrant an award.
25. The winners gave the audience encores.
26. Sam's group offered us a terrific number.

▶ **Apply/Writing**   Write a paragraph about your favorite kind of music. Include at least six indirect objects.

Review/Evaluation

For more review, see Tested Skills Practice, pages 523–527.

35 **Appositives** Write the letter of the answer that makes a correct statement about each sentence.
a. The appositive should be set off with one comma.
b. The appositive should be set off with two commas.
c. The sentence has no appositive.

1. Vatican City the world's smallest country has an area of 108 acres.
2. We visited Russia the largest country in the world.
3. Lhasa the capital city of Tibet is more than two miles above sea level.
4. Jan took pictures of Landscape Arch the world's longest natural bridge.
5. At low tide the D. River is the shortest river in the world.
6. Jupiter the largest planet in the solar system has a nine-hour day.
7. The brightest star in the sky is the Dog Star Sirius.
8. Lateiki the world's newest island appeared in the Pacific Ocean after a volcanic explosion in 1979.

36 **Combining Subjects/Predicates** Write the letter of the answer that states how each group of sentences can or cannot be combined.
a. Combine the subjects.
b. Combine the predicates.
c. The sentences cannot be combined in either of these ways.

9. Terns can fly great distances.
   Swallows can fly great distances.
   Geese can fly great distances.
10. Eagles have very keen eyesight.
    Eagles can see great distances.
11. Eagles build their nests in remote places.
    Eagles fiercely guard them.
12. The hummingbird sips nectar.
    The swallow eats flying insects.
    The eagle eats small animals and fish.

13. Vultures are scavengers.
    Giant petrels are scavengers.
14. Many birds migrate in spring and fall.
    Many birds may fly thousands of miles.
15. Penguins are flightless birds.
    Ostriches are flightless birds.
    Kiwis are flightless birds.

37. **Direct Objects and Subject Complements**   Write the letter of the answer that identifies the objects or complements in the following sentences.
   a. Single or compound direct object
   b. Single or compound predicate noun or pronoun
   c. Single or compound predicate adjective

16. Four years ago our family bought a summer cottage on Lake Bright Rainbow.
17. During the summer the cottage in the grove of tall trees is always cool and comfortable.
18. Sometimes our next-door neighbors share the cottage with us.
19. Paula Anderson is a very good swimmer.
20. She is a good diver also.
21. Dad caught eight trout and six bass.
22. The fish tasted delicious at supper.

38. **Indirect Objects**   Write the letter of the answer that identifies the underlined word in each sentence.
   a. The word is a direct object.
   b. The word is an indirect object.
   c. The word is neither of these.

23. Lizzie gave her parents a huge smile.
24. They had given Lizzie her very own guitar.
25. Her parents could not have given her a better gift.
26. She was extremely happy all that day.
27. Lizzie bought herself nylon guitar strings.
28. Her sister, Angela, gives adults guitar lessons.
29. Angela would teach her the basic fingering.
30. In return she would teach Angela a song.

Thinking/Writing Evaluation

30   **Cause and Effect**   Read the sentence and answer the questions.

Because Lou lost his keys he couldn't get into his apartment or drive his car.

1. What is the cause? **a.** Lou lost his keys.   **b.** Lou couldn't get into his apartment.   **c.** Lou couldn't drive his car.
2. What are the effects? **a.** Lou lost his keys and couldn't get into his apartment.   **b.** Lou lost his keys and couldn't drive his car. **c.** Lou couldn't get into his apartment or drive his car.

31   **Making Analogies**   Read the analogies and answer the questions.

     1. ice : slipping :: brakes : _____   **2.** dress : cotton :: bottle : _____

3. Which word completes the first analogy?   **a.** driving **b.** stopping   **c.** turning
4. Which word completes the second analogy?   **a.** break **b.** carton   **c.** glass

31
32   **Explanatory Paragraphs**   **A.** Read the paragraph from a business letter and answer the questions.

33
34   (1) I ordered a radio from your company on June 22.   (2) It arrived on July 13.   (3) Consequently, the volume knob wouldn't work.   (4) Now the radio works only at the loudest volume.   (5) I want the radio replaced or my money back.   (6) Therefore, I am returning the defective radio.   (7) Please settle this problem.

5. Which sentence has an incorrect transition word that can be replaced by the word *Soon?* **(a)** 3   **(b)** 4   **(c)** 7
6. Which word that completes the following analogy can replace *works* in sentence 4?   leave : depart :: works : _____   **(a)** stops **(b)** receives   **(c)** operates
7. Which closing would be appropriate for this business letter?   **(a)** Your pal,   **(b)** Respectfully yours,   **(c)** Best wishes,

32
33   **B.** Write an explanatory paragraph on one of the topics below. Apply what you have learned about explanatory paragraphs.

- how to change a car tire   • what causes a tornado
- one kind of tree found in your area

Curriculum Connection: Health

In Unit 19 you learned that parachuting can be dangerous. You do not have to jump out of a plane, though, to be in a dangerous situation. Sometimes danger exists in your very own home! More accidents occur in or around the home than anywhere else. These accidents take place because of carelessness or dangerously designed areas found in many homes. Some accidents occur because people fail to perform proper maintenance around the home. Make a note of potentially dangerous practices and places that may exist in your home.

▶ **Think**   Recall accidents that happened to you or to another family member in your own home. Did you or someone in your family ever slip on a bar of soap when entering a tub or shower? Did anyone in your family ever trip on a toy that a younger brother or sister left on a stairway? Did something ever fall on you when a closet door was opened? Make a list of accidents or "near misses" that occurred in your home. Think of ways to eliminate the causes of such accidents.

▶ **Discuss**   Meet with a group of classmates to discuss home accidents. Share experiences with each other. Discuss safety hazards that each person has encountered in his or her own home. Then talk about steps that can be taken to alert family members about home safety.

▶ **Find Out**   Check the card catalog in your library for subject cards labeled "Home Safety" or "Safety." Skim through two or three books that identify dangerous situations in your own home that you haven't thought of till now. Look also under the same headings in the *Readers' Guide to Periodical Literature* for magazine articles.

▶ **React: Make and Use a List**   Arrange all of the information that you have collected for a home safety meeting with your family. At this meeting you may identify the safety hazards that you have discovered in your own home. Enlist the aid of your family members in coming up with plans to eliminate the dangerous situations you have found. Be sure to volunteer for some of the fix-up work yourself. You might want to make up a few posters to remind family members of safety practices.

Explanatory Writing

Theme: Americans All

It is both the native born and the immigrants, **Americans all,** who give our country its varied flavor. Throughout this section you will find reminders of our diverse nation. You will learn how a Chinese-American woman cooks two Chinese dishes. You will also discover how another woman restores American flags. Finally, you will have a chance to write your own how-to explanation.

1 Literature: How-to Explanation

Americans all have favorite dishes that they pass down to their children. If you ever prepared an old family recipe, you probably followed a sequence of steps. In the following passage, a young Chinese-American woman cooks two favorite dishes for her college friends. Read the excerpt to find out what she makes.

from **Fifth Chinese Daughter**
by Jade Snow Wong

Besides the rice, she was planning only two dishes—egg foo young and tomato-beef. She started her preparations. Chinese dishes were always assembled from similar-sized particles. Vegetables were definitely diced, or shredded, or in chunks, depending on the nature of the meat with which they would be keeping company. They were chosen to give balanced crisp and soft textures and contrasting colors to a dish.

For the egg foo young, everything was shredded for quick cooking. So two onions were sliced thin, and a cup of celery slivered on a bias. The ham was cut into long shreds about one-eight inch thick. Proceeding with the precooking, Jade Snow fried the onions slightly in the frying pan and added the ham until both were barely cooked through. Lifting out this mixture, she put in the celery with a little water and covered it until that was barely cooked through, but still crisp. Two or three minutes only were given each vegetable. Then these three ingredients were beaten up with enough eggs—about six—to bind them together. A little soy sauce and chopped green onions were added for flavor and color, and the dish was ready for final cooking later on. Any firm meat could have been used in place of the ham—shredded or leftover chicken, roast pork, shrimp, or crab, but never beef, which would have been too juicy. A few cooked peas or bean sprouts could have been added to or substituted for the celery and onions. There were no specific proportions to Chinese cooking; just imagination according to personal preference, common sense, and knowledge of basic principles were necessary.

The tomato-beef followed a somewhat different method of preparation. She sliced, marinated, and quickly browned the beef with garlic and oil over very high flames as she had seen Mama do. Since the tomatoes had to be cut in quarters or eighths to preserve their identity after cooking, the large yellow onion and green pepper were also cut in chunks to go with the tomatoes properly. When an hour had passed, there was an array of colorfully filled bowls set out on the kitchen table: the yellow egg mixture dotted with pink and green, a bowl of red tomatoes, one of onions, another of green pepper, and one of browned beef. This freshly cut and precooked food sent delicate and exotic aromas through the house.

In addition, there were two bowls of gravy mixes. One, a basic brown sauce, was made with a tablespoon each of soy sauce and cornstarch mixed with a cup of water. The other was the basic sweet-and-sour sauce for the tomato-beef dish. To make this sauce, a little more cornstarch was used for a thicker consistency. For a cup or so of sauce, two spoonfuls of vinegar and four rounded tablespoons of brown sugar were added. Sometimes more sugar or more vinegar was used—the proportions depending on the dish. Since the tomatoes were likely to be sour, Jade Snow was using more sugar and less vinegar than she would use for spareribs, sweet and sour.

Soon a chatter of voices announced the coming of the guests, who trooped through the back door, and declared their eagerness to help. While they set the table in the living room, Jade Snow proceeded with the final cooking. As only one frying pan was available, she first fried the egg foo young gently in patties like pancakes, using just enough peanut oil to keep them from sticking, and as they became browned she set them in the warm oven and covered them.

She then started the tomato-beef dish by browning the onion wedges. She added tomatoes and green peppers, and let the mixture come to a boil for a couple of minutes to cook the tomatoes. Pouring on the sweet-and-sour sauce, she waited until it had turned clear. Then the flame was turned off, and the beef was added last. She dished up the tomato-beef, and used the pan to cook the other brown soy gravy to pour over the egg foo young.

Such a simple dinner these dishes made, but how the girls appreciated it. They enjoyed the fire, the candlelight, and the gaiety and confidences, as only four college girls with a sense of fellowship can do during a free evening.

Discussing

1. What did Jade Snow Wong cook?
2. How was the food cut for the egg foo young?
3. What kind of meat could be used to make egg foo young?
4. How was the food cut for the tomato-beef dish?
5. Tell about a favorite recipe in your family.

Analyzing: Imagery

You have learned that writers create imagery by using words that appeal to the senses. Read the following sentences from *Fifth Chinese Daughter*. Tell which sense—sight, sound, smell, taste, feel—each sentence appeals to.

1. When an hour had passed, there was an array of colorfully filled bowls set out on the kitchen table: the yellow egg mixture dotted with pink and green, a bowl of red tomatoes, one of onions, another of green pepper, and one of browned beef.
2. This freshly cut and precooked food sent delicate and exotic aromas through the house.
3. Soon a chatter of voices announced the coming of the guests, who trooped through the back door and declared their eagerness to help.

Writing

Imagine that you were one of the guests at the dinner described in the passage from *Fifth Chinese Daughter*. Write a thank-you note to the hostess. Explain what you especially liked about the dinner.

Extending

Speaking and Listening Even though Americans come from different cultural, racial, and ethnic backgrounds, we are Americans all. Meet with a small group of classmates to discuss what kinds of things come to mind when you think of Americans. Later, compare your group's list with another group's. It will be interesting to see how many items are the same and how many are different.

Reading *The American Book of Days,* by Jane M. Hatch, is about what we, Americans all, enjoy—holidays and festivals. This book contains articles about great events, holidays, celebrations, our nation's history, and distinguished citizens.

2 Listening to and Giving Directions

When you give directions, make sure they are clear and easy for others to follow. When you listen to directions, listen for the sequence of steps and for key words and phrases.

▶ **Focus**   In the excerpt from *Fifth Chinese Daughter* you read directions on how to make egg foo young and tomato-beef. Besides reading directions each day, you are involved in listening to them or giving directions yourself.

When you listen to directions, it is important to remember the sequence in which to do things. It will help if you picture the actions in your mind as you listen. It is also important to focus on key words and phrases. Read the following guidelines for listening to directions.

Guidelines for Listening to Directions

1. Listen for the sequence of steps, being alert for key words such as *first, next, before,* and *after.*
2. Listen for key words and phrases that indicate distance *(three blocks, one mile),* direction *(right, straight),* and landmarks *(the next traffic light, a little yellow house).*
3. Try to visualize the position of directional terms, such as *as the top right corner, one-half inch from the left,* and *in the center of the top line.*
4. Listen for numbers that tell how much, how big, and how long such as *ten centimeters, six drops,* and *one-half hour.*
5. Listen for terms that tell you how to proceed such as *outline, diagram, summarize, explain how,* and *research.*
6. Listen for places such as *page 333, Chapter 5,* and *in a test tube.*
7. Listen for unfamiliar words and their definitions.
8. Note special instructions such as *Skip one line between each item,* or *Fold your paper lengthwise.*
9. Take notes and ask questions if you are the least bit unsure about what you are to do or how you are to do it.

When you give directions, you need to provide others enough information so that they can repeat the process on their own. It is important, then, that your directions are clear, to the point, and correctly sequenced. Study the following guidelines for giving directions.

Guidelines for Giving Directions

1. Divide the entire process into separate actions.
2. Think of the order in which you do the steps in the process.
3. Sequence the steps in their proper order. Use short sentences or phrases.
4. Use transition words and phrases to signal that you are moving from one step to the next. Some examples of these words are shown in the Word Bank.
5. Check your directions for any technical words you may have used, and provide simple definitions for them.
6. Work out an introduction, in which you explain your topic, and a brief conclusion.
7. Decide on a visual aid—a sketch, diagram, picture, or object—to make your directions clear and more interesting.

Listen to your teacher read "A Painstaking Road to a New Old Glory," a newspaper article about restoring flags. Notice how each step in the process is described separately. Visualize the process and listen for transition words and definitions of unfamiliar words. Take notes as you listen.

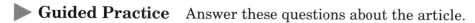 **Guided Practice**   Answer these questions about the article.

1. What sequence should the following steps be in?

   The flag is pasted to a fine silk netting.
   The flag is ironed.
   The flag is washed in cold water.
   The flag is marked with lines.
   Previous repairs are removed.

2. What is scrim? ethyl acetate?
3. For how long does Nancy Cyr soak the flag in water?
4. For how long does she let the paint dry?

Word Bank
first
second
next
then
finally
after
now
last

▶ **Practice   A.** Write in order the directions for each process. Insert appropriate transition words.

1. Making Cookies
   a. Put cookies in the oven for twelve minutes.
   b. Drop small balls of dough on cookie sheet, at least two inches apart.
   c. Mix butter and eggs.
   d. Add dry ingredients to butter-and-egg mixture.
2. Building a Sandbox
   a. Cut wood into four five-foot lengths.
   b. Position the box and fill with coarse gravel.
   c. Cover the gravel with sand as desired.
   d. Form the pieces of wood into a square and nail them together.
3. Changing a Flat Tire
   a. Raise the car with a jack.
   b. Put on the spare tire.
   c. Unscrew the bolts that attach the old tire, and remove tire.
   d. Replace the bolts tightly.
   e. Lower the car to the ground with the jack.

B. Prepare notes for a brief talk in which you give directions for doing something. Choose one of the following topics, or use one of your own. Draw or find a picture that will make your explanation clearer.

4. how to get to your home from school
5. how to set up an aquarium
6. how to make popcorn
7. how to change a flat bike tire
8. how to put up a tent
9. how to play "Capture the Flag"

▶ **Apply/Oral Language**   Give the talk for which you prepared notes in Practice B to a partner. As you listen to your partner's talk, take notes on how clear it is. Are the steps in proper order? Are there enough steps? Have transition words been used? Discuss each other's presentations and revise as needed.

3 Words from Names

Many of the words we use come from the names of people and places.

▶ **Focus** Fruits, flowers, clothes, games, and toys are some of the things around us that take their names from people or places. Some of these names are still proper nouns and always capitalized. Others have become common nouns and are not capitalized.

The word *sequoia*, for example, is used to describe redwood trees, many of which are found in Sequoia National Park in California. These trees are named after the American Indian scholar Sequoya.

As you learned in Section 1, an etymology is sometimes indicated at the end of a definition and enclosed in brackets. It shows the history of a word and how it came into the English language. The etymologies of many words show that they may have originated as the names of people or places.

Food and Plant Names
cantaloupe
Cheddar cheese
dahlia
frankfurter
graham cracker
hamburger
lima bean
lyonnaise
magnolia
mayonnaise
Melba toast
peach
sandwich
tangerine
zinnia

Fer ris wheel (fer′is), a large upright wheel rotating about a fixed axis, with swinging seats hanging from its rim, used in carnivals, amusement parks, at fairs, etc. [< George W. G. *Ferris,* 1859-1896. American engineer, the inventor]

▶ **Guided Practice** Discuss these questions about the etymology of the dictionary entry above.

1. What is a *Ferris wheel*?
2. What is the etymology of *Ferris wheel*?
3. What was the man's occupation?

▶ **Practice** **A.** Write the name of the plant or food that originated from the underlined word. The words in the box will help you.
Example: This flower was discovered by Joel <u>Poinsett</u>.
Answer: poinsettia

1. This picnic item comes from <u>Frankfurt</u>, Germany.
2. Johann <u>Zinn</u> discovered this flower.
3. Would you like this food, made by Sylvester <u>Graham</u>?
4. This dairy product was first made in <u>Cheddar</u>, England.
5. Pierre <u>Magnol</u> named this tree.

6. These fried potatoes come from <u>Lyon</u>, France.
7. In <u>Lima</u>, Peru, you might find this bean.
8. If you went to <u>Tangiers</u>, Morocco, you might eat this fruit.
9. Do they eat this meat in <u>Hamburg</u>, Germany?
10. This fruit might be found in <u>Cantalupo</u>.
11. Anders <u>Dahl</u>, a Swedish botanist, named this flowering plant.
12. This dressing was named after the seaport <u>Mahón</u>.
13. This thin, dry bread takes its name from Dame Nellie <u>Melba</u>.
14. This fruit's name came from the Old French, <u>peche</u>.
15. This food was first eaten by John Montagu, the fourth Earl of <u>Sandwich</u>.

B. Study the following descriptions of characters from history and literature. Then complete each sentence with one of their names.

Example: Frankenstein tried to create a human being but produced a monster instead.

Answer: He's a real Frankenstein, because all his projects end up in disaster.

Descriptions:

a. <u>Pollyanna</u> could always find the bright side of everything.
b. <u>Robin Hood</u> rescued unfortunate people and punished wrongdoers.
c. <u>Solomon</u> was a king known for his wisdom.
d. <u>Midas</u> was a mythical king whose touch turned things to gold.
e. <u>Scrooge</u> always found ways to spend as little money as possible.

Sentences:

16. Stanley was a regular _____ at the meeting, speaking out for the poor and against the injustice he saw in the welfare laws.
17. Carolotta seems to have the _____ touch, for all of her business ventures bring her a great deal of money.
18. When the basement flooded, Nancy acted like a _____, pointing out that now we could freeze the floor over and skate on it.
19. Our manager is a _____, always finding ways to cut down on spending.
20. The class turned to Ms. Chambers because of her wisdom, for she so often was a real _____ in her suggestions.

C. Study the definitions and etymologies below and answer the questions.

Example: Which word is a musical instrument?

Answer: saxophone

Rudolf Diesel

Adolph Sax

den im (dem′əm), *n.* **1** a heavy, coarse cotton cloth with a diagonal weave, used for overalls, upholstery, sports clothes, etc. **2 denims,** *pl.* overalls or pants made of this cloth [< French *(serge) de Nimes* (serge) from Nimes, town in France]

die sel or **Die sel** (dē′zl, dē′sl), *n.* **1** diesel engine. **2** a truck, locomotive, train, etc., with a diesel engine. —*adj.* **1** equipped with or run by a diesel engine: *a diesel tractor.* **2** of or for a diesel engine: *diesel fuel.* [< Rudolf *Diesel.* 1858-1913. German engineer who invented the diesel engine]

gup py (gup′ē), *n. pl.* **-pies,** a very small, brightly colored fish of tropical fresh water, often kept in aquariums. The female bears live young instead of laying eggs. [< Robert J. L. *Guppy.* Trinidad scientist of the 1800s who supplied the first specimens for public viewing]

sax o phone (sak′sə fōn), *n.* a woodwind instrument having a curved metal body with keys for the fingers and a mouthpiece with a single reed. [< Adolphe *Sax,* 1814-1894, Belgian inventor]

tux e do (tuk sē′dō) *n., pl.* **-dos** or **does.** **1** a man's coat for semiformal evening wear, made without tails, usually black with satin lapels. **2** the suit to which such a coat belongs. [′ *Tuxedo* Park, New York]

21. What three words get their names from people?
22. From what town and country does the word *denim* come?
23. What word gets its name from a park?
24. Which of the five words names a living thing?
25. One of these three dates is the approximate year that the saxophone was invented: 1740, 1840, 1940. Choose the one you think is correct and explain your choice.
26. Which is the only word with an American connection?
27. Which is the only word that can still have a capital letter?

▶ **Apply/Writing** Think of five people you know well who have a special quality you admire. Give each of their names an adjective form. For example, you might admire *Sandra* for her logical thinking. You could make up the adjective *sandrian* to mean "clear thinking." Use each of your new adjectives in a sentence.

Example: "Her sandrian approach helped her solve the problem."

Our Living Language
Words from Foreign Languages

> Dear Michael,
> Please pick up some sandwiches from the delicatessen on 1st Avenue. Get 4 hamburgers (no mayonnaise) and 3 orders of coleslaw.
>
> Mom

You've probably seen notes like this or have been given shopping lists from your parents. Did you know that many of the words you use every day are from foreign languages? *Delicatessen* and *hamburger* come from German; *coleslaw* comes from Dutch; and *avenue* and *mayonnaise* come from French.

People came from England to settle in America. Other settlers came from Holland, Spain, and France. They were soon followed by people from all over the world. The English-speaking settlers learned new words from other immigrant groups. The European settlers also learned names of animals, plants, and foods from Native Americans. Here are just a few examples of English words from foreign languages.

Native American	*Dutch*	*Spanish*	*French*	*German*
moose	stoop	ranch	mirage	kindergarten
chocolate	sleigh	rodeo	prairie	bratwurst
squash	boss	plaza	menu	pretzels
tomato	Santa Claus	barbecue	parrot	sauerkraut

Word Play   Make up a list of your favorite foods. Use a dictionary to look up the etymology of these words.

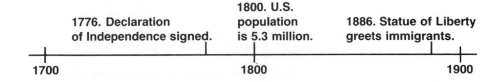

1776. Declaration of Independence signed.

1800. U.S. population is 5.3 million.

1886. Statue of Liberty greets immigrants.

1700   1800   1900

4 Writing a How-to Report

A how-to report explains how to do or make something according to a step-by-step process.

In this unit you will write a how-to report similar to the one you read by Jade Snow Wong in Lesson 1. You can make your report clear and easy to follow by explaining steps in a logical sequence and by using transition words and phrases to connect the steps.

Before you begin to write your report, decide who your **audience** will be—a friend who already knows something about your topic, a child or another person who is unfamiliar with it, or someone who has a particular interest in it. Make sure you have a clear idea of your **purpose.** This will help you keep to the point so that your directions are as clear as possible.

1. Prewriting

▶ **Choose a Topic**   Think about things you like to do or have learned to make. You may want to think about a topic many Americans are interested in, such as baseball. You might ask friends or relatives for suggestions. List all the topics you come up with. Then choose two or three topics from your list, and jot down the basic steps for each. With these topics and basic steps in front of you, ask yourself:
1. Which topic do I most enjoy explaining?
2. Is one topic more likely to be understood than the others?
3. Which topic will probably interest the most people and maybe even encourage a few to try making or doing what I write about?

▶ **Develop Ideas**   Once you have chosen a topic, organize your information. Think about the steps involved in the process. **Use the thinking skill of visualizing** to form mental pictures of each step.

One way to organize ideas is to put them on index cards. If the process you are explaining requires materials, list them on an index card. Now write each step on a separate index card. Number the cards in sequence. Then below each step, write information or details that you want to include.

If your topic were how to mount a map on plywood, your index cards might look like the ones on the next page.

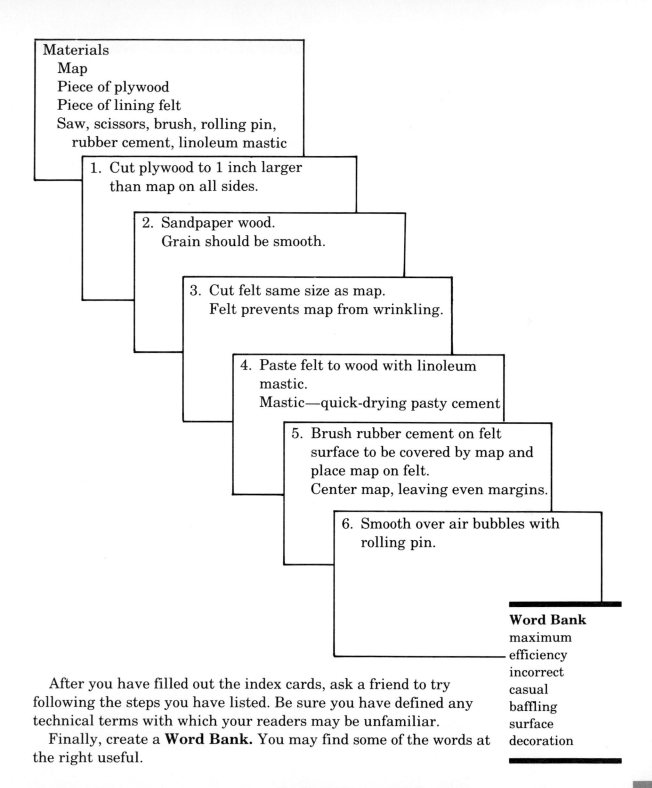

Materials
  Map
  Piece of plywood
  Piece of lining felt
  Saw, scissors, brush, rolling pin,
    rubber cement, linoleum mastic

1. Cut plywood to 1 inch larger
   than map on all sides.

2. Sandpaper wood.
   Grain should be smooth.

3. Cut felt same size as map.
   Felt prevents map from wrinkling.

4. Paste felt to wood with linoleum
   mastic.
   Mastic—quick-drying pasty cement

5. Brush rubber cement on felt
   surface to be covered by map and
   place map on felt.
   Center map, leaving even margins.

6. Smooth over air bubbles with
   rolling pin.

Word Bank
maximum
efficiency
incorrect
casual
baffling
surface
decoration

    After you have filled out the index cards, ask a friend to try
following the steps you have listed. Be sure you have defined any
technical terms with which your readers may be unfamiliar.

    Finally, create a **Word Bank.** You may find some of the words at
the right useful.

2. Writing

When you are ready to begin writing the first draft of your how-to report, start by writing two sentences that capture your readers' attention. Tell them exactly what process you will be explaining. You might also mention how many steps are in the process. A one- or two-sentence conclusion will round off your report smoothly.

▶ **Study the Draft** Before you begin to write, read this first draft, describing how to mount a map on plywood. Notice how the writer has based this report on the index cards that were filled out on page 297. Note also the introduction and conclusion, the inclusion of materials, as well as the use of transition words. Because this is a first draft, there are some errors and crossed-out words.

How to Mount a Map on Plywood

~~Remodling~~ Remodeling an old room that is not being used can be the answer to a space problem. What can you do if you need more space in your home? One thing you can do to change an old rooms' appearence is to ~~put~~ mount a map on wood and hang it on the wall. Everyone can make this decoration theirself.

Few has trouble following these six steps for mounting a flag. The materials you will need are a map, a piece of plywood that is larger than the map, a piece of lining felt that is larger than the map, a saw, scissors, a brush, a rolling pin, rubber cement, and linoleum mastic.

First, cut a thin piece of plywood so that its one inch larger than the map on all sides. Then sandpaper the wood. The result will be a smooth grain. Next, cut the felt the same size as the wood. paste the felt to the wood with linoleum mastic a quick-drying pasty cement. The felt prevents the map from wrinkling or craking. Now brush rubber cement on the felts surface and center the map on the left, making sure to leave even marjins. Slowly ~~take away~~ smooth out any air bubble's with a rolling pin.

After the rubber cement has dryed you're map is ready to hang. If you follow these steps, you will have a wall decoration that you can give as a gift or keep for youself.

▶ **Write a Draft**   Now write the first draft of your how-to, using the information on your index cards. Write on every other line so you have room to make changes. Don't worry about spelling, punctuation, or grammatical errors. You can correct them later.

3. Revising

▶ **Read and Confer**   Read your draft aloud to yourself and indicate any changes that you want to make. Look for ways to improve your draft by adding, deleting, or rearranging information. Ask a classmate to read your work. Use the following questions to discuss your draft.

Conference Questions
1. Has the writer begun by mentioning all materials needed?
2. Has the writer included all necessary steps in the process?
3. Are the steps in sequential order? Are transition words used?
4. Are special terms defined?
5. Are the directions easy to follow? Could they be made clearer?
6. Should any information be rearranged?

▶ **Make Changes**   Use your conference suggestions to make any changes you think will improve your report. Here is a strategy that will help you to make those changes.

STRATEGY: Read over your how-to report line by line. Place a ruler under each line as you read. That way all your attention will be concentrated on that one line. Notice how the writer used an arrow (→) to rearrange information.

> → ~~Remodling~~ Remodeling an old room that is not being used can be the answer ~~to a space problem?~~ What can you do if you need more space in your home? One thing you can do to

▶ **Proofread and Edit**   Check your report for errors in spelling, grammar, and punctuation. Use the following questions and proofreader's marks.

Proofreading Questions
1. Did I use apostrophes correctly in possessive nouns?
2. Did I use pronoun homophones such as *it's* and *its* correctly?
3. Did I use pronouns such as *himself* and *ourselves* correctly?
4. Did I check that pronouns and verbs agree?
5. Did I spell possessive nouns and pronouns correctly?
6. Did I check plural nouns and all other words for correct spelling?

▶ **Make a Final Copy**   When you have made all corrections and improvements, make a final copy of your report in your best handwriting.

4. Presenting

- Present your report to the class. Use visual aids such as pictures, diagrams, or photographs to help explain your topic.

- Create a how-to library in your classroom. Students should make their reports into booklets for others to read in their free time.

See the Writer at Work on pages 558–569 for more ideas on presenting and the other steps in the writing process.

Proofreader's Marks

Make a capital.

Make a small letter.

⊙ Add a period.

Add a comma.

Add quotation marks.

Add something.

Take out something.

Move something.

New paragraph.

Correct spelling.

Revising and Editing Workshop

Connecting Writing and Grammar

- In Unit 22 you read a how-to excerpt.
- In Unit 23 you wrote a how-to report.

Now it's time to use your skill as an editor to improve another writer's first draft. Read this how-to report carefully. As you read, ask yourself these questions.

✔ Are all steps in sequential order?
✔ Do pronouns and verbs agree?
✔ Are possessive nouns and pronouns spelled correctly?

(1) American Indian tribes sometimes make theirselves cooking and eating utensils out of hardened clay. (2) No one make better pottery than the Pueblo Indians. (3) The Zuñi tribe, who's pottery can be expensive, make beautiful bowls. (4) We admirers of Indian pottery can make such artifacts ourself.

(5) First, prepare the clay. (6) The result will be clay that is soft and smooth and free of air bubbles. (7) Press and squeeze the clay with your hands. (8) Now your ready to actually begin making the bowl.

(9) Make a base for your bowl by forming a piece of clay into a flat, round shape about one inch thick. (10) Your bases size will determine the size of you're bowl. (11) Roll more clay into a long, ropelike coil. (12) Attach the long piece to the base and start spiraling it upward. (13) Attach each coil to the one below it with slip. (14) Make more long pieces' as you need them, forming the bowl into the shape you wish. (15) Smooth the bowls coils so that the inside and outside surfaces become flat.

(16) Let the bowl dry for several days'. (17) When its dry, decorate the bowl with an American Indian design.

▶ Revising the Draft

1. The steps in the second paragraph are not arranged in a clear order. Rewrite the sentences so the directions are easy to follow.
2. The order of the steps in the third paragraph is not clear because the writer did not use transition words. Add transition words to the paragraph.
3. The writer did not define *slip*. Look this word up in a dictionary. Add a definition for *slip* to the draft.
4. Add, delete, or rearrange any other information you think would improve the draft.

▶ Editing the Draft

5. The writer made errors in the use of possessive and plural nouns. Apostrophes were used with plural nouns and not used with possessive nouns. Correct the four sentences that contain incorrectly written possessive and plural nouns.
6. The draft contains two mistakes in the use of pronouns such as *myself* and *herself*. Correct the sentences with these errors.
7. Find a sentence that contains an error in the agreement between a pronoun and a verb. Rewrite the sentence correctly.
8. The writer did not use pronoun homophones such as *their* and *they're* correctly. Correct four sentences that contain this type of error.

▶ Working Together on the Draft

Meet with a group of your classmates. Discuss the changes you made in the draft. Listen to the changes your classmates made. Then rewrite the draft on page 302. Include all the revisions you think are important.

▶ Evaluating Your Own Writing

Now review your own writing. Look over the how-to report you wrote in this unit and any other written work you have. Did you spell possessive and plural nouns correctly? Did you use pronoun homophones correctly? The lessons that follow will help you with these writing problems.

5 Possessive Nouns

Possessive nouns show ownership. They are formed with an apostrophe and the letter s ('s) or with an apostrophe alone (').

▶ **Focus** **Possessive nouns** are used to tell who or what owns something. They are formed with an apostrophe and *s* or with only an apostrophe.

Possessive nouns name someone or something, as all nouns do. But they are also like adjectives because they modify, or limit, other nouns. Read these sentences.

> The **boy's** dog was brown.
> The **collie's** collar was red.
> Our **class's** picnic will be next week.

The possessive noun *boy's* modifies the noun *dog*. The possessive noun tells which dog or whose it is—the dog belonging to the boy. What does the possessive noun *collie's* tell? What does *class's* tell?

You will recall that nouns have singular and plural forms. Possessive nouns also have singular and plural forms. The chart shows how to form singular and plural possessive nouns.

Singular Possessive Nouns

If the noun is singular, add **'s**.

cousin	**cousin's** book	Chris	**Chris's** honesty
dish	**dish's** design	Mike Jones	**Mike Jones's** car

Plural Possessive Nouns

If the noun is plural and ends in *s*, add only an apostrophe.

citizens	**citizens'** rights	cities	**cities'** mayors
classes	**classes'** schedules	Joneses	**the Joneses'** car

If the noun is plural and does not end in *s*, add **'s**.

women	**women's** votes	children	**children's** games

▶ **Guided Practice** Tell whether an apostrophe or an apostrophe and *s* should be added to each noun to make it a possessive noun.

lasses   father   thieves   jockey   men   wolves

▶ **Practice**   **A.** Rewrite the paragraph below. Use a possessive noun for each underlined group of words.
Example: The bravery <u>of the soldiers</u> was incredible.
Answer: The soldiers' bravery was incredible.

(1) Every soldier praised the courage <u>that belonged to Washington</u>.   (2) The army <u>of Cornwallis</u> met Washington and his men in battle.   (3) The hopes <u>of the soldiers</u> soared when they saw Washington.   (4) His leadership encouraged the men, and the bravery <u>that belonged to the army</u> returned.

B. Write the possessive form of the nouns in parentheses.
Example: the (sailors) hats   *Answer:*   sailors'

5. (James) supplies
6. a (businessman) briefcase
7. the (princess) land
8. a (farmer) cattle
9. the (actress) costume
10. the (oxen) horns

11. those (people) attitudes
12. the (families) homes
13. the (builders) successes
14. the (students) manners
15. our (brothers) coats
16. the (Dickenses) house

C. Make two columns on your paper with the headings shown in dark type below. Write the singular possessive form and the plural possessive form of each noun in parentheses.
Example: the (dog) home

Answer:	**Singular Possessive Form**	**Plural Possessive Form**
	the dog's home	the dogs' home

17. my (teacher) pupils
18. the (fisherman) catch
19. the (plumber) jobs
20. the (artist) work
21. the (dancer) shoes

22. the (glass) cracks
23. the (doctor) patients
24. the (woman) education
25. the (country) people
26. the (baby) toys

▶ **Apply/Writing**   Imagine you attended a party where everyone picked prizes from a grab bag. Write four sentences telling what prizes people chose. Include a possessive noun in each sentence. Use some of the names below in your sentences.

Maurice	Ross	Betsy	Kris
Kathy	Ernie	Tess	Roy

40   More practice on page 528.

6 Plural or Possessive

An apostrophe is used to form the possessive of a noun. It is not ordinarily used to form the plural of a noun.

▶ **Focus** Plural forms and possessive forms sound the same but are formed differently. Notice the sentences below. An apostrophe is used only with the possessive forms of the nouns.

> **Singular possessive form:** A **walrus's** tusks are used like tongs.
> **Plural form:** Some populations of **walruses** have been hunted almost to extinction.
> **Plural possessive form:** Eskimos sometimes uses **walruses'** skins for tents and boats.

The plural form *walruses* and the plural possessive form *walruses'* are used to show more than one. The singular possessive form *walrus's* and the plural possessive form *walruses'* are used to show ownership. In which two forms is an apostrophe used?

Read the sentences below and decide which words in dark type need apostrophes.

> **Icebergs** float slowly. **Ships** sail to the Arctic.
> An **icebergs** size varies. A **ships** strength is tested in a storm.

Remember, when you write plural possessives, follow two steps. First, write the plural form. Then add just an apostrophe if the plural ends in *s*. If the plural doesn't end in *s*, add an apostrophe and an *s*.

▶ **Guided Practice** Tell which underlined words should be plurals and which possessive. Tell how to form the possessive nouns.

1. In 1899 <u>Alaska</u> gold attracted many <u>prospector</u>.
2. For many <u>year</u> gold was <u>Alaska</u> most important product.
3. Most <u>mine</u> yields were not as great as <u>miner</u> expected.
4. However, many <u>miner</u> stayed to become permanent <u>inhabitant</u> of Alaska, and the <u>territory</u> population doubled in a ten-year period.
5. Alaska was one of the last two <u>state</u> to join the Union.

▶ **Practice** **A.** Choose and write the correct form of the noun for each sentence.

Example: The (towns, town's) boundaries extend into the country.
Answer: town's

1. The (oceans, ocean's) waters became choppy.
2. Then (wave's, waves) washed over the deck.
3. Deck (chairs, chair's) were blown about.
4. The (storm's, storms) fury tossed the ship over the seas.
5. The (passengers, passengers') faces showed worry.
6. The (ships, ship's) captain wasn't alarmed.
7. He had fought many (battle's, battles) with the weather.
8. He asked people to go to their (cabins, cabin's).
9. Everyone followed Captain (Jones, Jones's) orders.
10. The (winds, wind's) force grew stronger.
11. All of the (sailors, sailors') skills were needed.
12. The (engine's, engines) hummed through the night.
13. The (navigators, navigator's) kept the ship on course.
14. By dawn the (sun's, suns) rays began to shine through clouds.
15. Later in the day, the (skies, skies') were blue.

B. Read this report about Thomas Edison's inventions. Then rewrite it, correcting the words that need apostrophes. You will find eight words to correct.

(16) Thomas Alva Edisons first patented invention was an electronic vote recorder. (17) This invention improved the method of totaling voters ballots. (18) Later, Edison improved the financial worlds communication by designing a better stock ticker. (19) In time, Edison set up this countrys first industrial research laboratory. (20) Using the labs equipment, he developed a telephone transmitter and the phonograph. (21) He also developed the worlds first commercially successful electric light bulb. (22) The publics response to his inventions was tremendous. (23) Edisons ideas have made possible many electronic devices.

▶ **Apply/Writing** Write a description of your neighborhood. Use both plural and possessive nouns. These phrases may help you.

Charles's dog   neighbors' cars   people's homes

40 More practice on page 528. **307**

7 Pronoun Homophones

Homophones are words that sound alike. They have different meanings and are usually spelled differently.

▶ **Focus**   Some possessive pronouns and contractions are homophones. **Homophones** are words that are pronounced the same, but are spelled differently and have different meanings.

Read the following sentence groups and explanations. Notice how the words that sound alike are formed differently.

> Can you judge a book by **its** cover?
> **It's** an important part of a book.

Its is the possessive form of the pronoun *it* and does not have an apostrophe. *It's* is a contraction for *it is* or *it has*.

> Where is **your** science book?
> **You're** assigned two chapters.

Your is the possessive form of the pronoun *you* and does not have an apostrophe. *You're* is a contraction for *you are*.

> These are **their** art books.
> **They're** all books about surfing.
> The books are **there** on the table.

Their is the possessive form of the pronoun *they* and does not have an apostrophe. *They're* is a contraction for *they are*. *There* is an adverb which answers the question "Where?" and does not have an apostrophe.

> **Whose** books are these?
> **Who's** the author of this story?

Whose is the possessive form of the pronoun *who* and does not have an apostrophe. *Who's* is a contraction for *who is* or *who has*.

▶ **Guided Practice**   Tell what word fits in each sentence and whether it is a possessive pronoun or a contraction.

1. The cat hurt ____ paw.
2. ____ at the door?
3. ____ going, aren't you?
4. Have them sign ____ names.
5. ____ idea was that?
6. ____ raining again.

▶ **Practice**   **A.** Write the correct word for each sentence.
Example: (Its, It's) unusual for a mother to have twins.
Answer: It's

1. You and (you're, your) family may use special words.
2. (You're, Your) able to understand each other.
3. (Its, It's) not unusual for twins to have a private language.
4. Sometimes twins (who's, whose) lives have been isolated know how to talk only with each other.
5. When people are (their, there), the twins ignore them.
6. (Their, There) private vocabulary is called "twin talk."
7. (It's, Its) special sounds can make it sound foreign.
8. A person (who's, whose) a specialist in speech can help teach the twins how to talk with others.
9. The specialist records the twins when (their, they're) talking to each other.
10. The specialist will learn each word and (it's, its) meaning.

B. Follow the directions for Practice A.

11. Twin talk fascinates anyone (who's, whose) studying language.
12. The sounds of twin talk are strange to (you're, your) ears.
13. Many times (there, they're) hard to understand.
14. (It's, Its) possible for twin talk to be made up of words from different foreign languages.
15. (You're, Your) not sure from what language the words came.
16. Someone (whose, who's) a foreign-language expert might know.
17. (It's, Its) not known exactly how twin talk develops.
18. Both fraternal and identical twins were (there, their) at the conference.
19. (Its, It's) harder to tell identical twins apart.
20. Joy is a friend of mine (whose, who's) mother is a twin.
21. I asked Joy's mother and aunt if (its, it's) fun being twins.
22. They said that (their, they're) relationship is very special.
23. Do you know anyone (who's, whose) a twin?

▶ **Apply/Writing**   Write five or six sentences like those in Guided Practice. Exchange papers with a partner and fill in the blanks in each other's sentences. Check your sentences to be sure you have spelled possessive pronouns and contractions correctly.

41   More practice on page 529.

8 Reflexive and Intensive Pronouns

A reflexive pronoun reflects the action of the verb back to the subject. An intensive pronoun adds intensity to the noun or pronoun just named.

▶ **Focus**   Reflexive and intensive pronouns end in *-self* or *-selves*. Study the chart below showing the forms of these pronouns.

	Singular	**Plural**
1st person:	myself	ourselves
2nd person:	yourself	yourselves
3rd person:	herself, himself, itself	themselves

Reflexive pronouns serve as reflectors, as their name suggests. They reflect back to the subject. Read these examples.

The children taught **themselves** Italian.

I forced **myself** to sit still.

Sometimes we use a pronoun ending in *-self* or *-selves* to intensify, or emphasize, the noun or pronoun it refers to. This pronoun is called an **intensive pronoun**. Look at these examples.

Did you lift that **yourself?**
The President **himself** will address the meeting.

Remember these facts about reflexive and intensive pronouns.

- There are only eight correct reflexive and intensive pronouns. Never use incorrect forms like *hisself, ourself,* or *theirselves.*

- Reflexive and intensive pronouns should not be used in place of personal pronouns.

  Henry went with John and **me**. (Not: John and myself)
  Lois and **he** were early. (Not: Lois and himself)

▶ **Guided Practice**   Choose the correct form of the pronoun.

1. Tom and (I, myself) will paint the mural.
2. We painted the mural (ourself, ourselves).

▶ **Practice A.** Identify each reflexive or intensive pronoun in the sentences below.

Example: Have you ever seen yourself on television?

Answer: yourself—reflexive pronoun

1. In media class, the teacher had us videotape ourselves.
2. She herself gave each one of us an event to pantomime.
3. Some people can apparently discover themselves through mime.
4. Several in the group had seen themselves on TV before.
5. Jerry had never watched himself on TV.
6. The teacher told Jerry he would do fine if he would be himself.
7. Jerry himself did not share in her confidence.
8. We then prepared ourselves for the taping.
9. Some students allowed themselves several days to practice.
10. The students themselves were eager to begin.
11. I myself practiced for one week.
12. Many of us did not act like ourselves, but like other pupils.
13. You often find yourself amused when someone imitates you.

B. Choose the correct pronoun form from the choices given.

Example: Ted (hisself, himself) painted the picture.

Answer: himself

14. Has Larry ever had a portrait of (himself, hisself) painted?
15. Our family enjoyed the portrait of (ourself, ourselves).
16. Some people like to do portraits of (themselves, theirselves).
17. Ted and (I, myself), for example, painted self-portraits last year.
18. We (ourselfs, ourselves) thought we did well.
19. Some famous artists have painted (theirself, themselves).
20. Van Gogh painted several portraits of (hisself, himself).
21. Some artists have drawn caricatures of (theirselves, themselves).
22. A new artist painted Ted and (me, myself).
23. Ted and (he, himself) are good friends now.
24. They (theirselves, themselves) are going to put on a show.

▶ **Apply/Writing** Imagine you are a reporter for the entertainment section of your local newspaper. You are covering a new magic act in town. Write a paragraph about the act, including your reactions to it. Use several reflexive and intensive pronouns.

42 More practice on page 530.

9 Indefinite Pronouns

An indefinite pronoun may or may not have an antecedent. Some indefinite pronouns are singular, and others are plural.

▶ **Focus** The word *indefinite* means "vague, not sure or certain." A pronoun that may refer to a noun but does not indicate a definite person or thing is called an **indefinite pronoun**. Notice the pronouns in dark type in the sentences below.

> Of the two hundred filmmakers, **few** have seen the new movie.
> Years ago **someone** suggested making a movie about outer space.

In the first sentence, the indefinite pronoun *few* refers to its antecedent *filmmakers*, but it does not tell how many filmmakers have seen the new movie. In the second sentence, there is no antecedent for the indefinite pronoun *someone*.

Indefinite pronouns can be singular or plural. Some of the most commonly used indefinite pronouns are shown in the chart below.

Indefinite Pronouns				
Singular			**Plural**	
another	either	one	both	others
anybody	everyone	somebody	few	several
anyone	neither	someone	many	
each	no one	something		

Indefinite pronouns can be troublesome because people tend to think of most of them as plural forms. As the chart suggests, though, many of them are singular and take singular verbs. Some pronouns—*all, any, most, none,* and *some*—can be either singular or plural, depending on how they are used. You will learn more about agreement of indefinite pronouns and verbs in Unit 33.

▶ **Guided Practice** Identify each indefinite pronoun.

1. Does anyone want to go with me?
2. I hope someone will volunteer.
3. Several of you have offered to help before.

► **Practice**   **A.** Write the sentences below and underline the indefinite pronoun in each one.
Example: I hope <u>everyone</u> will compete.

1. Anyone can attend the event.
2. How could anybody miss it?
3. Someone might forget.
4. No one announced the place.
5. Many knew that.
6. Several asked about it.
7. Something should be done.
8. Neither knows about it.
9. Others have already heard.
10. Each will soon know.

B. Write the indefinite pronoun you find in each item below. Then write the antecedent that makes that pronoun clearer.
Example: These cameras are expensive, but others are cheap.
Answer: others, cameras

11. Tourists were in town. Many visited the World Trade Center.
12. Tourists went to the top of the building. Several took photos.
13. The twins didn't take photos because both forgot the film.
14. My brothers wouldn't go. All are afraid of heights.
15. My sisters like the view, and each has seen it before.

C. Write the indefinite pronoun in each sentence below, and tell whether it is singular or plural.
Example: Everyone has responsibilities.
Answer: Everyone, singular

16. Everyone knows about doing chores.
17. Each has agreed on a job.
18. Few would neglect carrying their own loads.
19. Several think their time is limited.
20. Others believe their schedules are not full.
21. Anybody forgets duties at times.
22. Either is able to do the tasks well.
23. Neither was pleased with the schedule.
24. Many are confident of their own abilities.

► **Apply/Writing**   Choose three of the words below. Write the indefinite pronouns that can be made with them. Then use each indefinite pronoun you made in a sentence.

thing   any   body   some   every

42   More practice on page 530.   **313**

Review/Evaluation

For more review,
see Tested Skills Practice,
pages 528–530

37 **Possessive Nouns**   Write the letter of the form of the noun that completes each sentence correctly.

1. The rangers found the ____ backpacks arranged carefully in a circle.
   a. hikers   **b.** hiker's   **c.** hikers'

2. The ____ silence was eerie.
   a. forests   **b.** forest's   **c.** forests'

3. None of the ____ were chirping or twittering.
   a. birds   **b.** bird's   **c.** birds'

4. The two ____ discovery alerted the town.
   a. rangers   **b.** ranger's   **c.** rangers'

5. Police Chief ____ orders were quickly obeyed.
   a. Rosses   **b.** Ross's   **c.** Rosses'

6. The ____ parents were awakened and informed of the serious situation.
   a. childrens   **b.** children's   **c.** childrens'

7. The ____ were stunned by the bad news.
   a. families   **b.** family's   **c.** families'

8. The ____ fears for their children were great.
   a. parents   **b.** parent's   **c.** parents'

9. The ____ duties were assigned by the chief of police.
   a. men   **b.** men's   **c.** mens'

10. The ____ were organized into small groups.
    a. searchers   **b.** searcher's   **c.** searchers'

11. The ____ noses sniffed the ground.
    a. bloodhounds   **b.** bloodhound's   **c.** bloodhounds'

12. The ____ first rays were brightening the sky.
    a. dawns   **b.** dawn's   **c.** dawns'

13. Several state ____ cars roared into the town square and screeched to a halt.
    a. troopers   **b.** trooper's   **c.** troopers'

14. All the ____ doors were quickly flung open.
    a. cars   **b.** car's   **c.** cars'

15. The missing ____ clambered out into the square.
    a. hikers   **b.** hiker's   **c.** hikers'

38 **Pronoun Homophones**   Write the letter of the answer that identifies the word needed to complete each sentence.

16. The Jones School Drama Club was rehearsing ____ annual play.
    a. its   **b.** it's   **c.** neither of these
17. ____ the third time they are presenting *The Wiz*.
    a. Its   **b.** It's   **c.** neither of these
18. "Put more feeling into ____ singing, Julie," the director said.
    a. your   **b.** you're   **c.** neither of these
19. "Remember, ____ the star of the show," he added.
    a. your   **b.** you're   **c.** neither of these
20. "The other actors are putting ____ trust in you," he continued.
    a. there   **b.** they're   **c.** their
21. " ____ really depending on you," the director said.
    a. There   **b.** They're   **c.** Their
22. "I'll do my best up ____ on stage," the star said.
    a. Their   **b.** They're   **c.** neither of these
23. " ____ the actor that is playing the wizard?" the girl asked.
    a. Who's   **b.** Whose   **c.** neither of these
24. Then she asked, " ____ costumes are these?"
    a. Who's   **b.** Whose   **c.** neither of these
25. " ____ is the designer of these costumes?" she demanded.
    a. Who's   **b.** Whose   **c.** neither of these

39 **Using Reflexive, Intensive, and Indefinite Pronouns**   Write the letter of the answer that identifies each underlined pronoun.
a. Reflexive   **b.** Intensive   **c.** Indefinite
d. None of these

26. Dad cut <u>himself</u> shaving this morning.
27. <u>Few</u> of the flowers we planted are growing.
28. The mayor <u>herself</u> will send the invitations.
29. The players congratulated <u>theirself</u> for winning the series.
30. <u>No one</u> ever answers your phone when I call.
31. <u>Several</u> of the cities submitted plans for the Olympics.
32. Did Len <u>hisself</u> return my bike?
33. We found <u>ourselves</u> on a road in the middle of the desert.
34. <u>Each</u> of the judges wrote the winner's name on a slip of paper.
35. Louis and Sherry counted the ticket money <u>themselves</u>.

Writing Evaluation

39. This boy is photographing a rhino in a game preserve in Africa. In this preserve where animals roam free, photographers take pictures from inside or on top of a vehicle. You probably have your own methods for photographing pets or other animals. Write a how-to explanation of six or seven steps and title it "How to Photograph Animals."

1. Before you write, think about the steps you want to include. Try to visualize each step.
2. Write your how-to explanation, using the following questions.
   - ✔ Does the opening sentence state the process that will be described?
   - ✔ Are all the steps in the process included?
   - ✔ Are these steps in sequential order?
3. When you have finished writing, spend a few minutes checking and revising your how-to explanation.
   - ✔ Can you answer "yes" to all the questions above?
   - ✔ Are plural and possessive nouns spelled correctly?
   - ✔ Are pronoun homophones used correctly?

Curriculum Connection: Social Studies

In "A Painstaking Road to a New Old Glory," you heard about how Nancy Cyr restores flags. The article explains the process she uses in a step by step order. The sequence of steps is extremely important in the type of writing that explains something.

Nancy Cyr has an interesting occupation—she restores old flags. Some of the flags she works on could have been made in colonial America. Readers like to learn about their nation's history. Nancy Cyr is someone who gives Americans all a glimpse at their past.

▶ **Think**   Think about what life was like in America two hundred years ago. Identify some modern products that you are reasonably sure also existed in colonial America. You might, for example, think of soap and clothing. Then think about how these products were made. Where do you think the materials were obtained?

▶ **Discuss**   Meet with your classmates to identify other products that were produced in eighteenth-century America. Brainstorm the topic to enlarge your initial list. You might expand your list to include such items as brooms, baskets, blankets, shoes, chairs, pillows, and tables. Then divide into groups of four.

▶ **Find Out**   Each group should choose one of the objects that came to light during the brainstorming session. Then find out how this object was made in colonial America. You may find information in the encyclopedia or in books in your library. Check the subject cards in your library's card catalog. Collect information about the materials, skill, and time needed to make the object. Take careful notes on what you learn.

▶ **React: Make a Booklet**   Each group will write a how-to explanation on the object it has researched. Make sure that the sequence of steps in the process is clearly indicated. Each report should be illustrated with graphics that will make the process easier to understand. After presenting these reports orally to the class, they should be combined in a how-to booklet.

Tested Skills Maintenance

35 **Appositives**   Write the following sentences. Use commas to set off the appositive phrases. Underline each phrase once. Underline the noun it describes or identifies twice.

1. The dahlia a plant with showy flowers blooms in autumn.
2. It is named for Anders Dahl a Swedish botanist.
3. Joel R. Poinsett an American diplomat introduced the poinsettia plant in the United States.
4. Timothy a coarse grass is grown for hay.
5. The grass was cultivated in the early 1700s by Timothy Hanson an American farmer.

36 **Combining Subjects/Predicates**   Combine the sentences in each group to make single sentences with compound subjects or compound predicates.

6. Jana studies ballet. Marta studies ballet.
7. Harry can tap-dance. He can also juggle.
8. Tom plays drums. Dick plays drums. Jerry plays drums.
9. The boys dance in the chorus. They sing in the chorus too.
10. Sue takes piano lessons. She practices every night.

37 **Direct Objects and Subject Complements**   Write the direct object or subject complement in each sentence and tell which it is.

11. My mother teaches mathematics and art to third graders.
12. She seems happy in her job.
13. The third graders like her very much.
14. She became a teacher three years ago.
15. My teacher, Mr. Grundy, knows my mother from college.

38 **Indirect Objects**   Copy each sentence. Label the subject *S*, the verb *V*, the indirect object *IO*, and the direct object *DO*.

16. Selma wrote a film star a fan letter last month.
17. He sent her an autographed photograph three weeks later.
18. Selma showed Molly the actor's picture the other day.
19. Molly then made Selma a frame for the picture.
20. A friend lent them a newsletter from the star's fan club.

31 **Making Analogies**   For each item, write the pair of words that expresses the same relationship as the example above it.

21. knife : chef
    (a) tree : root **(b)** student : teacher **(c)** wrench : mechanic
22. rain : flooding
    (a) brook : water **(b)** itch : scratching **(c)** ball : bat
23. paw : cat
    (a) hoof : sheep **(b)** cat : whiskers **(c)** car : bus
24. needle : tailor
    (a) jacket : coat **(b)** saw : lumberjack **(c)** glasses : eyes
25. pleasure : smile
    (a) hunger : teeth **(b)** test : grade **(c)** sorrow : tears
26. lens : camera
    (a) corn : kernel **(b)** page : book **(c)** car : wheel

32 **Writing an Explanatory Paragraph**   Rewrite the paragraph below. Fill in each blank with a transition word or phrase from those shown below the paragraph.

Anatole Lipinski started his career in government when he was elected to the state legislature. _____(27)_____ he ran for the office of state treasurer and won. _____(28)_____ in that office, he was elected U.S. senator. He served in the Senate for twelve years. _____(29)_____ he is running for governor.

Now   After four years   Then

34 **Writing a Business Letter**   Read the paragraph below, explaining Justin Maloney's need to write a business letter. Then write the letter. The address of the mail-order house is supplied. You will need to make up most of the information for the other parts of the letter.

On March 2 Justin ordered a small desk fan for a Mother's Day present. It arrived on April 14. The package was undamaged, but one of the fan blades was badly bent. Justin is returning the fan. He wants a replacement by May 9, if possible. Justin is writing to Direct-to-You, Inc., 1469 Arroyo Road, Phoenix, AZ 85032.

Explanatory Writing

Theme: Taking a Chance

Imagine what life would be like if no one were willing to take chances. In Unit 25 you will read about a girl who takes a chance as a competitive athlete and learns a new sport. You will also hear about a brave woman who takes a chance when an unexpected visitor shows up at a dinner party. What other people have you encountered in your reading who risked **taking a chance?** Perhaps one of these adventurous people will provide you with an engaging subject for the research report you will write in Unit 26.

1 Literature: Feature Story

Competitive athletes are always testing their skills and taking a chance that they may win or lose an event. The following feature story about a competitive athlete will give you information as well as entertain you. The story is about Elizabeth Cull, who performs rhythmic gymnastics. Do you know what rhythmic gymnastics is? Read the feature story to find out.

Rhythmic Gymnastics
by Herma Silverstein

The stage lights dim, the piano plays a happy tune, and suddenly ribbons swirl, snake, and spiral in the air. The darkened stage comes alive with soaring circles and streamers of color. When the lights brighten, the spectators gasp. Six girls—three twirling long silk ribbons and three spinning colorful Hula-Hoops—are dancing to the music in synchronized ballet steps.

Elizabeth Cull of Los Angeles, California, is one of these girls. As she and two others toss their ribbons like lances, the other three fling their Hula-Hoops backward over their heads. Elizabeth and her teammates ring the hoops with their arms while the other girls catch the brightly colored ribbons by sticks attached to the ends. All six girls perform the stunt without losing a single beat in their synchronized leaps, splits, and tumbling rolls onto the floor.

Are they doing gymnastics? Are they doing ballet? Are they doing a juggling act? Yes! to all the above.

These girls are performing a sport called rhythmic gymnastics in which ballet, baton twirling, acrobatics, juggling, and synchronized gymnastic exercises are all rolled into one.

The 1984 Olympics in Los Angeles, California, marked the first appearance of rhythmic gymnastics in Olympic competition. Yet the sport itself was first practiced by the ancient Greeks, who performed group gymnastic exercises using balls. Later, Europeans practiced rhythmic gymnastics as a noncompetitive exercise. Eventually, Eastern European countries established official rules for rhythmic gymnastics, and the first world championship was held in 1963 in Budapest, Hungary.

In comparison to artistic gymnastics, in which athletes perform *on* gymnasium equipment, rhythmic gymnasts perform *with* equipment—a six-meter silk ribbon, a pair of plastic clubs, a rubber ball, a Hula-Hoop, and a jump rope. Except for the ribbon, one item of equipment is eliminated every season, so that gymnasts actually perform only four routines in competition.

In scoring the event, judges look for originality in the dance routines and a wide variety of stunts, such as rolling, swinging, and throwing the apparatus.

A score of ten is considered perfect, and points are deducted for such faults as stepping off the mat, dropping the equipment, getting tangled in the equipment, and—the horror of all rhythmic gymnasts—twirling the ribbon into a knot.

One of the hardest parts of rhythmic gymnastics is learning how to keep your body and the equipment moving at all times. This requires skilled eye-hand coordination. Elizabeth Cull says at first it's like patting your head with one hand while rubbing your stomach with the other.

When Elizabeth started rhythmic gymnastics, she already had some previous artistic gymnastic training, plus three years of ballet lessons. Her coach felt she could handle being placed in a more advanced group. What a shock, however, when Elizabeth walked into the gymnasium on her first day of practice and discovered that the "advanced group" included some of the top-ranked rhythmic gymnasts in the United States!

She soon discovered though, that these gymnasts had the same kind of team spirit as athletes in other sports. The girls helped Elizabeth learn the basic techniques, which not only helped her score better but also resulted in a higher overall score for her team.

"That's what teamwork is all about," she says. "Sharing your know-how with someone less advanced is putting the best interests of the team first."

For her part, Elizabeth viewed the other gymnasts' talents as proof of what could be accomplished if she practiced hard. Elizabeth did—working out five hours a day every day.

Like athletes in most sports, rhythmic gymnasts learn their routines one step at a time. Elizabeth Cull spent hours just tossing the clubs and catching them, until she could catch the clubs by their long, skinny ends practically with her eyes closed. (Catching the clubs by their wide ends is a penalty.)

"You really have to love a sport," Elizabeth says, "or performing the same movement over and over can get boring. Everyone wants to do the tricky stunts. But it's the athletes who can 'grin and bear' the boredom of repetition who win gold medals."

Although the stunts, called *elements,* sometimes appear easy, Elizabeth says they are actually tricky to master. "If you want to feel just how tricky," she says, "find a volleyball-sized rubber ball. Then hold one arm out to your side, and position the ball on the inside of your wrist. Let the ball roll down your arm, across your chest, and out to the wrist of your other outstretched arm. Give yourself ten points, and every time you have to touch the ball to keep it moving on course, subtract three points."

Today, as more and more young men and women take up competitive Olympic sports that require full-time training, they are often asked if they mind giving up practically all of their free time in order to practice. Elizabeth Cull expresses the viewpoint of many such athletes when she says, "I don't think about giving up my free time so much as I think about how many experiences I've been able to enjoy that I wouldn't have otherwise . . . traveling all over the world to gymnastic meets, making new friends, and feeling super when I master a new trick. Do I regret my decision to train as a competitive athlete? No way. I'm glad I'm a rhythmic gymnast. The truth is I am having a *ball!*"

Discussing

1. What is rhythmic gymnastics?
2. When and where was its first world championship held?
3. What equipment do rhythmic gymnasts use?
4. What chance did Elizabeth Cull take when she started doing rhythmic gymnastics?
5. Elizabeth Cull talks about the importance of teamwork. Tell about a situation where you contributed to a team effort.

Analyzing: Cause and Effect

You have learned that an effect tells what happened and a cause tells why it happened. Complete the following chart about some cause-effect relationships in "Rhythmic Gymnastics."

Causes	Effects
	Elizabeth scored better. The team achieved a higher overall score.
One item of equipment is eliminated every season.	
Elizabeth spent hours tossing and catching clubs.	

Writing

Imagine you are Elizabeth Cull for a day. Write a paragraph explaining what your day is like.

Extending

Speaking and Listening   Discuss these questions with a group of classmates. Then have someone present the group's answers to the class: Is it ever a good idea to take a chance? When might it be a good idea? When is it definitely a bad idea?

Reading   *Harriet Tubman: Conductor on the Underground Railroad,* by Ann Petry, is about Harriet Tubman's life and work. This is the story of a courageous woman who each day took a chance and led slaves through the underground railroad to freedom.

2 Listening to Predict Outcomes

Predict what might happen next in a passage by listening for clues.

▶ **Focus**   You have already learned how to draw conclusions from clues a writer provides. Many of these clues give insights into a character's personality. For example, in "Rhythmic Gymnastics," the writer tells you that Elizabeth Cull works out five hours a day; you can conclude that Elizabeth is a hard worker. When you know what either fictional or nonfictional characters are like, you can imagine what they will do next. When you use clues to make these types of guesses, you are **predicting outcomes.**

The ability to predict outcomes will make you an alert and active reader and listener. When listening, try to stay one step ahead of the story as it is being read. Be alert for clues as they will provide you with a basis for making predictions. Here are some helpful guidelines for listening to predict outcomes.

Guidelines for Listening to Predict Outcomes
1. Remember details and think about what they mean.
2. Make decisions as the story unfolds, but listen for new information that could cause you to change your mind.
3. Notice key words and phrases that provide information about a character or situation.
4. Take note of actions or other details that could affect the outcome of the story.

Listen as your teacher reads the first part of the story "The Dinner Party."

▶ **Guided Practice**   Discuss the answers to these questions.

1. What is the discussion about at the dinner table?
2. How would you predict that this discussion will figure into what happens later in the story?
3. What might you predict about the American?

▶ **Practice**   **A.** Listen as your teacher reads the next part of the story. Then answer the following questions.

1. What does the American notice that none of the other guests see?
2. Where is the cobra hiding?
3. How do you know that Mrs. Wynnes knows about the cobra?
4. What does the American do when he realizes there is a cobra in the room? Why does he do this?
5. Do you think anyone in the room is taking a chance? Explain.
6. Who is the man with "perfect control" to which the host refers? Why does he say this?
7. Do you think the American agrees with the host? Explain.
8. Make a prediction about how Mrs. Wynnes will answer the American.

B. Listen as your teacher reads the end of the story. Answer the questions below.

9. How do your predictions about Mrs. Wynnes match what actually happens in the story?
10. Who was surprised by Mrs. Wynnes' answer?
11. What chance did the American take?
12. What chance did Mrs. Wynnes take?

C. Imagine that the story continues. Answer the following questions, basing your answers on clues you found in the story.

13. What will the young girl, the colonel, and the American each say to the hostess?
14. What will Mrs. Wynnes say to her guests?
15. What will be the topic of discussion now?

▶ **Apply/Oral Language**   Form groups of four or five classmates. Each person should make up a story about taking a chance. Make sure the story has details about the characters and their actions that will be useful as clues to listeners. Take turns telling the stories, without providing endings. Listeners should write down their predictions about each story's outcome. Then have everyone give their endings. Compare predictions and actual endings; as a group decide whether there were enough clues to make a good prediction.

3 Word Roots

Many English words are based on roots that come from Greek and Latin.

▶ **Focus**   If you learn word roots from Greek and Latin, the meanings of many unfamiliar English words will be easier to figure out. The charts on this page and the next show some roots from Greek and Latin that are used to make English words. Notice that some words are formed from two or more Greek or Latin roots. Some dictionaries call forms such as *auto* and *graph* combining forms.

Greek Word/ Root—Meaning	English Word/ Root—Meaning
autos—self	*autocracy*—government by oneself
bios—life	*biography*—account of a person's life
kratos—rule, power	*democrat*—person who supports government by the people
chronos—time	*chronology*—science of measuring time
kyklos—wheel, circle, ring	*cycle*—bicycle, tricycle, motorcycle
dēmo—people	*democracy*—government that is run by the people who live under it
etymos—true, real	*etymology*—study of word origins
geō—earth	*geology*—science of the earth
graphein—to write, draw, describe	*graphic*—shown by a graph
hydōr—water	*hydrant*—fireplug
logos—word, speech, reason	*biology*—science of life
mikros—small	*microphone*—instrument that magnifies small sounds
pathos—suffering, feeling, disease	*pathology*—study of disease
phōnē—sound	*phonic*—having to do with sound
phōtos—light	*photograph*—picture made with a camera
skopein—look at	*telescope*—instrument for viewing distant objects
tēle—far	*telecast*—broadcast by television

Latin Word/ Root—Meaning	English Word/ Root—Meaning
anima—life, breath	*animate*—give life to
capere—take	*capture*—take by force
cedere—to yield	*concede*—allow to have, yield
centum—hundred	*century*—one hundred years
creatum—made, produced	*create*—bring into being
currere—to run	*current*—flow of water, air, or liquid
dicere—say	*dictate*—say to another person who writes down the words
ducere—lead	*conductor*—leader, guide
facere—to make, do	*fact*—thing known to have really happened
fidere—to trust	*confide*—hand over in trust
flectere—to bend	*reflect*—turn back or throw back
forma—form	*formula*—set form of words
gradi—to walk	*progress*—to move forward
jacere—to throw	*project*—throw or cast forward
manus—hand	*manicure*—care of the hands
mittere—send, put	*commit*—do, deliver
portare—carry	*porter*—person employed to carry loads or baggage
premere—to press	*impress*—make marks on by pressing
rumpere—to break	*rupture*—a breaking
scribere—write	*subscribe*—sign one's name
specere—to view	*spectator*—observer
spirare—breathe	*respire*—breathe
struere—arrange	*structure*—arrangement of parts
venire—come	*convene*—gather together
vertere—to turn	*convert*—turn to another use
vocem—voice	*vocal*—having to do with the voice
volvere—to roll	*revolve*—move in a circle

▶ **Guided Practice**   Answer these questions.

1. Where can the Greek or Latin root appear in a word?
2. What might the word *autograph* mean? *captive?*

► **Practice** **A.** Notice the underlined word in each sentence. Write the word and tell which Greek or Latin word or root that it comes from. Also give a meaning for the word. Use the charts on pages 328 and 329 to help you.

Example: Her older brother was <u>inducted</u> into the army.
Answer: inducted, ducere, Latin led into military service

1. They drove away in a new, shiny <u>automobile</u>.
2. His picture was very <u>creative</u>.
3. The prisoner was given thirty days of <u>manual</u> labor.
4. The audience was <u>captivated</u> by Hiram's solo performance.
5. Lionel was asked to <u>remit</u> a check for the overdue bill.
6. He discussed the topic with great <u>animation</u>.
7. The scientist looked at the slide under a <u>microscope</u>.
8. We'll meet for lunch at the <u>convention</u>.
9. The doctor <u>prescribed</u> a new medicine for Ted.
10. You cannot believe Pat, who is a <u>chronic</u> liar.
11. The school will <u>recycle</u> that paper so it can be used again.
12. The committee needs to <u>evolve</u> a plan for finishing the project.
13. Please make a <u>photocopy</u> of that bill for our files.
14. The <u>construction</u> of the office will begin next month.

B. Copy the following English words. Next to each word write the Greek or Latin word it comes from. Then write the meanings of five of the words and use each in a sentence. Consult a dictionary to check your meanings.

Example: inform
Answer: inform, forma, tell, Did he <u>inform</u> you of our change in plans?

15. scope	20. euphonious	25. hydrofoil
16. portage	21. centimeter	26. factory
17. geographer	22. spectacle	27. vociferate
18. courier	23. aspire	28. reverse
19. diction	24. confidential	29. paragraph

► **Apply/Vocabulary** Choose three of the words from Practice B that you did not write meanings for. Look these words up in a dictionary. Then in your own words write two or three sentences that tell what each word means. Do not use the word or its root in your sentences. Exchange papers with a classmate and try to guess which words your classmate wrote about.

Our Living Language

How Words Are Invented

> After I *baby-sit* for my nephew, my
> sister promised, she'll take me in her
> new *hatchback* to buy a *stereo*.

Many words have entered our language by compounding, or joining two or more words to form a new word. Long ago, people began selling goods in a cart they pushed in the street. So the word *pushcart* came into use. The words *baby-sit* and *hatchback* are recent additions to the English language. What is a compound for restaurant food that is quickly prepared? an object that scares away crows? a ship moved by steam?

In addition to making words longer, words have been made shorter, or clipped, over the years. *Stereophonic system* was shortened to *stereo*. An unusual item or *curiosity* became known as a *curio*. *Zoo* is a shortened form of *zoological garden*.

Another method of inventing words is to use the name of the inventor or the place of origin. The man who introduced blue jeans or *Levi's* was Levi Strauss. The scent we know as *cologne* originally came from Cologne, a city in Germany.

Finally, some words have been formed by combining parts of two words. This method is called blending. A *moped* is a blend of the words *motor* and *pedal*. *Simulcast* is a combination of *simultaneous* and *broadcast*. *Smog* is a blend of *smoke* and *fog*.

Word Play Write the words for each clue given below.

1. shortened from *omnibus*
2. motor + hotel =
3. a small fish from Sardinia
4. instrument named after Adolphe Sax

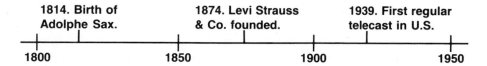

| 1814. Birth of Adolphe Sax. | | 1874. Levi Strauss & Co. founded. | | 1939. First regular telecast in U.S. | |

1800   1850   1900   1950

4 Writing a Feature Story

A feature story is a factual article written to entertain the reader or to give information in an interesting way.

In the last unit you read a feature story. In this unit you will write one of your own. Feature stories often appear in newspapers, but these stories do not report front-page news. A feature story engages a reader's interest by entertaining and informing the reader at the same time. It may report an incredible, touching, sad, or uplifting story about a person, place, event, or other subject.

Spend a few moments thinking about your **audience** and **purpose.** Ask yourself questions like these and decide how you would answer them.

Audience
1. Who will read my writing? Are they about my age, older, or younger?
2. Do they know much about my subject? If not, how much background and explanation should I include in my story?
3. How can I appeal to the interest of my audience?
4. What words and details can I use that are appropriate for this audience?

Purpose
1. What do I want to accomplish with this piece of writing?
2. Do I have a clear idea where I'm headed? How can I make my direction clear to the reader?
3. Do my notes keep to the topic?
4. Do I have the right information and materials to cover my topic?
5. Do I care about my topic?

1. Prewriting

▶ **Choose a Topic**   Where can you find a good subject? The newspaper, the evening news on television, a history book—all are possible sources. Whenever an idea to write about comes to you, jot it down in your journal. Then you will always have a list of good writing ideas on hand. Try to include specific topics rather than general subject areas, so that your list is more useful.

Take the topic "people" as an example. It is a vague subject, not a likely choice for a feature story. You need a specific "story," an event or an angle of some kind to write about. What if you were to choose one person—say someone who has a unique or exciting job that may require taking a chance? That could lead to a topic.

▶ **Develop Ideas**   To develop the topic, ask yourself questions, such as the following:

1. Who is the person?
2. What does the person do on the job?
3. What kind of person wants this job?
4. What kind of chances does the person take?

Make arrangements to observe the person at his or her job. Read materials about the career field in which this person is involved. For example, if you were thinking about a zoo veterinarian, you would want to read about veterinarians, veterinary medicine, and zoos. Take notes during your observation and from your reading. No one can remember everything. That is why writers jot down details. Your notes need only be words and brief phrases such as "injured alligator," "four years veterinary school," and "love of animals."

Then **use the thinking skill of classifying** to organize your notes. Arrange your notes under heads such as *Qualifications,* *Responsibilities,* and *Chances.*

Finally, make a **Word Bank.** The one at the right may provide nouns that you might find useful as you describe people in unusual circumstances in your feature story. Add other nouns to the Word Bank is you wish.

Word Bank
misery
recognition
independence
bravery
apology
endurance
fame
talent

2. Writing

▶ **Study the Draft**   Before you begin writing, read this first draft of a feature story. Notice how each paragraph tells about a different aspect of Dr. Frank. At this stage, the writer did not worry about neatness and correctness and just tried to get ideas on paper.

Next Patient, Please

Dr. Warren Frank arrived at his office at 8:30 A.M. He had been hoping to get some paperwork done. Before seeing any patients. However, a ~~miner~~ minor emergency forced him to change his plans. A seven-foot alligator had ~~hurt~~ injured its foot.

Dr. Frank is the veternarian at the City Central Zoo. Before working at the zoo Dr. Frank was in private practise treating people's pets. He studyed veterinary medicine for four years after finishing colege.

What is a typical day like for Dr. Frank? "Thats hard to say," the vet says with a grin. "There's so many unexpected things that ocur." Even though there are no "typical days a day may be like this.

Dr. Frank begins his day by going over reports, checking the progress of animals in the hospital, and he takes phone calls. He is interpted when a keeper brings in a crane, which Dr. Frank treats with an injured wing. Then another keeper brings in a cheetah for an exam. Keepers hold her down while the vet examines her. If she becomes frightened and afraid, she could be dangerous and unsafe to handle. After the exam, Dr. Frank goes on his rounds, looking in on the animals in the exibits. Dr. Frank then returns to the hospital but examines two new deer who just arrived at the zoo. Finally, the ~~tired~~ exhausted vet calls it a day. Finally, the hungry vet goes home.

What kind of person becomes a zoo veternarian? The answer is someone who loves animals, is a hard worker, and is willing to take a chance (after all, these are wild animals). Someone like Dr. Frank becomes the vet at a zoo.

▶ **Write a Draft**   Now write your own first draft. Write on every other line of your paper. That will allow room for any changes you may wish to make. Use your notes as you write. Try not to worry too much about making mistakes. For now, simply try to get your ideas on paper.

3. Revising

▶ **Read and Confer**   Ask a classmate to read your draft and answer the questions that follow. Use the answers to improve your draft.

> **Conference Questions**
> 1. Does the opening capture the reader's attention?
> 2. Are the details organized clearly? Should any be deleted?
> 3. Does the story inform as well as entertain?
> 4. Should anything be added to make the writing more interesting?

▶ **Make Changes**   Consider the suggestions made by your conference partner. Here is a strategy that may help strengthen your writing.

STRATEGY: One way to make your writing more interesting is to add adjectives and adverbs. Do a quick study of your feature story. Would it be more descriptive and specific if the nouns and verbs were modified by adjectives and adverbs? Notice how the writer of "Next Patient, Please" improved the draft.

> an injured wing. Then another keeper brings in a ^young^ cheetah for an exam. Several Keepers hold her down while the vet ^gently^ examines her. If she becomes frightened, ~~and afraid,~~ she could be dangerous ~~and unsafe to handle.~~

► **Proofread and Edit**   Now check your feature story for mistakes in spelling, capitalization, and punctuation. Use the checklist below and the proofreader's marks at the right to help you.

Proofreading Questions

1. Did I use commas correctly in sentences?
2. Did I combine short related sentences into compound sentences?
3. Did I put modifiers close to the words they modify?
4. Did I avoid wordiness?
5. Did I present items of equal importance the same way in a sentence?

► **Make a Final Copy**   When you make a neat copy of your own feature story, give your story a title that will attract readers' attention. Be sure to include all of the revisions you have made.

4. Presenting

One way to present feature stories is to have the class create a book. Your class may wish to give the book a title such as *Some Specials in Life, Stories That Don't Make the Front Page,* or *Presenting Particular People, Places, and Plans.* Make sure the title reflects the content of the feature stories in the book. Prepare a title page and table of contents for your book. For ideas on preparing and binding the book, see The Writer at Work, page 569.

Another way to present your feature story is to write it on a sheet of paper designed like a newspaper page. Use your title as a headline. Draw thin columns down the page and copy your story within them. Look at a newspaper for design ideas. You might also ask your classmates to write their feature stories as parts of the paper.

Proofreader's Marks

≡ Make a capital.

/ Make a small letter.

⊙ Add a period.

⋀ Add a comma.

∨ Add quotation marks.

⋀ Add something.

Take out something.

Move something.

New paragraph.

Correct spelling.

Revising and Editing Workshop

Connecting Writing and Grammar

- In Unit 25 you read a feature story.
- In Unit 26 you wrote a feature story.

Now it's time to use your skill as an editor to improve a first draft. Read this feature story carefully. Ask yourself these questions.

✔ Does this story inform as well as entertain?
✔ Are commas in sentences used correctly?
✔ Are modifiers close to the words they modify?

Reptile Rapport

(1) Lori Mann has just gotten to work.   **(2)** Even though she is the first to arrive she is not alone.   **(3)** She can feel eyes watching her and looking at her as she walks toward the office.   **(4)** She turns toward a pair.   **(5)** They blink slowly and then open wide.

(6) Lori Mann is in the Reptile House at the Hill Street Zoo. **(7)** I think reptiles are snakes and alligators.   **(8)** Lori is a zoo keeper which means she is responsible for feeding, cleaning, and she watches over certain animals.

(9) The first thing Lori does in the morning is to check each snake.   **(10)** If one looks unhealthy, she contacts the veterinarian, and the zoo that Lori works at is large enough to have its own vet.   **(11)** Usually the veterinarian comes to the Reptile House.   **(12)** If a snake needs an examination that is poisonous, Lori uses a snake hook to take it out of its cage.   **(13)** She puts the snake on the floor or on a table.   **(14)** She holds the snake's neck down with a special instrument, getting it to bite down on a sponge.   **(15)** She then grabs it behind the head and holds it safely while the vet examines it.

(16) Lori must be alert and wide-awake at all moments.   **(17)** She eats well and goes to bed early.   **(18)** She does not want to take a chance and get bitten.   **(19)** Some snakes can bite through their own lower jaws and into a finger of the person holding them down.

(20) Lori has always been interested in animals, especially snakes.   **(21)** Because Lori loves animals so much she looks forward to work each day.

Revising the Draft

1. The writer does not tell what type of reptile Lori takes care of. Add this information to the second paragraph.
2. Add this information about Lori to the last paragraph of the draft: Lori grew up on a farm and worked in pet shops. In college, she took courses in biology and zoology.
3. Delete an unnecessary detail in the fourth paragraph.
4. The writer did not read about reptiles and, therefore, did not know which animals to classify as such. Use a dictionary, encyclopedia, or other reference source to find out which animals are reptiles. Rewrite the sentence about reptiles, using the correct information.
5. Add, delete, or rearrange any other information you think would improve the draft.

Editing the Draft

6. The writer did not use commas at the beginning of two sentences to set off groups of words. Correct these sentences.
7. Find a compound sentence in the third paragraph that is made up of two unrelated sentences. Correct the error by breaking the sentence into two sentences and deleting the conjunction.
8. Find a sentence that is confusing because the modifier is not close to the word it modifies. Rewrite the sentence correctly.
9. Correct a sentence in which the writer did not use the same structure for items in a series. Use the same structure.
10. Two sentences contain unnecessary words. Correct these sentences by eliminating the wordiness.

Working Together on the Draft

Meet with a group of your classmates. Discuss the changes each of you made in the draft. Then rewrite the draft on page 338. Include all the revisions you think are important.

Evaluating Your Own Writing

Now review your own writing. Look over the feature story you wrote in this unit and any other written work you have. Did you have any problems with misplaced modifiers? Did you have any problems with wordiness? The lessons that follow will help you with these writing problems.

5 Simple and Compound Sentences

A simple sentence has a complete subject and a complete predicate. A compound sentence consists of two or more simple sentences.

▶ **Focus**   You will recall that a **simple sentence** has a complete subject and a complete predicate. Either the subject or predicate or both may be compound. Study these subjects and predicates.

S   V
The detective│chased the thief.
S   V   V
The detective│chased and caught the thief.
S   S V   V
The detective and his partner│chased and caught the thief.

To make a **compound sentence,** join simple sentences. A coordinating conjunction such as *and, but,* or *or* may be used to join them. The conjunction is usually preceded by a comma.

> The detective and his partner chased the thief, but only the detective actually caught him.

Two parts of a compound sentence may also be joined by a semicolon instead of a comma and coordinating conjunction.

> The chief congratulated the detective; he was a hero.

▶ **Guided Practice**   Tell whether these sentences are simple or compound.

1. The detective got a medal; the thief got ten years.
2. Tom and Jill read about it in the newspaper.
3. Tom reads the paper every day, and Jill does too.

▶ **Practice A.**   Write each simple sentence on the next page. Place *S* above each subject and *V* above each verb. Tell whether the sentence has a compound subject or a compound verb.
Example: The wind and the rain blew viciously.

S   S V

Answer: The wind and the rain blew viciously. Compound subject

1. The ducks and geese flew south.
2. Some birds swam or hunted for grain.
3. Many flocks landed and ate in a bird refuge.
4. Loud honks and quacks filled the air.
5. The hunters and bird watchers followed the birds' flight.
6. Occasional fog and heavy snow slowed their flying speed.
7. The birds glided and drifted on the air currents.
8. The weather warmed and mellowed in the south.
9. Quiet lakes and active rivers awaited them.
10. Familiar sights and sounds welcomed their arrival.

B. Tell whether each sentence is simple or compound. You should find eight simple sentences and seven compound sentences.
Example: The parrot spoke, but the child didn't answer.
Answer: Compound sentence

11. Mr. Gleason runs a pet store, and his two children help him.
12. Eric and Lida feed, groom, and train the animals.
13. Eric prefers grooming animals, but Lida likes feeding them.
14. Sometimes Eric assists his father; sometimes Lida does.
15. Lida feeds the parrot, and Eric teaches it words.
16. Parrots and mynas can imitate human speech.
17. Fish, dogs, and cats sell very well.
18. Puppies are the best sellers, but they are fairly expensive.
19. Fish and birds are less expensive pets.
20. Two cats live permanently in the store.
21. The cats are playmates, and both are good mouse hunters.
22. The store is closed on Sundays, Mondays, and holidays.
23. Then Mr. Gleason visits the store twice during the day.
24. Eric may become a zoo keeper, or he may become a veterinarian.
25. Lida would like to be an animal trainer.

▶ **Apply/Writing**   Follow the guidelines below to write four sentences. Then exchange papers with a classmate. Correct each other's papers.

1. a simple sentence with a compound subject and one verb
2. a simple sentence with a compound subject and a compound verb
3. a compound sentence

6 Independent Clauses

A part of a sentence that has a subject and a verb and makes sense by itself is called an independent clause.

▶ **Focus** In the previous lesson, you learned that a compound sentence is made up of two or more simple sentences, usually joined by a comma and a coordinating conjunction. When a simple sentence becomes a part of a compound sentence, it is called an **independent clause.** An independent clause has a subject and verb and makes sense by itself. It can be taken from the compound sentence and stand alone as a simple sentence.

>   **S**   **V**   **S**   **V**
> The hound | was weary, and he | panted.
> I called to him, but he didn't move.

The hound was weary and *he panted* are two independent clauses. Each makes sense by itself and can stand alone as a simple sentence. What are the subject and verb of *The hound was weary?* of *he panted?* What are the two independent clauses in the second sentence? What are their subjects and verbs?

Independent clauses are usually joined by a comma and a coordinating conjunction like *and, but,* and *or.* They may also be joined by a semicolon.

▶ **Guided Practice** Tell the subject and verb of each clause.

1. Jeff purchased a book about dogs, and I bought one about cats.
2. My book has many pictures, but only photos are in color.
3. That cat is a Siamese; mine is an Abyssinian.

▶ **Practice** **A.** Write the sentences. Underline each independent clause once. Underline the comma and conjunction, or the semicolon, twice.
Example: Cats vary in size, and many have wild colorings.
Answer: Cats vary in size, and many have wild colorings.

  1. Wild cats often hunt at night, but some prefer dusk or dawn.
  2. Cats see well in daylight, but their eyes also adjust.

3. Cats may meow softly, or they may shrill loudly.
4. Grassland leopards are tan with black spots; forest leopards are much darker.
5. Lions live in Africa, but most of them are in national parks.
6. Tigers are good swimmers, and they may cross rivers for food.
7. Most cats can extend their claws, but the cheetah cannot.
8. Domesticated cats do well as house pets, and wild cats fare best in their natural habitats or in zoos.
9. A cat's rough tongue is suited to eating, but it is equally useful for grooming the cat's fur.
10. Angora cats have long hair; Siamese cats have short hair.
11. Tabbies may have stripes, or they may be just black and white.
12. Most cats have tails, but a Manx cat does not.
13. Cats purr when happy, but they spit and hiss when angry.
14. A cat's hearing is good, and its sense of smell is excellent.
15. Cats hate baths, but they keep themselves clean.

B. Write each sentence. In each independent clause, label the subject *S* and the verb *V*. Place a comma before each conjunction that joins independent clauses.

Example: Dan shops at The Plaza but Cindy shops at The Mall.

               S   V   S   V

Answer: Dan shops at The Plaza, but Cindy shops at The Mall.

16. Cindy wanted a hat but she got a dress instead.
17. Cindy found jeans on sale and she bought two pairs.
18. Dan's father works at Benton's and Dan buys his clothes there.
19. His father sells shoes but he prefers the suit department.
20. Dan may become a salesman but he likes recreational sports.
21. He admires professional athletes and he likes most coaches.
22. Dan skis well and he plays basketball with equal skill.
23. Cindy practices ballet and she sometimes writes music.
24. She likes ballet but music interests her more.
25. One is a possible profession and the other is a likely hobby.

▶ **Apply/Writing**   Write three sentence beginnings that consist of an independent clause followed by a comma and a conjunction. Then exchange papers with a partner. Complete each of your partner's sentences by adding another independent clause.

Example: Eric likes to play chess, but

7 Dependent Clauses

A dependent clause has a subject and a predicate but does not make sense by itself.

▶ **Focus**   A **dependent clause** has a subject and a verb, but cannot stand alone. All of the following word groups are capitalized and punctuated as sentences, but not all of them make sense by themselves.

> We gathered wood for a fire.
> The fire was lit, and the food was unpacked.
> After we ate.

The first group of words is a simple sentence. It makes sense by itself. The second group of words is a compound sentence. Each of its independent clauses can stand alone and make sense by itself. The third word group is a dependent clause. It cannot stand alone as a sentence. It needs to be attached to an independent clause in order to make sense.

> **After we ate,** we put out the fire.

Dependent clauses begin with words like *which, who, that, before,* and *since.* A dependent clause may come at the beginning of a sentence, in the middle, or at the end.

> **Before we started,** we checked our backpacks.
> The person **who told us about a good campsite** was a ranger.
> We set up our tents **when we arrived there.**
> Some other campers **that we met** shared their campfire with us.

A dependent clause at the beginning of a sentence is usually followed by a comma, as in the first sentence.

▶ **Guided Practice**   Identify the clauses in the following sentences as dependent or independent.

1. Laura was in charge because she is an expert camper.
2. Although she was in charge, she was not bossy.
3. We found the stack of firewood that the ranger had mentioned.
4. My cousin Jan was the one camper who recognized the poison ivy.

▶ **Practice** **A.** Tell whether each group of words is a simple sentence or a dependent clause.

Example: Light gleamed through the trees.
Answer: Simple sentence

1. Because the owls were awake in the forest.
2. Every sound in the distance frightened us.
3. The wind brushed our cheeks.
4. After a gentle rain fell over the area.
5. That glimmered darkly on the leaves.
6. We dashed through the dark woods on our way home.
7. Dry branches cracked beneath our feet.
8. Though we didn't notice at first.
9. Lightning flashed when least expected.
10. Which illuminated eerie, looming shapes in the shadows.
11. A frightened rabbit hopped before us through the bushes.
12. After someone accidentally stumbled over its burrow.
13. Because we were very noisy during the rainstorm.
14. Fluttering birds chirped in alarm.
15. Since it was getting light in the east.
16. Someone saw smoke rising from a chimney in the distance.
17. Before an hour had passed.
18. The cabin to the left of us was in view.
19. Though we were very tired and hungry.
20. Everyone ate a hearty breakfast before nine o'clock.

B. Tell whether the underlined parts of these sentences are dependent or independent clauses.

Example: Everyone rose early <u>because the alarm went off</u>.
Answer: Dependent clause

21. It was time to leave, but <u>the bus had not arrived</u>.
22. A group leader whistled <u>because he wanted everyone's attention</u>.
23. <u>People could rest</u>, or they could take a short walk.
24. All the people chose to walk <u>since they could nap on the bus</u>.
25. A red bus came up the drive, and <u>everyone rushed back</u>.

▶ **Apply/Writing** Write five sentences, each containing one independent clause and one dependent clause.

8 Complex Sentences

A sentence that has one independent clause and one or more dependent clauses is a complex sentence.

▶ **Focus** Though a dependent clause has a subject and a verb, it cannot stand alone. It has to be joined with an independent clause to make a sentence. A sentence with one independent clause and one or more dependent clauses is called a **complex sentence.** Look for the dependent clauses in these two sentences.

> The locket **that Ted found in the desk** was his grandmother's.
> **Before he could examine it,** his candle, **which had been flickering,** dimmed and went out.

What is the dependent clause in the first sentence? What are the two dependent clauses in the second sentence?

A dependent clause may come before, after, or within the independent clause in a complex sentence. Look for the independent and dependent clauses in these sentences.

> While he searched for his matches, Ted heard strange noises.
> He lit the candle after he made several tries.
> Although he searched carefully, the locket, which had been on the desk, was nowhere in sight.

▶ **Guided Practice** Answer these questions about the three example sentences above.

1. What are the dependent clauses in the first two sentences? Which dependent clause comes first? Which comes last?
2. In the third sentence, what dependent clause comes within the independent clause? What is the independent clause?

▶ **Practice** **A.** Rewrite each sentence on the next page by adding a dependent clause to form a complex sentence. Use the word in parentheses to introduce the dependent clause that you make up for each sentence.

Example: Ted had to find the locket. (because)
Answer: Ted had to find the locket because it was valuable.

1. Ted could find the locket. (if)
2. He heard strange noises. (before)
3. The locket could have been stolen. (although)
4. Ted might have to call the police. (if)
5. Ted found the culprit in the closet. (after)
6. It was a squirrel. (that)

B. Read each sentence below. If the sentence is complex, copy it and underline the dependent clause. Do not copy the other sentences.
Example: Flying squirrels, <u>which are nocturnal,</u> come out only at night.

7. Although the tree squirrel is a wonderful acrobat, it sometimes misses its mark.
8. If a squirrel should fall, its tail will fan out and function as a parachute.
9. Some squirrels have a permanent home and a temporary one.
10. A temporary nest, which is a loose pile of twigs and leaves, is cool enough for hot weather.
11. Because temporary nests fall apart easily, squirrels build several during the summer.
12. Squirrels prefer nests in tree holes, but sometimes there aren't enough around for all of them.
13. An outside nest is called a "dray."
14. Although tree squirrels do not hibernate in the winter, they may stay in their nests for several days at a time.
15. Tree squirrels, who are omnivorous, can eat almost anything.
16. The seeds and nuts that squirrels bury in the fall are used for food all winter.
17. Squirrels are great foresters because many of these seeds and nuts grow into new trees.

▶ **Apply/Writing**   For each of the simple sentences below, write **(1)** a simple sentence with modifiers, **(2)** a compound sentence, and **(3)** a complex sentence.
Example: Morris climbed.
Answer: **1.** Morris climbed the tree cautiously. **2.** Morris climbed the tree cautiously, but he couldn't get down. **3.** When Morris climbed the tree cautiously, he was trying to get the kitten.

Carlos wrote.   Fay organized.   Sandy shouted.

9 Adjective and Adverb Clauses

An adjective clause is a dependent clause that modifies a noun or pronoun. An adverb clause is a dependent clause that modifies a verb.

▶ **Focus** A dependent clause can do the work of an adjective by describing a noun or pronoun. Such a clause is called an **adjective clause.** Adjective clauses usually begin with words like *that, which, who, whom,* or *whose,* called **relative pronouns.** Read these sentences.

> This is the bicycle **that I bought.**
> The tires, **which were flat,** had to be repaired.
> It was I **who repaired the tires.**

In the first sentence the clause *that I bought* modifies *bicycle.* The clause is necessary to the basic meaning of the sentence because it tells which bicycle. Notice that the clause is not set off by a comma. In the second sentence the clause *which were flat* modifies *tires.* This clause is set off by commas because it is not necessary to the basic meaning of the sentence, which is *The tires had to be repaired.* What word does *who repaired the tires* modify in the third sentence?

A dependent clause can act as an adverb by modifying a verb. Such a clause is called an **adverb clause.** Adverb clauses tell how, when, where, or why an action happened.

> I rode my bicycle **before I ate breakfast.**

> I stopped **where there was a good view of the sunrise.**

> I hurried home **because I was hungry.**

What does the adverb clause in each sentence tell about the action?
Adverb clauses begin with **subordinating conjunctions.** Some of these are listed below.

Subordinating Conjunctions				
after	because	since	until	where
although	before	though	when	wherever
as	if	unless	whenever	whether

An adverb clause that begins a sentence is followed by a comma.

I always use hand signals **when I bicycle.**
When I bicycle, I always use hand signals.

▶ **Guided Practice**   Identify each clause as adjective or adverb.
Tell what relative pronoun or subordinating conjunction begins it.

1. I adjusted the handlebars because they were too low.
2. Gene, who sold the bike to me, gave me a map.

▶ **Practice**   **A.** Copy the adjective or adverb clause in each sentence.
Tell what kind of clause it is.
Example: Pete Durgan lived alone until one snowy night in December.
Answer: until one snowy night in December   Adverb

1. Pete opened his back door because he heard a cat crying.
2. The cat, which was shoulder-deep in snow, looked miserable.
3. Although he didn't particularly like cats, Pete called to it.
4. Before Pete could blink, the cat was in his kitchen.
5. The cat purred gratefully when Pete offered it some leftovers.
6. "You can stay until I find your owner," Pete told the cat.
7. Pete put an ad in *The Express,* which was the local newspaper.
8. Whenever the phone rang, Pete answered it nervously.
9. Since no one ever claimed the cat, Pete named it Fred.
10. The cat that came in from the cold is now Pete's best friend.

B. Turn each simple sentence into a complex sentence by adding an
adjective or adverb clause. Begin each clause with the relative
pronoun or subordinating conjunction in parentheses. Be sure to
punctuate the clause correctly.
Example: Les closed the window. (because)
Answer: Les closed the window because the room was cold.

11. Jeff took a walk in the woods. (after)
12. He will return soon. (if)
13. We don't know. (where)
14. Kevin has a compass. (who)
15. Try the trail to the lake. (that)

▶ **Apply/Writing**   What makes a good friend? Write five complex
sentences to answer this question. Begin each sentence with one of
the subordinating conjunctions shown on page 348.

10 Combining Sentences

Sometimes two sentences with related ideas can be combined into a compound sentence.

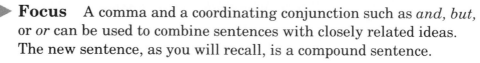

▶ **Focus**   A comma and a coordinating conjunction such as *and, but,* or *or* can be used to combine sentences with closely related ideas. The new sentence, as you will recall, is a compound sentence.

Congress passed a bill.	Congress passed a bill, **but**
The President vetoed it.	the President vetoed it.
Congress passed a bill.	Congress passed a bill, **and**
The President signed it.	the President signed it.
Will he sign the bill?	Will he sign the bill, **or**
Will he veto it?	will he veto it?

Notice that *but* shows contrast in the first sentence. The conjunction *and* shows addition in the second sentence, and *or* shows choice in the third sentence. Where is the comma placed in each combined sentence above?

Be sure that the ideas in the sentences you combine are closely related. You cannot combine the ideas in the following sentences. The price of the tickets had nothing to do with the band's leaving the hall.

The band left the hall.	The tickets were expensive.

You can combine these two closely related ideas.

The band left the hall.	The band left the hall, and
The fans went home.	the fans went home.

▶ **Guided Practice**   Which sentence pairs can be combined? What conjunction would you use in each case?

1. Rover chased the mail carrier. He didn't bite him.
2. The carrier dropped some mail. We helped him pick it up.
3. He continued on his route. I need to buy some stamps.
4. The incident didn't bother the carrier. He would have said so.
5. Our usual carrier didn't come today. It was Dad's day off.
6. Mr. Hill is our carrier. I need to write to my cousin.

► **Practice**   **A.** Combine each pair of related sentences. Use a comma and the conjunction *and, but,* or *or* as indicated.
Example: I am proud of my senator. She often upsets me. (but)
Answer: I am proud of my senator, but she often upsets me.

1. The Senate has one hundred members. The House of Representatives has over four hundred. (and)
2. Every state has two senators. The number of representatives depends upon a state's population. (but)
3. Senators are elected statewide. Representatives are elected by local districts. (and)
4. Congress has a great deal of power. This power is balanced by other branches of government. (but)
5. Congress makes laws. The President carries them out. (and)
6. Congress can go along with the President's ideas. It can refuse to cooperate. (or)
7. Congress can cooperate with the President. Sometimes it does not. (but)
8. Cooperation is usually best. This is not always true. (but)
9. The President can sign a bill. He can veto it. (or)

B. Study the six sets of sentences below and combine the four sets that are related. Two pairs should not be combined.
Example: Some crews plowed the streets. Others salted them.
Answer: Some crews plowed the streets, and others salted them.

10. The storm hit the town without warning. The town was founded in 1868.
11. Would the plows clear the streets? Would the streets remain packed with snow?
12. Commuters jumped into their cars. Some cars were red.
13. Cars skidded into snowbanks. Trucks slid through stop signs.
14. Citizens shoveled walks. The snow quickly covered them again.
15. The snowstorm departed. The weather bureau issued an all-clear bulletin.

► **Apply/Writing**   Write five pairs of sentences about a storm. Combine them to form compound sentences. Be sure to use a comma and a conjunction such as *and, but,* or *or* to combine your sentences.

11 Combining Sentences with Modifiers

Short sentences that have adjectives, adverbs, and prepositional phrases can sometimes be combined into a single, more interesting sentence.

▶ **Focus** Combining sentences can make your writing more interesting and your sentences more forceful. Study the three ways to combine the sentences that describe the lion. Notice where the adjectives are placed.

The lion was old.	The lion was **old, toothless,** and **weary.**
The lion was toothless.	The **weary old** lion was **toothless.**
The lion was weary.	The **toothless** old lion was **weary.**

Each combined sentence has a different emphasis. The first sentence presents the lion's traits equally. The second sentence emphasizes that the lion was toothless. The third sentence emphasizes that the lion was weary. What you wish to emphasize should determine the way you combine sentences.

Sentences can be combined when they contain adverbs that describe the same verb. Study the following example. Notice the commas that separate the adverbs in the fourth sentence.

Andrea worked swiftly.	Andrea worked **swiftly, carefully,** and **accurately.**
Andrea worked carefully.	
Andrea worked accurately.	

Prepositional phrases in sentences can also often be combined.

The convict ran down the street.	The convict ran **down the street and across the bridge.**
The convict ran across the bridge.	

What verb is modified by the prepositional phrase in the above sentence?

▶ **Guided Practice** Combine the following sentence groups.

1. The boy was short. The boy was blond. The boy was homely.
2. He leaped high. over the fence. He leaped onto the trampoline.
3. He jumped vigorously. He jumped expertly. He jumped intensely.

▶ **Practice**   **A.** Combine the groups of sentences below. Then go back and combine each group again in a different way.

Example: The iron fence was rusty. The iron fence was broken.
Answer: The iron fence was rusty and broken.
              The rusty iron fence was broken.

1. The house was old. The house was empty. The house was on a hill.
2. The windows were dirty. They were cracked. They were partially open.
3. Dennard entered cautiously. He entered timidly. He entered through the door.
4. The living room was chilly. The living room was empty.
5. The curtains looked wispy. The curtains looked faded.
6. The floor squeaked faintly. The floor squeaked eerily. The floor squeaked again.
7. The stove in the kitchen was black. It was filthy. It was in the corner.
8. The noise he heard was dreadful. The noise was mysterious.
9. Dennard left without looking back. He left immediately. He left through the window.
10. From a distance the house appeared innocent. It appeared harmless.

B. Read the paragraph below carefully. Decide which sentences should be combined. Use the ways to combine sentences you learned in this lesson.

   Jan walked across the campus. She walked swiftly. She walked confidently. Her black hair shone in the sunlight. Her hair was curly. She walked up the steps. She walked into the principal's office. She placed her books on the counter. The secretary greeted Jan quickly. She greeted Jan cheerfully. Jan glanced thoughtfully at the principal's door. "Is Mrs. Ortez here?" Jan inquired.

▶ **Apply/Writing**   Write an ending to the story about Jan. Use sentences with adjectives, adverbs, and prepositional phrases that can be combined. Give your ending to a partner. Have him or her combine adjectives, adverbs, and phrases where possible.

12 Improving Sentences

Make your sentences clear, smooth, and concise.

▶ **Focus** In writing sentences, keep modifiers close to the words that they modify, use balanced structures, and avoid wordiness. Here are some ways to improve your sentences.

1. Be careful not to use **misplaced modifiers.** Look at these sentence pairs. Each first sentence contains a modifier that seems to modify the wrong word because it is misplaced in the sentence. The modifier is placed correctly in each second sentence.

> They could see the road **barely** ahead of them.
> They could **barely** see the road ahead of them.

> The shark swam in front of us **in the aquarium.**
> The shark **in the aquarium** swam in front of us.

Why are the second sentences less confusing?

2. Make items of equal importance in a sentence balanced. This is called **parallel structure.** Compare these pairs of sentences.

> His explanation was **clear, concise, and gave much information.**
> His explanation was **clear, concise, and informative.**

> She made her point **carefully, precisely, and with force.**
> She made her point **carefully, precisely, and forcefully.**

Why are the second sentences parallel as compared to the first?

3. Check your sentences for **wordiness**—the use of more words than necessary to express ideas clearly and accurately.

> The statue seemed enormous **in size.**
> Sue was often tardy **and not on time.**
> **In the event that** it rains, the picnic will be rescheduled.

The words in dark type in the first two sentences should be deleted. What one word could replace the words in dark type in the third sentence?

▶ **Guided Practice** Explain how to improve the paragraph at the top of the next page.

On the anniversary of my birth I gave a party in my backyard. Setting up tables and chairs was a good idea on the lawn. The guests had cake, ice cream, and drank milk or lemonade when it was served.

▶ **Practice**   **A.** Improve the sentences by making words parallel, by eliminating wordiness, or by repositioning misplaced modifiers.

Example: Last fall in October Uncle Phil took Art and me with him to the zoo.

Answer: Last October Uncle Phil took Art and me to the zoo.

1. We drove in my uncle's new car there.
2. We arrived at exactly 10:30 A.M. in the morning.
3. The day was sunny, warm, and it was also windy.
4. One zoo visitor was studying the monkeys with binoculars.
5. One monkey entertained its audience of onlookers with its antics.
6. We thought the large birds were beautiful at the lagoon.
7. Just as we passed, a gorilla screamed loudly and in a menacing manner.
8. The polar bears were sunning by their pool in the sun.
9. The giraffes moved slowly and with grace.
10. All the animals in the zoo fascinate me in one way or another.

B. Rewrite the following paragraph, correcting misplaced modifiers, making words parallel, and deleting wordiness.

(**11**) The house was old, shabby, and a desolate place. (**12**) The original color of the house was recognizable hardly. (**13**) Now the paint was faded and gray in color. (**14**) The front porch sagged and slanted downward. (**15**) The steps were wobbly and cracked on the side of the house. (**16**) We entered the house slowly, hesitatingly, and in a reluctant way. (**17**) Inside, we found the house needed even more work and repair.

▶ **Apply/Writing**   Write a paragraph describing a place you have visited. Tell what it was like and how it made you feel. Choose a partner. Check each other's work to be sure you have correctly used modifiers and parallel structure and have avoided wordiness.

Review/Evaluation

For more review, see Tested Skills Practice, pages 531–535

44 **Independent and Dependent Clauses**   Write the letter of the answer that identifies the underlined part of each sentence.
a. Independent clause   **b.** Dependent clause   **c.** Neither

1. Tim will bake Lee's birthday cake, and <u>Erin will decorate it</u>.
2. I'll borrow Mom's recipe <u>before they begin</u>.
3. We'll wash our hands <u>and get started immediately</u>.
4. Tim used <u>yogurt</u>, so the cake won't have so many calories.
5. <u>Because Tim needed ginger</u>, I rushed to the store.
6. Tim sifted some of the ingredients <u>after he measured them</u>.
7. I creamed the butter <u>and gradually added the sugar</u>.
8. <u>One at a time</u>, Tim beat two eggs into the mixture.
9. We mashed ripe bananas <u>until they were smooth</u>.
10. Erin lit the oven, but <u>she forgot to grease the cake pans</u>.
11. Tim poured the batter <u>into the pans</u>, and he set them in the oven.
12. When the cake layers were baked, <u>he let them cool</u>.
13. Erin made the frosting <u>while the cake was cooling</u>.

45 **Complex Sentences**   Write the letter of the answer that identifies each sentence.
a. Complex sentence   **b.** Another kind of sentence

14. While I was shopping for Lee's birthday present, I had serious problems.
15. I left my wallet at home and couldn't pay for the gift.
16. I became very clumsy because I was so embarrassed.
17. I knocked over a display of stuffed animals when I stumbled against it.
18. Of course, I felt extremely dumb, but I cleared up the mess.
19. Since Lee's birthday party was at eight o'clock, I dashed for the bus.
20. Mrs. Atkins, who is my next-door neighbor, gave me bus fare.
21. As I got to the bus stop, the bus was just pulling up.
22. The ride to Lee's street was short, and I knew I arrived on time.
23. Before I could ring Lee's doorbell, the door popped open.
24. Lee had been waiting for me because I was the last arrival.
25. The party was a lot of fun, and the cake was a big hit.

Combining Sentences   Write the letter of the answer that applies to combining each set of sentences.

a. Make a compound sentence with two independent clauses.
b. Combine modifiers to make one sentence.
c. The sentences cannot be combined in either of these ways.

26. Some pupils gave reports on reptiles. Others reported on birds.
27. Would you like a bird as a pet? Would you rather have a dog?
28. Birds can fly gracefully. Birds can fly effortlessly. Birds can fly swiftly.
29. Birds can enjoy the sky. Birds can enjoy the water. Birds can enjoy the land.
30. Birds dine on worms, seeds, and fish. Insecticides are killing many birds.
31. Most species of birds search for food during the day. Some species hunt for food at night.
32. Baby birds are greedy. Baby birds are helpless. Baby birds are ugly.

Improving Sentences   Write the letter of the answer that explains why each sentence should be improved.

a. The sentence has a misplaced modifier.
b. The structure of the sentence is not parallel.
c. The sentence has unnecessary words.

33. In June early in the summer, my father finished his very first sailboat.
34. The man gave Dad advice in the red shirt.
35. Dad always worked energetically, carefully, and with great purpose.
36. He painted his sailboat yellow and blue carefully.
37. The sailboat glided through the water rapidly, smoothly, and it was graceful.
38. We hoisted the sails for the first time at 3:15 P.M. in the afternoon.
39. The sails filled as we sailed around the lake with the wind.
40. All of us waved excitedly and with glee at the people on the boats we passed.

Writing Evaluation

In this picture, a skydiver is experiencing the thrill of a free fall. Write a feature story of three or four paragraphs about this person. Include one quotation that the skydiver may have stated about the kinds of chances he or she takes in skydiving.

1. Consider the audience and purpose for this feature story. Create a Word Bank to describe the skydiver in the picture.
2. Write your feature story, using the following guidelines.
   ✔ Will the opening capture a reader's attention?
   ✔ Are the details organized clearly?
   ✔ Will a reader have enough details to understand the story?
   ✔ Does the story inform as well as entertain?
3. When you have finished writing, spend a few minutes checking and revising your composition.
   ✔ Can you answer "yes" to all the questions above?
   ✔ Have you used commas in sentences correctly?
   ✔ Have you combined sentences correctly?

Curriculum Connection: Art

Paul Revere was one of the heroes of the period leading up to the American Revolutionary War. He is perhaps best remembered as the midnight rider of Henry Wadsworth Longfellow's poem. By taking a chance, Paul Revere warned the communities west of Boston that British soldiers were marching toward the countryside. However, you may not know that Paul Revere was also one of the new nation's leading craftsmen. He was an accomplished designer and silversmith whose products were sought after in colonial America. Collectors today highly prize silverware that bears Revere's name.

Silversmithing was a profitable craft in the American colonies. It attracted several hundred workers in eighteenth-century New England. These skilled artisans turned out products of the highest quality. They catered to the needs of the prospering population for useful and decorative utensils. Silversmithing was one of the first arts practiced in the new nation.

▶ **Think** Consider what needs people had for silver objects in eighteenth-century America. Think about the kinds of pieces that were crafted. What might these pieces have been used for?

▶ **Discuss** With a group of four classmates, discuss aspects of early American silvermaking that could be researched. Consider what a knowledge of colonial silver products could teach us about the people who used these objects and the times in which they lived.

▶ **Find Out** Your local library is certain to have several books on silver produced during the colonial period in America. Learn what you can about the people who crafted silver, the pieces they produced, and their design features. Concentrate on at least three typical pieces.

▶ **React: Give an Oral Report** Talk to your class about early American silver. Explain who the artisans were, how they worked, and what they produced. Obtain illustrations or prepare your own for at least three typical pieces. Explain their design features. Point out how the pieces were typical of this early American art form. Indicate recurring motifs, such as the pineapple, which represented hospitality.

Quarterly Test

Sentence Parts

35 **A.** Write **a** if the appositive needs one comma and **b** if it needs two commas. Write **c** if there is no appositive in the sentence.

1. Pat met us at Hilo the big island's city in a jeep.
2. We traveled to Mauna Kea an extinct volcano in Hawaii.
3. Then we were going to climb Kilauea the drive-in volcano.

36 **B.** Write **a** if the sentences can be combined by using the subjects and **b** if they can be combined by using the predicates. Write **c** if they cannot be combined in either way.

4. Pat put on his backpack. I put on my hiking boots.
5. We followed the narrow trail. We found the waterfall.
6. Pat swam in the mountain pool. I swam in the mountain pool.

37 **C.** Write the letter that identifies the underlined word or words in
38 each sentence.
    a. Direct object   **b.** Subject complement   **c.** Indirect object

7. Pat showed <u>me</u> the sacred caves in the mountains.
8. The caves seemed <u>dark</u> and <u>mysterious</u>.
9. He took several <u>pictures</u> of the paintings in the caves.

Nouns and Pronouns

40 **D.** Write **a** for each plural noun, **b** for each singular possessive noun, and **c** for each plural possessive noun.

10. sons-in-law	**12.** James's	**14.** chiefs
11. glasses'	**13.** countries'	**15.** Smith's

41 **E.** Write the letter of the name of each underlined pronoun:
42   **a.** Reflexive   **b.** Intensive   **c.** Indefinite   **d.** Possessive

16. <u>Several</u> of Carol's friends are visiting her at home today.
17. They are spending <u>their</u> lunch hour at her bedside.
18. Yesterday she slipped on the ice and injured <u>herself</u>.
19. The principal <u>himself</u> drove Carol home.

Sentences and Clauses

44 **F.** Write **a** if the underlined clause is an independent clause. Write **b** if it is a dependent clause.

20. When the bells rang, people rushed to the town square.
21. People covered their ears, and the children started screaming.

45 **G.** Write **a** if the sentence is a complex sentence. Write **b** if it is another kind of sentence.

22. That is the couple that will lead the discussion.
23. He practices medicine, and she is a newspaper columnist.

46 **H.** Write **a** if the sentences can be combined into a compound sentence. Write **b** if they can be combined into a simple sentence with modifiers.

24. Helen addressed the envelopes. Ann put the stamps on them.
25. They worked hard. They worked fast. They worked carefully.

47 **I.** Write **a** if a sentence has a misplaced modifier, **b** if it needs parallel structure, and **c** if it is too wordy.

26. The day was bright, clear, and with coldness.
27. As a rule, Ann and Clarice are generally prompt and on time.

Thinking Skills/Paragraphs

30 **J.** Write **a** if the cause is underlined and **b** if the effect is.

28. I broke my radio, so now I need a new one.
29. I can't buy it today because I don't have enough cash with me.

31 **K.** Write the letter of the word that completes each analogy.

30. whale : mammal :: redwood: _____ **a.** forest   **b.** branch   **c.** tree
31. cold : frostbite :: bee: _____ **a.** insect   **b.** sting   **c.** flower

32 **L.** Read the explanatory paragraph in a business letter. Write **a** if an underlined transition expression is correct and **b** if it is not.

   (32) Earlier I reserved a room at your hotel for May 9.   **(33)** Just as a case of flu, I cannot be there.   **(34)** Therefore, cancel my room for May 9.   **(35)** Instead, reserve one for May 28.

Persuasive Writing

Theme: Spare Time

Most people wish they had more **spare time.** What do you do during your free moments—participate in sports, care for pets, take lessons, enjoy art or music? Throughout this section you will encounter people in their leisure moments. In Unit 29 you will have an opportunity to write a persuasive paragraph. You might want to persuade someone to try something you like to do in your spare time.

1 Literature: Persuasive Writing

Tom's parents have a chance to go to Europe in their spare time. They can only take this trip, though, if Tom will stay at his Aunt Millie's farm. Tom does not want to do this. First, Tom's mother tries to convince him that he will have a good time at the farm. She is not successful. Tom's father tries next. Read the following passage to find out what Tom's father says to try to persuade Tom to go to the farm.

from **The Midnight Fox** *by Betsy Byars*

"This is a wonderful opportunity," my dad said enthusiastically. "Wonderful! There's a pond there—did you know that? You can go swimming every day if you like."

"I'm not much of a swimmer," I reminded him. This was the understatement of the year. Having a body that would not float would be a great handicap to anybody.

"Well, you can learn! That is why this is such a wonderful opportunity." Then he said earnestly, "If you go to the farm with the right attitude, Tom, that's the main thing. With the right attitude, two months on a farm can make a world of difference in you both mentally and physically."

"I like myself the way I am." I continued working on my model, which was what I had been doing when this conversation started.

"Put down the model, Son."

I put down the model but kept it in my hands so he would know I was very eager for the conversation to be over.

"Son, this trip means a lot to your mother. She has never had a real vacation in her whole life. Remember last summer when we were all packed to go to the Smokies and you got the measles?"

"Yes."

"And she stayed home and nursed you and never complained once about it, did she?"

"Well, no."

"Now she has a chance for a real trip and I want her to have it. I want her to go to Europe and see everything she's wanted to see all her life. And I don't want her to be worried about you the whole time. As long as she thinks you don't want to go to the farm, she is going to worry."

► **Discussing**

1. What arguments did Tom's father use to try to persuade Tom to go to the farm?
2. How does Tom respond to the idea of swimming each day?
3. Why does Tom keep the model in his hands?
4. Do you think going to the farm is a good opportunity for Tom? Why or why not?
5. Tell about a time that a family member tried to persuade you to do something you didn't want to do.

► **Analyzing: Persuasive Writing**

Persuasive writing states an opinion about a topic and tries to convince others to think the same way. Persuasive writing appears in many forms, including advertisements, book reviews, and letters to the editor of a newspaper. It attempts to convince an audience, the people to whom the writing is aimed, that the opinion is reasonable and acceptable. You are more likely to persuade someone to see your viewpoint if you give good, strong reasons for your opinion.

In the passage that you read, Tom's father wants Tom's mother to go to Europe. What reasons does he give to try to persuade Tom to see his viewpoint?

► **Writing**

Imagine you are Tom's Aunt Millie. Write a letter to Tom, persuading him to come to the farm.

► **Extending**

Speaking and Listening   Meet with a group of four or five classmates to discuss what each of you likes to do in his or her spare time. Each person should choose a different activity. Try to persuade the group that what you do is the best activity. After everyone has had an opportunity to speak, find out if anyone has been persuaded to try a new activity.

Reading   *Life in Rural America,* prepared by the Special Publications Division of National Geographic Society, tells about how ranchers, farmers, and people who live in small towns work and spend their spare time. Country living is described through essays and photographs.

2 Fact and Opinion

Statements of fact can be checked for accuracy. Statements of opinion cannot be proved true or false.

▶ **Focus**   Persuasive writing contains statements of fact and statements of opinion. **Statements of fact** can be proved true or false.

> Tucson is a city in Arizona.
> Tucson is a city in Mississippi.
> Styler jeans cost $45.00 at Pants a Plenty on Mills Road.

The first statement of fact above can be proved true, the second can be proved false, and the third can be proved true or false by going to the Pants a Plenty store on Mills Road.

A **statement of opinion** expresses belief or judgment. A statement of opinion can be supported but not proved either true or false.

> Tucson is a **great** city.
> Styler jeans cost **too much.**

Words and phrases like *great* and *too much* are clues that those statements are opinions, not provable fact. Other opinion words are *wonderful, ugly, boring, should,* and *must.* Words like these express judgments, for you cannot prove that something is "great" or "should" happen.

Statements that contain both fact and opinion are called **mixed statements.**

> *The Monster Show,* which is broadcast on Saturday nights, is a terrible program.

The first part of the sentence above, up through *nights,* states a fact. The last part, *is a terrible program,* is an opinion. You can find mixed statements in many places, including advertisements, letters to the editor, and editorials. Be sure you understand what is fact and what is opinion in mixed statements.

▶ **Guided Practice**   Rewrite the mixed statement above as two statements: a statement of fact and a statement of opinion.

▶ **Practice** **A.** Decide which of the following paragraphs contains only statements of fact, which contains only statements of opinion, and which contains mixed statements.

1. Ludwig van Beethoven, born in Germany, was the best musician who ever lived. His work is especially incredible considering that he was afflicted with deafness during his adulthood. He conducted the first performance of his magnificent Ninth Symphony in Vienna in 1824, but could hear neither the music nor the applause.

2. Franklin Delano Roosevelt was the thirty-second President of the United States. He contracted polio when he was thirty-nine years old. Eleven years later, he was elected President. His hobbies included reading novels by Mark Twain and writing a movie script.

3. The greatest music ever is being made now. All other music is boring. The music of the 1980s will always be the best. The synthesizer is the greatest instrument ever.

B. The sentences below are mixed statements. Rewrite each statement as a statement of fact and a statement of opinion.
Example: Unicycles, which have one wheel, are silly.
Answer: Unicycles have one wheel. Unicycles are silly.

4. Before the invention of television, many Americans worked crossword puzzles, a wonderful hobby.

5. See the best movie of the year, *Cinder-the-Cat,* opening at your theater Wednesday.

6. One of the all-time top films, *Gone with the Wind,* is based on the novel by Margaret Mitchell.

7. The most exciting bicycle on the market, Doublewheel, is on sale.

8. I saw a great ballet, *Rodeo,* by Aaron Copland.

9. Joe watches football—a silly game—every autumn Saturday and Sunday.

10. Chockfullosugar Cereal, which Alex eats, is awful.

▶ **Apply/Thinking Skills** Find an advertisement in a magazine or newspaper. On a separate paper, list the statements of fact, statements of opinion, and mixed statements you find in the ad. Look for opinions made to look like facts.

3 Detecting Bias

Biased writing presents just one point of view, usually unfairly.

▶ **Focus** Persuasive writing may be balanced or biased. **Balanced writing** presents facts that support both sides of an issue. **Biased writing** may present facts, but those facts support only one side, or give only one opinion, of the issue. Biased writing often uses loaded words—words like *fantastic* and *worthless* that not only describe something but also try to influence the reader's view.

Besides loaded words, biased writing may contain faulty generalizations. A **generalization** is a broad or general statement that is based on several specific facts. For example, if the dogs on your block are constantly barking, chasing cars, and digging up lawns, you can make the generalization that the dogs on your block are causing problems. This is a **valid generalization** because it is based on the facts. However, if you made the generalization that all dogs in the world are troublemakers, you made a **faulty generalization**—a generalization that is not supported by the facts.

Learn to recognize bias when you read and to avoid it when you write. Check for loaded words and unfair generalizations. Works like *always, never, all,* and *nobody* often show bias whereas words and phrases like *may, perhaps,* and *some* admit disagreement and are usually found in balanced writing.

Decide whether the following statements are biased or balanced.

A. Our city must have a bicycle path. This would offer safety for bicyclists and would draw the town together because people would bicycle together. Also, people would drive less, and thus reduce pollution. Only idiots would argue against this proposal.

B. There are arguments for and against the bicycle path. On the one hand, it will offer a safe path for bicyclists. On the other hand, it will use up a valuable section of our park.

C. We have absolutely no space for a worthless bicycle path. Not enough people would use the path to justify digging up our fantastic park. Trees and bushes would be destroyed. Nobody really needs a bike path so why wreck our park to make one.

► **Guided Practice**   Discuss answers to these questions.

1. Which two of the paragraphs above are biased? How do you know?
2. Which paragraph is balanced? How do you know?

► **Practice**   **A.** If a sentence shows a balanced point of view, write Balanced. If it contains loaded words or an unfair generalization, rewrite it to make it more balanced.

Example: All Saturday morning television is awful.
Answer: Some Saturday morning television is awful.

Example: Some people prefer not to watch television.
Answer: Balanced

1. Television does terrible things to children's minds.
2. All children like to watch television.
3. All cartoons are amusing.
4. No cartoons are amusing.
5. All television detectives are childish and moronic.
6. There is nothing to be learned from television.
7. There is possibly something to be learned from television.
8. Children should be allowed to watch all programs.

B. Read each of the following paragraphs. Identify one as biased and one as balanced. Be prepared to support your answers.

9. Scary cartoons always cause children to have nightmares. When kids see witches and monsters maim and destroy each other during the day, their dreams are filled with murders and disasters. Therefore, children never should be allowed to watch television.
10. Some scary cartoons cause certain children to have nightmares. When these sensitive kids see witches and monsters fight and threaten each other during the day, they sometimes dream about fights and disasters at night. These children might be better off if they watched shows that are less violent.

► **Apply/Thinking Skills**   Find a brief editorial or a letter to the editor either in a magazine or newspaper. Decide whether it is biased or balanced. List your reasons. Then rewrite any biased sentences so that they are balanced.

4 Finding Books in the Library

The card catalog will help you locate books in the library.

▶ **Focus**   When you want to persuade someone to accept your opinion, it helps to present as many facts as possible. The most logical place to find such facts is often your library. The **card catalog** lists all the books in a particular library. This alphabetical file contains at least three cards for each nonfiction book in the library: an **author card,** a **title card,** and one or more **subject cards.** Each of the cards gives the author, book title, publisher, and place and date of publication. In some libraries, a computer screen shows the catalog system.

Although each card contains the same information, this information is given in different order. If you knew the name of an author who wrote a book on May Lou Retton, you would look for the author card. If more than one author wrote a certain book, a card is given for each author.

If you knew the title of a book on Mary Lou Retton, you would look for the title card. A book titled *Mary Lou Retton: Power Gymnast* would be found alphabetically in a drawer labeled *M*. The book's title is on the top line of the title card.

If gymnasts is the general topic you're interested in, you would

000–099 General
Works
100–199
Philosophy
200–299 Religion
300–399 Social
Sciences
400–499 Language
500–599 Science
600–699
Technology
700–799 The Arts
800–899
Literature
900–999 History
and Geography

look for a subject card under a heading like *Gymnasts* and *Gymnasts—Biography*. The subject would be on the top line.

In the upper left corner of each card is a **call number.** This number helps you find the book on the library's shelves. One numerical classification system is called the **Dewey decimal system.** Dewey decimal system numbers are grouped into specific subject areas. In a library using this system, the shelves would be labeled with the numbers at the left.

▶ **Guided Practice**   Answer the following questions.

1. What kind of card would you look for if you wanted to find a book by Betsy Byars?
2. Under what letter in the card catalog would you look to find a book titled *The Teenager's Guide to Hobbies for Here and Now?*
3. Under what numbers in the Dewey decimal system would you expect to find a book on modern dance? on biology?

▶ **Practice**   Study the card catalog cards below. Use the information on them and on the previous page to answer the questions.

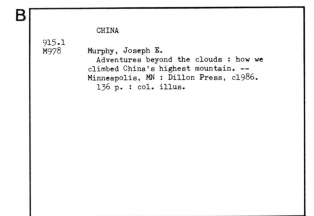

A
```
629.45
R544    Ride, Sally.
            The space in back / by Sally Ride and Susan
        Okie. -- New York : Morrow, 1986.
            96 p. : col. illus.
```

B
```
            CHINA
915.1
M978    Murphy, Joseph E.
            Adventures beyond the clouds : how we
        climbed China's highest mountain. --
        Minneapolis, MN : Dillon Press, c1986.
            136 p. : col. illus.
```

1. Which is an author card? Which is a subject card?
2. Who is the author of the book on card A?
3. How many pages does the book on card A have?
4. If you knew only the title of the book on card A, how would you find it?
5. What is the call number of the book on card B?
6. What is the title of the book on card B?
7. Where in the card catalog would you find other books by Joseph E. Murphy?
8. How would you find more books on the topic of China?
9. Under what letter would you find the title card of the book on card A? on card B?
10. If the books in the library are arranged in Dewey decimal order, would you find book A or book B first on the shelf?

▶ **Apply/Study Skills**   Visit your local or school library. Choose one fiction book and one nonfiction book. Look up in the card catalog (or on the computer) the title card of the fiction book and the subject card of the nonfiction book. Copy these cards. Label the author, title, publisher, and call number.

5 Writing a Persuasive Paragraph

A persuasive paragraph tries to convince others to accept an opinion by giving strong reasons in support of that opinion.

▶ **Focus**   You read persuasive writing every day in advertisements, movie reviews, editorials, and letters to editors. You usually begin a **persuasive paragraph** with a topic sentence that states your opinion about a subject. The rest of the paragraph gives supporting reasons, including facts, to support your opinion. These reasons should be ordered from least convincing to most convincing

Topic sentence: School athletes should participate in school sports but should not be excused from taking a full schedule of other subjects.

Reasons: 1. Athletes should not base all their hopes on having sports careers.
2. "Dr. B," the famous basketball star, urges all school athletes to prepare for an alternative career.
3. A well-rounded student makes a better, more confident athlete.
4. Students are better prepared for life when they take part in the whole school program.

Use the following guidelines to help you write a persuasive argument.

1. Express your opinion clearly in a topic sentence.
2. Give relevant, accurate reasons or facts as evidence.
3. Give specific examples from your personal observations or experience.
4. Quote statements of authority, such as the comments of experts or the results of public-opinion polls.
5. Order reasons from least convincing to most convincing.
6. Use transition words and phrases that signal your supporting evidence. These include *first, next, finally, because, since, more important, furthermore,* and *therefore.*
7. Present a balanced argument. Avoid loaded words or faulty generalizations.

▶ **Guided Practice** Answer these questions about school athletes.

1. What will be the effect on students who take part in a whole school program?
2. What transition words and phrases could be added to each of the reasons given?
3. Do you consider the final reason the most convincing? Why or why not?

▶ **Practice** **A.** Read the topics listed below and choose five topics about which you have an opinion. Write a topic sentence that expresses your opinion for each.

1. homework
2. city recreation centers
3. choosing friends
4. snakes as pets
5. grades
6. movies on home videos
7. college
8. school sports

B. Choose two topic sentences from those you have written in Practice A. List three reasons that support your opinion, from least convincing to most convincing.

▶ **Apply/Writing** Use the work you have done in Practice B and in the previous lessons to write a persuasive paragraph. Choose one of your topics from Practice B for your paragraph. Use the following checklist to evaluate your work.

Persuasive Paragraph Revision Checklist
✔ Have I stated my opinion clearly in a topic sentence?
✔ Did I support my opinions with good reasons, including facts?
✔ Are my reasons organized from least convincing to most convincing?
✔ Have I used transition words in ordering my reasons?
✔ Have I used the correct forms of the verbs *be, have,* and *do?*
✔ Did I present a balanced argument? Have I avoided loaded words and faulty generalizations?

6 Writing a Summary Paragraph

A summary tells main ideas and omits irrelevant details.

▶ **Focus**   In a **summary paragraph,** only the most important ideas are stated. A summary is always much shorter than the original. When you write a review of a novel, short story, or film, as you will in Lesson 7, you use the skill of summarizing. Follow these guidelines.

Guidelines for Summarizing

1. After you read something ask yourself, "What is this about?"
2. Find the main idea. If this idea is not directly stated, you must infer it.
3. Begin your summary with a topic sentence that states the main idea. Add sentences that supply supporting details.
4. Avoid unnecessary details.
5. To summarize lists of things or actions, find a category that covers what is on the list. For example, do not say a character coughed, sneezed, felt dizzy, had the chills, and felt weak. Instead, say the character had the flu.

Read the following summary of *Cinderella*.

   This is the story of patience and virtue being rewarded. The kind and sweet-tempered Cinderella was constantly mistreated by her stepmother and stepsisters. When she was forbidden to accompany her stepsisters to a magnificent ball, she wept. Suddenly a fairy godmother appeared, dressed her in splendid clothes, and transported her to the ball in a magic coach. The unknown beauty dazzled everyone, including a prince. She quickly departed just before midnight, leaving a glass slipper in her haste. In the following weeks, the love-struck prince searched everywhere for the beautiful woman whose foot would fit the slipper. Finally, he found Cinderella and made her his princess.

▶ **Guided Practice**   Answer the questions about the summary.

1. What is the main idea stated in the topic sentence?
2. Has any unnecessary information been provided?

▶ **Practice**   Read the following summaries of the excerpt from *A Midnight Fox*. Then answer the questions.

A. Tom's father tries to persuade his son to go to the farm so that he and Tom's mother can take a trip to Europe. One thing Tom's father mentions is that Tom will be able to go swimming each day. Tom resists his father's reasoning. Finally, Tom's father recalls a time that Tom's mother sacrificed a trip because Tom got sick. If Tom doesn't go to the farm, he could ruin this trip for his mother because she would worry about him.

B. First, Tom's father tells his son there's a pond at the farm. He says that Tom can go swimming every day. Tom reminds his father that he isn't much of a swimmer. Then Tom's father says that Tom can learn. He also says that two months on a farm could make a mental and physical difference in Tom. Tom responds that he likes the way he is and continues working on his model. Tom's father asks him to put the model down. Finally, Tom's father says that this trip means a lot to his mother. He reminds Tom that she didn't go to the Smokies, stayed home, nursed Tom when he got the measles, and never complained. Tom's father wants her to go to Europe and see everything she's wanted to see her whole life. If Tom does not go to the farm, she will worry.

1. Which summary has a main idea? What is the topic sentence that expresses this main idea?
2. Identify a detail that supports the main idea.
3. Find a sentence in both summaries that tells what Tom's father reminds Tom of. Which summary states this more briefly?
4. Which summary contains unnecessary details? Identify three.

▶ **Apply/Writing**   Write a summary paragraph about a short story you have read. Then use the checklist below to decide whether your summary accurately and briefly reflects the contents of the story.

Summary Paragraph Revision Checklist
✔ Have I included a topic sentence that states the main idea?
✔ Have I added details that support the main idea?
✔ Have I avoided unnecessary details?
✔ Have I used one or two words to cover lists of things or actions?
✔ Have I used irregular verbs correctly?

7 Writing a Review

A review summarizes and gives an opinion of a visual or written work.

▶ **Focus**   A review can help you decide what book to read next or what movie to see. In this lesson you will use what you have learned about summarizing and fact and opinion to write a review. A review gives the title, author's name, setting, major characters, and a summary of the story. A film review gives the director's and major actors' and actresses' names instead of the author's. A review also states the reviewer's opinion about the work and gives reasons to persuade others to accept that opinion.

Following is an excerpt from *A Gathering of Days,* by Joan W. Blos. Set in nineteenth-century New England, the story is told in journal form by thirteen-year-old Catherine. Catherine lives on a farm in New Hampshire with her father and sister Matty. Catherine's widowed father has met and is intending to marry a woman from Boston whose son, Daniel, is Catherine's age. Read about the approaching marriage, as told from Catherine's point of view.

from **A Gathering of Days** *by Joan W. Blos*

Monday, May 9, 1831

Again a letter for Father from *her!* And Father makes no secret of it; he is as eager as a boy, and specially goes to the bridge on Mondays so as to be there when the mail's handed down from the Boston coach.

Her letters are neatly sealed and folded, and with a well-schooled hand. Beside them my own look poor and untidy, hard tho' I may try.

Tuesday, May 10, 1831

A new pine dresser was installed today, a large and handsome piece.

Using salt and vinegar, we rubbed the pewterware till it shone, then set it out on the dresser. If we'll not use it until she comes, it will retain its lustre, and such is my intent.

Father goes in two weeks' time. He is very hard pressed these days to put all in order. It came to me 'tis the very last time that this, our house, will be ours alone, not also hers, and Daniel's.

Saturday, May 14, 1831

Father has had a jacket made lest he appear too rude a sort in city company.

"Will not your old one do," I asked, "the one you wore at Closing Day, and still put on for church?"

"Now, miss," he said, "we'll have none of your sulks, and none of your savings either. I tell you we are *fortunate* that Mistress Higham has accepted to make her home with us."

So the new jacket—sewn for a fee!—by a seamstress-woman in town. It is grey, as a sheep's wool is. The colour becomes him nicely. The stuff should wear very well, I think, it being closely woven.

Tuesday, May 17, 1831

"Shall I have need of this or that? Please ask Catherine if . . . ?" Yesterday's letter abounded with questions which Father read aloud. He seems not to think it odd that she should be so unknowing and so unashamed. "'Tis good," he approves, "that she thinks to ask. How many others would? Come then, Catherine, what shall I say? Or do you prefer to prepare a reply that I may carry with me, it being of women's work?"

Even Cassie who is my friend is wont to take her side! "After all, Catherine," she enjoins. "It must be ever so *diff'rent* for her, living in Boston till now."

Wednesday, May 18, 1831

Father departed this morning. Again he drove the Shipmans' team, both to hasten the journey and better present himself. The wagon itself we washed with care and have recovered the seat. The case in which Father packed his clothes bulged with the new-made woolen jacket, a fine linen shirt (of Mr. Shipman's), and other items, his own and borrowed, that he will wear for the wedding itself or in the course of his stay.

He gave us each a kiss on parting. "Look after your sister," were his words to me; then quickly he mounted the wagon seat and adjusted the reins. I did my best to return his smile, and waved till he was gone.

Sunday, May 22, 1831

On this day, in Boston, they married. I will not call her Mother.

Thursday, May 26, 1831

She is less tall than I expected—smaller, even, than Mrs. Shipman; and plainer than Aunt Lucy.

Daniel, too, is plain. He, however, is rather tall, with a sprinkling of freckles, and none too large a jaw. Just below the crown of his head his hair sticks out in a little tuft. D. brushes it often, in nervous gesture, but this avails him not.

"Yes, sir," "No, sir," and "Thank you, sir" were all he said today. 'Tis quite a different brother we've got than I had expected, knowing the Shipman boys.

Catherine's stepmother, Ann, learns of a quilt that Catherine and Cassie left in the woods for a runaway slave. Catherine explains why she took the quilt, and awaits her stepmother's response.

Monday, May 30, 1831

I am to make a replacing quilt. That she has decided & our father agreed. When I protested I could do it not—that I knew hemming, running, and felling, overstitch and buttonhole, but not to make a quilt—she smiled despite the solemn moment, and my urgency.

"All that should make it easy," she said. "Besides I am here now, to teach you."

Then she stretched out a hand to me. Whereat I cried, as I'd not done before—nor have I done for months and years—and when at last I looked at her I saw her own eyes glistened.

Now read this review of the entire book. Note how the student first summarizes the story, major characters, and plot and then tries to persuade others to accept her opinion of the work.

In the novel <u>A Gathering of Days</u>, by Joan W. Blos, thirteen-year-old Catherine struggles with her innermost feelings as her father prepares to marry a widow who has a son, Daniel, Catherine's age. Catherine, who lives with her father and sister in rural New Hampshire during the nineteenth century, resists the changes about to enter her life. She relates her story in diary form, where she expresses her confusion and hostility. Catherine's entries vividly detail her daily life and the events that finally make her resolve the conflict she feels.

<u>A Gathering of Days</u> is one of the most enjoyable books I've

read in a while. The use of diary entries to tell a story is both unique and effective. I could hardly put this book down. We all like to know about other people's secrets and you learn about Catherine's in A Gathering of Days. Because Catherine is such a likable character and because she seems so real, you will find yourself truly caring about what happens to her. You will realize that teenagers of long ago faced some of the same problems growing up that we do today. It is no surprise that this book won the Newbery Medal and American Book Award. It certainly wins my vote for a definite must read.

▶ **Guided Practice**   Answer these questions about the review of *A Gathering of Days*.

1. Which paragraph is a summary of the book?
2. What is the book about?
3. Which paragraph contains the reviewer's opinion?
4. What is the reviewer's opinion of the book?

▶ **Practice**   Answer these questions to plan your own review.

1. What is the name of the work you plan to review?
2. Who wrote it?
3. If it is a film, who are the major actors and actresses? Who is the director?
4. Who are the main characters?
5. What is the setting?
6. What is the main idea that the story is about?
7. List 5–8 details that summarize the plot.
8. Did you enjoy the work you reviewed? Why or why not?
9. Do you recommend that others read or see it? List your reasons.

▶ **Apply/Writing**   Write the review that you planned in Practice. Use the following checklist when you have finished.

Review Revision Checklist
✔ Did I include the title, author's (or director's, actors, and actresses') name, setting, and major characters?
✔ Did I summarize the plot briefly?
✔ Did I state my opinion clearly and give reasons for it?
✔ Did I use troublesome verbs such as *lie* and *lay* correctly?

Revising and Editing Workshop

Connecting Writing and Grammar

- In Unit 28 you read an example of persuasive writing.
- In Unit 29 you wrote a persuasive paragraph, a summary paragraph, and a review.

Now it's time to use your skill as an editor to improve another writer's first draft. Read this persuasive paragraph carefully. As you read, ask yourself these questions.

✔ Is the writer's opinion stated in a topic sentence?
✔ Are the correct forms of the verbs *be, have,* and *do* used?
✔ Are the past and past participle forms of irregular verbs formed correctly?

(1) In 1987 *Growing Up* magazine reported that boys and girls are born with different interests, but this is stupid. (2) I be shocked at this conclusion. (3) Boys and girls ain't born this way. (4) You must of heard that parents and teachers treat boys and girls differently. (5) I has observed this frequently. (6) All boys are given worthwhile toys like trucks and building blocks by parents, while all girls are showered with useless stuffed animals and tea sets. (7) In play groups, little boys have chose to play with trucks. (8) Little girls have took dolls. (9) A son is always encouraged by his father to play rougher games and to participate in sports. (10) A man will admit that he gone to ball games with his father. (11) A woman can't say that she has went to ball games. (12) A daughter is never encouraged by her parents to participate in active games. (13) A daughter don't complain about this either! (14) Some math and science is learned by all boys and girls in American schools. (15) However, teachers always set down with boys and explain the difficult problems. (16) They spend more time learning boys these subjects. (17) Too bad they never done this with girls. (18) Is it any wonder that boys and girls behave differently?

▶ Revising the Draft

1. The draft does not contain a topic sentence that states the writer's opinion. Add one to the draft.
2. The draft is biased because the writer has used several loaded words and faulty generalizations. Delete these and add words such as *may, perhaps, some,* and *often* to make the writing balanced.
3. The writer did not use words and phrases to signal supporting evidence. Add transition words and phrases to the draft.
4. Add, delete, or rearrange any other information you think would improve the draft.

▶ Editing the Draft

5. The past and past participle forms of the verbs *go, choose,* and *take* are used incorrectly. Correct the four sentences that contain these errors.
6. Two sentences do not use forms of the verb *be* correctly. Correct the sentences with these errors.
7. Two sentences do not use forms of the verb *have* correctly. Correct the sentences with these errors.
8. Two sentences do not use forms of the verb *do* correctly. Correct the sentences with these errors.
9. The writer confused forms of the verbs *set* and *sit* and the verbs *teach* and *learn*. Correct the two sentences that contain these errors.

▶ Working Together on the Draft

Meet with a group of your classmates. Discuss the changes you made in the draft. Listen to the changes your classmates made. Then rewrite the draft on page 380. Include all the revisions you think are important.

▶ Evaluating Your Own Writing

Now review your own writing. Look over the persuasive paragraph, the summary paragraph and the review you wrote in this unit plus any other written work you have. Did you have any problems with the past and past participle forms of irregular verbs? Did you have any problems using the verbs *be, have,* and *do?* The lessons that follow will help you with these writing problems.

8 Principal Parts of Irregular Verbs

The past and past participle forms of irregular verbs do not end in *-ed*.

▶ **Focus**   All verbs have four principle parts. They are the present, the present participle, the past, and the past participle. The past and past participle forms of regular verbs end in *-ed*, for example, *followed, have followed* and *prepared, have prepared*.

The past and past participle of irregular verbs are not formed in the same way. The chart below shows principal parts of common irregular verbs.

Present	Present Participle	Past	Past Participle
run	(is) running	ran	(has, have, had) run
come	(is) coming	came	(has, have, had) come
become	(is) becoming	became	(has, have, had) become
go	(is) going	went	(has, have, had) gone
begin	(is) beginning	began	(has, have, had) begun
see	(is) seeing	saw	(has, have, had) seen

Two guidelines will help you use the past and past participle forms of irregular verbs correctly.

1. Don't use the part participle form without an auxiliary verb such as *have, has,* or *had.*

   Ian **has become** a whale lover. (Not: Ian become)
   We **have seen** the whales out at sea. (Not: We seen)

2. Don't use the past form with an auxiliary verb.

   Ian **began** a book about whales. (Not: Ian has began)
   He **went** to the science museum. (Not: He had went)

Some irregular verbs can be grouped according to the patterns by which they change. Try to learn these patterns. Note that the past participle is always used with a helping verb like *has, have,* or *had.* (Since the present participle presents no problem it is not included in the chart.)

Present	Past	Past Participle
grow	grew	(has, have, had) grown
know	knew	(has, have, had) known
throw	threw	(has, have, had) thrown
blow	blew	(has, have, had) blown
fly	flew	(has, have, had) flown
draw	drew	(has, have, had) drawn
wear	wore	(has, have, had) worn
tear	tore	(has, have, had) torn
swear	swore	(has, have, had) sworn
ring	rang	(has, have, had) rung
sing	sang, sung	(has, have, had) sung
sink	sank, sunk	(has, have, had) sunk
swim	swam	(has, have, had) swum
spring	sprang, sprung	(has, have, had) sprung
drink	drank	(has, have, had) drunk
shrink	shrank, shrunk	(has, have, had) shrunk

What spelling changes occur in the *grow* group of words? in the *wear* group? in the *ring* group? Which four verbs in the *ring* group have two acceptable past forms? *Grow* changes to -*ew* and then to -*own* or -*awn, wear* to -*ore,* then -*orn; ring* changes only vowels.

▶ **Guided Practice**   Tell whether the past or past participle form of the verb in parentheses should complete each sentence.

1. Yesterday Ian ____ a blue whale for the first time. (see)
2. It had ____ near his boat. (swim)
3. I have myself ____ interested in studying whales. (grow)
4. I had ____ to the marine museum one day. (go)
5. There Ian and I ____ into each other. (run)
6. Ian ____ many facts about whales. (know)
7. He had ____ a wonderful picture of a whale. (draw)

▶ **Practice**   **A.** Complete each sentence with the correct past or past participle form of the verb in parentheses.

Example: Track has _____ a very popular sport. (become)
Answer: Track has become a very popular sport.

1. Sharon had _____ to one track meet. (go)
2. A week later she _____ to another one. (go)
3. She _____ someone who was a runner. (know)
4. She had _____ this person in both races. (see)
5. Soon Sharon _____ a runner herself. (become)
6. She _____ to work out every day after school. (begin)
7. She _____ herself into the activity. (throw)
8. With her teammates, she _____ five miles a day. (run)
9. She had _____ to get stronger and faster. (begin)
10. The day of the race _____ near. (draw)
11. Finally, the big day had _____. (come)
12. Sharon _____ a pair of new running shorts. (wear)
13. She had _____ her old ones. (tear)
14. Her entire family had _____ to watch her first race. (come)
15. Before the race, everyone _____ the national anthem. (sing)
16. The starting bell had _____ loudly. (ring)
17. Sharon _____ forward ahead of the other runners. (spring)
18. The coach had never _____ her run so well. (see)
19. That day she _____ the 220-meter race and won. (run)
20. After the race, she _____ several glasses of water. (drink)
21. The next year she _____ the state champion. (become)
22. Her team _____ to the national meet in Idaho. (fly)
23. Her career in track _____ as a spectator. (begin)
24. Now she has _____ one of the best runners in the country. (become)

B. Write the correct past or past participle form of the verb.
Example: The players (drank, drunk) water during the time-out.
Answer: drank

25. The referee had (blew, blown) the whistle.
26. The quarterback dropped back and (threw, thrown) a pass.
27. He had (threw, thrown) the ball to the receiver.
28. The receiver (ran, run) to catch the ball.
29. The receiver had (sprang, sprung) high in the air but still missed the ball.

30. The audience (began, begun) to shout and boo the players.
31. Clearly the crowd had (became, become) upset.
32. The team (drew, drawn) into a close huddle.
33. In the huddle the quarterback had (sank, sunk) to his knees.
34. At first he had not (knew, known) what play to call.
35. An idea (grew, grown) in his mind while he knelt there.
36. The players (went, gone) back to their positions.
37. The quarterback (began, begun) to give signals.
38. He had (sang, sung) out the signals loudly and clearly.
39. A cry of disappointment (rang, rung) out from the crowd.
40. The quarterback had (threw, thrown) the ball to a running back.
41. The running back had not (saw, seen) a tackler behind him.
42. Both players had (went, gone) down.
43. The ball had (flew, flown) out of the running back's hands.
44. Everyone had (knew, known) it would be a close game.

C. Rewrite each sentence to make the verb correct.
Example: The tire had sprang a leak.
Answer: The tire had sprung a leak.

45. I had grow to love my old car.
46. I had swore never to get rid of it.
47. At one time it flown over the highways.
48. Now its engine has wore out somewhat.
49. It has blow many tires.
50. The muffler has sink closer to the ground.
51. The seat belt buzzer has rang its last warning.
52. Among my friends I have sang its praises.

▶ **Apply/Writing**   Write at least five sentences telling about what you do in your spare time. Use the past or past participle form of some or all of the verbs below.

know   become   wear   run   go   swim   spring

9 More Irregular Verbs

The irregular verbs *break*, *drive*, and *bring* represent three more patterns.

▶ **Focus**   In each group of irregular verbs shown below, the changes from present to past to past participle are similar. Study the chart and look for the patterns.

Present	Past	Past Participle
break	broke	(has, have, had) broken
speak	spoke	(has, have, had) spoken
steal	stole	(has, have, had) stolen
freeze	froze	(has, have, had) frozen
choose	chose	(has, have, had) chosen
drive	drove	(has, have, had) driven
eat	ate	(has, have, had) eaten
fall	fell	(has, have, had) fallen
ride	rode	(has, have, had) ridden
write	wrote	(has, have, had) written
give	gave	(has, have, had) given
take	took	(has, have, had) taken
bring	brought	(has, have, had) brought
think	thought	(has, have, had) thought
buy	bought	(has, have, had) bought
teach	taught	(has, have, had) taught
lead	led	(has, have, had) led
lend	lent	(has, have, had) lent
leave	left	(has, have, had) left
find	found	(has, have, had) found
say	said	(has, have, had) said
sting	stung	(has, have, had) stung
swing	swung	(has, have, had) swung

► **Guided Practice**   Answer these questions about each group of words in the chart on page 386.

1. For the first group of words, what pattern do you notice when the verb changes from the present to the past and then to the past participle?
2. What pattern do you notice for the second group of verbs?
3. What pattern do you notice for the third group of verbs?

► **Practice**   **A.** Write each sentence, using the correct past or past participle form of the verb in parentheses.
Example: Zack and Zena (ate, eaten) lunch at their grandmother's.
Answer: Zack and Zena ate lunch at their grandmother's.

1. Zack and Zena had (chose, chosen) to ignore each other.
2. They had not (spoke, spoken) for over an hour.
3. They had (ate, eaten) lunch in angry silence.
4. Finally, their grandmother (drove, driven) the two home.
5. Zack thought Zena had (took, taken) his book.
6. Zena believed Zack had (broke, broken) her bike.
7. Finally, Zena (spoke, spoken) angrily to Zack.
8. "You (broke, broken) my bike," she said.
9. "Well, you (stole, stolen) my book," replied Zack.
10. The two (froze, frozen) in their tracks.
11. At least they had (broke, broken) their silence.
12. "I have not (stole, stolen) your book," Zena said.
13. "Remember, you (gave, given) it to me to read," she continued.
14. Zack forgot he had (gave, given) Zena the book.
15. He had (chose, chosen) the book himself from a stack in his room.
16. Zack (spoke, spoken) next.
17. "I (rode, ridden) your bike to the store."
18. "On the way there, I (fell, fallen)."
19. "I (chose, chosen) not to tell you because I was embarrassed."
20. "I am sorry that I have (fell, fallen) with your bike."
21. Zena (gave, given) her brother a hug.
22. Then she said, "I have (wrote, written) for a new reflector."
23. "I (wrote, written) the letter two days ago."
24. Now Zack has (gave, given) Zena money for a new reflector.
25. Zack and Zena have (drove, driven) each other crazy many times.

B. Write the sentences. Use the correct past or past participle form of the verbs in parentheses.

Example: We (speak) about Socrates in class today.
Answer: We spoke about Socrates in class today.

26. I have (buy) a book about him.
27. This Greek philosopher and teacher has (give) much to us.
28. His ideas have (bring) us wisdom and knowledge.
29. He has (teach) us important lessons.
30. Socrates had (choose) to live a humble life.
31. In addition to dressing plainly, he (eat) simply.
32. Socrates believed that it was people's natures that (lead) them to behave correctly.
33. He had (think) that people acted wrongly because of ignorance.
34. He (say) that the unexamined life is not worth living and that no person knowingly does evil.
35. He (teach) many students by questioning them.
36. He had (lead) his students to answer their own questions.
37. He (speak) to his listeners in the streets, marketplace, and gymnasiums.
38. Socrates's students (find) him to be a respectable teacher.
39. However, the general public (think) he should not be trusted.
40. He had (fell) from honor among influential Athenians.
41. His ideas had (sting) the rulers.
42. The Athenians (bring) Socrates to trial.
43. Socrates (give) good arguments during the trial.
44. He had not (freeze) on the witness stand.
45. The jury (find) Socrates guilty of corrupting the young and being disrespectful to religion.
46. They (give) him the death sentence.
47. Socrates (choose) to carry out the sentence himself.
48. He (swing) his arm up in a toast and then drank a poison.
49. Socrates never (write) a book.
50. Others have (write) about his beliefs.
51. Socrates has (lend) his name to a special kind of teaching.
52. He has (leave) behind many lessons that are still studied.

▶ **Apply/Writing**   Write a description of a misunderstanding between two friends. Include forms of at least four of the following verbs: *bring, speak, eat, give, lead, lend,* and *take.*

10 Forms of *be*

Use the forms of the verb *be* correctly.

▶ **Focus**   These forms of the verb *be*—*am, is, are, was, were*—can be used as a linking verb or as an auxiliary verb.

> Nina **is** a student.   Nina **is studying** American history.

Study the chart for forms of *be* to use with subject pronouns.

	Pronoun	Present	Past	Past Participle
Singular	I	am	was	(have, had) been
	you	are	were	(have, had) been
	he, she, it	is	was	(has, had) been
Plural	we	are	were	(have, had) been
	they	are	were	(have, had) been

> I **am** the first. (Not: I is)   You **were** second. (Not: You was)
> We **are** the prize winners. (Not: We is)

Use the present participle *being* with the auxiliary verbs *am, is, are, was,* and *were*. Use the past participle *been* with *has, have,* and *had*.

> He **is being** silly. (Not: He being)
> He **has been** that way all day. (Not: He been)

The form *be* should not be used in place of *am, is,* or *are*.

> He **is** foolish. (Not: He be)

The word *ain't* is not a correct form and should not be used in place of *isn't* or *aren't*.

> Jerry **isn't** going with us. (Not: Jerry ain't)
> His friends **aren't** leaving yet. (Not: His friends ain't)

▶ **Guided Practice**   Tell how to correct each sentence.

1. You is the first to know.
2. He been elected treasurer.
3. He being humble about it.

▶ **Practice** **A.** Write the verb in parentheses that correctly completes each sentence.

Example: A kind of karate (is, are) the Wing Chun style.
Answer: is

1. Two women (was, were) the originators of it.
2. The name of its first teacher (was, were) Yim Wing Chun.
3. She (had been, been) the teacher of Ng Mui.
4. Ng Mui and others (is, are) the ones who popularized the art.
5. We (is, are) about to go to a karate tournament today.
6. Concentration (is, be) the most important ability in karate.
7. Probably you (will be, being) most familiar with judo and karate.
8. They (have been, been) considered common arts of self-defense.

B. Rewrite each sentence, correcting the form of *be* where needed.

Example: The word *judo* are a Japanese word.
Answer: The word *judo* is a Japanese word.

9. The meaning of *judo* are "gentle way."
10. Judo were for fighting, but now it's a sport.
11. The idea of it ain't to overpower your opponent.
12. The moves been designed to use the opponent's strength to your own advantage.
13. Courtesy and confidence is gained from judo.
14. New students being given a white belt to wear.
15. Black belts ain't worn by anyone except masters of the art.
16. Judo be an Olympic event for the first time in 1964.
17. That year Tokyo been the site for the Olympics.
18. Did you know some moves in karate was originally imitations of the movements of animals?
19. One master were impressed by the way a praying mantis defended itself.
20. Other moves is imitations of a white crane's movements.
21. That *karate* means "an empty hand" ain't well known.
22. Karate be both an exercise and a sport.

▶ **Apply/Writing** Write eight sentences telling what you know about the arts of self-defense or some other topic. Use these forms of *be* in your sentences: *am, are, is, was,* and *were.*

11 Forms of *have*

Use the forms of the verb *have* correctly.

▶ **Focus**   Forms of the verb *have—have, has, had*—can be used by themselves as main verbs or as auxiliary verbs to form verb phrases.

> Chiyoko **has** a question.
> Chiyoko **has asked** a question.

Study the chart to learn what form of *have* to use with subject pronouns.

	Pronoun	Present	Past	Past Participle
Singular	I	have	had	(have, had) had
	you	have	had	(have, had) had
	he, she, it	has	had	(has, had) had
Plural	we	have	had	(have, had) had
	they	have	had	(have, had) had

> Emma **has** the answer. (Not: Emma have)
> We **have heard** it. (Not: We has heard)
> I **had** another question. (Not: I has)

Do not write the word *of* in place of the word *have* in phrases like *would have, should have, could have,* and *must have.*

> Joshua **must have** heard the answer. (Not: must of heard)

▶ **Guided Practice**   Tell which form in parentheses is correct to use in each sentence.

1. We (has, had) visitors last week.
2. They (have, had) visited us last year too.
3. You (could have, could of) met them.
4. The Burkes (has, have) gone home now.
5. Their visit (has, have) left our family excited.
6. I (has, had) the time of my life.

► **Practice**   **A.** Write the verb that completes each sentence correctly.

Example: The students (has, have) their reports ready.
Answer: have

1. Flora (have, had) her report on H. G. Wells ready at least a week early.
2. She (hasn't, haven't) read much science fiction before this.
3. I (has, have) loaned her the novel *The Time Machine.*
4. The bookstores all (have, has) copies of that novel.
5. I (haven't, hasn't) read his novel *The Island of Dr. Moreau.*
6. Flora (have, has) promised to lend it to me.
7. Our library (have, has) copies of *The Invisible Man.*
8. Wells (have, has) written many books besides novels.
9. Those books (haven't, hasn't) been read as much as the novels.
10. Several of his novels (have, has) been made into movies.
11. Flora (haven't, hasn't) heard the recording of the broadcast of *The War of the Worlds.*
12. She should (of, have) read about it in his biography.

B. Rewrite each sentence, using the correct form of *have.*
Example: H. G. Wells should of lifted weights as a child.
Answer: H. G. Wells should have lifted weights as a child.

13. Wells have poor health as a child.
14. Early in life he must of had an interest in science.
15. We know he have worked in a drapery factory and as a science teacher in a small school.
16. Many of his books has scientific-sounding titles.
17. He have written one book called *The First Men in the Moon.*
18. I think Wells would of been a good science teacher.
19. Wells also have ideas about the world of the future.
20. In one of his novels he have written about a time machine.
21. You has heard of that machine, haven't you?
22. Do people in real life has a chance to ride in time machines?

► **Apply/Social Studies**   Write a paragraph about a day on an imaginary planet. Tell what the planet has and does not have, and explain two things you would have or should have done there.

12 Forms of *do*

Use the forms of the verb *do* correctly.

▶ **Focus** Three forms of the verb *do* are *do, does,* and *did.* These forms can be used alone as main verbs or as auxiliary verbs.

> Janitors **do** the work.
> A janitor **does** things professionally.
> The janitor **did fix** the furnace.
> He **did** it quickly.

Study the forms of *do* in the chart below.

	Pronoun	Present	Past	Past Participle
Singular	I	do	did	(have, had) done
	you	do	did	(have, had) done
	he, she, it	does	did	(has, had) done
Plural	we	do	did	(have, had) done
	they	do	did	(have, had) done

Study the example sentences, which show correct uses of forms of the verb *do.*

> Our janitor **did** all the cleaning. (Not: Our janitor done)
> He **had done** a good job. (Not: He done)
> He **has done** it by himself. (Not: He has did)
> He **doesn't complain.** (Not: He don't complain)

▶ **Guided Practice** Tell how to correct each sentence.

1. Their team don't win many games.
2. They have did their best.
3. We done our best too.
4. The coach don't ask for anything more.
5. He says we done a good job this year.
6. It do make us proud to hear that.

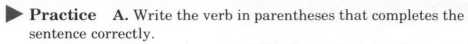

▶ **Practice** **A.** Write the verb in parentheses that completes the sentence correctly.

Example: (Do, Does) you know anything about Sir Ronald Ross?
Answer: Do

1. Ross (had done, done) research on malaria.
2. (Do, Does) you think most people know he discovered the malaria parasite?
3. He (don't, doesn't) get talked about often.
4. Many scientists (do, does) know about Ross's discovery.
5. Scientists (don't, doesn't) forget about Giovanni Grassi either.
6. Grassi (did, done) research on malaria also.
7. (Does, Do) the name Charles Laveran mean anything to you?
8. He was another scientist who (had done, had did) research on malaria.
9. Laveran (did, do) important work on other diseases too.
10. Grassi did not receive a Nobel prize, but Laveran and Ross (did, do).
11. Malaria (don't, doesn't) worry people as much as it used to.
12. It (doesn't, don't) worry me.
13. I (does, do) not think you can catch malaria from another person.
14. I (do, does) know what the symptoms are.

B. Write each sentence below. Use *do, does, did,* or *done* to complete the sentences.

Example: Giovanni Grassi has _____ important work on malaria.
Answer: Giovanni Grassi has done important work on malaria.

15. Grassi had _____ work on eels and white ants.
16. He _____ recognize malaria as a problem in Italy around 1898.
17. Few scientists had _____ studies on mosquitoes.
18. _____ you know there are over thirty kinds of mosquitoes?
19. Grassi _____, and he tried to find the ones causing malaria.
20. He _____ his work in the nastiest swamps in Italy.
21. In time he had _____ over one hundred experiments.
22. _____ his work seem interesting to you?

▶ **Apply/Science** Write a paragraph about a scientific discovery you know or have heard about. Use *do, don't, does, doesn't, did, and didn't* as helping and main verbs in the paragraph.

13 Troublesome Verb Pairs

Some pairs of verbs are confusing because they have similar meanings or because they look alike.

▶ **Focus**   Notice the difference in the principal parts of each pair of verbs below. These verb pairs are frequently confused. The examples and definitions will help you use the verbs correctly.

Present	Past	Past Participle
lay	laid	(has, have, had) laid
lie	lay	(has, have, had) lain

Lay your coat over there. ("put or place")
Lie down for a nap. ("rest or recline or be at rest")

set	set	(has, have, had) set
sit	sat	(has, have, had) sat

Set your books on that table. ("put something somewhere")
Sit here and rest awhile. ("sit down")

let	let	(has, have, had) let
leave	left	(has, have, had) left

Let me help you. ("allow")   I **leave** at six. ("go away")

lend	lent	(has, have, had) lent
borrow	borrowed	(has, have, had) borrowed

Lend me a pen. ("give")   I **will borrow** one from Pat. ("get")

teach	taught	(has, have, had) taught
learn	learned	(has, have, had) learned

Rob **taught** me to play chess. ("give knowledge")
I **learned** to play chess from Bob. ("gain knowledge")

bring	brought	(has, have, had) brought
take	took	(has, have, had) taken

Bring the book here. ("carry something toward")
You **can take** the book home. ("carry something away")

rise	rose	(has, have, had) risen
raise	raised	(has, have, had) raised

Rise when the judge enters. ("get up")
Please **raise** the window. ("lift something up; make higher")

▶ **Guided Practice** Tell which verb in parentheses is the correct one to use in each sentence.

1. You have (laid, lain) in the sun long enough.
2. You should (set, sit) in the shade awhile.
3. Will you (lend, borrow) me some tanning lotion?
4. (Bring, Take) the towel over here.
5. Is Juan (teaching, learning) you to swim?
6. He won't (let, leave) me swim by myself yet.
7. The water in the lake (rises, raises) higher every year.

▶ **Practice** **A.** Write the verb in parentheses that correctly completes each sentence.

Example: I (lain, laid) my science book on the table.
Answer: laid

1. An experiment I did (taught, learned) me about plants.
2. Mr. McRoberts, our science teacher, (brought, took) a white carnation from home.
3. He (laid, lay) the carnation on the table.
4. He (borrowed, lent) me his penknife to slit the carnation stem vertically.
5. I (set, sat) half the stem in a glass of plain water and the other half in a glass of water with blue ink in it.
6. I didn't (leave, let) any water touch the flower.
7. Then I (let, left) the carnation in water overnight.
8. That night as I (laid, lay) in bed, I wondered what would happen to the carnation.
9. After twenty-four hours, I (took, brought) the carnation out of the water and looked at the petals.
10. On the side where the stem (lay, laid) in blue water, the petals were blue.
11. I (taught, learned) that there are little tubes inside the carnation's stem.
12. The water (rises, raises) through these tubes into the petals and leaves.
13. The next day Mr. Roberts (lent, borrowed) me a book about plant experiments.
14. I (set, sat) at my desk for hours and read it.
15. I finally (lay, laid) the book down to try another experiment.

B. Write the verb in parentheses that correctly completes each sentence.
Example: I (learned, taught) to play softball last week.
Answer: learned

16. My brothers, Sid and Ernie, (taught, learned) me the basics.
17. They (borrowed, lent) a softball and a bat from our gym teacher.
18. He (let, left) us practice on the athletic field after school.
19. Some softball players (lay, laid) on the grass.
20. Sid told me to (rise, raise) the bat to shoulder height.
21. I (rose, raised) my bat even more before Sid pitched to me.
22. I swung and watched the ball (let, leave) my bat.
23. Ernie simply (set, sat) there and watched the ball.
24. I (laid, lay) the bat next to him.
25. Now I (borrow, lend) the softball and bat every day and work on my hitting.

C. Write the verb form needed to complete each sentence. Use the principal part and verb given in parentheses.
Example: Ken has _____ the table. (past participle of *set*)
Answer: set

26. Gina _____ the garlic bread on the table. (past of *lay*)
27. Sara has _____ the lasagna out of the oven. (past participle of *take*)
28. Mom has _____ down the napkins. (past participle of *lay*)
29. We were out of cheese, so we _____ some from our neighbor. (past of *borrow*)
30. Please ask Uncle Leo to _____ here. (present of *sit*)
31. I _____ next to my grandmother at the table. (past of *sit*)
32. My brothers each had _____ a second helping of lasagna. (past participle of *take*)
33. We _____ the dishes into the kitchen. (past of *bring*)
34. Dad asked Barry and me to _____ the dishes near the sink. (present of *lay*)
35. I wonder if Mom has _____ down for a nap. (past participle of *lie*)

▶ **Apply/Writing** Decide which pair of verbs gives you the most trouble. Then write a sentence using each verb correctly. Exchange papers with a classmate and check each other's work.

14 Active and Passive Verbs

Active verbs are used most often because they express action directly and naturally. Passive verbs are used less often.

▶ **Focus** A verb is called **active** when the subject of a sentence is the doer of the action. A verb is called **passive** when the subject receives the action.

> Diego **hit** the ball.

Diego, the subject of the sentence, performed the action. *Hit* is the active verb. *Ball* is the direct object of the sentence. It receives the action.

Now look at the sentence below.

> The ball **was hit** by Diego.

Ball still receives the action, but in this sentence it is the subject. The verb *was hit* is passive. Passive verbs consist of some form of *be,* such as *was,* plus a past participle.

Writers generally use active verbs because they express action in a direct, natural way. There are two cases, however, when writers prefer to use passive verbs.

- A passive verb is used to emphasize the receiver of the action over the doer of the action.

> The winning run **was scored** by the Trenton catcher.

- A passive verb is used when the doer of the action is unknown or unimportant.

> Some equipment **had been taken** from the locker room.

▶ **Guided Practice** Which of the sentences below have active verbs? Which have passive verbs?

1. Sandi broke the record a second time.
2. Toby played the game well.
3. The record was broken by Sandi.
4. A speech was given by the coach.
5. Mr. Baker handed Sandi her trophy.

► **Practice** **A.** Write the verb in each sentence. Tell whether it is active or passive.

Example: Marcus wrote the play.
Answer: wrote—Active

1. The play was directed by Rudy.
2. Rita played the lead.
3. The costumes were made by Elena and Louise.
4. Sam sold tickets to all his friends.
5. Sam's parents also bought tickets from him.
6. The scenery was built by Sam and Tim.
7. Jane and Judy collected the props.
8. The cast rehearsed the play for two weeks.
9. A good performance was given by the cast.
10. The proceeds were donated to charity.

B. Rewrite the sentences below, changing the passive verbs to active verbs.

Example: A hobby show was held by our class.
Answer: Our class held a hobby show.

11. Shells were collected by Bonnie.
12. The shells were displayed by her on a velvet cloth.
13. Two large albums of foreign stamps were brought by Willis.
14. The stamp collection had been started by his father.
15. Hand-carved marionettes were exhibited by Maya.
16. The marionettes had been carved by her father.
17. The marionettes were worked for us by Maya.
18. A prize was awarded by the judges to the best exhibit.
19. The prize was won by Barry Handelman.
20. A miniature theater was built by him.
21. Students from other classes were invited by us to see the hobby exhibit.
22. The exhibit was considered a great success by all the class members.

► **Apply/Writing** Write a paragraph about your hobby or one you would like to start. Use both active and passive verbs. Exchange papers with a classmate. Underline all the passive verbs in your partner's paragraph.

Review/Evaluation

For more review,
see Tested Skills Practice,
pages 536–540.

52 **Irregular Verbs** Write the letter of the verb form that completes
each sentence correctly.

1. John and Peter had _____ toward the boat.
   a. swam   **b.** swum
2. Some sea gulls _____ above them.
   a. flown   **b.** flew
3. Some other gulls had _____ the waves.
   a. ridden   **b.** rode
4. Peter had _____ hundreds of gulls following a fishing boat once.
   a. saw   **b.** seen
5. The cries of the sea gulls had _____ Peter's attention.
   a. drew   **b.** drawn
6. These birds _____ more numerous every year.
   a. grow   **b.** grown
7. Sea gulls have _____ a nuisance in many coastal cities.
   a. became   **b.** become
8. Ornithologists have _____ to study these birds more closely.
   a. began   **b.** begun
9. John and Peter _____ themselves into the boat.
   a. threw   **b.** thrown
10. Two weeks ago the boat had _____ a leak.
    a. spring   **b.** sprung
11. It had almost _____.
    a. sink   **b.** sunk
12. Luckily, John's father _____ how to repair it.
    a. know   **b.** knew
13. Suddenly a strong wind _____ harshly against the boys' bodies.
    a. blew   **b.** blown
14. A menacing cloud had _____ in size.
    a. grew   **b.** grown
15. The sky had _____ dark.
    a. become   **b.** became
16. The forecasted storm had _____!
    a. came   **b.** come
17. John and Peter _____ home.
    a. gone   **b.** went

53 **Forms of *be, have,* and *do*** Write **a** if a form of *be, have,* or *do* is used correctly in the sentence. Write **b** if it is not used correctly.

18. You must of heard of Alexis Ackeroyd.
19. She be an artist.
20. Her paintings are in galleries downtown.
21. She done the portrait of our governor and his wife.
22. My family has been to all the exhibitions of her paintings in this city for the past ten years.
23. We has had one of Alexis's paintings in our living room for about two years.
24. Dad don't like the painting very much.
25. I is in agreement with him.
26. Alexis ain't painted anything new lately.

54 **Troublesome Verb Pairs** Write the letter of the verb that completes each sentence correctly.

27. Uncle Hal has (**a.** learned, **b.** taught) me how to stop hiccups.
28. I (**a.** let, **b.** left) Uncle Hal put a paper bag over my head, though I couldn't imagine how this would help me stop hiccupping.
29. He led me to the couch in the living room, and he said, "Now (**a.** lie, **b.** lay) down and relax."
30. I thought Uncle Hal had (**a.** set, **b.** sat) down, but I was wrong.
31. Uncle Hal said, "You have (**a.** lain, **b.** laid) there long enough."
32. "When I count to ten, you can (**a.** take, **b.** bring) the bag off your head and look at what I have for you."
33. Uncle Hal had (**a.** laid, **b.** lain) a rubber snake on my chest.
34. A scream (**a.** let, **b.** left) my throat, and my hiccups were gone.

55 **Active and Passive Verbs** Write **a** if the sentence has an active verb. Write **b** if it has a passive verb.

35. The portrait of my father was painted by Alexis Ackeroyd.
36. I recently discovered the true identity of Alexis Ackeroyd.
37. That name was taken by my mother many years ago to hide her real identity.
38. Mom finally admitted the truth to me.
39. She just wanted to paint without fame or fortune.
40. The secret will be kept by me.

Thinking/Writing Evaluation

48   **Detecting Bias**   Read the sentences and answer the questions.

(1) The flood did millions of dollars worth of damage and left sixty homeless.   (2) All the flood victims think the governor is stupid for waiting a week to provide aid.   (3) Even though he was unable to provide immediate help, he is now making every effort to aid the victims.

1. Which sentence contains loaded words?   **a.** sentence 1
   b. sentence 2   **c.** sentence 3
2. Which sentence expresses a more balanced view? **a.** sentence 1
   b. sentence 2   **c.** sentence 3

49   **Persuasive Paragraphs**   **A.** Read the paragraph and answer the questions.

(1) Schools should be kept open at night and on weekends for many good reasons.   (2) First, the school buildings wouldn't be wasted for so many hours.   (3) Second, taxpayers' money would be put to better use.   (4) Most important, young people could use school gyms instead of hanging around the streets; consequently, they would avoid danger and trouble.

3. Which sentence is the topic sentence and expresses the writer's opinion?   **a** sentence 1   **b.** sentence 2   **c.** sentence 3
4. Which sentence gives the weakest reason?   **a.** sentence 2
   b. sentence 3   **c.** sentence 4
5. Which sentence gives the most convincing reason?   **a.** sentence 2   **b.** sentence 3   **c.** sentence 4

49   **B.** Write a persuasive paragraph on one of the topics below. Apply what you have learned about persuasive paragraphs.

why people should have an annual medical checkup
why students shouldn't go to school on weekends
why students should be allowed to grade each other's papers

Curriculum Connection: Social Studies

If you look closely at two of Catherine's journal entries in the excerpt from *A Gathering of Days,* you will see that her father left for his marriage in Boston on May 18, 1831. A later entry states that the marriage took place on May 22, four days after his departure. While the passage doesn't tell us where in New Hampshire Catherine's farm was located, it is reasonable to assume that it was probably close to the Groton, Keene, and Hanover Road, an old right-of-way that connected Boston with towns in New Hampshire. Catherine's farm was probably between 50 and 60 miles from Boston. Her father could not have spent much time in Boston before the wedding because in 1831 it probably took him three full days to travel to Boston. The problem was the roads.

Even as late as 1870, the great majority of roads in New England were little more than clearings through forests. There were very few level stretches, and tree stumps were often left in the middle of the cleared sections. A journey from New York to Boston, a distance of 250 miles, normally took six days, provided that the weather cooperated and the traveler was willing to keep moving for eighteen hours per day. This was an improvement over the situation that existed in 1775. In that year postal officials boasted that it would take only three weeks for a letter to travel the 300 miles between Boston and Philadelphia.

▶ **Think**   Consider the importance of good roads. Think about the effect that they have on your community. Imagine what life would be like if roads were today what they were one hundred years ago.

▶ **Discuss**   Participate in a class discussion about the importance of roads in modern America. Discuss how life would be different if good roads did not link cities and towns.

▶ **Find Out**   Gather information about early American roads. Start with the encyclopedia and then use your library's card catalog to identify other books that you can consult. Take careful notes on how the roads were built and on the problems that travelers faced.

▶ **React: Report**   Prepare an oral report on early American roads, using the information that you gathered. You might want to illustrate your report with maps or drawings. Be prepared to summarize your report in class orally.

Tested Skills Maintenance

40 **Possessive Nouns** Write the correct plural or possessive form of each underlined noun.

1. The <u>play</u> cast consisted of amateur <u>actor</u>.
2. The <u>heroine</u> pleas did not change the <u>villain</u> mind.
3. The <u>villain</u> evil laugh drew <u>hiss</u> from the audience.
4. The audience clapped their <u>hand</u> at the <u>hero</u> entrance.
5. As plays go, <u>melodrama</u> are not among my <u>favorite</u>.

41 **Pronoun Homophones** Write the homophone that completes each sentence: you're, your, who's, whose, it's, its, they're, their. Tell whether each word is a possessive pronoun or a contraction. Remember to use capital letters correctly.

6. _____ sure, aren't you?
7. _____ car is that?
8. _____ going to snow.
9. The dog wagged _____ tail.
10. Do you have _____ own books?
11. _____ going with you?
12. _____ late, aren't they?
13. Have them show _____ IDs.

42 **Using Reflexive, Intensive, and Indefinite Pronouns** Write the reflexive, intensive, or indefinite pronoun or pronouns in each sentence and tell what kind each is.

14. Did Ron himself make the chili?
15. We helped ourselves to another bowl.
16. Each made himself a huge sandwich.
17. The food was prepared by Jan herself.
18. Did everyone have enough to eat?

39 **Writing a How-to Report** Write the following steps in order. Insert appropriate transition words to help make the sequence clear.

Stripping paint off a chair
19. After the chair has dried, you are ready to refinish it.
20. Apply the remover with the paintbrush.
21. Wash off remaining remover with mild detergent.
22. As the paint loosens, scrape it off gently with the wire brush.
23. Gather materials—paint remover, paintbrush, wire brush.

44 **Independent and Dependent Clauses**   Write whether the underlined sentence parts are independent or dependent clauses.

24. I did not know much about magic before <u>I met Kenji</u>.
25. He has lent me some books, and <u>I am learning from them</u>.
26. Kenji is teaching me tricks, but <u>I am not very good yet</u>.
27. A card trick is the only trick <u>that I do well</u>.
28. I am assisting Kenji at his next show, <u>which is on Friday</u>.

45 **Complex Sentences**   Write *Compound* or *Complex* for each sentence. For each complex sentence, write the dependent clause.

29. Italo opened a restaurant when he came to this country.
30. His restaurant, which is open daily, is flourishing.
31. It is a good eating place if you like generous servings.
32. Unless you have a reservation, don't go on Saturday night.
33. Come along with us next Tuesday, or try it for yourself.

46 **Combining Sentences**   Combine each set of sentences into one sentence.

34. The cabin was old. The cabin was empty. The cabin was half-hidden in the woods.
35. Hikers sometimes peered in the broken windows. No one ever entered the cabin.
36. Then one day two boys approached the cabin slowly. The two boys approached the cabin cautiously.
37. They pushed open the sagging door. They went into the cabin. They looked around.
38. Suddenly a squirrel ran out of the fireplace. The squirrel ran around the room. The squirrel ran out the door.

47 **Improving Sentences**   Improve the sentences by making the underlined words parallel, by repositioning the underlined misplaced modifiers, or by eliminating wordiness.

39. The girl likes science <u>in the brown shirt</u>.
40. <u>Last spring in the month of May</u> she won a science contest.
41. She does all her work quickly, ably, and <u>with thoroughness</u>.
42. This student is an excellent athlete and <u>musical</u>.
43. She <u>almost</u> participates in all our school contests.

Persuasive/Analytical Writing

Theme: Making Choices

Which shirt should I wear? What shall I eat for lunch? Which book do I want to read? We are all constantly **making choices** about a variety of things in our lives. In Unit 31 you will read about the choice a determined racer makes during an exhausting race in the Alaskan Wilderness. In Unit 32 you will make a choice of your own when you decide upon a topic for a research report.

1 Literature: Article

*The article that follows is from a 1986 issue of **National Wildlife**. In it we learn about a remarkable young woman who made a life-and-death choice in order to win one of the most difficult, grueling races in the world. Like any good article, this one is both entertaining and informative. As we follow the exciting race, we learn a good deal about the Alaskan wilderness and the people and animals who inhabit it. The editors of the magazine, rather than a single author, wrote the article. Read to find out what choice Libby Riddles made and what gave her the confidence to make this choice.*

Dogging It Through the Wilderness
*by the editors of **National Wildlife***

In March of 1985, a determined, 28-year-old Alaskan named Libby Riddles won a 1,000-mile dogsled race by taking a shortcut. Though she broke no rules, Riddles risked a harsh penalty: freezing to death.

Heading into a blizzard 225 miles from the finish line in Nome, Riddles commanded her lead dog to abandon the established trail and turn onto the ominous stretch of offshore ice blanketing Alaska's Norton Sound. Though blinded by the blizzard, her highly

trained team led her safely across the frozen sheet as night set in. In their wake, they left behind a field that had started with some 60 men and women racers, and nearly 1,000 dogs. The tactic led to a $50,000 prize.

The five dogsledders who tried to follow Riddles weren't so fortunate. They spent a harrowing night in the middle of frozen Norton Sound. "Our dogs became frazzled," said one racer the next day. The five mushers were forced to huddle beneath overturned sleds, as 70-mile-per-hour winds battered them throughout the ordeal. "After that night out on the ice," sighed competitor Rick Swenson, "I'm just glad to be alive."

Enduring Alaska's annual Iditarod race is indeed an achievement. Braving a course that winds along a historic gold rush trail from Anchorage to Nome, competitors must cope with breath-freezing cold, unpredictable storms, the exhaustion of more than two weeks in the wilderness, and occasional encounters with defensive moose. Throughout the race, the mushers rely on the abilities of some remarkably intelligent, durable dogs—descendants of animals that came to North America with natives thousands of years ago. . . .

Over the years, Libby Riddles consistently has shown that she is one of the better prepared racers. A Minnesota native who came to Alaska at the age of 16, she is one of the few Iditarod competitors who have turned professional, living off race winnings. She had finished the 1980 and 1981 races respectably—but not well enough to pay back her investment in supplies.

To win, Riddles thought, she needed what she called "a different type of dog that was faster and tougher." So she moved from interior Alaska to the harsh northwest coast, teaming up with champion musher Joe Garnie, an Inupiat Eskimo and mayor of the windblown town of Teller. The treeless landscape and frozen shore there duplicated conditions in the Iditarod's toughest leg—the 270-mile sprint along the coast to the finish line at Nome.

Like many racers, Riddles bred her own dogs, a mixture of hardy old native strains and modern breeds. Her new home was ideal for molding leaders and making them "mentally tough," she said, "because if you can teach dogs to lead out on the open flat ice, they can go anywhere."

At the start of last year's race, which always begins on the second Saturday in March, a long line of teams filled Anchorage's Fourth Avenue with a jostling menagerie of dogs and mushers. Riddles had one of her trusted dogs in the lead harness. Close behind, as the "swing dog," or co-pilot, in the second harness, was another favorite. Thirteen teammates followed two abreast, with the strongest members—the "wheel dogs"—closest to the sled. Some of the racers eyed each others' teams while they traded reports of near-record snowfalls. The heavy, crusted snow had driven large numbers of moose to the packed trail of one of the event's early legs. The talk made novice driver Monique Bene nervous. The 34-year-old musher had traveled to Anchorage from a small town 30 miles east of Paris. "I'm afraid of the moose, you know?" she confided, "because I have heard many, many stories about them."

At a word from the drivers, the teams snapped into action, plummeting through the starting chute at two-minute intervals. At first, they headed for the temperate, south-central lowlands; later, they would cross the huge, snow-clogged Alaska Range.

After leaving the great interior basin, dogs and mushers traversed a long windswept valley that leads to the northwest coast. It was the last leg that won the race for Riddles. Once she reached the desolate coastline, her team—trained to withstand the most severe winds—was able to outpace the others by traveling as the crow flies across the hazardous Norton Sound. Eighteen days after leaving Anchorage, she sprinted into Nome. Rough weather made her four days slower than the record time, but she finished unscathed.

Frenchwoman Monique Bene fared much worse: in a terrifying attack that turned her fears into prophecy several days into the race, a moose stomped her team. The territorial animal then stood over Bene, who lay huddled for hours until an approaching musher scared it away. Forced to drop off several injured dogs at a checkpoint, Bene nevertheless finished bravely in last place.

Since 1973, several dozen dogs, out of the thousands entered, have died in Iditarod races, from accidents and from the harsh conditions of the trail. But the mushers share those conditions; several years ago, for example, racer Joe Redington suffered a broken leg when a moose stomped him and several of his team. Race rules require one 24-hour layover, and veterinarians are on call to help injured dogs.

The isolation of the trail brings the drivers closer to their teams. Besides setting the six-mile-per-hour pace, the best lead dogs sometimes help make choices when a trail forks. Riddles's lead dogs felt their way across Norton Sound while Riddles couldn't even see them through the snow.

The dogs actually win the race, according to Riddles, who talks like a canine coach. A large part of winning, she says, "involves pure and simple dog training and care. The main thing is concentrating on your dogs all year round. That's what I do," she adds with some modesty.

Riddles's competitiveness earned the respect of the Women's Sports Foundation, which named her Professional Sportswoman of the year in 1985; her devotion to dog care won her a veterinarian-sponsored award from race officials. The greatest praise, however, came from those racers who were left behind as her tough dogs crossed Norton Sound—drivers who know what Alaska's wilderness is like. Retired businessman Burt Bomhoff appeared subdued after his ordeal. "Being out on the ice—which is trackless, shelterless, no trees—is awesome," he said. Added Joe Redington, one of the race's founders: "She done it the hard way!"

▶ **Discussing**

1. What choice did Libby Riddles make 225 miles from the finish line? What did she rely upon that enabled her to make this choice?
2. Name some conditions that competitors in the Iditarod race have to cope with?
3. Why did Libby Riddles move from interior Alaska to the northwest coast?
4. What happened to Monique Bene?
5. If you were Libby Riddles, how would you feel after the first few minutes after you finished the race?
6. Tell about a time you were trying to win something. What choices did you have to make?

▶ **Analyzing: Setting**

Setting is the time and place in which things happen. Answer these questions about the setting of the article.

1. When and where did the race take place?
2. Where did the race begin? What was the scene like there?
3. Name some specific ways the setting affected various participants in the race.

▶ **Writing**

Imagine that you are Monique Bene. Write an account of what happened to you when you encountered a moose during the race.

▶ **Extending**

Speaking and Listening Meet with a small group of classmates to discuss the topic Making Choices. Talk about how much time it takes to make a choice. Identify choices that can be made in a short amount of time and choices that require more thought and time. Then think about the time you use when you make choices. Do you devote too much time making choices about unimportant matters? Do you spend enough time making choices about more important, serious things?

Reading *The Kissimmee Kid,* by Vera and Bill Cleaver, is a story about making choices between justice and family loyalty. It is a story about what a twelve-year-old girl does when she learns that her brother-in-law is doing something unlawful.

2 Idioms

An idiom is an expression that means something different from the ordinary meanings of the words that make it up.

▶ **Focus**   When Libby Riddles and her dog team crossed Norton Sound, they traveled "as the crow flies." This does not mean that they flew through the air, of course. It means that they traveled in a straight line. *As the crow flies* is an **idiom**—an expression that means something different from the meanings of the words that make it up. Notice the idioms in the paragraph that follows.

> I like stories where every scene is exciting, where new things happen **at every turn.** Stories with happy endings, where everything **turns out** all right for the characters, appeal to me. On the other hand, I dislike stories where events are told **out of turn.** The events in a story should be told **in turn,** from first to last. I always **turn down** stories with plots that are difficult to follow.

The expressions in dark type are all familiar idioms. A native speaker of English will understand the meanings of most familiar idioms. People to whom English is a second language, however, may find these idioms puzzling at first glance.

When you run into an unfamiliar idiom in your reading, look for context clues. For example, the phrase "where every scene is exciting" suggests that "at every turn" means something like "on every occasion"—which it does.

If context clues don't work, look up the idiom's meaning in a dictionary. Most dictionaries will list an idiom under its most important word. The idioms in the example paragraph can all be found under the same entry word. Which entry word do you think this is?

- Use context clues to figure out the meanings of unfamiliar idioms.
- If you are still not sure of the meaning, look up the idiom in the dictionary under the most important word.

▶ **Guided Practice**   What are the meanings of the last four idioms in the example paragraph? What context clues suggest each meaning?

▶ **Practice   A.** Rewrite each sentence, replacing the underlined idiom with a word or phrase that defines it. You may use a dictionary.
Example: Harry ran away with first prize.
Answer: Harry easily won first prize.

1. I hope you will see to your homework soon.
2. Her parents decided to take in a movie that night.
3. Tammy jumped at the chance for a promotion.
4. People say Nancy takes after her mother as far as looks go.
5. Pick out your new clothes with care.
6. I ran across my friends at the shopping mall.
7. Mom rolled up her sleeves and set about changing the tire.
8. I'm glad I set aside money for a camera.
9. Wilson set forth his ideas clearly and effectively.
10. The Yankees pulled off a rare triple play.

B. Rewrite each sentence. Replace the underlined word or phrase with an idiom from the box. Use a dictionary if you need help.
Example: Our plans have completely failed.
Answer: Our plans have completely fallen through.

tied down	made up	gave in
fallen through	carried on	draw a fine line
check in	shake up	made off with
touched off	fallen on	stands up for

11. The pesky squirrel stole my peanuts.
12. The group forgot to register at the hotel desk.
13. Janet didn't want to be confined to a long-term contract.
14. His angry remark started a hot argument.
15. Eventually the team surrendered to the coach's judgment.
16. The actors continued even though the scenery fell over.
17. Farmers have experienced hard times in our state this year.
18. Martha always defends her ideas with great enthusiasm.
19. We make a precise distinction between good and bad writing.
20. We must completely change the management of this company.

▶ **Apply/Vocabulary**   Find an entry word in a dictionary that has at least five idioms listed. Use each idiom in a sentence.

3 Holding a Panel Discussion

A panel discussion is a discussion of a particular issue by a selected group of people speaking before an audience.

▶ **Focus**   A **panel discussion** is an organized way of exchanging and presenting views on a particular issue. Usually a group of three to five people serve as members of the panel. A chairperson helps organize and guide the panel members through the process of preparing and presenting the issue. Additionally, the chairperson monitors the time for each member's presentation.

Each member of the panel is assigned one aspect of the topic to research independently. Then he or she prepares an opinion based upon his or her findings. Often a panel has a planning session or rehearsal before the presentation. At this time, each member can summarize the material he or she will cover and the group can determine what additional work needs to be done to make the total presentation effective.

The panel presents its topic seated together. The chairperson announces the topic of discussion, introduces the panel members, and then outlines the rules to be followed during the presentation. The audience can ask the panel questions and panel members can question each other. However, depending on the topic and time limitations, it may be necessary to save questions until the end of the entire presentation.

During the panel discussion the chairperson must make sure that no one opinion or speaker is allowed to dominate. Also, the chairperson should encourage the audience to ask questions or address comments to the panel. Once everyone has had an opportunity to voice an opinion, the discussion is ended. A vote may be taken to determine how the audience feels about the issue at hand. In the closing remarks the chairperson gives a brief summary of the main points made and thanks the audience for their participation.

The guidelines on the following page can help you prepare a panel discussion for your class.

Guidelines for a Panel Chairperson

1. Research the topic well so you can help panel members develop their presentations.
2. Take notes on each member's speech during the rehearsal so you can write a concluding summary.
3. Help determine time limits. During the discussion, be firm in keeping panel members to these limits.
4. Make sure both speakers and audience keep to the topic.

Guidelines for a Panel Member

1. Make sure you understand and research the aspect of the topic you are presenting.
2. Prepare your talk thoroughly. Rehearse with another panel member until you feel comfortable and confident. Be aware of time limits.
3. State your opinion clearly during the discussion. Offer details to support your opinion.
4. Listen carefully to other participants. Ask thoughtful questions.

▶ **Guided Practice**   Answer these questions.

1. What is the role of a panel chairperson
2. What is the role of a panel member?

▶ **Practice**   **A.** Brainstorm topics for a panel discussion with your class. List on the board the aspects to cover for each topic. Follow this example.

Topic:	The school dress code should be abolished.
Aspects:	The code denies freedom of expression.
	Without a code, some students may dress in a way that distracts other students.
	Codes teach students how to dress appropriately.

B. Choose one of the topics from Practice A. Form a small group with others who are interested in the same topic. Select a chairperson and decide who will cover each aspect of the topic. Research and outline what you will say. Have a rehearsal.

▶ **Apply/Oral Language**   Present your panel discussion to the rest of the class.

Our Living Language

Words from Literature

> Oh! but he was a tight-fisted hand
> at the grindstone, Scrooge! a squeezing,
> wrenching, grasping, scraping, clutching,
> covetous old sinner.
> —*Charles Dickens*

Have you ever heard a person called a Scrooge or an Ugly Duckling? Some fictional characters become so well known that their names enter our language. Scrooge was the mean old miser in Charles Dickens's story *A Christmas Carol*. In Hans Christian Andersen's tale, the Ugly Duckling becomes a beautiful swan.

Do you know someone who is extremely kind but often daydreams and has impractical ideas? You could call such a person *quixotic*. The word comes from Don Quixote, the hero of the novel by the Spanish writer, Cervantes.

Gargantua was a friendly giant in a novel by the French writer, Rabelais. The Lilliputians, on the other hand, were only six inches tall. They were created by Jonathan Swift in his novel, *Gulliver's Travels*. Can you guess what *gargantuan* and *lilliputian* mean?

Word Play Tell what each of these words from literature means.

1. *puckish* (from Puck, a mischievous child in one of Shakespeare's plays)
2. *herculean* (from Hercules, a strong hero in Greek and Roman myths)
3. *utopian* (from utopia, an ideal place described by Sir Thomas More)

4 Choosing a Topic

When you write a research report, choose a topic that interests you. Then take time to narrow your topic.

▶ **Focus** In this unit you will prepare to write and then write a research report. The first step in preparing your report is choosing your topic. Begin by making an **interest inventory,** a list of topics that interest you.

The next step is to check that each topic on your list is narrow enough to handle in six to eight paragraphs. Try webbing or clustering each topic that needs to be narrowed. Here is an example of a web in which the broad topic Animals is narrowed to the more manageable topic Working Dogs.

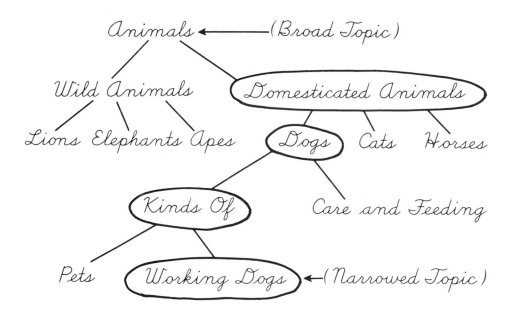

Next, write a list of from five to eight questions that you would like your report to answer. With these questions in hand, you will know exactly what to look for when you do your research. On the next page is a list of questions on the topic Working Dogs.

1. What work did dogs do long ago?
2. What work do they do now?
3. How do dogs help people who are handicapped?
4. How do dogs herd animals?
5. How are sled dogs trained?

▶ **Guided Practice**   Discuss how each broad topic that follows could be narrowed for use in a research report. Then discuss some questions that a report on each narrowed topic might answer.

1. Our Solar System   2. Movies   3. Safety   4. Presidents

▶ **Practice**   **A.** Narrow each topic to one that could be covered in a research report of from six to eight paragraphs. Draw webs if you think they will help you.
Example: Photography   *Answer:* Early Cameras

1. South America   6. Texas
2. Great Inventors   7. Careers in Medicine
3. Jungle Animals   8. Bees
4. Weather   9. Bicycles
5. Athletics   10. Mirrors

B. Write three good questions to use in researching each of the following topics.
Example: Early Airplanes
Answer: Who built the first engine-driven airplane?
            How do the first planes compare with modern planes?
            What were early airplanes used for?

11. Martin Luther King, Jr.   16. Marie Curie
12. The Civil War   17. Education in China
13. Life in a Mexican Village   18. African Art
14. Japanese Poetry   19. Death Valley
15. Ocean Tides   20. Careers in Law Enforcement

▶ **Apply/Prewriting**   Make an interest inventory of topics you might use for a research report. Narrow each topic that seems too broad. Choose the one you would most like to write about. Then write from five to eight questions that you would like your report to answer. Save your work.

5 Using Reference Sources

Reference books help you find specific information.

▶ **Focus** When you want to find out about a topic—for a school research project or simply for your own information—there are many books that can help you. **Reference sources** such as dictionaries, encyclopedias, atlases, and almanacs are located in a reference section of the library. The key to using reference sources is knowing which one to use for the information you want. For example, you would use an encyclopedia for general information, an almanac for current statistics, and an atlas for detailed maps. Frequently used reference works are described in this lesson.

Encyclopedia Because an encyclopedia contains articles on a wide range of subjects, it usually is a good place to start looking for information. If your topic is *Working Dogs,* for instance, you will find background information by reading a general article about dogs. Cross-references at the end of the article may point out related articles in the encyclopedia.

Articles in the encyclopedia are organized in alphabetical order. If the encyclopedia consists of more than one volume, find the volume that includes the key word in the name of your topic. The key word for an article about Libby Riddles is *Riddles*. Most encyclopedias also present an index of subject titles in the last volume.

Almanac An almanac is a source to use when you quickly want to find a few facts or statistics. Consult an almanac to answer questions like these: How large is the Statue of Liberty? Who won the gymnastics gold medal on the parallel bars for the most recent Olympic games? In an almanac, facts are organized in an index under headings such as *Olympics* or *U.S. Government*. Because many almanacs are revised each year, use the current edition for the most up-to-date information.

Atlas An atlas is a book of maps. You can use an atlas to find the location of a place, information about the geographical features of an area of land, the populations of cities, and the distance from one place to another. World atlases contain maps of countries and continents all over the globe. Road atlases contain highway maps of states, countries, or regions within countries.

The Readers' Guide to Periodical Literature   This is an index that will help you find magazine articles. It lists articles from about two hundred periodicals—publications that appear regularly but not daily. The articles are indexed by name of the author and by subject. Here is part of an entry for the subject *Dogs.*

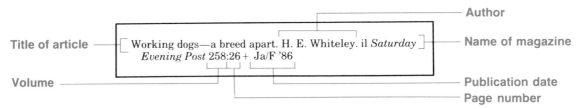

Title of article — Working dogs—a breed apart. H. E. Whiteley. il *Saturday Evening Post* 258:26 + Ja/F '86

Author

Name of magazine

Volume

Publication date

Page number

Books of Quotations   Books such as *Familiar Quotations* and *The Home Book of Quotations* list famous quotations. The quotations may be arranged by subject or author. Quotations may be indexed at the back of the book by authors and key words.

The Vertical File   This is a file of such materials as pamphlets, charts, newspaper clippings, and magazine articles about topics of current interest. Information is arranged alphabetically according to subject.

Nonprint Media   Reference sources are not limited to the printed materials described thus far. Nonprint media can include collections of films, filmstrips, records, tape cassettes, microfilm and microfiche.

▶ **Guided Practice**   Discuss answers for the questions below.

1. Which reference source would you consult if you wanted to know who was the winner of the Rose Bowl in 1983?
2. Which reference source would include an article on spacecraft?
3. Which reference source would you consult if you wanted to find a map of Alaska?
4. Which reference source would help you find a magazine article that was published last year?
5. Which reference source would you use if you wanted to find a particular newspaper article on a recent election?

▶ **Practice** Choose the reference source in parentheses that would be best to consult for the following information.

Example: a list of sunrise times for 1987 (atlas, almanac)
Answer: almanac

1. a map of Alberta, Canada (atlas, vertical file)
2. information about the history of motion pictures (encyclopedia, nonprint media)
3. a 1959 magazine article on Hawaii becoming a state (atlas, *Readers' Guide*)
4. a pamphlet on current health trends (almanac, vertical file)
5. a film of the first walk on the moon (encyclopedia, nonprint media)
6. some recent magazine articles about trends in music (encyclopedia, *Readers' Guide*)
7. the author who wrote, "Neither a borrower, nor a lender be" (book of quotations, encyclopedia)
8. the final standings of the East Division American League in 1986 (*Readers' Guide,* almanac)
9. some general information about the state of Alabama (encyclopedia, almanac)
10. slides showing the Rocky Mountains (*Readers' Guide,* nonprint media)
11. a back issue of your local newspaper on microfilm (encyclopedia, nonprint media)
12. a map showing the geographical features of the United States (vertical file, atlas)
13. the most recent statistics on how much corn is grown in the United States (atlas, almanac)
14. a well-known quote by George Washington (encyclopedia, book of quotations)
15. a clipping from a magazine about how new tax laws will affect us (vertical file, nonprint media)
16. a magazine article by Garrison Keillor (*Readers' Guide,* book of quotations)

▶ **Apply/Study Skills** Go to a library and find two different types of reference sources (such as an almanac and an encyclopedia). Write a list of three questions that each source could answer.

6 Taking Notes

Summarize information in your own words as you take notes.

▶ **Focus**   The next step in preparing your report is to find information on your topic and take notes. Read the following passage from a book. Then notice how the information from this passage has been recorded on the note card that follows.

> Good sheep dogs have both "eye" and "style." The style allows the dog to approach a flock without scaring them. The dog moves in a crouched position rather than rushing and causing the sheep to scatter. When the dog is close, its "eye" comes into play, for a good dog can stare so intently at the sheep that they are literally hypnotized and will not move.

<u>Working Dogs</u>
by George S. Fichter, p. 10
Good sheep dogs need "style" + "eye."
1. <u>Style</u> = approach flock in crouch
   so won't scare sheep.
2. <u>Eye</u> = close to flock, dog stares
   at sheep — can hypnotize.

The note is written on an index card. Use index cards so that your notes will be easy to sort. The number at the top tells which question from the top of page 419 the information relates to. The title, author, and page of the source follow. Book and magazine titles are underlined. Titles of articles are enclosed in quotation marks. Include this information on each note card above the note.

The information on the note card is a summary of the information in the passage. When you **summarize** you use your own words to note main ideas and details. Summarize when you take notes for your research report. When you do, take note only of information that will help to answer the question.

The card on page 423 was made from information in a nonfiction book. Here are examples of cards made from other kinds of sources.

1 <u>National Wildlife,</u> "Dogging It Through the Wilderness," by the editors. Feb.-Mar., 1986, p. 44 Sled dogs need qualities: 1. mentally tough 2. leadership 3. "a mixture of hardy old native strains and modern breeds "	*2* "Dog," <u>World Book Encyclopedia,</u> 1986, Vol 5, p. 224 19 breeds of working dogs 1. Dobermans and mastiffs—police dogs 2. Malamutes, Siberian huskies pull sleds 3. St. Bernards—rescue work

Notice that the facts on each card are broken down and numbered. Number the facts on each card so you will not confuse them later. When you use the exact words of a source, be sure to enclose the words in quotation marks.

As you do your research, you can add or drop questions to change the focus of your report. Remember, do not make your topic too broad or too narrow.

> **Think Back: Summarizing**
>
> In Unit 29 you learned about summarizing, giving the main points of something. Use the skill of summarizing when you take notes for your research report.

▶ **Guided Practice**   Discuss these questions about the note cards in this lesson.

1. What abbreviations and symbols were used on the cards?
2. What are some other abbreviations and symbols you might use to make notetaking easier?

▶ **Practice**   Read each passage below. Decide which question on page 419 it answers. Write the number of the question and the source of the information. Follow the form shown on the note cards in this lesson. Then summarize only the information that will help to answer the question.

1. From the entry "Guide Dog" on pages 784–785 of Volume 4 of *The New Encyclopaedia Britannica,* 1982.

At the age of approximately one year, the dog is trained for three to four months to mold the animal's behavior to its owner's handicap. The dog learns to adjust to a harness, stop at curbs, gauge its owner's height when traveling in low or obstructed places, and disobey a command when obedience will endanger its master. Although several breeds, including Doberman pinschers, retrievers, and boxers, have been successfully educated as guide dogs, German shepherds are the most used.

2. From pages 42–43 of the book *All About Dogs* by Carl Burger.

As the centuries went by, early men discovered new ways to make life more comfortable and secure. They advanced beyond being mere hunters of wild game and gatherers of wild vegetables and fruits. Animals other than the dog were domesticated: herds of cattle and horses, flocks of sheep, and various kinds of fowl. People began to cultivate food crops: different sorts of vegetables and grain to feed themselves and their domestic animals.

Men found that dogs could be trained to guard and herd the flocks. New weapons, such as the bow and arrow, led to new hunting methods. For all these purposes dogs were increasingly useful. Among tribes that followed their flocks from one grazing ground to another, dogs drove the herds and guarded them from thieves and wild beasts. In addition, they were set at new and more menial tasks. They became bearers of burdens and haulers of loads. When the tribe moved, the dogs were pressed into service to help carry the household goods.

▶ **Apply/Prewriting**   Research the questions you wrote in Apply of Lesson 4. Note the question and source at the top of each index card. Then summarize the important information.

7 Organizing Information

Use classifying skills to organize your information.

▶ **Focus**   Now decide which note cards you will actually use. Review each card and ask yourself: Does this information really help answer the question? Is it important and interesting enough to include in my report? Keep in mind that you have only six to eight paragraphs in which to present your information. Remove any cards that don't measure up. Aim for a total of no fewer than ten and no more than thirty cards.

Next, decide on the order in which you will present your information. Your notes are already sorted into piles, one for each question. Look through each pile and decide on the order in which you plan to deal with the questions. The writer who researched Working Dogs decided to present the questions in this order. Notice that a question was added to the original list.

1. What work did dogs do long ago?
2. What work do they do now?
3. How do dogs help save people's lives?
4. How do dogs help people who are handicapped?
5. How do dogs herd animals?
6. How are sled dogs trained?

The first two items are in **time order.** Reports on the lives of famous people, on historical events, and on how-to projects often use time order.

The writer decided to present the last four items in **order of importance,** with the most important ideas presented first, and less important ideas following. This order is often used for research reports that present a series of examples.

Problem and solution reports begin by presenting a problem and go on to suggest possible solutions. A report on air pollution, for example, might use this kind of order.

Cause-and-effect reports explain why an event happened, or what happened as a result of some event. A report on the Civil War might focus on its causes. A report on automobiles might focus on what effects automobiles have had on our lives.

▶ **Guided Practice**   Discuss the order of importance of the last four questions in the list on the previous page. Would you put the questions in a different order? Why or why not?

▶ **Practice**   **A.** The following notes were collected for a research report. Rearrange them in the order you think they should be presented in the report. Write what kind of order you used. List first the item that gives the topic of the research report.

1. Ban cars entirely from certain areas of the inner city
2. The problem of noise pollution in large cities
3. Make laws on auto mufflers stricter
4. Pass laws against playing portable radios on buses
5. Move airplane flight paths farther from populated areas

B. For each report topic below, decide on a good method of organization. Write *Time order, Order of importance, Problem and solution,* or *Cause and effect* to tell which method you chose. Then explain briefly why you chose that method.

6. Preventing Fires in the Home
7. How a Caterpillar Becomes a Butterfly
8. The Birth of a Hurricane
9. Ways to Improve Your Memory
10. Life in a Mexican Village
11. The Development of the Bicycle
12. How Clouds Form
13. The Beliefs of Martin Luther King, Jr.
14. The Sinking of the *Titanic*
15. Birds of Northern California

▶ **Apply/Prewriting**   Go over your notes. Pick the cards you will use in your report. You may want to use one of the four kinds of order presented in this lesson for your report.

8 Outlining

Use sequencing skills to organize your information into an outline.

▶ **Focus** Now you are ready to make an **outline**—a general plan for your report. Study the outline for a report on Working Dogs. Notice that the writer used the questions on page 426 as the basis for the outline. Then read the guidelines for outlining.

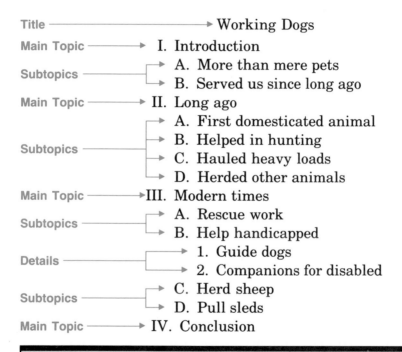

Title ──────────────▶ Working Dogs

Main Topic ──────▶ I. Introduction

Subtopics ──────▶ A. More than mere pets
                          B. Served us since long ago

Main Topic ──────▶ II. Long ago

Subtopics ──────▶ A. First domesticated animal
                          B. Helped in hunting
                          C. Hauled heavy loads
                          D. Herded other animals

Main Topic ──────▶ III. Modern times

Subtopics ──────▶ A. Rescue work
                          B. Help handicapped

Details ──────────▶ 1. Guide dogs
                          2. Companions for disabled

Subtopics ──────▶ C. Herd sheep
                          D. Pull sleds

Main Topic ──────▶ IV. Conclusion

Guidelines for Outlining
1. Capitalize the first word of each line.
2. Write each main topic with a Roman numeral and a period.
3. Write each subtopic with a capital letter and a period.
4. Write each detail with a number and a period.
5. Indent each subtopic and detail.
6. Make sure subtopics support main topics and that details support subtopics.
7. Each time you list subtopics or details, list at least two.

▶ **Guided Practice**   Look back at the questions on page 426 and discuss how each one was put into the outline on Working Dogs on the previous page.

▶ **Practice**   Look over the outline for a report and the information in the box. Copy the outline, filling in the blanks with the information in the box. One blank has been filled in for you.

Walt Disney

I. Introduction
II. Early Life
   A. ____
   B. ____
   C. ____
   D. ____
III. Motion Pictures
   A. Cartoon
      Characters
      1. ____
      2. <u>Minnie Mouse</u>
      3. ____
   B. Nature Films
      1. ____
      2. ____
IV. Amusement Parks
   A. ____
   B. ____
V. Conclusion

1. Disney World in Florida
2. Made first cartoons at 19
3. Born in Chicago
4. Donald Duck
5. Showed animals in nature
6. At 16 studied art
7. Minnie Mouse
8. Rare scenes of animal life
9. Disneyland in California
10. Moved to Missouri when a child
11. Mickey Mouse

▶ **Apply/Prewriting**   Make an outline from the notes you organized in the last lesson. Make the first main topic *Introduction* and the last *Conclusion*. Be sure to use correct outline form.

9 Writing a Research Report

A research report contains an introduction, a body, a conclusion, and a bibliography.

In this lesson you will write a research report. When you write a research report you gather and organize information from reference sources on a specific topic, as you have been doing so far in this unit. Then you write about this information in your own words. You list the reference sources at the end of the report in a bibliography.

At this time consider your **purpose** and **audience.** Assume that your readers share your interest in the topic, but not your knowledge. Take care to fill them in on the meanings of any special vocabulary words. Above all, be clear. If your ideas are clearly organized and simply stated, your report will be interesting to your readers.

1. Prewriting

▶ **Choose a Topic** In Lesson 4 you made an interest inventory and from it chose a topic for your report. In the process you made sure your topic was narrow enough to deal with in six to eight paragraphs. You also wrote a series of questions to use as a guide in doing your research.

▶ **Develop Ideas** In Lesson 5–8 you researched your questions, organized your notes, and made an outline from them. You **used the thinking skills of summarizing, classifying, and sequencing.** Your next step is to review your notes and outline. First, review your notes to make sure you have enough information. You may need to do more research on certain points. Then review your outline. Are all the main topics, subtopics, and details in the best possible order? Does another, better order occur to you? Make changes if you need to.

Now make a **Word Bank** to help you get started writing. Be sure to include any words that are new to you, such as special vocabulary words or proper names. At the left is a Word Bank prepared by the writer who chose the topic Working Dogs.

Word Bank
domesticated
disabled
prey
crisis
fearless
compete
mere
draft
malamute
St. Bernard

2. Writing

▶ **Study the Draft** Read the first draft of this research report on Working Dogs. Notice that the introductory paragraph tells what the report will be about and that the concluding paragraph restates the most important points in the rest of the report. The outline is shown alongside the draft. Notice that the main idea for each paragraph is either a main topic or a subtopic from the outline.

Working Dogs

There's over forty million dogs in the United States. Most of them is kept soley as pets. For they give love and compainonship to their owners. However, dogs can become excellent workers. In fact, ~~smart~~ intelligent dogs have always ~~enjoyed~~ thrived on serving people in some way through a variety of chores.

In ancient times, dogs were already helping people. The dog was the first animal that was domesticated. With their keen sense of smell, dogs could track prey for hunters. Larger, stronger dogs could be trained as draft animals. Also, dogs helped ancient people by herding their flocks.

~~Now~~ In modern times, there are

I. Introduction
  A. More than mere pets
  B. Served us since long ago

II. Long ago
  A. First domesticated animal
  B. Helped in hunting
  C. Hauled heavy loads
  D. Herded other animals

ninteen breeds of working dogs preforming a ~~huge~~ wide variety of tasks. St. Bernards, powerful dogs first bred in the Swiss Alps, are trained to rescue people trapped in snow. A fearless St. Bernard named Barry saved over forty people during his lifetime.

Dogs help people who are handicaped. They guide people who are blind from place to place. They helps people who are deaf by letting their masters know when the telephone is ringing or when someone is at the door. They also ~~help~~ aid people who are disabled by bringing them things they can't reach.

Some dogs is trained to herd animals and pull sleds. Sheep dogs herd sheep with what is called "eye" and "style." Style mean the dog approaches the flock in a crouch so it won't scare them. Eye mean the dog can stare at the sheep in a way that almost hynotizes them. Both malamutes and huskies is sled dogs. These dogs must be brave and ~~strong~~ hardy to pull sleds through the frozen wildernesses of Alaska and Canada and other cold, harsh lands.

Ever sinse ancient times dogs have been trained to help people. They have hunted and herded animals, pulled heavy loads, saved lives, and made life easier for people who are handicapped. Dogs can be more than mere pets. They can be valuble workers helping in many ways.

Bibliography

Burger, Carl. *All About Dogs*. New York: Random House, 1962.

"Dogging It Through the Wilderness." *National Wildlife* (February–March, 1986), pages 40–45.

Fichter, George S. *Working Dogs*. New York: Franklin Watts, 1979.

"A Friend For Kris." *National Geographic World* (August, 1985). pages 25–29,

"Guide Dog." *The New Encyclopaedia Britannica*, 1982, Vol. 4, pages 784–785.

▶ **Write a Draft** Work from your note cards and outline as you write your draft. Write on every other line to leave room for corrections. Notice the bibliography for Working Dogs above. Use it and the guidelines on the next page when you write your bibliography.

Guidelines for Writing a Bibliography
- List sources alphabetically by the author's last name. If no author is listed, use the title of the article.
- Underline the names of books, magazines, and newspapers. Put quotation marks around the titles of articles.
- List page numbers for articles in newspapers, magazines, and encyclopedias. Do not list page numbers for books unless you have used information from one specific chapter in the book.
- Put the date of issue of magazines and newspapers in parentheses.
- Use commas and periods correctly.

3. Revising

▶ **Read and Confer**   Read your draft over to a conference partner. Bring your outline along. Discuss your draft and outline with your partner, keeping the following Conference Questions in mind. Take notes on your discussion.

Conference Questions
1. Does the introductory paragraph give the reader a good idea of what the report will be about?
2. Does the concluding paragraph restate the most important points in the rest of the report?
3. Does the report follow the outline? If not, should the writer make changes so that it does?
4. Has the writer used his or her own words throughout the report?
5. Should the writer add context clues to explain the meanings of any special vocabulary words?

▶ **Make Changes**   Read over your draft again and use your conference notes to help you revise. You may also want to use the following special revision strategy for research reports.

STRATEGY: Circle any words that your readers might not know. Provide a context clue for each one. Here is how the writer of the report on Working Dogs used this strategy.

> *animal that was domesticated.* ^or tamed by people^ *With*
>
> *their keen sense of smell. dogs could*
> *track ^animals that were^ prey for hunters. Larger. stronger*
> *dogs could be trained as draft animals.* ^to pull heavy loads^

Proofreader's Marks

≡ Make a capital.

/ Make a small letter.

⊙ Add a period.

⌄ Add a comma.

⌄⌄ Add quotation marks.

∧ Add something.

ℓ Take out something.

→ Move something.

¶ New paragraph.

sp Correct spelling.

▶ **Proofread and Edit** Check your report for any errors you might have made in spelling, punctuation, capitalization, and the form of your bibliography. Use the proofreader's marks and the questions below.

Proofreading Questions
1. Are all my sentences complete and correctly punctuated?
2. Did I use correct subject-verb agreement in sentences in which the subject follows the verb?
3. Did I use correct subject-verb agreement in sentences that contain words like *family* and *anyone?*
4. Did I spell each word correctly?

▶ **Make a Final Copy** Recopy your report. Since a research report is more lengthy and formal than other kinds of papers, you may want to type your final copy.

4. Presenting

The writer of the report on Working Dogs read her report to her social studies class, which had studied Alaska and Canada earlier in the year. Read your report to one of your classes.

10 Giving an Oral Report

A good oral report depends upon clear, focused writing and effective communication skills.

▶ **Focus**   Another way to share your research report is by making an oral presentation. Giving an oral report is not the same as merely reading your research report aloud, as you will learn about in this lesson. Usually an oral report is not as long as written report; you should allow about 5–10 minutes to present your material. Also, unlike a written report, your audience will not have the opportunity to turn back to a certain paragraph to help clarify or remember a particular idea. Therefore, you must keep your language simple and focus on covering only a few main ideas.

The following steps will help you plan and present an oral report.

1. Plan your report carefully. Help you audience get the "big picture" before you launch into the details of your topic. Introduce your report by giving an overview of your main ideas and a summary of the points you are going to make. Include an opening statement that will catch your listeners' attention. End your talk with a summarizing statement similar to the opening one, to help your audience review all the information you have presented. Use transition words and phrases such as *first, then, as a result,* and *finally* to help your listeners follow your ideas.

2. Write your presentation in an easy-to-give manner. Determine for yourself how to pare down the material from your written report. You may, for example, begin by underlining key ideas and examples in the research report. You might even go back to your original outline and add details as needed to its main topics and subtopics. Whichever method you choose for condensing your ideas, put your statements on note cards you can read while standing in front of the group. Avoid holding too many papers or cards, so you do not lose your place. Remember to number your cards to keep them in order. Include graphic aids such as charts or illustrations to further clarify your ideas. Make sure these aids are legible enough to be seen by the audience at the back of the room.

3. Practice your talk. Ask a friend or family member to help you rehearse or do so in front of a mirror. Speak clearly, watching how you use your voice. Avoid mumbling or speaking too quickly. Remember to make eye contact with the audience. If you feel nervous, take a deep breath and try to relax.

▶ **Practice** **A.** Use the research report you wrote in Lesson 9 or choose one of the topics below to prepare a plan for an oral report. If you choose one of the following topics, allow time for research. Put your ideas on note cards.

circus life
choosing a career that takes you outdoors
a country you'd like to visit
animals that help people
endangered species of animals

B. Get together with another classmate to rehearse your oral talk. Use the note cards you wrote in Practice A. Take turns rehearsing the talk with your partner. Use the following questions to evaluate each other's talks. Revise your talk as necessary.

1. Does the opening statement engage the audience's interest?
2. Does the overview clearly state the main ideas?
3. Have enough details been provided that develop each main idea that was mentioned in the overview?
4. Does the report use transition words and phrases such as *first, then, as a result,* and *finally* to help the audience follow the discussion?
5. Does the ending summarize the main points of the talk as stated in the overview statement?
6. Would a graphic aid make the report clearer?

▶ **Apply/Oral Language** Present your oral talk to the rest of the class.

Revising and Editing Workshop

Connecting Writing and Grammar

- In Unit 31 you read an article.
- In Unit 32 you learned how to prepare for writing a research report and then you wrote one.

Now it's time to use your skill as an editor to improve another writer's first draft. Read these paragraphs from a research report carefully. As you read, ask yourself these questions.

✔ Does the introductory paragraph tell what the report will be about?

✔ Do subjects and verbs agree in sentences in which the subject follows the verb?

✔ Do subjects and verbs agree in sentences that contain indefinite pronouns such as *some* and *no one?*

(1) Climbers must be well prepared. (2) Rocky slopes and icy inclines constitutes their world. (3) Therefore, the equipment that they take along with them are of utmost importance. (4) It must be light, strong, and packed carefully. (5) Sir Edward P. Hillary reached the summit of Mount Everest in 1953. (6) Mount Everest is the world's highest peak. (7) Climbers may need ice axes, sleeping bags, cooking gear, and crampons.

(8) There is many adventurous people who enjoy mountain climbing. (9) Special knowledge, skills, and equipment is needed for this activity. (10) Because mountain climbing can be dangerous, there's many precautions that must be taken.

(11) Climbs take different amounts of time to complete. (12) Some takes one day. (13) Low, easy mountains is good for short climbs. (14) A taller, more challenging mountain takes longer. (15) No matter where climbers climb, they should follow good safety rules. (16) No one climb alone. (17) There is too many dangers and problems to be faced. (18) Also, a climber should not try to climb a mountain that is too difficult for him or her.

▶ Revising the Draft

1. The information in the draft is not organized clearly because the writer did not put the introductory paragraph first. Rearrange the paragraphs so they are in the correct order.
2. Delete two sentences in one of the paragraphs that do not keep to the main idea of that paragraph.
3. The writer did not explain that crampons are metal frames with spikes. Add this information to the draft.
4. Add, delete, or rearrange any other information that you think might improve the draft.

▶ Editing the Draft

5. Incorrect subject-verb agreement occurs in three sentences in which the subject follows the verb. Correct the sentences that have this type of error.
6. Correct three sentences in which plural verbs should be used to agree with compound or plural subjects.
7. Correct a sentence in which a singular verb should be used to agree with the singular noun.
8. Correct two sentences in which the verbs do not agree with the indefinite pronouns.

▶ Working Together on the Draft

Meet with a group of your classmates. Discuss the changes you made in the draft. Listen to the changes your classmates made. Then rewrite the draft on page 438. Include all the revisions you think are important.

▶ Evaluating Your Own Writing

Now review your own writing. Look over the research report you wrote in this unit and any other written work you have. Did you have any problems with subject-verb agreement in sentences where the subject follows the verb? Did you have any problems with subject-verb agreement in sentences that contain indefinite pronouns? The lessons that follow will help you with these writing problems.

11 Subject-Verb Agreement

A singular subject agrees with a singular verb. A plural subject agrees with a plural verb.

▶ **Focus**   When the subject and verb of a sentence are both singular or both plural, they agree in number. This is called **subject-verb agreement.** Read the sentences below.

> The <u>road</u> **is** icy. (singular subject; singular verb)
> The <u>roads</u> **are** icy. (plural subject; plural verb)

Pronouns generally follow this rule. However, *I* and *you* always take plural verbs.

> <u>I</u> **iron.**   <u>She</u> **scrubs.**   <u>You</u> **watch.**   <u>We</u> **complain.**

Use the following two rules to help you make compound subjects and their verbs agree.

Rule 1. Most compound subjects joined by *and* or *both . . . and* are plural and are followed by plural verbs.

> <u>Sarah and Helga</u> **drive** to the mountains on weekends.
> <u>Both Sarah and Helga</u> **like** the area very much.

Rule 2. A compound subject joined by *or, either . . . or,* or *neither . . . nor* is followed by a verb that agrees in number with the closer subject. Study these sentences.

> <u>Either Sarah or Helga</u> **drives** to the mountains on weekends.
> <u>The twins or the girls</u> **drive** to the mountains on weekends.
> <u>Neither Brian nor the twins</u> **go** with the girls.
> <u>Neither the twins nor Brian</u> **goes** with the girls.

In the first sentence both subjects are singular, so the verb is singular. In the second sentence both nouns are plural, so the verb is plural. Why is the verb plural in the third sentence? Why is the verb singular in the fourth sentence?

▶ **Guided Practice**   Choose the correct form of the verb.

1. Both Sarah and Helga (drives, drive) carefully.
2. Brian or his friends (brings, bring) sandwiches.
3. Neither the girls nor Brian (does, do) much climbing.

▶ **Practice** **A.** Write the correct singular or plural form of the verb in parentheses.

Example: Either a dog or a cat (makes, make) a good companion.
Answer: makes

1. Two dogs and a cat (lives, live) in that house.
2. They (is, are) always playing together.
3. Neither the dogs nor the cat (likes, like) strangers.
4. Mr. Terry and one dog (takes, take) long walks.
5. Either Mr. Terry or his housekeeper (feeds, feed) the animals.
6. Neither the cat nor the dogs (strays, stray) far from home.
7. Either the dogs or the cat (sleeps, sleep) with Mr. Terry.
8. Both my mother and father (disapproves, disapprove) of my dog sleeping with me.
9. Both cats and dogs (is, are) easy to care for.
10. Neither the cat nor the dogs (is, are) any trouble.

B. Follow the directions for Practice A.

11. Juan and his sisters (wants, want) to put on a pet show.
12. Neither his parents nor the neighbors (objects, object).
13. Both Cindy and Maria (has, have) agreed to help.
14. They (has, have) put on a show before.
15. Two boxers and a cat (is, are) entered already.
16. Either the twins or Jamie (has, have) entered a snake.
17. Jamie or the twins (is, are) also entering a myna bird.
18. Either a blue ribbon or some treats (is, are) to be first prize.
19. Both Ron and the twins (expects, expect) to win a prize.
20. I (know, knows) that it will be a good pet show.
21. You (remember, remembers) what fun it was last year.

▶ **Apply/Writing**   Use the compound subjects below to make some sentences of your own. Be sure your subjects and verbs agree.

some artists and writers
either Karen or the boys
both the boys and Karen
neither the girls nor Cal
either the cyclist or the runners
both the runners and the cyclist

12 Subjects Separated from Verbs

Agreement between subject and verb is not affected by words or phrases that come between the subject and the verb.

▶ **Focus**   Subjects and verbs must agree in number. A common agreement problem occurs when the subject of a sentence is separated from the verb by a prepositional phrase. Notice that the subject and verb in the sentence below agree.

<u>Reports</u> of a gigantic earthquake **were** greatly exaggerated.

The verb *were* is plural to agree with the plural subject *reports*. The prepositional phrase *of a gigantic earthquake* comes between the subject and the verb. Although the noun *earthquake* appears just before the verb, it does not affect the number of the verb. The verb agrees in number with the subject.

Here are some other examples of subjects separated from verbs.

The <u>report</u> about many injured people **was disproved.**
The <u>objection</u> of the city manager and the two commissioners **has received** much publicity.
That newspaper <u>column</u> of questions and answers **gives** all the necessary information.
The <u>cars</u> in the driveway next to the house **belong** to our visiting relatives.

Why are the verbs in the first three sentences singular? What are their subjects? What is the subject of the fourth sentence? Does the verb agree with that subject? Why or why not?

▶ **Guided Practice**   Tell why the underlined verb in each sentence is singular or plural.

1. That bag of old letters and bills <u>was thrown</u> out.
2. The curtains in Boyd's and Jerry's bedrooms <u>need</u> to be washed and pressed.
3. The other picture of Inez and her brothers <u>belongs</u> to me.
4. The problem with mosquitoes and other insects <u>is growing</u> worse.
5. Ten of the rabbits in the rabbit room at the animal shelter <u>have been adopted</u>.

▶ **Practice**   **A.** Write the correct form of the verb in parentheses.
Example: Tracks of a large animal (has, have) been found.
Answer: have

1. Scientists from a nearby university (has, have) examined them.
2. The spokesperson for the scientists (says, say) that the tracks resemble those of a dinosaur.
3. A reporter for two magazines (wants, want) an interview.
4. The citizens of the town (welcomes, welcome) the excitement.
5. A group of parents (has, have) formed a dinosaur watch.
6. One parent of six-year-old twins (states, state) that his children will stay home from school until the animal is found.
7. A parent of two boys (describes, describe) the news as scary.
8. Rumors of a prank (is, are) beginning to spread.
9. The opinion of my friends (is, are) that someone is fooling us.
10. An animal with such big feet (has, have) not been seen yet.

B. Rewrite the sentences. Correct the agreement mistakes.
Example: The stories of great pranks is found in this book.
Answer: The stories of great pranks are found in this book.

11. The history of pranks are a fascinating one.
12. Victims of a prank quite often does not know they're being fooled.
13. Once, scientists from a British university was fooled by the skull of an animal.
14. A 1938 radio drama about Martian invaders have been broadcast every Halloween to fool listeners.
15. Reports of a UFO invasion still scares many people.
16. People in an Illinois town has believed in "Big Foot."
17. Descriptions of "Big Foot" has varied greatly.
18. The footprints of the creature is found in the snow.
19. A picture of the footprints show their huge size.
20. The students from the local high school was making the footprints with a handmade monster foot.

▶ **Apply/Writing**   Copy several sentences from exercises in this book that have subjects separated from verbs by prepositional phrases. Circle the subject and verb in each sentence, and underline the prepositional phrase. Do all the subjects and verbs agree?

13 Sentences in Inverted Order

The position of a subject in a sentence does not affect subject-verb agreement.

▶ **Focus**   In most sentences the subject comes before the verb. In some, though, especially in questions, the verb or part of the verb usually comes first, and the subject follows. When the subject follows the verb, the sentence is said to be in **inverted order.** To make sure that such sentences have subject-verb agreement, reverse the order.

Down the street **strolls** <u>Jean</u>.	<u>Jean</u> **strolls** down the street.
Does <u>Jean</u> **practice** today?	<u>Jean</u> **does practice** today.
Where **are** her <u>instruments</u>?	Her <u>instruments</u> **are** where?

In the first sentence pair the verb *strolls* agrees with the singular subject *Jean*. The verb phrase *does practice* in the second pair agrees with the singular subject *Jean*. In the third pair the plural verb *are* agrees with the plural subject *instruments*.

In sentences that begin with *here* or *there*, the words *here* or *there* are not subjects. To find the subject, reverse the order of the sentence.

There **are** no <u>seats</u>.	No <u>seats</u> **are** there.
Here **is** a <u>book</u> of songs.	A <u>book</u> of songs **is** here.

The plural verb *are* agrees with the plural subject *seats*. What are the subject and verb in the next sentence?

Remember that *here's* and *there's* are contractions of *here is* and *there is*.

Incorrect:	Here's the <u>programs</u>. There's our <u>seats</u>.
Correct:	Here **are** the <u>programs</u>. There **are** our <u>seats</u>.

▶ **Guided Practice**   Identify the subject and verb in each sentence. Tell whether they agree.

1. When does Natusa go to science class?
2. Here's a copy of her schedule.
3. There's your books on the table.
4. Does Ollie know about the meeting?
5. Where has Sandy and Duncan gone?

▶ **Practice** **A.** Write the correct form of the verb in parentheses.
Example: Who (was, were) the first musicians?
Answer: were

1. (Do, Does) you know the history of music?
2. (Was, Were) music developed before writing?
3. What (was, were) the first musical instruments?
4. (Does, Do) music historians know if cave people had drums?
5. Where (has, have) the earliest instruments been found?
6. In those ruins (dig, digs) the archaeologists.
7. (Is, Are) there any ancient drums or other instruments?
8. What (have, has) these researchers reported?
9. There (have, has) always been music in ceremonies.
10. What (do, does) people like about the sound of music?
11. In the box (is, are) some suggestions for music research.
12. There (are, is) many people oddly affected by music.

B. Copy the sentences below, underlining the subject in each. Then find the six sentences with mistakes in subject-verb agreement, and correct the verb to make it show agreement.
Example: Here are your guide for today.

  is
Answer: Here are your guide for today.

13. Are there still many volcanoes active in the world today?
14. Here in Hawaii are the famous volcano Kilauea.
15. Has there been many eruptions of this volcano over the years?
16. There are tourists who come just to see the eruptions.
17. Up in the air shoots the lava.
18. Here's the footprints of some soldiers who were caught in an eruption.
19. Where is the viewing center for visitors to safely watch the volcanoes?
20. There was no casualties during the last few eruptions.
21. On the hillsides grow new trees.
22. Here's the reports about another new eruption.

▶ **Apply/Writing** Write six questions about music or volcanoes. Exchange questions with a classmate and write the questions as statements to check the subject-verb agreement.

14 Agreement with Collective Nouns

A collective noun names a group made up of individual people or things. It may be either singular or plural.

▶ **Focus**   A noun that names a group or collection of people or things is called a **collective noun.** Study the list.

gang	herd	band	audience	school	committee
crew	flock	class	army	fleet	crowd
pack	faculty	group	club	family	troop

When a collective noun is the subject of a sentence, it can be used with either a singular or plural verb. It depends on the writer's intended meaning. Study these example sentences.

> Our family **enjoys** hiking in the woods.
> The committee **has made** a decision.

The subjects *family* and *committee* are collective nouns. Each names a group made up of individuals. In these sentences, though, the family and the committee act as *one*, not as individuals. For that reason a singular verb is used with each.

Now study these sentences with collective nouns. Is the verb in each singular or plural?

> Kim's family **have** all **been** sick at various times this winter.
> All the committee **have signed** the petition.

The verb in each sentence is plural. In the first sentence the several individual members of the family were sick. What is the meaning in the second sentence?

▶ **Guided Practice**   What is the subject and verb in each sentence? Why is the verb singular or plural?

1. A crew of workers is cleaning up.
2. That group disagree about almost everything.
3. The crowd has made a path for the heroes.
4. The Rockville team plays a very fast game.
5. The audience take their seats.

▶ **Practice**   **A.** Write the singular or plural verb or helping verb that correctly completes each sentence.

Example: The team of scientists (is, are) speaking in the auditorium.
Answer: The team of scientists is speaking in the auditorium.

1. Our class (is, are) writing a history of birds and animals.
2. The whole school (is, are) involved in a conservation project.
3. The faculty (is, are) busying themselves with preparations.
4. One committee (was, were) formed to study the names of birds.
5. The family of cats (is, are) the focus of those students.
6. A different group of students (is, are) reading books about caribou in Alaska.
7. A pack of wild dogs (is, are) the subject of Lola's report.
8. One team of students (is, are) learning about birds.
9. Recently, a flock of geese (has, have) stopped by the river.
10. A crowd (has, have) gathered to watch these birds.

B. Complete each sentence below with a collective noun. Tell if the noun you use is singular or plural.

Example: The _____ of voters has made up its mind.
Answer: group, singular

11. The _____ of applicants for the job was small.
12. A(n) _____ of ants is invading our picnic lunch.
13. The _____ of citizens have already voted.
14. The community _____ offers night classes.
15. The _____ of twenty was recruited by the president.
16. My _____ have gone to separate meetings.
17. The hobby _____ at my church is giving a demonstration.
18. This stage _____ seems better than that one.
19. Our new _____ have been on break all morning.
20. A(n) _____ of ships sails tomorrow morning.
21. A(n) _____ of politicians are sending them off.
22. The _____ of parents was standing in the auditorium.
23. A(n) _____ of frightened homeowners was frantically building a wall of sandbags to keep back the flood waters.
24. The _____ of protesters are arguing among themselves.

▶ **Apply/Writing**   Write two sentences each for some collective nouns like *orchestra, herd, pair,* and *team*. First use each noun with a singular meaning, and then use it with a plural one.

15 Agreement with Indefinite Pronouns

When an indefinite pronoun is used as a subject, the verb in the sentence must agree with it.

▶ **Focus**   As you may remember, indefinite pronouns are words such as *both, each, everyone,* and *few.* An indefinite pronoun can be singular or plural.

Some singular indefinite pronouns are shown below. When they are subjects, they take singular verbs, as the sentences show.

anybody	either	neither	one
anyone	everybody	nobody	somebody
each	everyone	no one	someone

Everyone <u>trains</u> hard.   **No one** <u>complains</u> much.
Each <u>has</u> a special diet.   **Nobody** <u>wants</u> to lose the game.

Some plural indefinite pronouns are *both, few, many,* and *several.* The examples below show these pronouns followed by plural verbs.

Few of the athletes <u>complain</u>.   **Several** of us <u>are</u> here.
Both of our coaches <u>encourage</u> us.   **Many** <u>are</u> young.

The indefinite pronouns *all, any, most, none,* and *some* can be either singular or plural, depending on their meaning in a sentence. Notice the meaning of the pronouns in the examples.

Singular
Most of the training <u>was</u> hard.
Some of the competition <u>is</u> slow.

Plural
Most of the athletes <u>are</u> young.
Some of the competitors <u>are</u> fast.

In the sentences on the left, the pronouns *Most* and *Some* tell how much. They refer to nouns—*training* and *competition*—that have a singular meaning. The same indefinite pronouns are used with a plural meaning in the sentences on the right. There they tell how many and refer to nouns—*athletes* and *competitors*—that can be counted.

One way to select the proper verb for sentences like these is to identify the noun to which the indefinite pronoun refers. Determine if the noun is singular or plural. Then select the verb that agrees in number with the noun.

▶ **Guided Practice** Tell what form of the verb in parentheses belongs in each blank. Use present tense.

1. No one _____ him seriously. (take)
2. Some of the problems _____ insoluble. (look)
3. Most of the book _____ dull. (be)

▶ **Practice** **A.** Write the subject of each sentence. Then write the verb in parentheses that correctly completes the sentence.

Example: Nobody in class (know, knows) about Alexander von Humboldt.
Answer: Nobody knows.

1. Everybody in Europe (recognize, recognizes) his achievements.
2. All of his work (was, were) fascinating.
3. Everyone (understand, understands) the dangers of mining.
4. One of von Humboldt's inventions (was, were) a miner's helmet.
5. Each of his helmets (has, have) a device to detect dangerous gases.
6. Any of his explorations (is, are) interesting to read about.
7. Some of his travels (was, were) in South America.
8. Several (was, were) across the frozen regions in Russia.

B. Follow the directions for Practice A.

9. Everybody (need, needs) to learn how to write clearly.
10. Several of the country's leading educators (has, have) recommended that students write something every day.
11. One of the best ways (is, are) to keep a journal.
12. Many of the journal entries (turns, turn) into compositions.
13. Most of the writing (serves, serve) only as practice.
14. Some of the work (is, are) wonderful.
15. All of the compositions (shows, show) improvement.
16. No one (knows, know) how to produce great writers.
17. Someone (is, are) studying how great writers got started.
18. Each of the writers (has, have) kept records of his early years.
19. (Has, Have) either of your parents read this book?
20. Both of mine (say, says) it helped them a lot.

▶ **Apply/Writing** Write two sentences each for the pronouns *all, any, some,* and *most.* First tell how much, then how many.

Review/Evaluation

For more review, see Tested Skills Practice, pages 541–543.

57 **Subject-Verb Agreement**   Write the letter of the verb that agrees with the subject of each sentence.

1. Both the engineer and the construction crew _____ the dam's location carefully.
   a. is selecting   **b.** are selecting
2. Their decision about the dam's location _____ great importance to the whole region.
   a. has   **b.** have
3. The farmers in the area _____ more water for their crops.
   a. need   **b.** needs
4. A dam in the right location _____ cheap water for the crops.
   a. provide   **b.** provides
5. It also _____ a lake for the townspeople's recreation.
   a. creates   **b.** create
6. Neither the mayor nor the council members _____ the dam.
   a. oppose   **b.** opposes
7. Conservationists from the area _____ with the mayor and the council members.
   a. disagree   **b.** disagrees
8. The mayor or a council member _____ in the auditorium tonight.
   a. speak   **b.** speaks
9. The voters of the region _____ the issue in the fall election.
   a. decide   **b.** decides
10. Either the mayor or the conservationists _____ right.
    a. is   **b.** are

58 **Subject-Verb Agreement: Inverted Order**   Write the letter of the subject of each sentence.

11. Is there another team practice today?
    a. there   **b.** practice
12. Does any student know the answers to my questions?
    a. student   **b.** answers
13. Here is the most recent schedule of team practices for the fall season.
    a. practices   **b.** schedule

14. Onto the field run the players.
    a. field   **b.** players

15. When does our team play the Eagles and the Hawks again?
    a. team   **b.** Eagles and Hawks

16. Where have Bob and Jack gone with my bat?
    a. Bob and Jack   **b.** bat

17. Are there any new left-handed starting pitchers on the team this year?
    a. any   **b.** pitchers

18. There is the roster of pitchers on the locker-room wall.
    a. There   **b.** roster

19. When are the batting practices scheduled?
    a. batting   **b.** practices

20. Over the pitcher's head flies the ball.
    a. head   **b.** ball

59 **Subject-Verb Agreement: Indefinite Pronouns** Write the letter of the verb or verbs that complete each sentence correctly.

21. Most of the students at school _____ hobbies.
    a. has   **b.** have

22. Some of the students' hobbies _____ very ordinary.
    a. is   **b.** are

23. Few _____ really unusual hobbies.
    a. has   **b.** have

24. Everyone _____ his or her pastime is special.
    a. think   **b.** thinks

25. One of the hobbyists _____ and _____ fingerprints.
    a. collects, studies   **b.** collect, study

26. Each of the fingerprints _____ a unique pattern.
    a. has   **b.** have

27. Several of the patterns _____ fairly common.
    a. is   **b.** are

28. Some of the patterns _____ like a series of loops.
    a. look   **b.** looks

29. Many _____ in a spiraling pattern.
    a. turn   **b.** turns

30. _____ any of the patterns exactly identical?
    a. Are   **b.** Is

Writing Evaluation

56   This picture shows a scientist studying an erupting volcano. Use the information below to make an outline for a research report on Harnessing Energy from Volcanoes.

1. Make the main topics by summarizing the questions. Make the subtopics by summarizing the facts. Include an introduction and a conclusion.
2. When you have finished, spend a few minutes checking and revising your outline. Use these questions as guidelines.

✔ Have you arranged things in the best possible order?
✔ Have you used the correct form for an outline?
✔ Have you restated the questions as main topics?
✔ Have you included an introduction and conclusion?

Questions
- What causes volcanoes? • What is the job of scientists who study volcanoes? • How can energy from volcanoes be used?

Facts
- Volcanic steam can be used to generate electricity for industry.
- Hot rock called lava explodes from the earth's crust.
- Scientists collect samples of the lava.
- Volcanic pressure builds deep within the earth.
- Lab technicians study the hardened rock.
- Volcanic energy is used for heating buildings.

Curriculum Connection: Mathematics

The article you read in Unit 31 describes Alaska's annual Iditarod race. This is probably the longest and most grueling race in the world. It is fitting that it takes place in Alaska, a vast and powerful land and America's largest state. In fact, Alaska is so large that it covers almost as much area as one-fifth of the forty-eight continental states. In addition to size, there are some other noteworthy things about Alaska. The settlement of Point Barrow is the northernmost point in the United States. Mount McKinley is the highest peak in North America. One-third of Alaska lies north of the Arctic Circle. The Aleutian Islands, which are part of Alaska, actually stretch into the Eastern Hemisphere.

▶ **Think**   Spend some time considering how to communicate such information about Alaska as discussed above. If you are looking for a way to communicate this information so that people can grasp it quickly, consider how graphs of various kinds can help you.

▶ **Discuss**   Meet with four classmates to discuss how graphs may be used to communicate factual information about Alaska. Examine your math text. Locate and review information about bar graphs, broken-line graphs, and circle graphs. Consider what kinds of information each of these graphs can show about Alaska. A bar graph, for example, could show the size of Alaska in square miles as compared to five other states. A broken-line graph could show population growth over a number of five- or ten-year periods. A circle graph could show the ethnic mix of Alaska's population.

▶ **Find Out**   Collect information on one aspect of Alaska from appropriate reference sources. Almanacs and reference books called *statistical abstracts* include the kind of information you will need.

▶ **React: Make a Graph**   Develop a graph to present information about Alaska. Be sure that your graph is carefully labeled and clearly communicates your information. Below is an example.

Alaska Population 1950–1980				
	1950	1960	1970	1980
400,000				
300,000				
200,000				
100,000				

Tested Skills Maintenance

52 **Irregular Verbs**   Write the correct past or past participle form of the verb.

1. A letter from my pen pal (came, come) yesterday.
2. It had (went, gone) to a wrong address first.
3. Akemi (became, become) my pen pal last year.
4. She has (wrote, written) me several letters so far.
5. I have (grew, grown) interested in her activities.
6. She has (rode, ridden) in horse shows.
7. I (saw, seen) a horse show for the first time last week.
8. Akemi has (took, taken) a picture of her horse for me.
9. Akemi and I have (spoke, spoken) to our parents about visiting each other.
10. As soon as my parents said yes, I (began, begun) to save for the trip.

53 **Forms of *be, have,* and *do***   Write the correct form of the verb in parentheses that is needed to complete the sentence.

11. _____ you at the game last Saturday? (be)
12. She _____ n't go to games very often. (do)
13. They _____ n't been to one so far. (have)
14. _____ n't you live near the stadium? (do)
15. Once they _____ sure you lived nearby. (be)
16. We _____ n't been swimming for a week. (have)
17. He _____ n't like to swim in the lake. (do)
18. _____ you at the swim-team tryouts last week? (be)
19. I _____ n't, but they _____. (be)
20. She _____ n't think she can make the team this year. (do)

54 **Troublesome Verb Pairs**   Write the verb in parentheses that correctly completes the sentence.

21. Tony (lay, laid) in the grass and watched the game.
22. Jamie and I (set, sat) in the bleachers.
23. Jamie (lent, borrowed) me his sunglasses.
24. I asked him to (let, leave) me keep score.
25. He said I could (bring, take) the scorecard home.

26. Jamie has (taught, learned) me all I know about baseball.
27. The first hitter walked to the plate and (rose, raised) his bat.
28. The pitcher (lay, laid) the ball over the plate.
29. The hitter (let, left) it go by without swinging.
30. The coach has (learned, taught) him when not to swing.

55 **Active and Passive Verbs**   Rewrite the sentences, changing the active verbs to passive and the passive verbs to active.

31. The poster picture was drawn by Noreen.
32. The lettering was done by Martin.
33. Mr. Baker printed the posters.
34. They were distributed around town by Raymond.
35. Store owners put them in windows.
36. The posters were seen by passers-by.

30 **Cause and Effect**   Identify the cause and effect in each sentence. Write first the cause and then the effect.

37. Tanya didn't turn in her report on time; consequently, her grade was lowered.
38. Because his plane from Detroit to Chicago was late, Dad missed his connecting flight in Chicago.
39. Les couldn't mow the lawn because it rained all day.
40. Sal broke her arm; therefore, she couldn't dance in the ballet.
41. The schools were closed for two days after two feet of snow fell.

48 **Detecting Bias**   If a sentence shows a balanced point of view, write *Balanced*. If the sentence shows a biased point of view, write *Biased*.

42. Some people seldom read a newspaper.
43. All newspaper readers are well-informed.
44. Many readers feel that comic strips are entertaining.
45. No comic strips are worth reading.
46. All newspapers are well written.
47. Watching the news on television is a silly waste of time.
48. Some people seldom watch news broadcasts.
49. News broadcasts can never be a substitute for newspapers.
50. Perhaps the popularity of evening news broadcasts killed off afternoon editions of newspapers.

Persuasive/Analytical Writing

Theme: A Far Other Time

Have you ever wished that you'd been born in **a far other time,** past or future? Although life may appear different from age to age, there are some things that remain the same. Consider age-old fables, legends, and myths, such as those you will read in this section. You will probably respond to these much the same way as young people did many centuries ago. You will also have an opportunity to put your opinions into writing when you write a literary response essay in Unit 35.

1 Literature: Folk Literature Analysis

*People in every culture from a far other time have passed down fables and legends. **Fables** teach lessons, or morals. The characters are usually animals or objects from nature that act and speak like humans. Many times they represent particular human qualities such as wisdom and greed. **Legends** recount exciting adventures and noble deeds about a culture's heroes. Legends may be based on real events and usually tell of people who actually lived, but often exaggerations are added. Legends embody the beliefs and ideals of the people who tell them. The first three stories in this lesson are fables—the first from Russia, the second from India, the third by Aesop, a Greek slave said to have lived in the sixth century B.C. The last story is a legend. Read the fables to learn what lessons they teach. Read the legend to learn about No Eyes's brave deed.*

The Fox and the Thrush *retold by Mirra Ginsburg*

A hungry fox saw a thrush sitting high in a tree.

"Good morning, dear thrush," said the fox. "I heard your pleasant voice, and it made my heart rejoice."

"Thanks for your kindness," said the thrush.

The fox called out, "What did you say? I cannot hear you now. Why don't you come down on the grass? We'll take a nice, long walk and have a good, friendly talk."

But the thrush said, "It isn't safe for us birds on the grass."

"You are not afraid of me?" cried the fox.

"Well, if not you, then some other animal."

"Oh, no, my dearest friend. There is a new law in the land. Today there is peace among all beasts. We are all brothers. None is allowed to hurt another."

"That's good," said the thrush. "I see dogs coming this way. Under the old law, you would have had to run away. But now there is no reason for you to be frightened."

As soon as the fox heard about the dogs, he pricked up his ears and started running.

"Where are you going?" cried the thrush. "We have a new law in the land. The dogs won't touch you now."

"Who knows," answered the fox as he ran. "Perhaps they have not heard about it yet."

The Partridge and the Crow
retold by Maude Barrows Dutton

A crow flying across a road saw a partridge strutting along the ground.

"What a beautiful gait that partridge has!" said the crow. "I must try to see if I can walk like him."

She alighted behind the partridge and tried for a long time to learn to strut. At last the partridge turned around and asked the crow what she was about.

"Do not be angry with me," replied the crow. "I have never before seen a bird who walks as beautifully as you can, and I am trying to learn to walk like you.

"Foolish bird!" responded the partridge. "You are a crow, and should walk like a crow. You would look silly indeed if you were to strut like a partridge."

But the crow went on trying to learn to strut, until finally she had forgotten her own gait, and she never learned that of the partridge.

The Dog and the Wolf
retold from Aesop by Thomas Bewick

Discouraged after an unsuccessful day of hunting, a hungry wolf came on a well-fed mastiff. He could see that the dog was having a better time of it than he was and he inquired what the dog had to do to stay so well fed. "Very little," said the dog. "Just drive away beggars, guard the house, show fondness to the master, be submissive to the rest of the family and you are well fed and warmly lodged."

The wolf thought this over carefully. He risked his own life almost daily, had to stay out in the worst of weather, and was never assured of his meals. He thought he would try another way of living.

As they were going along together the wolf saw a place around the dog's neck where the hair had worn thin. He asked what this was and the dog said it was nothing, "just the place where my collar and chain rub." The wolf stopped short. "Chain?" he asked. "You mean you are not free to go where you choose?" "No," said the dog, "but what does that mean?" "Much," answered the wolf as he trotted off. "Much."

Far Looker

by Mari Sandoz

When the son of Tall Deer was born, the Sioux warrior gave away many ponies. He gave ponies to all those of his village who were poor, for was not his son, No Eyes, of the Chosen Ones? Many children came every year to the tipis of the great Sioux people, but only a few were set off from the rest because they would never hear the barking of the village dogs, or learn to make words, or see the sun on the buffalo grass. These, it was well known, were the bearers of great gifts for the preservation of their people. And so Tall Deer made all the village glad with him.

Soon this boy of the Chosen Ones learned to know many things beyond common man. He could feel spring on his cheek when the tipis were yet in snow, could smell the smokeless enemy fire that none could see, could hear the far crunch of the ice under the feet of the elk when meat was low in the village. Often in the night he was allowed to roam, for darkness and day were as one to him.

Then one night the fall he was nine, when the ponies were fat and the village full of winter meat, he smelled the burning of the smokeless fire. He was away from his village, up the wind, and his own people had no reason to burn the fire of the sneaker of the night. Swiftly he thought. It must be an enemy war party, out for horses, meat, and scalps. He sniffed the air, slipped off his moccasins and circled out wide, like the bow of a great man. Then his feet felt pony tracks, many times his toes in number, and the broken earth still moist. He followed the trail, losing the fire smell, finding it again. Several times he put his ear to the earth for the sound of pony feet. At last he found them, many ponies feeding, two men on guard, making low words he did not know, and many sleeping men breathing nearby, many men and no women—a war party.

No Eyes knew what this meant—attack at the first small wind of dawn upon his unsuspecting village, robes waved to scatter the pony herd, whooping warriors riding up the canyon to cut off escape, riding down the tipis of his people, with the twanging of the bow string, the swinging of the war club. Swiftly the boy dropped his robe, slipped into his moccasins and began to run. He ran lightly, not swiftly, knowing he must last, avoiding bush and stone and tree, running along the crest of the ridge as the coyote lopes.

An hour later, before the time for the enemy's coming, there was robe-waving among the ponies of the enemy's herd, and wild young Sioux riding the surprised sleepers down. By the time the sun was warm on the face, and the cooking fires burning fine before the tipis, the captured ponies were all admired and divided. Then Tall Deer walked slowly through the village in his noblest blanket of blue cloth with a white banding of beads. He was making a song, calling for his friends to feast with him, for now his son who had been No Eyes would be Far Looker, one whose far seeing had indeed saved his village and his people.

▶ **Discussing**
1. What lesson does each fable teach? What was No Eyes's brave deed?
2. In "The Fox and the Thrush," is the fox being honest? How do you know?
3. In "The Partridge and the Crow," what does the crow admire about the partridge? What advice does the partridge give?
4. In "The Dog and the Wolf," what things does the dog have to do in order to be fed and lodged? What must he give up?
5. In "Far Looker," how does No Eyes track the enemy?
6. Tell about a personal experience that one of the stories in this lesson brings to mind.

▶ **Analyzing: Theme**

The **theme** of a literary work is its main idea. Usually the theme is implied, but sometimes it is directly stated. The moral of a fable is usually its theme. What is the theme of each of the following?

1. "The Fox and the Thrush" **a.** Don't trust anyone. **b.** Don't always believe what you hear.
2. "The Partridge and the Crow" **a.** It is better to fly than to strut. **b.** It is better to be yourself than to imitate someone else.
3. "The Dog and the Wolf" **a.** It is better to be free and starving than to be a slave and well fed. **b.** Everyone is free to choose his or her own way of life.
4. "Far Looker" **a.** The Sioux are great warriors. **b.** One can accomplish great deeds in spite of a disability.

▶ **Writing**

Choose one fable whose moral appeals to you. Write a few sentences explaining why you think the moral is important.

▶ **Extending**

Speaking and Listening   Meet with a small group of classmates to discuss what daily life might be like in a far other time. Select a year either in the past or in the future. Describe what a day would be like.

Reading   *Journey to the Centre of the Earth,* by Jules Verne, is about a group of explorers who travel down the funnel of a volcano and find evidence of life that existed in a far other time.

2 Discussing a Myth

A myth is a traditional story often involving supernatural beings that explains a phenomenon of nature.

▶ **Focus**   Like the folk literature you read in Lesson 1, myths are very old stories that have been handed down from generation to generation. Different versions of the same myth have been told by different storytellers and writers.

Myths are set in a timeless past and are generally not intended to be amusing. They explain the beliefs of a particular group of people about nature and contain supernatural elements. Myths, like fables, may give lessons in how people should behave.

In this lesson you will discuss a myth. When people examine and discuss a literary work in a group situation, they often come away with a deeper understanding and appreciation of that work. Someone may express an idea that no one else thought of.

Because everyone interprets what he or she reads differently, there may be some disagreement in a discussion. Remember, though, a discussion is not an argument. Its purpose is to share ideas and information. The following guidelines will help you when you have your discussion about the myth.

Guidelines for a Discussion
- If you need information for the discussion, get it beforehand.
- Be sure you know what you're talking about. Use facts and examples to support your statements.
- Speak clearly and loudly enough for everyone to hear.
- Stick to the topic. Be aware of where the discussion is headed.
- Be polite. Don't interrupt when others are speaking.
- Listen closely to what others have to say. Ask them about their ideas.
- If you disagree with someone, say so politely.

▶ **Practice** **A.** Listen to your teacher read the myth "Arachne."
Then divide into small groups to discuss it, using the questions
below. Use the discussion guidelines on the preceding page.

1. What phenomenon of nature is explained in this myth?
2. What is the setting of "Arachne"?
3. For what was Arachne famous? How did she feel about her
   skill?
4. What kind of person was Arachne?
5. Why did Athene come to earth disguised as an old woman?
6. What did Athene weave? Why did she weave this?
7. Who won the contest? How did Arachne react to this?
8. What was Arachne's punishment? Do you think Arachne
   deserved this? Why or why not?
9. What is the lesson of this myth?
10. Do you think people should be proud of their accomplishments?
    When do they go too far with this?
11. What real life situations can you think of where pride was
    someone's undoing?
12. What other stories—new or old—have you read that have a
    theme similar to the one in "Arachne"?
13. What details would need to change if "Arachne" took place in a
    modern setting?

B. With the same group of classmates from Practice A, create a
myth. Choose one or two of the suggestions below as possible topics
for the myth, or the group can make up a topic of its own. Choose
one person to take notes. Brainstorm ideas that would explain how
this element of nature came to be. Select a timeless setting and
decide if your myth will teach a lesson. When you have finalized
your myth, present it to the rest of the class.

14. why cats and dogs fight
15. why parrots talk
16. why leaves fall off trees when autumn comes
17. why the sea is salty
18. why snow is white

▶ **Apply/Oral Language** Read a myth and tell the class about it.
Be sure to relate what phenomenon of nature is explained.

3 Prefixes and Suffixes

Recognizing prefixes and suffixes can help you figure out word meanings.

▶ **Focus** Words are often made up of several parts—a root and one or more prefixes and suffixes. Sometimes if you look at the separate parts of an unfamiliar word, its meaning will become clear. For example, consider the word *premeditation,* or *pre + meditate + tion.* The word *meditate* means "to think about or plan," and the prefix *pre-* means "before." The suffix *-tion* means "act of" and is added to the word *meditate* to form the noun *meditation.* When you combine the meanings of these parts, you get a definition for *premeditation:* "the act of planning beforehand."

Listed below are common prefixes and suffixes along with some of their meanings. Use them to answer the exercises on the next page.

Prefixes		Suffixes	
dis-	opposite of; not	-ary	having to do with
en-	cause to be	-ent	one that _____
il-	not (used before *l*)	-ful	full of _____
im-	not (used before *m, p*)	-ible	that can be _____ed
ir-	not (used before *r*)	-ish	like a _____
mis-	bad; wrong	-ize	make
over-	too; too much	-less	without a _____
re-	again	-ment	condition of being _____ed
un-	not	-ous	full of
under-	not enough	-ship	condition or skill of

Follow these spelling rules for adding prefixes and suffixes.

- When a prefix is added to a root word, the spelling of the root does not change.
- When a suffix beginning with a vowel is added to a word ending in silent *e,* the *e* is dropped (advisable). The exception is if the *e* is preceded by *c* or *g* (outrageous).
- When a suffix is added to a word ending with a consonant plus *y,* the *y* is usually changed to *i* (steadily).

▶ **Guided Practice**   In the following line from "The Dog and the Wolf," what does the word *unsuccessful* mean?

Discouraged after an unsuccessful day of hunting, a hungry wolf came on a well-fed mastiff.

▶ **Practice**   **A.** Look at the italicized word in each sentence. Use your knowledge of roots, prefixes, and suffixes to help define the word. You may need to use a dictionary for some words.
Example: Manny told us the decision was *irreversible*.
Answer: something that cannot be reversed

1. Our boss will *disapprove* of our long lunch hours.
2. That printing is too large, but I was told it is *irreducible*.
3. Paul Bunyan was a folk hero of *legendary* strength.
4. When Jake saw the election results, he knew he had been *overconfident* about his chances of winning.
5. The teacher criticized our *childish* behavior on the trip.
6. The man's handwriting was *unreadable*.
7. Because Ned kept distracting her with his jokes, Sara was afraid she would *miscount* the tickets.
8. Notice the fine *workmanship* on this antique chair.
9. This is a *restatement* of the original sentence.

B. Follow the directions from Practice A to define each italicized word. Then write another sentence using each word.
Example: It was a *joyous* occasion when Nancy returned from her trip.
Answer: full of joy   The joyous child smiled brightly.

10. Sam hopes to become a foreign *correspondent* for a newspaper.
11. *Thunderous* applause greeted the orchestra.
12. There was loud *disagreement* among the members of the group.
13. Contaminated water could *endanger* the lives of thousands of people in the surrounding area.
14. Drivers may *misinterpret* signs that are poorly worded.

▶ **Apply/Writing**   Choose three of the following prefixes and suffixes: *en-, il-, ir-, -ent, -ize, -ship, -ment*. Write a paragraph about something you find difficult to do. Use four words that contain the suffixes and prefixes you have chosen.

Our Living Language

English Is Alive and Well

> My computer uses a floppy disk. I just
> wrote a new program for it. I'll give you
> a printout.

Do you understand the paragraph above? Do you think an English-speaking person who lived in the 1800s would understand it? A living language never stands still. Some words familiar to you were unknown to people one hundred years ago.

Words are being invented all the time. Some new words to enter our vocabularies are *chairperson, videotape, hype* (from *hyperbole*), and *quasar* (a blend of *quasi* and *stellar*). Words called *acronyms* are formed by using the initial letters of several words: *sonar* (from **so**und **na**vigation **r**anging), NASA (from **N**ational **A**eronautics and **S**pace **A**dministration).

As we approach the year 2000, English is alive and well. In the 1980s, words such as *byte, Dumpster, house-sit, interface, teletext,* and *Yuppie* entered our dictionaries. Recent English words are entering foreign languages too. Soon, words like *self-service,* and *soundtrack* will be understood everywhere. In the years to come, English will undoubtedly continue to be a vital force—a living language.

Word Play Use the ideas below to invent some words of the future.

1. a video machine that records your dreams
2. a robot that walks dogs
3. a medicine that makes you immune to all diseases
4. clothes that never need cleaning

4 Forming a Thesis Statement

A thesis statement is a sentence that expresses the main idea and focus of an essay.

▶ **Focus**   In the next lesson, you will write a literary response essay. In the essay, you will respond to folk literature that you have read. An essay of this type is developed around a thesis. This **thesis** is the major idea expressed and then supported throughout the composition. An essay's thesis is presented in a sentence called the **thesis statement,** a general statement that tells what the essay is about. The purpose of a literary response essay is to prove the validity of the thesis statement with details from literature. The thesis statement does not give a plot summary but rather your position on what you've read.

The thesis statement is usually the first sentence in an essay. It lets the reader know the focus of the essay. How can you form a thesis statement? First, reread the stories in Unit 34, or one from another book. As you read, note a moral, character, image, or bit of dialogue that appeals to you. Now examine your notes and try to write a sentence that expresses the big idea that you would like to make in your essay. Make sure your thesis statement is clear, concise, and specific.

A thesis statement should be short, clear and specific. Study the three thesis statements below, based on the legend "Far Looker." Which one is best?

    A. Some legends are about Indians.
    B. "Far Looker" is an excellent example of a legend.
    C. No Eyes smelled smokeless fire, slipped off his moccasins, followed pony tracks, and discovered a war party.

The best thesis statement is B. It is short, clear, and specific and summarizes the main ideas of the essay. It is important to realize that your thesis statement may change before you begin your actual writing. This can occur after you work with your notes and become aware of a part of your topic that you want to emphasize or omit.

▶ **Guided Practice**   Tell what is wrong with the other two thesis statements for "Far Looker."

► **Practice**   **A.** Study each group of three thesis statements based on the fables in Unit 34. Then tell which one is best.

1. "The Fox and the Thrush"
   a. Foxes should be hunted because they destroy birds.
   b. The thrush protected itself well by reacting to the fox with cleverness rather than fear.
   c. Fables are more interesting when the characters are at odds with each other.
2. "The Partridge and the Crow"
   a. The moral of "The Partridge and the Crow" is effectively taught.
   b. The partridge in "The Partridge and the Crow" thought that the crow was silly.
   c. Partridges are beautiful birds.
3. "The Dog and the Wolf"
   a. Wolves have a harder life than dogs do.
   b. The wolf decides that he'd better keep things the way they are, and he also realizes that there's no need for him to envy the better-fed dog.
   c. Fables usually make their point in few words.

B. Read this summary of the Aesop fable "The Dog and the Shadow" and write your own thesis statement based on it.

A dog crossing a bridge over a stream with a piece of meat in his mouth happened to see his reflection in the water. He thought it was another dog with another piece of meat. He dropped his own piece and jumped at the other so he could have two pieces of meat. As a result, he got neither—one being a shadow and the other being carried away by the current.

► **Apply/Prewriting**   Choose one of the thesis statements presented in this lesson and write down two details that help support it. Adjust the thesis statement slightly if the two details bring to mind a different emphasis.

5 Writing a Literary Response Essay

You can express your ideas and opinions about a work of literature in a literary response essay.

In previous lessons in this book, you have read and written a number of things, including a short story, a poem, and a how-to explanation. In this lesson, you will write a **literary response essay** that presents your ideas about a work of literature—in this case, a fable. As you prepare to write this essay, try to recall the literature and writing skills you have learned about throughout this book.

Before you actually begin to write your essay, decide who your **audience** will be. Make sure you have a clear idea of your **purpose.** Remember, the purpose of a literary response essay is to present and support a valid thesis related to a literary work.

1. Prewriting

▶ **Choose a Topic**   First, choose a fable to discuss in your essay. Choose one of the fables you worked with in the preceding unit or find another fable that appeals to you.

Once you have decided on a fable to write about, read it over two or three times. Then **use the thinking skill of summarizing** to write a brief summary of the fable and some thoughts about it. As you study the fable, remember to draw conclusions about characters and their motivations. Be aware, too, of cause and effect. Ask yourself questions like these:

1. Why does this fable appeal to me?
2. What personality traits do the characters have? How do these traits affect their behavior?
3. Are the characters appropriate for the parts they play? Why or why not?
4. Am I sympathetic to the characters? Why or why not?
5. Do I agree with the lesson, or moral?
6. How might the moral apply to my everyday life? to life in general?

Now, look over what you have written and choose a topic that interests you and about which you have enough information and ideas. For example, you may decide to write about the characters or the moral of a fable.

Next, develop a thesis statement for your essay. As you learned, a thesis statement should express the focus of your essay. Possible thesis statements for the fable "The Partridge and the Crow" are these:

1. The gentle way in which "The Partridge and the Crow" is written may not be strong enough to carry its warning effectively.
2. The moral in "The Partridge and the Crow" applies well to developing one's talents.
3. The characters in "The Partridge and the Crow" act very much like humans do.

▶ **Develop Ideas**   With a specific topic and a thesis statement in mind, you can begin to organize your thoughts about the fable you have chosen. Try outlining your ideas. The following sample four-part outline is for an essay based on "The Partridge and the Crow."

   I. Thesis Statement: the moral—"Be yourself"—applies to developing one's own talents
  II. Plot Summary
     A. Crow admires partridge's walk
     B. Tries to imitate partridge
     C. Loses own identity
 III. Practical Application
     A. Tony (swimmer) admires Steve (soccer player)
     B. Tony practices soccer and neglects swimming
     C. Tony loses swimming skills and doesn't make the soccer team
 IV. Conclusion

Create a **Word Bank.** Consider using the words in the Word Bank at the right.

Word Bank
beliefs
affection
rash
haggard
imitate
virtue
admire

2. Writing

▶ **Study the Draft**   The following essay is a first draft written from the preceding outline. Notice how the thesis statement expresses the focus of the fable. Note also the use of transition words and phrases such as *then*, *for example*, and *consequently* to connect sentences. Remember that a first draft will probably contain errors and changes.

Use Your Talents

"Be yourself" — the moral of the fable "The Partridge and the Crow" — is a phrase that sure applies to developing one's talents. The animals in this here tale do and say things that can teach us about ~~ourselfs~~ ourselves.

A crow admires a partridge's strutting walk, and she tries to be like the crow and imitate it. The partridge calls her a "foolish bird" for trying to be something she isn't. The plot of the fable is simple and direct. The crow keeps trying, unsucessfuly, until she can no ~~further~~ longer walk like a crow either. In trying so hard to ~~mimic~~ imitate someone else, the crow loses the ability she once had.

In the same way, a person who tries too hard to imitate someone else may

---

lose their own abilities or talents. For example, Tony, whom is an excellent swimmer, might admire his friend Steve's skill on the soccer feild. Tony has a real good chance of wining the state swim meet, but he practises soccer insted of swimming. Consequently, he is not in no shape for the swim meet, and his skills are not no good enough for the soccer team.

The fable "The Partridge and the Crow" ~~helps us remember~~ is a dramatic remindor for you and I. We should use our own talents before trying to imitate the talents of others.

▶ **Write a Draft** Now you are ready to write your essay. Begin with your thesis statement and consult your outline to determine if each main topic could be used as the main idea of a paragraph. Use transition words and phrases such as *although* and *in this case* as you move from paragraph to paragraph. Conclude your essay with a sentence that reinforces your thesis statement. Finally, think of a title. Remember to write on every other line so you have space to make changes. Consult your notes so you include the information you intended.

3. Revising

▶ **Read and Confer** Read your first draft to make sure your ideas are clearly stated and well organized. It usually helps to put your first draft away for a while before rereading it. Then meet with a partner and read your drafts aloud to each other. Use the following questions to discuss improvements.

> **Conference Questions**
> 1. Does the thesis statement clearly present the essay's focus?
> 2. Are enough details included to support the thesis statement?
> 3. Are the details organized around two or three general ideas?
> 4. Has the writer used transition words and phrases appropriately?
> 5. Is there an effective concluding sentence?
> 6. Should any information be added, deleted, or rearranged?

▶ **Make Changes** Use your conference notes and the strategies below to improve your essay. You have learned about these strategies in other writing process lessons. Notice how the writer of "Use Your Talents" used these strategies.

STRATEGIES: Use a red pencil to make your changes stand out. Use arrows (→) to rearrange information that is out of order. Use a (∧) to add transition words. Use a (   ) to delete unnecessary words.

> First
> ∧A crow admires a partridge's strutting
> walk. and she tries to ~~be like the crow~~
> Then
> ~~and~~ imitate it. ∧The partridge calls her
> a "foolish bird" for trying to be
> something she isn't. (The plot of the
> fable is simple and direct.) The crow

▶ **Proofread and Edit** Check your draft for mistakes in spelling, capitalization, and punctuation. Use the proofreader's marks and the following questions to help you.

Proofreader's Marks

≡
Make a capital.

/
Make a small letter.

⊙
Add a period.

‸
Add a comma.

⋁⋁
Add quotation marks.

⋀
Add something.

℮
Take out something.

↷
Move something.

⨍
New paragraph.

⊛
Correct spelling.

Proofreading Questions

1. Did I use subject and object pronouns correctly?
2. Did I use pronouns that agree with their antecedents?
3. Did I use *who* and *whom* correctly?
4. Did I use adjectives to modify nouns and pronouns and adverbs to modify verbs, adjectives, and other adverbs?
5. Did I use *this, that, these,* and *those* correctly?
6. Did I use only one negative word in a sentence?
7. Did I spell every word correctly?

▶ **Make a Final Copy** Is your essay as good as you can make it? Then write the final draft in your best handwriting.

4. Presenting

It should be interesting to learn what different reactions students have to the same fable.

1. Group the essays by fable and have someone read aloud, for instance, all the literary response essays written about "The Fox and the Thrush." Then compare and contrast the reactions. Next, have someone read aloud all the essays in response to "The Partridge and the Crow," and so on.
2. You might want to collect the essays in a classroom binder for others to read in their free time. You can group them by fable to make comparisons and contrasts easier. Try your hand at illustrating the part of your fable that represents the moral most graphically. For example, show the dog chained to the fence for "The Dog and the Wolf."

Revising and Editing Workshop

Connecting Writing and Grammar

- In Unit 34 you read fables and a legend and heard a myth.
- In Unit 35 you wrote a literary response essay.

Now it's time to use your skill as an editor to improve another writer's first draft. Read this literary response essay carefully. As you read, ask yourself these questions.

✔ Does the thesis statement clearly present the essay's focus and the writer's attitude?
✔ Are subject and object pronouns used correctly?
✔ Are *this*, *that*, *these*, and *those* used correctly?

Learning from Fable Characters

(1) In "The Tortoise and the Hare," the title characters speak and act like humans with very different personalities. (2) The hare is conceited. (3) He boasts loudly about how fast they can run. (4) The tortoise, who the story is also about, is modest and quiet. (5) He knows he is much slower than the hare. (6) The tortoise agrees to a race. (7) The hare, whom is so sure he will win, stops for a rest and falls asleep. (8) The tortoise plods past the sleeping hare, and it is him who wins the race. (9) The patient and determined tortoise accomplishes more than the careless hare, who assumes he doesn't never need to try.

(10) These kind of fable teaches us a lesson about ourselves. (11) It is you and I who will benefit from the moral. (12) If one is overconfident, they may not achieve their goals; anything worth winning takes determination and perseverance. (13) This here moral can apply to all of us. (14) Every day you and me strive for some kind of goal—a good grade, an athletic achievement, or some other accomplishment.

▶ Revising the Draft

1. The writer did not include a thesis statement. Add an opening paragraph to the draft that presents the thesis statement and makes a transition to the second paragraph.
2. The writer did not include an effective concluding sentence. Add this to the draft.
3. To make the sentences read smoother, add transition words and phrases to the paragraph that tells what "The Tortoise and the Hare" is about.
4. Add, delete, or rearrange any other information you think would improve the draft.

▶ Editing the Draft

5. The writer did not use personal pronouns correctly. Correct two sentences in which object pronouns are used instead of subject pronouns.
6. Correct two sentences in which the pronouns do not agree with their antecedents.
7. The writer made errors using *who* and *whom*. Correct two sentences that contain this type of error.
8. The writer did not use *these* and *this* correctly. Correct two sentences that contain this type of error.
9. Correct the sentence that contains two negative words.

▶ Working Together on the Draft

Meet with a group of your classmates. Discuss the changes you made in the draft. Listen to the changes your classmates made. Then rewrite the draft on page 476. Include all the revisions you think are important.

▶ Evaluating Your Own Writing

Now review your own writing. Look over the literary response essay you wrote in this unit and any other written work you have. Did you have any problems using subject and object pronouns correctly? Did you have any problems using *who* and *whom?* The lessons that follow will help you with these writing problems.

6 Subject and Object Pronouns

Subject pronouns are used as subjects of sentences. Object pronouns can be used as direct objects, indirect objects, or objects of prepositions.

▶ **Focus**   When a pronoun is used as the subject of a sentence, the pronoun is in the nominative case and is called a **subject pronoun.** Notice the pronouns in the chart and then read the sentences.

Subject Pronouns			
Singular	I	you	he, she, it
Plural	we	you	they

I borrowed Marta's bike.   Bill and **I** rode bikes.

The sentence on the right has a compound subject. To check that you are using the correct pronoun in a compound subject, use the pronoun by itself with the verb. For the compound subject *Bill and I,* you would say *I rode,* which makes sense (Not: *me rode*).

Personal pronouns can also be used as direct and indirect objects and objects of prepositions. Then the pronoun is in the objective case and is called an **object pronoun.** Study the object pronouns in the chart and then read the sentences.

Object Pronouns			
Singular	me	you	him, her, it
Plural	us	you	them

When the sandwiches were ready, Kay ate **them.** (direct object)
Mrs. Rosario gave **me** and **her** some orange juice too. (indirect objects)
When Nolan arrived, we ate lunch with Mrs. Rosario and **him.**
(objects of preposition)

To check that you are using the correct pronoun in a compound object, say the sentence with just one pronoun as the object.

► **Guided Practice**   Tell which pronoun form in parentheses is the correct one to use in each sentence and why.

1. Jill and (I, me) are in the same history class.
2. Our teacher gave an assignment to (she, her) and (I, me)—a report on peasant life in the Middle Ages.
3. Toni and (they, them) are studying medieval home life.
4. (He, Him) and Manuel are researching knighthood.
5. Our teacher gave Jill and (I, me) a good grade.
6. She congratulated Toni and (they, them) on their report.

► **Practice**   **A.** Write the dialogue below, completing each blank with the subject or object pronoun that is appropriate.
Example: MORRIS: How are _____ today, Norris?
Answer: MORRIS: How are you today, Norris?

MORRIS   *(to himself):* ___(1)___ think I'll call my good friend Norris
to see how ___(2)___ is. *(The phone rings.)*
Hello . . . hello . . . Norris, can you hear ___(3)___ ?

NORRIS: Of course ___(4)___ am able to hear you, but just barely.
___(5)___ always seem to get a bad connection. The phone-
company people should pay ___(6)___ for the use of these
phones.

MORRIS: ___(7)___ should write ___(8)___ a letter about our phones.

NORRIS: ___(9)___ write the letter, Morris, and I'll sign ___(10)___ .

MORRIS: Why do ___(11)___ always have to do the writing, Norris?

NORRIS: The phone company and ___(12)___ are not on speaking
terms, that's why. Besides, your writing amuses ___(13)___ .

MORRIS: What do you mean ___(14)___ amuses you?

NORRIS: You always give the phone company and ___(15)___
something to laugh about.

B. Write the pronoun that can be substituted for the underlined word or groups of words.
Example: <u>France</u> was an important center for painters.
Answer: It

16. <u>Women</u> were not accepted as artists until quite recently.
17. People ignored <u>Mary Cassatt</u> for years.
18. Mary's parents raised <u>Mary and her brothers and sisters</u>.
19. Eventually, Mary and <u>her family</u> settled in Pennsylvania.

20. Mary surprised her parents when she decided to become an artist.
21. The decision was unusual for a woman of her time.
22. Mary's decision was supported by Mr. Cassatt and her older brother.
23. In 1866 Mary went to France with her parents and her sister.
24. In Paris Mary studied art done by Impressionists.
25. These painters experimented with the effects of light and color.
26. Edgar Degas, an Impressionist, and Mary became friends.
27. Degas introduced Mary to other painters and sculptors.
28. Her paintings show the influence of the French Impressionists.
29. Today people from around the world know Mary Cassatt and her paintings.

C. Write the correct form of the pronoun in parentheses.
Example: (He, Him) and Naomi both play the banjo.
Answer: He

30. Wallace and (she, her) have joined the school orchestra.
31. Naomi gave Sam and (I, me) tickets to the first concert.
32. The musicians and (we, us) were the first ones to arrive.
33. The ushers and (they, them) showed us to our seats.
34. Then the musicians invited Naomi and (we, us) backstage so we could watch them prepare for the performance.
35. Paula, Blair, and (I, me) all play the trumpet.
36. Paula and (he, him) are good musicians.
37. (She, Her) and her brother Frank are in the orchestra.
38. Our group met (she, her) and (he, him).
39. (He, Him) and Barney are accomplished clarinet players.
40. (We, Us) and (they, them) wanted to hear Frank play a solo.
41. Instead Naomi and (he, him) sang a duet.
42. Kyoko and (she, her) got the most applause.
43. Both (she, her) and Naomi have marvelous voices.
44. After the concert we congratulated the musicians and (they, them) on their performances.

▶ **Apply/Writing** Write a conversation like the one between Morris and Norris in Practice A. Try to use as many subject and object pronouns as you can in your conversation.

7 Pronouns as Subject Complements

A subject pronoun is used as a subject complement.

▶ **Focus**   As you know, when a word follows a linking verb and refers to the subject, it is called a **subject complement.** A pronoun that follows a linking verb such as *am, is, are, was,* and *were* and identifies the subject is used as a subject complement. A subject pronoun is always used as a subject complement in formal English. Compare the following pairs of sentences. The subjects are underlined; the subject complements are in dark type.

<u>She</u> is the **judge.**   The <u>judge</u> is **she.**
<u>They</u> are the **players.**   The <u>players</u> are **they.**
<u>Tim and I</u> are **alternates.**   The <u>alternates</u> are **Tim and I.**

In the sentences on the left, the subject complement *judge* refers to the subject *she,* the subject complement *players* refers to the subject *they,* and the complement *alternates* refers to the subject *Tim and I.* The subject and subject complement in each sentence refer to the same people. Therefore, the sentences can be turned around as they are at the right without changing the meaning. Notice that the pronoun forms do not change when the sentences are turned around. The same pronoun form—a subject pronoun—is used as subject and as subject complement.

If someone asks you "Who is it?" you probably use an object pronoun and say "It is me" or "It's me" rather than "It is I." When you are speaking to family or friends, "It's me" is acceptable. However, in writing or in more formal situations such as a job interview, use "It is I." Also use "It is she," "It is we," and so on.

▶ **Guided Practice**   Tell which form of the pronoun in parentheses is correct to use in formal situations.

1. It was (she, her) who had the idea.
2. It was (they, them) who made the posters.
3. It was Lucia and (I, me) who distributed them.
4. They thanked Lucia and (I, me).
5. It was (we, us) who helped.
6. The person who benefited most was (he, him).

▶ **Practice**   **A.** Write whether the underlined pronoun in each sentence is used as a subject or subject complement.

Example: According to Scooter, <u>he</u> and I must prepare a report.
Answer: Subject

1. <u>We</u> were puzzled about being chosen to do a report.
2. The only two students that were selected were Scooter and <u>I</u>.
3. <u>He</u> and I both liked the novelist Daniel Defoe.
4. It was <u>he</u> that we chose for our report.
5. <u>We</u> had both enjoyed reading *Robinson Crusoe*.
6. <u>It</u> is the novel based on the life of Alexander Selkirk.
7. It was <u>he</u> whom Defoe used to create Crusoe.
8. The main characters are Friday and <u>he</u>.
9. Scooter thought it was <u>he</u> who made the novel interesting.
10. <u>I</u> wrote about the lives of Selkirk and Defoe.

B. Write the pronoun that completes the sentence. Tell whether the pronoun used is a subject pronoun or object pronoun.

Example: Between Scooter and (I, me), we finished the report.
Answer: me—Object pronoun

11. Scooter and (I, me) practiced giving our report many times.
12. It was (I, me) who was nervous, not Scooter.
13. It was (he, him) who introduced the report.
14. The only two speakers today are Scooter and (I, me).
15. First, (he, him) will speak about the life of Daniel Defoe.
16. (I, Me) will also say something about Defoe.
17. About (he, him) we know very little.
18. (We, Us) know, however, that Defoe was a novelist, journalist, and secret agent.
19. It was (he, him) that Queen Anne threw in prison in 1702.
20. To Scooter and (I, me), *Robinson Crusoe* is his best novel.
21. To (we, us), Friday is one of the most important characters.
22. It is (he, him) who makes the story exciting.
23. The phrase "man Friday" comes from (he, him).

▶ **Apply/Writing**   Write sentences naming the best actress, the best musician, the best friend, and the best writer you know. Then replace those nouns with subject complements.
Example: My best friend is John. My best friend is he.

8 Pronoun Agreement

A pronoun should agree with its antecedent.

▶ **Focus**   As you know, an **antecedent** is the word to which a pronoun refers. When the antecedent is singular, the pronoun referring to it should be singular. When the antecedent is plural, the pronoun should be plural. Here are examples.

> The **duke** went out riding on **his** horse.
> The **duchess** attended to **her** horse at the stable.
> The **horses** served **their** owners well.

The pronouns and antecedents above also agree in gender. That means the masculine pronoun *his* refers to the masculine noun *duke*. The feminine pronoun *her* agrees with the feminine noun *duchess*.

What pronoun would you use to complete this sentence?

> If a driver is careful, _____ can avoid many accidents.

In formal English the pronoun *he* is used. However, because the noun *driver* in such a sentence might refer to either a man or a woman, some writers use the phrase *he or she*. Another, less repetitious, solution is to reword the sentence, if possible.

> If drivers are careful, **they** can avoid many accidents.
> A careful driver can avoid many accidents.

Although in everyday conversation you sometimes hear *they* or *you* used with a singular antecedent, this use of a plural pronoun should be avoided in writing.

> **Do not write:** If a driver is careful, **they** can avoid many accidents.
> If a driver is careful, **you** can avoid many accidents.

Singular indefinite pronouns like *each, anybody, everyone, either, someone,* and *neither* should be referred to by singular pronouns. Although in conversation plural pronouns are sometimes used, this should be avoided in formal speech and in all writing. Plural indefinite pronouns like *both, few, many* and *several* should be referred to by plural pronouns.

> **Each** of the girls displayed **her** entry. (Not: their)
> **Both** of the winners proudly held up **their** prizes. (Not: her)

▶ **Guided Practice**   Tell whether the underlined pronoun in each sentence is used correctly. Explain your answer.

1. Has either of the women had <u>their</u> turn yet?
2. Each of the boys offered <u>his</u> help.
3. If a person is wrong, <u>they</u> should admit the fact.
4. Many of the participants brought <u>their</u> radios.

▶ **Practice**   **A.** Write a pronoun that correctly completes each sentence in formal English.

Example: A female member of the expedition unpacked ——— gear.
Answer: her

1. Each person had ——— own backpack.
2. Several of the hikers carried heavy things in ——— packs.
3. Many of the women carried cameras around ——— necks.
4. Every explorer had ——— own goal.
5. One of the men went north with ——— guide.
6. Several of the hikers followed ——— guide along a river.
7. On the third day somebody lost ——— sleeping bag.
8. Someone had lost several of ——— maps.
9. Neither of the guides ever lost ——— patience.
10. The younger of the women picked ——— way carefully.
11. Both of the guides carried equipment on ——— heads at times.
12. Everyone knew that ——— should wear sunglasses.
13. At night no one was to leave ——— tent.
14. The explorers took time to write about ——— discoveries that day.
15. Each of the guides had ——— own tent.
16. No one complained about ——— food.
17. Some of the party did voice ——— other complaints.
18. Most said ——— were covered with insect bites.
19. One of the women brought out ——— first-aid kit.
20. If a jungle explorer forgets repellent, ——— is in trouble.
21. A few of the explorers said ——— would be glad to get home.
22. Everybody said ——— had a great time.
23. Many of the participants gave money toward ——— next expedition.
24. Does anyone from the expedition know where ——— will explore next year?

B. Write the pronoun that agrees with each indefinite pronoun in formal English.

Example: If someone on the boys' team volunteers, (they, he) should be prepared to work.

Answer: he

25. Everyone on the boys' team did (their, his) work.
26. Each of the girls spent (their, her) time at the car wash.
27. Many of the girls brought (their, her) towels and sponges.
28. Neither of the twins brought (their, her) old clothes.
29. Neither of them had time for (her, their) lunch.
30. All of the boys spent (their, his) time waxing and polishing.
31. Many of the boys also gave (their, his) time to work at the retirement home.
32. Each of the boys was using (their, his) parents' lawnmower.
33. Many of them spent (their, his) time trimming hedges.
34. Neither of the girls realized how much (their, her) contribution was appreciated.

C. If the antecedent and pronoun in a sentence agree, write *Correct.* If they do not agree, rewrite the sentence, correcting the pronoun.

Example: Each of the bakers has their own specialty.

Answer: Each of the bakers has his own specialty.

35. If a repair person will be late, they should call.
36. Few of the actresses knew their lines yet.
37. Each of the mechanics bought their own tools.
38. When a person is a doctor, they sometimes work long hours for several days in a row.
39. If you are a plumber, you must take care of your tools.
40. Neither of the chefs owned their own restaurant.
41. Before a lawyer can practice, they must pass a bar exam.
42. If any of the teachers disagreed, they didn't say so.
43. Many of the faculty help their students if necessary.
44. If a farmer has a good crop, they feel lucky.

▶ **Apply/Writing**   Write three or four sentences about a career you are interested in. Use singular indefinite pronouns as subject antecedents of other pronouns. Check to be sure the pronouns and antecedents agree.

9 Using *who* and *whom*

Who is generally used as a subject. Whom is used as a direct object or object of a preposition.

▶ **Focus**   *Who* is usually used as a subject of a sentence or clause.

> **Who** knows anything about books?
> The man **who** brought the message left immediately.

In the first sentence *who* is the subject of the verb *knows*. In the second sentence *who* is the subject of *brought* in the clause *who brought the message*.

The pronoun *whom* is used as the direct object of an action verb or with a preposition such as *for, from, to,* and *with*. Look at these two uses of *whom* in the sentences below.

> **Whom** do we call for information?
> Is this the man **whom** the bank president hired?
> From **whom** did you hear the news?

In the first sentence the pronoun *whom* is the direct object of the sentence (*we do call whom*). In the next sentence *whom* is the direct object of the verb *hired* in the clause *whom the bank president hired* (*the bank president hired whom*). In the third sentence the pronoun *whom* is the object of the preposition *from*.

Now read these sentences. How is *who* being used in the sentences on the left? How is *whom* being used in the sentences on the right?

Who is the next appointment?	**Whom** do you see at 3:00?
Those **who** arrived can sign in.	To **whom** do I give this?

In everyday conversation *who* is often used in place of *whom,* especially at the beginning of questions: *Who did you write?* However, in writing and formal speech, use *whom* as a direct object or object of a preposition: *Whom did you write?*

▶ **Guided Practice**   Tell how the underlined pronoun is used.

1. <u>Whom</u> did you sell the ticket to?
2. The one <u>who</u> sold the most tickets was Patty.
3. That is the actor <u>whom</u> I admire.

Example: (Who, Whom) called you yesterday?
Answer: Who

1. (Who, Whom) wants to ride downtown?
2. From (who, whom) did you get a ride?
3. (Who, Whom) gave you an invitation?
4. This is the girl (who, whom) Jon invited.
5. (Who, Whom) do you usually invite?
6. Ramon was the one (who, whom) thought of the idea.
7. I don't know anyone (who, whom) wouldn't like it.
8. Ramon and Pia are the ones (who, whom) we should thank.
9. (Who, Whom) arranged the flowers on the tables?
10. (Who, Whom) cooked these delicious foods?

B. Complete each sentence with *who* or *whom.*
Example: Do you know for _____ this hairstyle is named?
Answer: Do you know for whom this hairstyle is named?

11. Rudolph Diesel was the German engineer _____ invented the diesel engine.
12. For _____ was the state of Virginia named?
13. Jean Martinet was a military leader _____ people hated.
14. Someone _____ is too strict is called a martinet.
15. The man _____ ran from Marathon to Athens in 490 B.C. became famous.
16. People for _____ running is a sport enter marathons.
17. _____ was the Earl of Sandwich?
18. He is the person after _____ the sandwich was named.
19. _____ was Napoleon Bonaparte?
20. From _____ did you receive that biography about Napoleon Bonaparte's life?

▶ **Apply/Writing** Write several sentences describing people that you know or have heard about. They might be friends, sports figures, or people in the news. Use the word *who* in half of your sentences and *whom* in the other half. Try to give the person's occupation in the sentence. You might begin some of your sentences like this: *I admire Pablo Picasso, who was a . . .*

10 Adjective or Adverb

Use adjectives to modify nouns and pronouns. Use adverbs to modify verbs, adjectives, and other adverbs.

▶ **Focus**   Sometimes it is difficult to tell whether to use an adjective or an adverb after the verb in a sentence. The choice depends both on what word is being modified and what kind of verb is used. Look at the following sentences.

> The tiger **snarled ferociously.**
> The tiger **was ferocious.**

The verb *snarled* in the first sentence is an action verb. It is followed by the adverb *ferociously,* which tells *how* the tiger snarled. In the second sentence the verb *was* is a linking verb. It is followed by the predicate adjective *ferocious,* which modifies the subject noun *tiger.* The adjective describes the tiger.

Before you choose between an adjective or adverb following a verb, decide what word is being modified. Use an adverb (usually a form with an *-ly* ending) to modify an action verb.

> The chef **tasted** the hot soup **carefully.**
> You **read** that speech **perfectly.**

Use an adjective to modify nouns and pronouns.

> The hot **soup** smelled **delicious.**
> His **voice** sounded **confident** too.

The adjectives *sure* and *real* and the adverbs *surely* and *really* can be especially troublesome. Look at their use in the following pairs of sentences.

> Tino was **sure.**   He was **surely** certain.
> His account was **real.**   His account was **really** believable.

In the first sentence on the left, the adjective *sure* is a predicate adjective. It modifies the noun *Tino.* In the sentence on the right, the intensifier-type adverb *surely* modifies the predicate adjective *certain.* What does the adjective *real* modify in the second pair of sentences? What does the adverb *really* modify?

▶ **Guided Practice**   Tell whether the underlined modifier in each sentence is correct or incorrect and why.

1. Cam spoke <u>real</u> sincerely.
2. This suit fits <u>perfect</u>.
3. That peach tastes <u>sour</u>.
4. He really sleeps <u>sound</u>.
5. They are <u>sure</u> right.
6. We ate <u>hearty</u>.

▶ **Practice**   **A.** Write the word that correctly completes the sentence. Then tell whether the word is an adjective or an adverb.

Example: We did a (real, really) good job.
Answer: We did a really good job. Adverb

1. This engine usually starts (regular, regularly).
2. We should have worked more (careful, carefully).
3. Now the engine is running (smooth, smoothly).
4. Does it sound (smooth, smoothly) to you?
5. It started as (sudden, suddenly) as it stopped.
6. Don't you feel (happy, happily) to have it fixed?
7. Well, don't look so (smug, smugly).
8. We can repair any engine (easy, easily).
9. Jim worked (steady, steadily) on the repairs.
10. The engine now sounds (different, differently).

B. Write the sentences. Substitute for the blanks the modifiers *sure, surely, real,* or *really.*

Example: We are _____ pleased to meet you.
Answer: We are really pleased to meet you.

11. You were _____ right about the contest.
12. It was _____ difficult, wasn't it?
13. I am _____ that is the correct answer.
14. You are a _____ good contestant.
15. Do you have the _____ answer?
16. These are _____ good prizes.

▶ **Apply/Writing**   Write several sentences using the verbs below. Include in your sentences a choice of an adjective or adverb form, like the choices in Practice A. Then have a partner choose the correct adjectives or adverbs.

grow   taste   look   feel   appear   sound

11 *This, that, these, and those*

This and ***that*** are singular. ***These*** and ***those*** are plural.

▶ **Focus**   The adjectives *this, that, these,* and *those* modify nouns by telling *which one* or *which ones. This* and *that* are used to modify singular nouns or pronouns. *These* and *those* are used to modify plural nouns. Study these examples.

> **This** book on my desk explains how to make a fighter kite.
> **These** directions are too hard to follow.
> Was **that** movie you saw last week frightening?
> **Those** sound effects were quite scary.

The adjectives *this* and *these* refer to things close to the speaker or writer. *That* and *those* refer to things farther away.
Do not use *here* or *there* after *this, that, these,* and *those.*

> **This** glove is yours. (Not: This here glove)
> **That** package belongs to me. (Not: That there package)

Because *this* and *these* include the idea of "here," and *that* and *those* include the idea of "there," the words *here* and *there* directly after these adjectives are unnecessary.
Avoid using the pronoun *them* in place of the adjective *those.*

> **Those** skates are mine. (Not: Them skates)

Use the singular adjectives *this* and *that* to modify the singular nouns *kind* and *sort.* Use the plural adjectives *these* and *those* when these nouns are plural.

> I like **this kind** of running shoes. (Not: these kind)
> Don't buy **that sort** of shoes. (Not: those sort)
> **These kinds** of shoes are comfortable.
> **Those sorts** of shoes are uncomfortable.

▶ **Guided Practice**   Tell how to correct these sentences.

1. I don't like these kind of shorts.
2. Do you like them scissors?
3. Don thought that there book was yours.
4. This magazine over there is mine.

▶ **Practice** **A.** Rewrite the following, using *this, that, these,* and *those* in place of the blanks.

"Do you want some of ___(1)___ pie I'm serving?" Dad asked.

"No, thanks," I said, "but ___(2)___ pie over there looks great!"

"Are ___(3)___ desserts you're giving us made by your chef?" I asked the waiter.

"___(4)___ cakes from my cart are," he replied, "but ___(5)___ cupcakes on the shelf are store-bought."

B. Write the correct form of each adjective in parentheses. Then write the noun it modifies.

Example: Sylvia chose (that, those) set of books.
Answer: that set

6. Did you find (this here, this) book on the sale table?
7. I found (these, these here) magazines over near the door.
8. (This, These) kinds of magazines are hard to find.
9. I would like to read (that there, that) article.
10. (That, Those) kind of article is of interest to me.
11. I will buy (them, those) two magazines.
12. Julio bought (this, this here) book.
13. (Them, Those) volumes show cave paintings.
14. Cave dwellers drew (this, these) kind of scene.
15. (Them, Those) scenes helped them in their hunting trips.
16. They thought that (these, these here) pictures attracted animals.
17. (These, These here) animals died long ago.
18. Yet they live forever in (this, these) cave paintings.
19. (Them, Those) artists of long ago drew interesting pictures.
20. Many people have seen (this, these) sort of painting in books.
21. People are often amazed by (this, these) sorts of sketches.

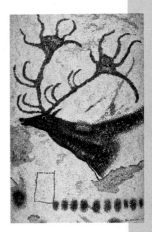

▶ **Apply/Writing** Write a paragraph to describe one of the pairs of topics below. Use *this, that, these,* and *those.*

- your most recent vacation and the one you took five years ago
- the bicycle you ride now and the bicycle you rode when you were younger
- the dinner you ate last night and a holiday dinner you have eaten in the last year

12 Using Negative Words

Use only one negative word when you mean "no."

▶ **Focus**   Negative words include *no, not, nothing, none, nobody, no one, neither, nowhere,* and contractions with *n't,* the shortened form of *not.* The use of two negative words in the same clause to express the meaning "no" or "not" is called a double negative. Read these examples.

> Wilma **never** reads **nothing** but books about horses.
> Benito could**n't** do **no** wrong, according to her.

In the first sentence the words *never* and *nothing* are both negative. So are the words *couldn't* and *no* in the second sentence. Only one word is needed to convey the meaning "no" or "not." Here is how these sentences can be corrected.

> Wilma **never** reads **anything** but books about horses.
> Wilma reads **nothing** but books about horses.

> Benito could do **no** wrong, according to her.
> Benito could**n't** do **any** wrong, according to her.

Sentences with double negatives can be corrected by dropping one of the negative words or by changing one negative word to a positive word like *anything, any, anywhere, either,* and *ever.*

Some negative words—*hardly, barely, scarcely*—do not begin with the letter *n.* These words should not be used with another negative word in a sentence.

> **Incorrect:** They had **scarcely no** food.
> **Correct:** They had **scarcely any** food.

▶ **Guided Practice**   Tell how to correct the double negative in each sentence. Suggest more than one way, if you can.

1. The poor man can't hardly walk.
2. Sandra hasn't never lied.
3. We aren't going nowhere this summer.
4. Why won't you have nothing to do with him?
5. They haven't no chance to win.

▶ **Practice**   **A.** Rewrite the sentences, using the correct word in parentheses.

Example: That runner has never won (no, any) prizes.
Answer: That runner has never won any prizes.

1. I won't eat (nothing, anything) that those chefs cook.
2. She hadn't (never, ever) felt this way before.
3. Don't they want (no, any) help?
4. Who says I never go (nowhere, anywhere)?
5. Why (don't, do) you want to eat nothing but broccoli?
6. No snowstorm (wasn't, was) expected that day.
7. They have barely (any, no) money left.
8. He knows nothing about (no, any) extra practice.
9. It seemed he couldn't do (nothing, anything) to please them.
10. We hardly have (no, any) time to finish the job.

B. Each of the following sentences contains a double negative. Rewrite each sentence correctly. Remember that there will often be more than one way to correct the sentence.

Example: Lou doesn't never play the drums no more.
Answer: Lou doesn't play the drums anymore.   or
             Lou never plays the drums anymore.

11. The Farbers didn't bring no thermos to the game.
12. There wasn't nobody at the ticket booth.
13. Our quarterback doesn't know nothing about sneak plays.
14. We barely had no time to get to our seats.
15. Doesn't the peanut vendor never come this way?
16. Our tackle doesn't ever hit no harder than necessary.
17. Our cheerleaders don't seem to have no pep for this game.
18. Our running game wasn't never as good as today.
19. Some days a team just can't seem to make no good plays.
20. The championship won't never belong to this team unless they play harder than they did this afternoon.

▶ **Apply/Writing**   Write a paragraph describing something that happened in school today or something that you did over the weekend. Do not make any of the sentences negative. Exchange papers with a partner. Rewrite each other's papers, making negative statements wherever they seem suitable.

Review/Evaluation

For more review,
see Tested Skills Practice,
pages 544–549.

62 **Subject and Object Pronouns**   Write the letter of the pronoun form or forms that complete each sentence correctly.

1. Gary and ____ signed up for the spring marathon.
   a. she   **b.** her
2. The coach gave ____ and ____ a lecture about daily practice.
   a. they, I   **b.** them, me
3. Gary and ____ ran six miles every day after school.
   a. I   **b.** me
4. Sally's sister and ____ ran for several hours on weekends.
   a. she   **b.** her
5. Whenever Gary and ____ ran together, his father went along.
   a. they   **b.** them
6. Coach Jackson gave ____ and ____ good advice.
   a. they, we   **b.** them, us
7. He gave keys to the gym to both ____ and ____.
   a. they, we   **b.** them, us
8. Sally and ____ thanked the coach for his help.
   a. we   **b.** us

63 **Pronoun Agreement**   Write the letter of the pronoun that agrees formally with the underlined antecedent in each sentence.

9. The <u>king and queen</u> ascended to ____ golden thrones.
   a. his   **b.** her   **c.** their
10. Then <u>each</u> of the ladies-in-waiting took ____ seat.
    a. his   **b.** her   **c.** their
11. If a court <u>jester</u> is funny, ____ can have a successful career.
    a. he   **b.** it   **c.** they
12. <u>Neither</u> of the princes danced with ____ mother that night.
    a. her   **b.** his   **c.** their
13. Every <u>one</u> of the women danced with ____ king, however.
    a. his   **b.** her   **c.** their
14. Has <u>either</u> of the princes lost ____ silver gloves?
    a. their   **b.** its   **c.** his
15. If a <u>woman</u> doesn't want to dance, ____ should say so politely.
    a. he   **b.** she   **c.** they

64 **Using *who* and *whom*** Write **a** if the missing word is *who.* Write **b** if the missing word is *whom.*

16. With _____ did the king dance first?
17. _____ is leading the royal orchestra?
18. The prince _____ lost his gloves while getting out of his carriage is dancing with Lady Lia.
19. The queen admired the jester _____ the king disliked.
20. We met Princess Nadia, _____ the king's son loves.
21. To _____ did she present the award?
22. The jester, _____ is really amusing, rarely smiles.
23. Prince Jerome, _____ everyone admires, will leave for Arcadia as soon as the evening is over.

65 **Using *this, that, these,* and *those*** Write the letter of the adjective that corrects the underlined error in each sentence.
a. this   **b.** that   **c.** these   **d.** those

24. <u>That there</u> is Princess Nadia talking to the queen.
25. I like <u>this</u> kinds of parties, don't you?
26. <u>Them</u> silver gloves over there belong to Prince Claudio.
27. <u>This here</u> rose was given to me by the queen.
28. <u>These here</u> women attend the king and queen.
29. <u>Those</u> kind of roses are specially grown by the queen, who allows no one else to grow them.
30. Do you like <u>that</u> sorts of decorations over there?
31. Yes, I like <u>those</u> kind of decorations.

66 **Using Negative Words** Write **a** if the sentence uses negative words incorrectly. Write **b** if the negative is correct.

32. Nobody saw no ghosts around here.
33. There aren't any such creatures as ghosts.
34. Witches never ride no brooms neither.
35. No one ever became a werewolf either.
36. Don't you never get scared?
37. I don't never get scared by things that don't exist.
38. Do you know nothing about poltergeists?
39. I haven't seen no proof that they exist.
40. Let's not talk about none of those creatures anymore.

Writing Evaluation

60
61

    This picture depicts "a far other time" when animals and people lived together in peace and harmony. Write an essay of at least three paragraphs that responds to this scene.

1. Use some prewriting strategies. Write a brief summary of the picture. Draw conclusions about the characters in the scene and their motivations. Decide if the painting presents a moral, and if so, how you feel about the moral. Make a Word Bank to help you describe the feeling of the painting.
2. Write your response essay, using the following guidelines.
  ✔ Does the thesis statement present the essay's focus and your attitude toward the painting?
  ✔ Is the thesis statement supported with specific details?
  ✔ Are the details in each paragraph based on a main idea?
  ✔ Are sentences and paragraphs connected with appropriate transition words and phrases?
  ✔ Is there an effective concluding sentence?
3. When you have finished writing, spend a few minutes checking and revising your response essay.
  ✔ Can you answer "yes" to all the questions above?
  ✔ Do all pronouns agree with their antecedents?
  ✔ Are subject and object pronouns used correctly?

Curriculum Connection: Health

In Unit 34 you read several fables, each of which has a moral. A moral is a brief message that summarizes the lesson taught in the fable. Fables and their morals are actually examples of what we call "folk wisdom." They teach basic lessons about human nature that generations of people have learned through experience.

Folk wisdom is also found in proverbs, which are brief statements of popular and basic truths. Proverbs are actually morals without stories attached. If you look through collections of proverbs, you will find that an amazingly large number deal with good nutritional practices. Many proverbs warn about eating too much or eating the wrong foods. Here are a few examples:

"Diet cures more than the lancet."
"Even sugar itself might spoil a good dish."
"Feed sparingly and defy the physician."
"An apple a day keeps the doctor away."
"More die by food than famine."
"Eat to live and not live to eat."

▶ **Think**   Consider the important role that good nutrition plays in your health. Think about times when you ate more than you should have or neglected an important food group in your diet.

▶ **Discuss**   Conduct a class discussion about the proverbs that appear above and about other proverbs. Classmates might want to suggest other proverbs that deal with sound eating practices and a healthy diet. You might also consult a collection of proverbs or examine a collection of familiar quotations.

▶ **Find Out**   Review what your health text has to say about good nutrition and proper diet. Pay particular attention to important nutrients and to foods that you should avoid or eat in limited amounts.

▶ **React: Write**   Based on your review of good nutritional practices, choose one of the proverbs presented here or one discovered in the class discussion. Use this proverb to write a fable. In your fable develop the moral expressed in the proverb. Choose animal characters that are effective in getting your moral across.

Endyear Test

Sentence Parts

[35] **A.** Write **a** if the appositive needs one comma and **b** if it needs two.

1. Ms. Dru Mr. Lane's private secretary greeted me at the door.
2. We walked into Mr. Lane's office a book-filled room.

[36] **B.** Write **a** if the sentences can be combined by using the subjects and **b** if they can be combined by using the predicates.

3. Ms. Dru entered Mr. Lane's office. I entered Mr. Lane's office.
4. Mr. Lane smiled. Mr. Lane greeted me. Mr. Lane shook my hand.

[37] **C.** Write the letter that identifies each underlined sentence part.
[38] **a.** Direct object   **b.** Subject complement   **c.** Indirect object

5. Uncle Kirk is a world <u>traveler</u>.
6. He sent Jane and <u>me</u> gifts from New Zealand.
7. Jane and I received <u>them</u> early this afternoon.

Nouns and Pronouns

[40] **D.** Write **a** for each plural noun, **b** for each singular possessive noun, and **c** for each plural possessive noun.

8. Rosses'	**10.** donkey's	**12.** knives	**14.** waitress's
9. spies'	**11.** fox's	**13.** mice's	**15.** tomatoes

[41] **E.** Write the letter that identifies each underlined pronoun.
[42] **a.** Reflexive   **b.** Intensive   **c.** Possessive   **d.** Indefinite

16. The President <u>himself</u> will lead the Labor Day parade.
17. Roberta and I found good seats for <u>ourselves</u>.
18. <u>Some</u> of the people will watch the parade from their porches.
19. <u>Their</u> house is too far away from the parade route.

Sentences and Clauses

[44] **F.** Write **a** if the underlined words are an independent clause and **b** if they are a dependent clause.

20. <u>When the parade started</u>, the people cheered.
21. <u>They applauded the President</u> as his limousine rolled by.

G. Write **a** if the sentence is complex. Write **b** if it is another kind of sentence.

22. The President, who was smiling broadly, waved to the people.
23. People took pictures and showed them to their friends.
24. The President was leaving the city when the parade was over.

H. Write **a** if the sentences can be combined in a compound sentence and **b** if they can be combined by using modifiers.

25. The President's car was long. It was new. It was bulletproof.
26. The President boarded the plane. The crew led him to his cabin.
27. The President looked tired. He didn't complain.

I. Write **a** if the sentence has a misplaced modifier, **b** if it lacks parallel structure, and **c** if it is too wordy.

28. The three triplets are still quite small in size.
29. Her speech was dull, wordy, and gave no information.
30. The man took the photograph in a white shirt.

Verb Usage

J. Write **a** if the verb in the sentence is correct. Write **b** if it is incorrect.

31. Teddy must of been at the Andersons' picnic yesterday.
32. Conrad learned Alice all about coins.
33. Natalia Stanislavsky be our new class president.
34. Lenny sat the grocery bags down on the kitchen counter.
35. Sheila has torn her favorite basketball jacket again.
36. Last night the manager left us into the movie for nothing.
37. Jessie wrote the bicycle manufacturers several letters.
38. Norman has went scuba diving every day this week.
39. Grandpa's clock has been broke for a long, long time.

K. Write **a** if the sentence has an active verb. Write **b** if it has a passive verb.

40. All of our sports equipment was destroyed in the fire.
41. The firefighters worked heroically for seven hours.
42. The fire was started by an overloaded electrical circuit.

Subject-Verb Agreement

57
58
59

L. Write **a** if the verb in the sentence is correct. Write **b** if it is incorrect.

43. Rumors of an escaped tiger has spread all over town.
44. Neither the officers nor the chief know anything about it.
45. There is absolutely no truth to these rumors.
46. Where does such ridiculous rumors come from?
47. Wise people usually ignore unconfirmed rumors.

Pronoun and Modifier Usage

62
63

M. Write the letter of the pronoun that makes each sentence complete.

48. Georgie and (**a.** them, **b.** they) are going climbing tomorrow.
49. Does everyone know where (**a.** he, **b.** they) should meet us?
50. Several climbers will bring (**a.** his, **b.** their) own gear.
51. Mr. Keynes gave Tim and (**a.** us, **b.** we) her telephone number.
52. Tim and (**a.** her, **b.** she) will be here in just a little while.

64

N. Write the letter of the word that makes each sentence complete.

53. (**a.** Who, **b.** Whom) is in the play?
54. He is an actor (**a.** who, **b.** whom) always forgets his lines.
55. (**a.** Who, **b.** Whom) do we see for costumes?
56. From (**a.** who, **b.** whom) did you get that script?

65
66

O. Write **a** if the sentence is correct and **b** if it contains an error.

57. This here vase is very ancient and valuable.
58. There isn't no other vase like it in the world.
59. Those kinds of paintings are very popular once again.
60. Them statues are over three thousand years old.
61. Hardly any of the art in this museum is more valuable.

Thinking Skills

30

P. Write **a** if the underlined words state a cause. Write **b** if they state an effect.

62. It was getting dark; hence we pulled up to a motel.
63. Because the motel was full, we couldn't get a room.
64. Since Dad was tired, Mom drove to the next motel.

31   **Q.** Write the letter of the word that completes the second word pair correctly.

65. lion : roar :: horse : **a.** gallop **b.** neigh **c.** reins
66. clown : circus :: teacher : **a.** pupils **b.** school **c.** books

48   **R.** Write **a** if the sentence is biased. Write **b** if it has a balanced point of view.

67. Perhaps rock music will be commonly played in orchestra concert halls someday.
68. The popular music of today has nothing good about it.

Paragraphs

32   **S.** Read the explanatory paragraph from a business letter. Write **a**
34   if each transition is correct and **b** if it is incorrect.

   (69) You sent the wrong color sweater, but I am writing you.
(70) In addition, you spelled my name wrong.   **(71)** Nevertheless, cancel my charge account.

33   **T.** Write the letter of each word that can be used to signal a cause or an effect in a paragraph.

72. **a.** the same as **b.** since **c.** through
73. **a.** hence **b.** similarly **c.** meanwhile

49   **U.** Write the letter of the one true statement about a persuasive paragraph.

74. **a.** It can appear in a TV review, an ad, or an editorial.
    b. It gives supporting reasons ordered in no special way.
    c. The topic sentence always appears at the end.

50   **V.** Write the letter of the only incorrect statement about a summary paragraph.

75. **a.** It is shorter than the original material you are summarizing.
    b. It has a main idea.
    c. It contains several details about everything in the material you are summarizing.

Kinds of Sentences *pages 32–33*

A sentence may be declarative, interrogative, exclamatory, or imperative.

Declarative: The cougar is one of America's largest animals.
Interrogative: Do they really grow up to eight feet long?
Exclamatory: You must be joking!
What an extraordinary feat that is!
Imperative: Tell us more about them.
Don't frighten me!

A. Read each sentence and write what kind it is.
Example: What do cougars eat? ***Answer:*** Interrogative

1. Is their favorite food deer?
2. Cougars stalk silently and can jump great distances.
3. Imagine a leap of forty feet.
4. Are they dangerous to humans?
5. Actually, humans have proven more dangerous to cougars.
6. Fewer than thirty remain in the Everglades.
7. What a shame that is!
8. Are they an endangered species?
9. Please don't destroy their habitats.
10. Save the Florida cougar now!

B. Copy the sentences and add the correct punctuation.
Example: Are cougars the same as mountain lions
Answer: Are cougars the same as mountain lions?

11. Are they also called panthers
12. How their numbers have dwindled
13. Ask any environmentalist about the cougars' plight
14. Once they inhabited most of North America
15. Now cougars live only in the wildest regions
16. Do more live in the mountains than in the swamps
17. They help the balance of nature by preying on plant-eating deer and other mammals
18. What cute-looking cubs they have
19. Look, but don't pet them
20. A cougar mother is never far away

Subjects and Predicates *pages 34–35*

All sentences have a simple and a complete subject and predicate.

A science class from our school | went on a field trip.

They | visited an unusual zoo.

A. Copy each sentence. Draw a line between the complete subject and predicate.

Example: Many people are superstitious about owls.

Answer: Many people | are superstitious about owls.

1. Owls fly silently and hunt at night.
2. An owl in a tree makes a good Halloween decoration.
3. Children and adults delight in the owl's characteristic call.
4. Owls symbolized wisdom to the ancient Egyptians and Greeks.
5. Their large eyes seem intelligent and help them in the dark.
6. They also have excellent hearing.
7. Barn owls are the farmer's best friends.
8. Mice, rats, and rabbits are the owl's usual food.
9. Their feeding habits benefit farmers and save valuable crops.
10. Owls catch and eat troublesome rodents.

B. Copy each sentence. Draw a vertical line between the complete subject and predicate. Underline the simple subject once and the simple predicate twice.

Example: Farmers often like owls and protect them.

Answer: <u>Farmers</u> | often <u>like</u> owls and <u>protect</u> them.

11. Some variety of owl inhabits almost every country.
12. Holes in trees are their usual homes.
13. Some inhabit burrows or build nests on the ground.
14. Barn owls live in barns and can be found near farm buildings.
15. Asia and Africa are home to many kinds of owls.
16. The snowy owl lives in the far north and blends with the winter scenery.
17. Some owls in tropical countries catch fish or even hunt reptiles.
18. Most owls make a common hooting sound.
19. Some owls actually hiss and whistle.
20. Owls, falcons, and hawks are all birds of prey.

7 # Correcting Sentence Fragments

pages 40–41

A group of words punctuated like a sentence but not expressing a complete thought is called a sentence fragment.

Incorrect: We spent much of our time. Packing for our trip.

Correct: We spent much of our time packing for our trip.

A. Write *S* if the group of words is a sentence and *F* if it is a fragment.

Example: Being away for only a week.

Answer: F

1. I practically emptied my dresser and closet.
2. Having a difficult time trying to decide what to pack.
3. Can you imagine taking two large suitcases?
4. For such a short vacation.
5. It's lucky that we have a large station wagon.
6. Even so, my mother was annoyed with me.
7. For taking up so much room in the car.
8. And leaving so little room for everyone else.
9. Fortunately, my little brother packs his favorite toys.
10. But seldom worries about what to wear.

B. Correct the sentence fragments below by joining each one to the sentence next to it. Change capitalization and punctuation when necessary. If an item is already correct, write *Correct*.

Example: Antarctica is a lonely continent. Belonging to no one.

Answer: Antarctica is a lonely continent belonging to no one.

11. You can visit it without a passport. Because no country claims it.
12. In 1911, there was a famous race. Between two nations.
13. Both Norway and Britain wanted to be first. At the South Pole.
14. The Norwegian Amundsen arrived. A month before his English rival.
15. The English team never returned. Scott and his party died in a storm.
16. Today, nations share Antarctica. Using it for scientific study.
17. Temperatures reach $-129°F$. Making it too cold to snow.

18. Antarctica gets only three inches of snow in a year. A remarkably small amount.
19. What seems to be blizzards is actually fallen snow. Blowing around in winds of one hundred miles per hour.
20. Penguins are Antarctica's most well-known life form. Though mosses and small spiders called mites live there too.
21. These creatures can be found on the Antarctic Peninsula. Which reaches north toward the southern tip of South America.
22. Here summer temperatures of 58°F have been recorded. Surprising most people.
23. Scientists are just beginning to discover Antarctica's mysteries. How long will it take to unlock its many secrets?

8 # Correcting Run-on Sentences *pages 42–43*

A run-on sentence contains two or more sentences written together without the proper punctuation between them.

Incorrect: Cross-country skiing is good exercise it also is a practical way to travel over snowy terrain.

Correct: Cross-country skiing is good exercise, but it also is a practical way to travel over snowy terrain.

A. Find the run-on sentences below and write them correctly. If a sentence is correct, write *Correct*.

Example: Helicopters have many uses they can perform many tasks.

Answer: Helicopters have many uses. They can perform many tasks.

1. Helicopters can go straight up and down, they can go forward and backward.
2. Helicopters are used for emergencies in cities and can ferry people between airports.
3. They hover over crops to prevent frost and are also used to dry out ballparks after rain.
4. The first helicopter was invented in China it was only a toy.
5. The artist Leonardo da Vinci drew a plan for a helicopter in the 1400s it was never built.
6. Four hundred years later, a steam-powered helicopter was built, it was too heavy to fly.

7. The first helicopter pilots could not control their machines, they used ropes fastened to the ground to steady them.
8. Today, helicopters are much more reliable they still are trickier to fly than airplanes.
9. A sudden down-draft can cause the crash of a low-flying craft.
10. The first successful American helicopter flew in 1939, it was invented by Igor Sikorsky.
11. New kinds of helicopters are still being invented, one can even land on water.
12. Some are used for moving soldiers and supplies into remote, rugged country.
13. Beaches are often patrolled by Coast Guard helicopters some have rescued swimmers and boaters in distress.
14. In fact, helicopters serve as the only means of air transportation in some areas.
15. The helicopter has become an important modern machine, no one considers it a toy anymore.

B. Read each item below and decide if it is a sentence or a run-on. Write *R* if it is a run-on and *S* if it is a sentence.
Example: Australia is the smallest continent it is also a country.
Answer: R

16. The English settled Australia, but the Dutch actually discovered it first.
17. The first European to explore Australia was Captain James Cook he also discovered Hawaii.
18. A native people were already living in Australia, they are called aborigines.
19. The aborigines invented the boomerang, a throwing weapon used for hunting.
20. Europeans found unusual animals there—the kangaroo, the platypus, and the koala bear, to name a few.
21. The north is hot and tropical, most European settlers choose to live in the cooler south.
22. Almost a third of Australia is desert and receives little rain.
23. Australia's biggest cities are Sydney and Melbourne neither is the capital.
24. The capital is Canberra it lies between these cities.
25. Australia includes Tasmania, a big island south of Melbourne.

Plural Nouns   *pages 76–77*

Many plural nouns are formed by adding *-s* or *-es* to the singular. Some nouns require a spelling change to form the plural.

coat—**coats**	wax—**waxes**	child—**children**
toy—**toys**	sky—**skies**	series—**series**
solo—**solos**	tomato—**tomatoes**	snowman—**snowmen**
chief—**chiefs**	knife—**knives**	son-in-law—**sons-in-law**

A. Write the plural form of each noun.
Example: circus   *Answer:* circuses

1. bay	6. country	11. ostrich	16. lunch
2. goose	7. lily	12. sportsman	17. safe
3. grandchild	8. sheep	13. potato	18. turkey
4. shampoo	9. donkey	14. ruby	19. piano
5. thief	10. igloo	15. calf	20. dress

B. Copy the sentences. Write the correct plural form for each word in parentheses.
Example: The (man) filled the (glass).
Answer: The men filled the glasses.

21. The (tomato) were so heavy that they broke the (branch).
22. My (grandparent) always have plenty of (kiss) for me.
23. Several (passer-by) looked at us as we cooled our (foot) in the fountain.
24. (Bench) were set up for the Fourth of July (picnic).
25. Were the plays (comedy) or (tragedy)?
26. We will need some (scissors) to complete these (project).
27. Our science teacher explained the (idea) behind (pulley).
28. (Settler) had hollowed out (shelf) beneath the (cliff).
29. The (sailor) sheltered their boats in (bay).
30. Buy two (loaf) of bread and some assorted (cheese) for the party.
31. In westerns, the (hero) are often (sheriff) or (deputy).
32. We could still hear both (oboe) over the sound of the (radio).
33. Please make some (copy) of these (page).
34. Are (fox) and (wolf) related to dogs?
35. They usually keep (deer) or (sheep) in the petting (zoo).

Identifying Kinds of Pronouns *pages 78–81*

A personal pronoun takes the place of one or more nouns. An antecedent is the word or words to which the pronoun refers.

Lisa told **her** mother that **she** would be home later.

Interrogative pronouns are used to introduce questions.

What is she doing?　　**Whom** is she visiting?

Relative pronouns introduce groups of words that act as adjectives.

The person **who** answered the phone didn't know.

Perhaps this note **that** she left will explain.

A. Write the personal pronoun in each sentence. Three sentences have two personal pronouns each.

Example:　Pat and Becky say they will help plan the class beach party.
Answer:　they

1. Tom has agreed to lend his radio.
2. All students will bring their own towels, blankets, and other swimming gear.
3. Some of the girls said they will make sandwiches and bring fresh fruit.
4. "My choice for lunch," remarked Paul, "is always frozen yogurt."
5. "I will fill my cooler with cold drinks and ice cream for everyone," offered Masako.
6. "What can we do to help?" asked one of the twins.
7. "Bring our dad's beach umbrella and suntan lotion," replied the other twin.
8. "Is one umbrella enough, or should I look for mine too?" asked Terri.
9. Sally said she will bring her volleyball and surf rider for people who want some exercise.
10. This party sounds as though it will be a great success, and everyone is encouraged to attend.

B. Write whether each underlined pronoun in the sentences on the following page is Interrogative or Relative.

Example:　<u>What</u> are you doing after school?　　*Answer:*　Interrogative
Example:　I'm late for practice, <u>which</u> is now.　　*Answer:*　Relative

11. <u>Who</u> coaches your Pony League team?
12. Mr. Edel, <u>who</u> also coached us last year, does.
13. Is he the man <u>who</u> once played semipro ball?
14. The positions <u>that</u> he played were third base and shortstop.
15. <u>What</u> does the coach think about your chances this year?
16. Our team, <u>which</u> finished third last year, has really improved.
17. We may be the team <u>that</u> wins the championship this year.
18. <u>Which</u> is your position, and <u>what</u> is your batting average?
19. I'm the pitcher <u>whose</u> fastball struck you out last week.
20. <u>Who</u> would have recognized you without your uniform?

C. Write the pronouns from each sentence. They may be personal, interrogative, or relative.

Example: We are the girls who volunteered to candystripe.
Answer: We, who

21. Which is your mother's office?
22. Hers is next to the room that has the X-ray machines.
23. Can we visit her while we are here?
24. I don't know which is her office.
25. Maybe the man who is pushing the cart can help us.
26. He seems to be very busy with his work.
27. Here is a sign that looks familiar to me.
28. Are you sure?
29. It says *Radiology,* which is the name of her department.
30. The arrow points in the direction that we came from.

D. Follow the same directions as for Practice C.

31. Who would have guessed I would walk right by it!
32. Its door is shut, and a warning light that I recognize is on.
33. What is their problem?
34. It means they are X-raying, and we must stay out.
35. Whose is the office with the file cabinets?
36. I think it is hers.
37. Finally we have found it!
38. Make room on the sofa, which is cluttered with books.
39. My brother has waited in her office before.
40. I hope she comes back soon because I am getting hungry.

Distinguishing Action/Linking Verbs

pages 110–111

Some verbs can be either action verbs or linking verbs.

Action: Herbert **looked** all over for his baseball mitt.
Linking: He **looked** glum about its loss.
Action: I **felt** under the dugout bench for the mitt.
Linking: I **felt** glad about finding it for him.

A. Copy the verbs from the sentences and write whether they are used as action or linking verbs.

Example: Petunias grow well in the sun. *Answer:* grow—Action

1. We grow petunias in a box on the back porch.
2. They smell surprisingly faint for a flower.
3. The flowers look so colorful there.
4. Look at all these fruit trees!
5. I myself grow weary of that crabapple tree.
6. The lawn looks messy with those tiny apples all around.
7. I tasted crabapple jelly once.
8. It tastes both tart and sweet.
9. In the springtime, the blossoms smell pleasant.
10. Two bluejays appear in the pear tree every morning.
11. Their calls sound throughout the yard.
12. They look for caterpillars and grubs.

B. Follow the same directions as for Practice A.

13. The jays appear quite content back here.
14. Sometimes they sound awfully noisy in the early hours.
15. Those purple plums look almost ripe.
16. Blue jays sometimes sound their cries loudly like roosters.
17. I feel hungry for a plum.
18. Please taste some.
19. The skins feel soft enough.
20. They certainly smell very fresh.
21. These plums taste delicious!
22. You grew them yourself!
23. Now I feel lazy.

Principal Parts of Verbs   *pages 116–117*

Verbs have four basic forms, which are called principal parts. They are used to form tenses.

| **Present:** | describe | **Present participle:** | (is) describing |
| **Past:** | described | **Past participle:** | (has) described |

A. Write the four principal parts of each verb.

Example: carry   ***Answer:*** carry, (is) carrying, carried, (has) carried

1. rest	**6.** shout	**11.** provide
2. wrap	**7.** complicate	**12.** jog
3. disappear	**8.** marry	**13.** slip
4. laugh	**9.** recognize	**14.** distract
5. snicker	**10.** clean	**15.** move

B. Copy the verb from each sentence. Then write which principal part it is formed from—Present, Present participle, Past, or Past participle.

Example: People have marveled at the works of Leonardo da Vinci.
Answer: have marveled—Past participle

16. This great Italian painter and inventor lived in the fifteenth century.
17. Most people remember him for his painting the *Mona Lisa.*
18. In fact, this work has inspired artists over the centuries.
19. Mona Lisa's smile still is intriguing people today.
20. Leonardo completed many other paintings too.
21. Unfortunately, only a handful survive.
22. Leonardo studied science as well as painting.
23. He displayed genius as an inventor and an engineer.
24. People today are realizing the modernness of his ideas.
25. He developed locks for a canal system for the city of Milan.
26. Milan has used the locks all these years.
27. Imagine the cleverness of Leonardo da Vinci.
28. Even now, armies are crossing rivers and canyons with portable bridges of his design.
29. His notebooks contain sketches for flying machines too.
30. People are examining these notebooks for possible ideas.

Verbs have present, past, and future perfect tenses.

Present Perfect:	have, has gone
Past Perfect:	had gone
Future Perfect:	will have gone

A. Copy the verb from each sentence. Then tell whether it is
Present perfect, Past perfect, or Future perfect.
Example: The water level of the Great Lakes has changed many times.
Answer: has changed—Present perfect

1. Once it had dropped five feet below its present level.
2. Today it has risen to an all-time high.
3. Few cities and towns have planned for this increase.
4. Hardly anyone had known of this change.
5. Thousands of acres will have eroded by 1995.
6. Scientists have guessed at some possible reasons.
7. More rain and snow have contributed to the problem.
8. In addition, man-made dams had stopped the normal flow of water to the sea.
9. People will have built miles of protective dikes by the end of this century.
10. Maybe the water level will have dropped by then.

B. Follow the same directions as for Practice A.

11. It has rained now for almost a week.
12. No one here has seen the sun in days.
13. Soon I will have forgotten its appearance.
14. I have carried an umbrella with me everywhere.
15. At least the streets will have gotten a good cleaning.
16. The ducks have seemed happy too.
17. The garden has benefited from it also.
18. I had wished to see a ball game today.
19. Instead I have listened to the rain against the windows.
20. It certainly has bored me to stay inside.
21. It has given me a chance to read and play games though.
22. Perhaps it will have stopped by tomorrow.

Functions of Adverbs   *pages 154–155*

Adverbs modifying verbs can function, or act, as adverbs of time, place, or manner. Adverbs modifying adjectives or other adverbs function as intensifiers.

Adverb of Time:	then	**Adverb of Place:**	here
Adverb of Manner:	noisily	**Intensifier:**	almost

A. Find the adverbs in the sentences below. The function of each adverb is indicated in parentheses.

Example: Nordic skiing is becoming more popular. (intensifier)
Answer: more

1. I skied eagerly across the snowy meadows. (manner)
2. My partner was quite nervous at first. (intensifier)
3. He made rather frequent mistakes. (intensifier)
4. He felt that he was skiing badly. (manner)
5. After a while, he was moving smoothly. (manner)
6. Signs of life could be seen everywhere. (place)
7. Moose tracks often marked our trail. (time)
8. Deer had hungrily nibbled at tree bark. (manner)
9. Squirrels were digging nearby for hidden acorns. (place)
10. We decided later to return home. (time)
11. Our trip had taken us far. (place)
12. We may go skiing tomorrow. (time)

B. Copy the adverb in each sentence. Tell whether it is an adverb of time, place, manner, or an intensifier.

Example: The storm had ended abruptly.   *Answer:* abruptly—Manner

13. The beach had looked clean yesterday.
14. Many items now littered the beach.
15. Unusual shells could be seen everywhere.
16. Collectors eagerly gathered them in plastic bags.
17. Several pieces of driftwood had washed ashore.
18. Some extremely large pieces resembled parts of wrecked boats.
19. I carefully scoured the beach for treasures.
20. Pirates could have buried gold here.
21. I am a very optimistic person.

Comparative Forms *pages 156–159*

Most adjectives and adverbs have a positive, a comparative, and a superlative form. The comparative form is used to compare two people or things. The superlative form is used to compare three or more people or things.

	Positive	**Comparative**	**Superlative**
Adjectives:	small	smaller	smallest
	careful	more careful	most careful
Adverbs:	fast	faster	fastest
	quickly	more quickly	most quickly

A. Write the adjectives and adverbs below. Beside each, write its comparative and superlative forms.

Example: angry   *Answer:* angry, angrier, angriest
Example: much   *Answer:* much, more, most

1. beautiful	6. sharp	11. highly	16. loudly
2. green	7. prompt	12. slowly	17. seldom
3. long	8. unusual	13. bad	18. good
4. humorous	9. serious	14. soon	19. warmly
5. few	10. fuzzy	15. nearly	20. calmly

B. Copy each sentence, using the comparative or superlative form of the adjective or adverb in parentheses.

Example: Halley's comet appeared (faint) this time than last.
Answer: Halley's comet appeared fainter this time than last.

21. This hurricane was the (destructive) one yet.
22. Can you run (fast) than Eddie?
23. The (tall) building in the world is the Sears Tower.
24. Roast beef is my (little) favorite dish.
25. The sun was (bright) today than yesterday.
26. The Giants are the (tough) team in the league.
27. Our school bus arrived (late) than usual.
28. Sometimes I think we have the (cold) weather in the country.
29. This dress is (pretty) than the blue one.
30. Who on your team can hit the ball (far)?
31. This is the (tasty) bread I have ever eaten.
32. A hungry Great Dane gobbled its food (greedily) of all.

Tested Skills Practice

Using *good, well, bad,* and *badly*
pages 160–161

Good and *bad* are adjectives. *Well* and *badly* are adverbs.

   Adjectives: I always enjoy a **good** science-fiction movie.
   Unfortunately, *Invasion of the Willow People* is a very
   bad one.
   Adverbs: The stars did not perform **well.** Most delivered their
   lines **badly.**

A. Read the sentences. Write the correct modifier in parentheses.
Example: Dad's nine-year-old car still drives (good, well).
Answer: well

  1. It is worth keeping, though the tires have worn (bad, badly).
  2. The car needed alignment (bad, badly), but now it's fixed.
  3. Dad has decided to buy a (good, well) set of tires.
  4. The engine runs (good, well) in spite of its age.
  5. The muffler rattled (bad, badly) before he replaced it.
  6. It stops immediately because it has (good, well) brakes.
  7. It used to bounce (bad, badly) until Dad bought new shocks.
  8. Now it rides (good, well).
  9. One (good, well) feature for long trips is its large size.
 10. Despite some (bad, badly) rust spots, I like its looks.

B. Follow the same directions as for Practice A.

 11. My city's baseball team has played (bad, badly) for years.
 12. Yet, fans continue to have (good, well) feelings about the team.
 13. They never seem to care if the team does (good, well) or not.
 14. The park fills up even if the team has a (bad, badly) season.
 15. I sometimes wonder whether the fans can see (good, well).
 16. This year, the team performed so (bad, badly) that they were
     twenty-one games behind in June.
 17. One can say that they lose (good, well).
 18. The batters hit (bad, badly), and the pitchers do not pitch very
     (good, well) either.
 19. Yet the cheerful fans continue to root for this club as if they
     were not such a (bad, badly) team.

Kinds of Prepositional Phrases

pages 193–195

A prepositional phrase can act as an adjective or as an adverb.
  A festival **in a city park** began **in the morning.**

A. Copy the prepositional phrases from the sentences. After each, write whether it is an adjective phrase or adverb phrase.

Example: By noon restaurants from many neighborhoods were selling unusual foods.

Answer: By noon—Adverb phrase
        from many neighborhoods—Adjective phrase

1. Long lines of people waited patiently for tickets.
2. Many of them had traveled in large numbers from the suburbs.
3. Booths in neat rows were stocked with exotic foods.
4. Behind tables, clerks and chefs worked feverishly in spite of the heat.
5. Smoke from barbecues and cookstoves wafted through the air.
6. The crowds around each booth filled the spaces between the rows.
7. Throngs of hungry customers moved slowly toward the booths.
8. Once served, they walked beyond the rows to picnic tables.
9. At these tables they feasted on several delicious treats.
10. Before them sat slabs of ribs, barbecued chicken, shish kebabs, and shrimp off the grill.

B. Follow the same directions as for Practice A.

11. Desserts like fruit tarts could be bought at other booths.
12. In addition to these, people bought ice cream.
13. Beneath a bandshell, entertainers performed until sunset.
14. Besides all this, the city had built a midway with rides.
15. Laughing children rode above the trees on the Ferris wheel.
16. Below them others played games with darts and baseballs.
17. Still others sat near the enormous dolphin fountain.
18. The spray from the fountain cooled the hot faces of the people.
19. At nightfall fireworks of every color filled the skies.
20. Everyone at this festival agreed it was the best one in our city's history.

A conjunction joins words or groups of words. The terms *coordinating conjunction* and *correlative conjunction* describe how certain conjunctions are used in sentences.

Coordinating: The actor left the stage, **but** applause continued.
Correlative: People **either** stood **or** sat clapping their hands.

A. Copy the conjunctions from the sentences. Write whether they are coordinating or correlative.

Example: Recently, he starred in a movie yet he is better known as a ballet dancer.
Answer: yet—Coordinating

1. Is Mikhail Baryshnikov a ballet dancer or a movie actor?
2. As a child in the Soviet Union, he was both a good fencer and a gymnast.
3. He liked sports, but his main talent was piano playing.
4. At twelve, he had switched to ballet, for he was sent to a special school.
5. He was old to begin ballet, but Mikhail worked hard.
6. In just three years, he was able to go to Leningrad and study with Pushkin.
7. Alexander Pushkin was a great teacher and dancer.
8. He taught both ballet and mime to promising students.
9. Days at the school were long, but Mikhail did not mind.
10. He worked every day until either ten or eleven at night.

B. Follow the same directions as for Practice A.

11. Would you work that hard, or would you give up ballet?
12. He won gold medals in competitions in both 1966 and 1969.
13. Neither his country nor the world recognized his talent.
14. Mikhail loved his country yet left it in 1974.
15. He left behind both his family and his friends.
16. He was performing in Canada but fled to the United States.
17. He asked for political asylum and received it quickly.
18. The decision to leave or return to the Soviet Union was hard.
19. Mikhail is content, yet sometimes he must miss his homeland.
20. Now he has freedom in both his life and his art.

Commas in Writing *pages 226–231*

Use a comma to show a pause or separation between words or word groups in a sentence. Use commas to separate items in addresses and dates. Also use commas in figures and in friendly letters.

> By the way, John, don't forget to write, call, or send a telegram.
> My summer address will be 165 Arbor Road, Roslyn Heights, New York 11577, until September 3, 1988.
> Dear John,   Yours truly, $16,702

A. Copy the following sentences, adding commas where necessary.

Example: Beverly Karen and I are going to a barbecue on the Forth of July my favorite holiday.

Answer: Beverly, Karen, and I are going to a barbecue on the Fourth of July, my favorite holiday.

1. In addition to hamburgers there will be hot dogs chicken ribs potato salad cole slaw and plenty of lemonade.
2. Mrs. Thomas our next-door neighbor always brings a watermelon and Mom bakes homemade bread.
3. By the way many people bake cakes and someone usually brings a popcorn machine.
4. My brothers believe it or not do some of the outdoor cooking.
5. Besides the food there is always a good softball game but my favorite of course is the volleyball game.
6. If you would go we could probably beat the boys.
7. When it's dark we walk over to the lake sit on blankets listen to a band concert and watch the fireworks.
8. Will you be my guest Jan or are you already busy?
9. I hope you can go yet I understand if you can't.
10. If you do Jan I promise you the best Fourth of July you can imagine.

B. Follow the same directions as for Practice A.

11. On August 1 1985 my aunt stepped off a plane in Beijing China.
12. China has the largest population of any country yet it is only slightly bigger in size than the United States.
13. Its three eastern seas are the Yellow Sea the East China Sea and the South China Sea.

14. Most of its cities are along this coast but many people also live in river valleys.
15. The Hwang Ho also known as the Yellow River and the Yangtze are two of the most famous rivers.
16. They are used for transportation irrigation and hydroelectric power.
17. Far fewer people live in western China for there are rugged mountains plateaus and deserts.
18. In fact only about 20 percent of China's land is farmable.
19. Because farmable land is scarce China has had a long history of famine disease and civil war.
20. Today China uses irrigation soil conservation and planting twice a year to solve its agricultural problems.
21. China has many large cities but only about one third of the people live in them.
22. Most of the people are farmers and live in the eastern southern or northern part of the country.
23. Shanghai Canton and Beijing the capital are well known.
24. Hong Kong a city on the southeast coast is also famous but it will remain under British rule until the end of this century.
25. China's richest natural resources—iron ore coal and oil—are important for its industries.

C. Copy the letter, adding commas where needed.

(26) 163 Morse Street
(27) Kenosha WI 53545
(28) March 11 1989

(29) Dear Steve

(30) Believe it or not our family is going to Disney World for spring vacation! (31) We made our reservations Monday March 21 1988 one year ago! (32) My mother has cousins in Nashville Tennessee and Atlanta Georgia whom we will visit on the way. (33) The whole trip by car is over 1500 miles and should take us three days each way. (34) I'll send you a post card when we get to Orlando Florida. (35) You can write to me at 112 Bee Line Drive Kissimmee Florida 32742.

(36) Your pal
Billy

Quotation Marks   *pages 235–236*

Quotation marks enclose a speaker's exact words. Quotation marks are also used to enclose some titles.

> The melody of "My Country 'Tis of Thee" is the same as "God Save the Queen."
> "Why the long face, Marty?" Vic inquired.

A. Copy the sentences, adding quotation marks where needed.

Example: I'm always broke during the summers, Marty explained.

Answer: "I'm always broke during the summers," Marty explained.

1. Have you thought about how to earn money? asked Marion.
2. I haven't decided, answered Marty, what kind of job I want.
3. You could cut lawns, Lucy suggested.
4. Oh no, Marty retorted. I can't stand blistered hands.
5. Why not baby-sit? suggested Vic.
6. I tried that, said Marty, but the baby got into the linen.
7. When his mother came home, she said I had no common sense.
8. You could deliver newspapers, suggested Marion.
9. My sister does that, added Vic. She doesn't mind it a bit.
10. I'd have to get up too early, answered Marty.
11. Then how about delivering groceries? asked Lucy.
12. Marty whined, Those bags are too heavy!
13. Hey, wait a minute! shouted Vic. You don't really want a job.
14. You want money, agreed Marion, but you won't work for it.
15. Vic joked, I think you want a job that pays for doing nothing.
16. I just want to make sure I get the right job, Marty said.
17. It doesn't have to be easy, he said, as long as it's not too hard.
18. Marty, we've told you about all the jobs we know, said Kathy.
19. Thanks, grinned Marty, but now I need a rest.
20. He explained, All this talk about work really makes me tired.

B. Copy the items below, adding quotation marks where needed.

21. the poem Casey at the Bat
22. singing The Star-Spangled Banner
23. a short story called Flight
24. the article Time-out
25. Poe's The Black Cat
26. Chapter 3, The Sahara
27. Eliot's Rum Tum Tugger

Capitalization: Nouns, Adjectives, Titles *pages 237–243*

Capitalize the first words in sentences, in direct quotations, and in the greetings and closings of letters.

> **Dear** Junko,
>> **Thanks** for the book. **Dad** said, "**She** really knows your taste."
>> **Your** friend,

Capitalize all proper nouns and all adjectives formed from proper nouns.

> The church that **Paul Revere** made famous is in the heart of an interesting **Italian** neighborhood in **Boston.**
> On **Inauguration Day,** the **President** of the **United States** is sworn in by the **Chief Justice** of thc **Supreme Court.**

Capitalize the first word and every important word in a title.

> Have you read *The Call* of the *Wild* by Jack London?

A. Copy each item, adding capital letters where needed.

Example: here's a letter for you.

Answer: Here's a letter for you.

1. dear betty,
2. guess what lou got?
3. his folks gave him a kitten.
4. do you want one?
5. very truly yours,
6. dear jane,
7. my mom says, "no way!"
8. my sister sue is allergic.
9. they make her sneeze.
10. your friend,

11. dear gramps,
12. i found a new job.
13. it's what you used to do.
14. i'm learning to shoe horses.
15. with love,
16. dear ron,
17. what good news!
18. you'll enjoy it too.
19. horses make good company.
20. all my love,

B. Copy from the sentences the words that need capitalization and write them correctly.

Example: nell brennan and I visited new york city for a week.

Answer: Nell Brennan, New York City

21. We landed on a muggy monday in july at kennedy airport.
22. uncle dave and aunt mary took us to the united nations on first avenue and forty-first street.

23. Later we visited the world trade center, which is bigger than the empire state building.
24. Since we were at the tip of manhattan, we walked to battery park for a view of the new york harbor.
25. Our neighbor in st. louis, dr. sam levitt, told us about ellis island, which we could see.
26. Thousands of european immigrants first landed there.
27. Grandma and grandpa wolinski spoke polish and german but no english when they arrived from poland on st. patrick's day.
28. To see the harbor, we decided on a ferry ride to staten island.
29. Uncle dave explained, "beyond the verrazano narrows bridge are the open waters of the atlantic ocean and then europe."
30. Aboard the ferry, we snacked on fruit and florida fruit juice.
31. Besides seeing ellis island, we could also see the u.s. coast guard base on governors island and, of course, liberty island.
32. Liberty island is where the *statue of liberty,* a gift from the french people, stands.
33. It was designed by the frenchmen frédéric auguste bartholdi and alexandre gustave eiffel, who built the eiffel tower.
34. My aunt explained that manhattan is also surrounded by rivers, the hudson river, the east river, and the harlem river.
35. After returning, we visited trinity church on broadway and federal hall, the first united states capitol building.
36. Then we walked to the new york stock exchange on wall street.
37. Since we were tired, we took a bus up broadway through chinatown and greenwich village to washington square.
38. Aunt mary pointed out new york university, where she received her master of arts degree in spanish and portuguese.
39. Despite our hunger and fatigue, she made us walk a few more blocks down sullivan street to bleeker street for a surprise.
40. Finally, we stopped at del rio's, a restaurant, for my absolute favorite, italian food for dinner.

C. Capitalize the titles correctly.

Example: *the light in the forest*   ***Answer:*** *The Light in the Forest*

41. "to build a fire"
42. *monday night football*
43. "the lady, or the tiger?"
44. "born in the u.s.a."
45. *the clan of the cave bear*
46. *that was then, this is now*
47. *the red badge of courage*
48. picasso's *guernica*

Appositives *pages 272–273*

An appositive is a noun or phrase that follows a noun and identifies or explains it. Appositives can be used to combine sentences.

> In 1893, Chicago hosted the Columbian Exposition, **a famous world's fair.**
>
> It commemorated the four-hundredth anniversary of the discoverer of America, **Columbus.**
>
> The main attraction, **an enormous Ferris wheel,** was built especially for the exposition by its inventor, **George Ferris.**

A. Copy the appositive from each sentence as well as the noun or pronoun that it explains.

Example: The Everglades, regions of marshlands and swamps, make up much of southern Florida's interior.

Answer: regions of marshlands and swamps, Everglades

1. The Everglades begin at Lake Okeechobee, the largest in the state.
2. Lake water mixed with rain water flows slowly southward to Florida Bay, a water body at the southern tip of the peninsula.
3. The most characteristic plant, sawgrass, is a sedge that grows in the shallow water and resembles a large blade of grass.
4. The glades look like a prairie, a large grassy plain.
5. Airboats, shallow boats powered by airplane engines, make their way through channels in the Everglades.
6. These marshy wetlands teem with life, both plant and animal.
7. The glades are the only home left for two endangered species, the American crocodile and the Florida panther.
8. During the dry season, aquatic life survives by retreating to alligator holes, deep pools dug out by alligators.
9. At the heart of the food chain is *peryphyton,* a floating mass of green algae.
10. *Peryphyton* provides food for small animals, and they, in turn, are eaten by larger animals, mostly turtles and fish.
11. The ibis, heron, and egret, types of wading birds, also feed at the alligator holes.
12. Of course, the alligator, "the keeper of the glades," does not go hungry either.

B. Copy the sentences, setting off appositives with commas.

Example: The anhinga a strange bird with a snakelike neck dives for fish in the alligator pools.

Answer: The anhinga, a strange bird with a snakelike neck, dives for fish in the alligator pools.

13. Another feature of Everglades scenery is the tropical hammock an island of trees.
14. Slightly elevated above the glades, these islands provide shelter for other animals mostly deer and small mammals.
15. Unusual trees mahogany and gumbo-limbo grow alongside thick clumps of palms in this unique jungle.
16. *Bromeliads* types of air plants hang from dense branches.
17. The colorful *Liguus* a tree snail also clings to the tree limbs.
18. Another air plant Spanish moss hangs from live oak trees.
19. Farther south, mangroves thick-growing trees that tolerate salt water form the last barrier between the Everglades and the sea.
20. Along the narrow beaches of Florida Bay are the hidden nests and telltale tracks of loggerheads giant sea turtles.
21. Here the Everglades America's true tropical wilderness ends.

36 Combining Subjects/Predicates
pages 274-275

Sentences with the same predicate or with the same subject can often be combined into one sentence.

   Sentences: Mexico is in North America. Canada is in North America.

   Combined Subjects: Mexico and Canada are in North America.

   Sentences: The United States is the fifth largest nation.
                       The United States borders both Canada and Mexico.

   Combined Predicates: The United States is the fifth largest nation and borders both Canada and Mexico.

A. Combine each group of sentences on the next page into one.

Example: The Seine River flows through Paris. The Seine River empties into the English Channel.

Answer: The Seine River flows through Paris and empties into the English Channel.

1. Ireland is a British Isle. Great Britain is a British Isle.
2. The Alps form a natural boundary of France. The Pyrenees form a natural boundary of France.
3. Italy is a peninsula. Turkey is a peninsula.
4. The Rhone flows into the Mediterranean. The Nile flows into the Mediterranean.
5. Germany was divided after World War II. Germany today has two separate governments.
6. The United Kingdom borders the North Sea. Denmark borders the North Sea. Norway borders the North Sea.
7. Many European cities lay in ruins after World War II. Many European cities had to be rebuilt.
8. The Dutch built seawalls. The Dutch reclaimed valuable land.
9. German is spoken in Switzerland. French is spoken in Switzerland. Italian is spoken in Switzerland.
10. Vikings once invaded the Mediterranean. Vikings conquered Sicily.

B. Follow the same directions as for Practice A.

11. The circus parade attracts many people. The circus parade has become a local tradition.
12. The crowd arrived early. The crowd camped on the sidewalks. The crowd waited all morning for the start of the parade.
13. Children cheered the colorful wooden wagons. Adults cheered the colorful wooden wagons.
14. Snarling lions paced nervously inside. Ferocious tigers paced nervously inside. Menacing panthers paced nervously inside.
15. A chimp in a skirt danced on an open float. Another in a tuxedo danced on an open float.
16. Gorillas gripped the bars of their wagons. Gorillas made faces at the crowd. Gorillas scratched their heads.
17. An amusing clown juggled apples. An amusing clown ate them at the same time.
18. A tightrope walker on a special float performed for the people. A trapeze artist on a second float performed for the people.
19. Circus ponies with acrobat riders followed behind. A chain of marching elephants followed behind.
20. The cheering crowd roared their approval. The cheering crowd waved merrily to the performers.

Direct Objects and Subject Complements *pages 276–277*

A direct object is a noun or pronoun that follows an action verb. A subject complement is a noun, pronoun, or adjective that follows a linking verb and refers to the subject.

Direct object: Peter saves **coins.** He keeps **them** in an album.

Subject complements: I am a **collector.** These coins are **mine.**
Some have become **rare** and **valuable.**

A. Copy and identify the direct objects and subject complements in the sentences. Write whether the subject complements are predicate nouns, predicate pronouns, or predicate adjectives.

Example: Two robins built a nest on the porch.   *Answer:* nest—DO

Example: It is mostly twigs.   *Answer:* twigs—SC, Predicate noun

1. The robins began it in March.
2. They chose a high, wooden beam under the roof.
3. Occasionally, they carried pieces of newspaper.
4. At first, it looked rather sloppy.
5. Their nest grew larger and neater over the months.
6. Soon the female robin laid four blue eggs in the bottom.
7. One parent never left the nest after that.
8. The new hatchlings are theirs, so the adults protect them.
9. Mealtimes are busy and noisy.
10. Mom becomes quite sentimental about the robins.
11. She eyes every neighborhood cat with suspicion.
12. The nestlings aren't ours, but I feel responsible for them.

B. Follow the same directions as for Practice A.

13. The mechanic drove the car into the garage.
14. She raised the hood and looked in.
15. First she tested the fan belts and hoses.
16. They seemed tight and secure, so she checked the fluids.
17. The car had leaked something onto the floor.
18. It was a black pool of engine oil.
19. A loose bolt seemed the cause of the problem.
20. The mechanic tightened it with her wrench and added more oil.

Indirect Objects *pages 278–279*

An indirect object is a noun or pronoun that tells to whom or for whom the action of the verb is done.

IO   DO   IO   DO

A guest gave our **class** a **talk.** She also showed **us** some **slides.**

A. Copy the sentences. Underline the subject once and the verb twice. Then label the direct and indirect object.

Example: Sue offered everyone some lemonade.

IO   DO

Answer: <u>Sue</u> <u><u>offered</u></u> everyone some lemonade.

1. Mr. Han built the school a bandstand.
2. We sent the mayor an invitation.
3. Ramon offered him a front-row seat.
4. Dorothy gave the class the idea.
5. The accordionist promised them a solo performance.
6. The old musician played us our favorite tunes.
7. A caterer sold the people box lunches.
8. The waiter brought the hungriest people a second helping.
9. The sale of lunches provided the man an income.
10. Vicki showed me her new plan.

B. Copy and identify the direct objects and indirect objects in the sentences. Two sentences have no indirect object.

Example: I always feed Skipper his supper.
Answer: supper—DO   Skipper—IO

11. I brought June her groceries.
12. My mother made me a delicious dinner.
13. I gave Skipper a little taste.
14. The hotel served the star breakfast in bed.
15. They prepared it especially for her.
16. Dad cooked us our favorite meal.
17. A relative sent the Richardsons a box of assorted cheeses.
18. The clerk sold me some sweet plums.
19. I gave a friend several of them.
20. My hamster stores extra food in its cheeks.
21. Julie loaned me a book about rodents.

Tested Skills Practice

Possessive Nouns   *pages 304–307*

Possessive nouns show ownership. They are formed with an apostrophe and the letter **s ('s)** or with an apostrophe alone (**'**).

Singular Possessive Nouns	**Plural Possessive Nouns**
a **desk's** legs	many **desks'** legs
Ms. Thomas's bicycle	the **Thomases'** bicycles
a **child's** shoes	**children's** shoes

An apostrophe is not ordinarily used to form the plural of a noun.

Plural: The **artists** displayed their works.
Possessive: The **artist's** signature is usually in a lower corner.
Possessive: Several **artists'** paintings won awards.

A. Write the possessive form of each noun in parentheses.
Example: (Willis) football
Answer: Willis's

1. all (nations) flags
2. several (torches) flames
3. the (band) music
4. (Betsy) shoes
5. some (contestants) entries
6. a (skier) tracks
7. my (team) toboggan
8. the (men) final
9. (Ross) roller skates
10. (everyone) applause
11. the (judge) decision
12. (James) award
13. both (families) photos
14. two (reporters) comments
15. many (buses) windows
16. few (runners) victories
17. each (couple) dance
18. many (people) cheers
19. the (women) relay race
20. most (newspapers) accounts

B. Write the plural possessive form of each singular noun in parentheses.
Example: his (puppy) coats
Answer: puppies'

21. few (workman) overcoats
22. some (baby) blankets
23. three (bicyclist) caps
24. two (goose) nesting places
25. many (mosquito) bites
26. six (rabbit) hutches
27. the (ox) harnesses
28. our (father-in-law) blessings
29. the (cloud) shadow
30. the (Morris) convertibles
31. both (chairwoman) decisions
32. some (athlete) medals

C. Write the correct plural or possessive form of the word in parentheses.

Example: We admired the (fisherman) catch. ***Answer:*** fisherman's

Example: They used (minnow) for bait. ***Answer:*** minnows

33. Derrick saw a (moose) tracks on the other side of the lake.
34. Two large (turtle) sunned themselves on wet rocks.
35. The (beach) sand looks white on bright summer (day).
36. Linda recognized the (Smiths) and (Jameses) campers.
37. Both boys helped dock the (sportsmen) boats.
38. Everyone enjoyed the (countryside) charm.
39. Two (family) sat near the (water) edge.
40. They will miss the (lake) quiet pleasures.

41 **Pronoun Homophones** *pages 308–309*

Homophones are words that sound alike. They have different meanings and are usually spelled differently.

Possessive pronoun:	This is **their** field.
Contraction:	**They're** finished now.
Adverb:	Will they let us play over **there?**
Possessive pronoun:	Where is **your** excuse?
Contraction:	**You're** late again.
Possessive pronoun:	**Its** tail is short.
Contraction:	**It's** just a little hamster.
Possessive pronoun:	**Whose** shoes are these?
Contraction:	**Who's** the forgetful one?

Copy the sentences, choosing the correct word in parentheses.

Example: (Whose, Who's) driving (your, you're) car?

Answer: Who's driving your car?

1. (Its, It's) almost all packed in (their, they're, there) truck.
2. Is (your, you're) van parked over (their, they're, there)?
3. Take this lamp, since (your, you're) such a careful driver.
4. (Its, It's) very delicate and so is that old China teapot (whose, who's) handle is cracked.
5. The movers, (whose, who's) record is good, have loaded (their, they're, there) truck.
6. (Their, They're, There) quick at (their, they're, there) work.
7. (Its, It's) only noon, and look (whose, who's) nearly finished.

42 # Using Reflexive, Intensive, and Indefinite Pronouns *pages 310–313*

A reflexive pronoun reflects the action of the verb back to the subject. An intensive pronoun emphasizes the noun or pronoun just named. Indefinite pronouns may be either singular or plural and may or may not have antecedents.

Reflexive: He found **himself** on a lonely trail.
Intensive: I **myself** enjoyed the solitude.
Indefinite: **Each** has his preference, but **many** prefer some company.

A. Copy the reflexive and intensive pronouns, and give each antecedent. Also write which kind each pronoun is.

Example: Runners should buy themselves a good pair of shoes.
Answer: themselves = Runners—Reflexive
Example: I myself have taken up the sport.
Answer: myself = I—Intensive

1. We pride ourselves on keeping fit.
2. Jogging is an exercise I myself do.
3. Perhaps you yourself are a jogger.
4. My brother Ted usually jogs by himself.
5. He needed to lose weight, but running itself wasn't enough.
6. I myself do not eat as much as he.
7. Some joggers entertain themselves with tiny cassette players.
8. I enjoy the silence but sometimes I hum to myself.

B. Copy the indefinite pronouns from the paragraph.

   (9) Did anyone see it land?   (10) Several think it was something or other from a strange planet.   (11) Few know for sure.
(12) Everyone has his own explanation.   (13) Someone picked up two shiny, metallic objects.   (14) Both were unusually hard, and neither looked familiar.   (15) Of course, no one had actually seen anybody.   (16) One thinks he saw somebody run; another says something flew over his head.   (17) Many don't believe either of them.   (18) If anyone has taken pictures, please submit them.

Independent and Dependent Clauses
pages 342–345

A part of a sentence that has a subject and a verb and makes sense by itself is called an independent clause. A dependent clause has a subject and a predicate, but does not make sense by itself.

> **Independent Clauses:** **Mary dusted the furniture, and I**
> **vacuumed the floors and rugs.**
> **Dependent Clause:** We took a break **when we finished.**

A. Copy the sentences, and underline the independent clauses. Put two lines under commas, conjunctions, and semicolons that join independent clauses.

Example: Most spiders have venom, but few are dangerous to humans.

Answer: <u>Most spiders have venom,</u> <u>but</u> <u>few are dangerous to humans.</u>

1. You may dislike spiders, or you may be a rare spider fan.
2. Spiders originally lived in the sea, but they adapted to life on land long, long ago.
3. People mistake spiders for insects, but spiders belong to a completely different species.
4. Spiders have eight legs, and their heads and chests are fused.
5. Insects have six legs, and their bodies are in three sections.
6. Spider webs make excellent traps for insects, but many webs look like works of art.
7. Spiders weave cocoons for their prey, and female spiders weave egg sacs too.
8. Most webs are sticky, but some feel more like wool.
9. Females lay hundreds of eggs, but only a small proportion survive to adulthood.
10. Spiders live anywhere; they are even found in Antarctica.

B. Read the sentences. If a sentence has a dependent clause, copy the clause on your paper.

Example: Although most spiders catch their own food, some do not.

Answer: Although most spiders catch their own food

11. Thief spiders do not catch insects because they do not build webs of their own.

12. These creatures must be clever, or they would not survive.
13. When they find another spider's prey, they steal it from the web.
14. Although webs have signal threads, thief spiders can avoid these natural "burglar alarms."
15. If a web does catch them, they can usually escape.
16. Scientists who are interested in spiders have studied them in some unusual ways.
17. Spiders wove webs in space while astronauts observed them.
18. Since there was no gravity in the spacecraft, web-spinning was tricky for the spiders.
19. The first few webs that they made were sloppy, but soon the spiders were weaving beautiful, unusual webs.
20. Because spiders can adapt to almost any conditions, they have survived for ages.

C. Read the items and write whether they are dependent clauses or simple sentences.

Example: I woke up early this morning   ***Answer:*** Simple sentence

21. when I arrived a little late at Al's Restaurant
22. I was nervous and worried about my first day at work
23. I had been there only once before
24. though some of my friends had worked there
25. the boss explained my job to me
26. since I was new and hadn't worked in this business
27. he was very patient and really calmed me down
28. before I took my first order at the counter
29. I tied my apron around my waist
30. although my hands were still shaking
31. when my first customer came in and placed her order
32. I could hardly believe it
33. because the order was so huge
34. she wanted so many kinds of sandwiches and beverages
35. that I nearly ran out of paper
36. after I delivered that order
37. which is the largest in my short experience as a counterman
38. everything else seemed easy by comparison

A sentence that has one independent clause and one or more dependent clauses is a complex sentence.

> **Until it was brought back to Spain in the 1500s,** the potato, **which is a valuable food source,** was unknown in Europe.

A. Read the sentences. Copy all complex sentences and underline the dependent clauses. Six of the eight sentences are complex.

Example: Though Europeans were unaware of its existence, the potato had been an important food for centuries.

Answer: <u>Though Europeans were unaware of its existence</u>, the potato had been an important food for centuries.

1. The Incas, who lived in the Andes Mountains of South America, considered the potato their staple food.
2. Potatoes will grow under harsh conditions and at high altitudes that would destroy other crops.
3. When the Spanish conquered the Incas, they also discovered the potato.
4. They brought it back to Europe, but it wasn't popular at first.
5. Many people who were superstitious thought it was evil because it grew underground.
6. After many famines struck Europe, the potato slowly gained acceptance as a food.
7. Its hearty nature made it ideal for the cool, damp climate.
8. Because the potato is so adaptable, it is grown today all over the world.

B. Make the sentences complex by adding dependent clauses. Use the word in parentheses to introduce each dependent clause.

Example: We pick vegetables from the garden. (when)
Answer: When they are ripe, we pick vegetables from the garden.

9. I noticed a family of rabbits in our garden. (when)
10. They were feasting on our lettuce and carrots. (while)
11. The rabbits ignored me and continued their feast. (although)
12. They would destroy many days of hard work. (if)
13. I chased the rabbits out of the garden. (when)
14. I felt a little bad about it. (because)

Tested Skills Practice

46 **Combining Sentences** *pages 350–353*

Sometimes two sentences with related ideas can be combined into a compound sentence. Short sentences with modifiers can sometimes be combined into a single, more interesting sentence.

Sentences:	Will I finish my report on time? Will it be late?
Combined:	Will I finish my report on time, or will it be late?
Modifiers:	I worked on it today. I worked on it at the library.
Combined:	I worked on it today at the library.

A. Combine the related sentences, using the best conjunction and a comma. Two pairs of sentences should not be combined.

Example: I spent several hours there. I finally finished.
Answer: I spent several hours there, but I finally finished.

1. First I checked the card catalog. Then I went to the shelves.
2. I wanted a certain book for my report. It was not there.
3. I asked the librarian about it. She found it checked out.
4. Would I have to look for the book somewhere else? Could I get the same information from a different source?
5. The librarian suggested an encyclopedia. She had been a librarian for many years.
6. The encyclopedia had the information. Unfortunately I couldn't take it home.
7. The article was quite long. I really wanted to leave.
8. Should I stay and read it? Should I hand in my report late?
9. I read the article. The notes I took were very helpful.
10. I turned in my report on time. Libraries are great places.

B. By combining the modifiers, write one sentence for each item.
Example: I worked slowly. I worked carefully. I worked until late.
Answer: I worked slowly and carefully until late.

11. I read at a table. I read in a corner of the library.
12. The room was large. The room was quiet. The room was empty.
13. I took notes on the article. I took notes in my looseleaf.
14. The librarian was helpful. The librarian was very knowledgeable.
15. Dad waited patiently. Dad waited in the car. Dad waited in front of the library.

Improving Sentences *pages 354–355*

Make your sentences clear, smooth, and concise.

Unclear:	Put the map **in the glove compartment from the hotel.**
Clear:	Put the map from the hotel in the glove compartment.
Not smooth:	The road was bumpy, dusty, and **it wound around.**
Smooth:	The road was bumpy, dusty, and **winding.**
Not concise:	The ride **was very long and took a lot of time.**
Concise:	The ride **took a long time.**

A. Improve the sentences by rewriting, deleting, or repositioning the underlined words according to the guidelines of the lesson.

Example: We camped for one week on a camping trip at Elks Lake.

Answer: We camped for one week at Elks Lake.

1. We got to our campsite early in the morning at breakfast time.
2. We set up our tents in an area near the lake with many trees.
3. We immediately went to the lake as soon as we could.
4. The water felt cool, cleansing, and it also was refreshing after our long ride.
5. I swam for about fifteen minutes and then sunned myself on a raft made out of wood.
6. A man swam to the raft with a sunburn.
7. Those swimmers have snorkles, fins, and are wearing masks.

B. Follow the same directions as for Practice A.

8. In spite of the fact that I was hungry, I went on a canoe ride for a long time.
9. A woman caught a fish that was huge in size in a red shirt.
10. Right after lunch, we went for a hike in the afternoon.
11. The trail led through a forest, a ravine, and it also went across a meadow.
12. By the time we finished and stopped hiking, I was tired, hungry, and wanted something to drink.
13. The camper gave me a glass that contained water near the supplies.
14. Later I helped prepare a dinner of fish, corn, and potatoes that we baked.

Tested Skills Practice
Verb Usage

The past and past participle forms of irregular verbs do not end in *-ed*.

Present	Past	Past participle
go	went	(have, has, had) gone
begin	began	(have, has, had) begun
throw	threw	(have, has, had) thrown
speak	spoke	(have, has, had) spoken
leave	left	(have, has, had) left

A. Copy the sentences, using the correct past or past participle form of the verb in parentheses.

Example: Max _____ a zoo keeper two years ago. (become)
Answer: Max became a zoo keeper two years ago.

1. Most of Max's days at the zoo have _____ smoothly. (go)
2. One day he _____ to the cheetah cage. (go)
3. He couldn't believe what he _____. (see)
4. "What has _____ of the cheetah!" Max exclaimed. (become)
5. He _____ as fast as he could to the director's office. (run)
6. The director had already _____ to worry. (begin)
7. She had _____ Max running toward her office. (see)
8. She also _____ frantic when she heard the news. (become)
9. Together they _____ a desperate search. (begin)
10. Just then, Donald _____ up to them. (come)
11. "The cheetah has not _____ away," Donald said quietly. (run)
12. "I _____ for a walk, and she _____ with me." (go, come)

B. Follow the same directions as for Practice A.

13. Natalie _____ she was going to be late again. (know)
14. Quickly she _____ a glass of milk. (drink)
15. She had _____ that she would not be late again. (swear)
16. The coach had _____ weary of her excuses. (grow)
17. She _____ up from the table and headed for the door. (spring)
18. Natalie practically _____ down the street to school. (fly)
19. When she reached the gym, her heart _____. (sink)
20. Her hopes had _____ to nothing. (shrink)
21. "I have _____ my promise," Natalie lamented. (break)

22. "I have _____ my last lap!" (swim)
23. By now she had _____ the gym doorbell several times. (ring)
24. In relief, Natalie suddenly _____ her equipment bag into the air. (throw).
25. "I should have _____ that practice is tomorrow!" she laughed. (know)

C. Follow the same directions as for Practice A.

26. Some people have _____ the wolf a bad name. (give)
27. Storybook authors have _____ about the wolf as a villain. (write)
28. This _____ many people to be afraid of wolves. (lead)
29. The wolf's bad reputation _____ because sometimes these animals killed livestock. (begin)
30. In the past, wolves _____ cattle from ranchers. (steal)
31. They also _____ into chicken houses. (break)
32. Civilization itself _____ wolves to these attacks. (drive)
33. Wolves have always _____ sick or wounded animals. (eat)
34. People have _____ away the wolf's natural food supply. (take)
35. This has _____ wolves with little else to eat. (leave)
36. Today the government has _____ of ways to protect the wolf because it is endangered. (think)

53 # Forms of *be, have,* and *do* pages 389–394

Use the forms of the verbs *be, have,* and *do* correctly.

	be	**have**	**do**
Present	am, is, are	has, have	does, do
Past	was, were	had	did
Past Participle	(has) been	(has) had	(has) done

A. Copy the sentences, using the correct form of *be*.
Example: My latest hobby _____ music.
Answer: My latest hobby is music.

1. Today there _____ many types of musical instruments.
2. Drums probably _____ the earliest to be invented.
3. It _____ not easy to say how many kinds now exist.
4. The flute has _____ around since ancient times too.

5. The first guitar probably ____ invented in the Middle East.
6. ____ you sure that I haven't told you about this before?
7. Of course, the electric guitar ____ much more recent.
8. It had ____ invented in America during this century.
9. My sister ____ a report on electronic instruments.
10. I ____ learning all I can about these too.

B. Copy the sentences, using the correct form of *have*.

11. People throughout the world ____ pets.
12. My neighbor ____ a dog, a macaw, tropical fish, and a lizard.
13. He has also ____ snakes, frogs, and rabbits for pets.
14. For years, some people ____ tried to make wild animals into pets.
15. State parks have ____ a big problem with illegal trapping.
16. Some poachers ____ even attempted to tame bears, wolves, coyotes, and falcons.
17. Our state ____ passed a law prohibiting this.
18. Before it passed, the government ____ felt that too many wild species were being endangered by people.
19. Most pet owners ____ more sensible, domestic pets.
20. Your living space ____ much to do with what kind of pet you should own.

C. Copy the sentences, using the correct form of *do*.

21. My friend Megan has ____ many magic tricks for her friends.
22. She ____ n't even charge us admission.
23. One time she ____ some card tricks.
24. I still ____ n't know how she always knew which card I was holding.
25. She said she would ____ some tricks with her hat.
26. She asked Toby if he was ____ anything special.
27. Since he wasn't, Toby ____ n't mind volunteering.
28. "____ you mind breaking three eggs into my hat?" Megan asked.
29. After Toby had ____ what she asked, she tapped the hat three times.
30. Though it ____ n't seem possible, she put the hat on her head, and nothing spilled out.

Troublesome Verb Pairs *pages 395–397*

Some pairs of verbs are confusing because they have similar meanings or because they look alike.

Lay down the cartons.
Set them down here.
Let me make some room.
Lend me your pencil.
Teach me backgammon.
Bring a raincoat when you come.
We **rose** for the national anthem.

I want to **lie** in the sun.
Will you **sit** in the shade?
Tom must **leave** on time.
You may **borrow** it again.
I **learned** tumbling in gym.
Take this note to Ms. Dee.
I want to **raise** the flag.

A. Copy the sentences, using the correct verb from each pair in parentheses.

Example: Marla (raised, rose) at seven this morning.
Answer: Marla rose at seven this morning.

1. She (brought, took) her tennis racket from her closet.
2. "(Leave, Let) me have your sun visor," she said to her sister.
3. "I have a tennis lesson this morning and need to (lend, borrow) it."
4. When Marla arrived at her lesson, she (set, sat) on the bench and waited for her instructor.
5. She (laid, lay) her jacket down on the bench next to her.
6. Other students started to arrive and (set, sat) down too.
7. The instructor was going to (teach, learn) them the basics.
8. Mr. Williams, the instructor, had (brought, taken) all of his equipment with him.

B. Follow the same directions as for Practice A.

9. The class (raised, rose) from the bench when Mr. Williams walked onto the court.
10. "Today I will (learn, teach) you the fundamentals of tennis."
11. "I see no one needs to (lend, borrow) a racket today," he said.
12. "Now (sit, set) yourselves in the position I (learned, taught) you yesterday," said Mr. Williams.
13. "Bend your knees and (rise, raise) your racket waist high."
14. "(Let, Leave) your shoulders relax!" he called out to Marla.
15. He tossed a ball that had (laid, lain) nearby over the net.

Active and Passive Verbs   *pages 398–399*

Active verbs are used most often because they express action directly and naturally. Passive verbs are used less often.

Active Verb: Papers **littered** the streets.

Passive Verb: The streets **were littered** with papers.

A. Copy the verbs or verb phrases from the sentences and write whether they are passive or active.

Example: The news was broadcast over the radio.

Answer: was broadcast—Passive

1. It rained very heavily yesterday.
2. Seven inches of rain fell in only a few hours.
3. The streets were flooded with water.
4. The airport was closed by the city.
5. Cars stalled at every intersection.
6. Some vehicles rolled completely under water.
7. Scuba divers checked them for trapped passengers.
8. Many basements were filled with storm water too.
9. Water even filled the baseball stadium to the third row!
10. Rescue volunteers have arrived from other cities.

B. Rewrite the sentences, changing the passive verbs to active verbs.

Example: Jupiter was visited by *Voyager II*.

Answer: *Voyager II* visited Jupiter.

11. Extraordinary pictures were taken by the satellite's cameras.
12. The pictures were sent over a billion kilometers by *Voyager*.
13. They were received by the Jet Propulsion Laboratory in Pasadena, California.
14. Many new facts were learned by researchers at the laboratory.
15. Detailed pictures of Jupiter's moons were studied by the scientists.
16. Saturn also has been visited by *Voyager II*.
17. Its rings have been analyzed by the laboratory's computers.
18. New theories of the rings' origins have been proposed by astronomers.

Subject-Verb Agreement *pages 440–443*

A singular subject agrees with a singular verb. A plural subject agrees with a plural verb. Agreement between subject and verb is not affected by words or phrases that come between the subject and the verb.

Plural: My **sister** and **I wonder** about life on other planets.
Singular: Neither my **dad** nor my **teacher believes** in aliens.
Plural: Some **experts** on this subject **disagree.**

A. Copy each sentence, using the form of the verb in parentheses that agrees with the subject.

Example: A geologist and an astronomer (has, have) a new theory.
Answer: A geologist and an astronomer have a new theory.

1. One of the scientists (was, were) lecturing to our class today.
2. Neither her observations nor her research (leaves, leave) her in doubt.
3. At least one of the millions of other planets probably (has, have) life on it.
4. Chance and probability (point, points) toward that conclusion.
5. Conditions for life probably (exists, exist) somewhere.
6. Both water and ice (has, have) been detected on nearby planets.
7. Carbon and nitrogen (is, are) also common in the universe.
8. A balance between hot and cold (makes, make) life more likely.
9. Life on other planets (remains, remain) a distinct possibility.
10. Her theories and hypotheses (seems, seem) reasonable to me.

B. Follow the same directions as for Practice A.

11. Students and teachers (was, were) intrigued by the lecture.
12. Many questions about alien life (was, were) asked.
13. Neither Mars nor Venus (has, have) favorable conditions for our form of life.
14. The moons of Jupiter (offers, offer) a better possibility.
15. The planets beyond Jupiter (appears, appear) to be too cold.
16. Neither her facts nor her conclusions (was, were) challenged by anyone present.
17. After all, the earth, one of the millions of planets, (does, do) contain life.

Subject-Verb Agreement: Inverted Order *pages 444–445*

The position of a subject in a sentence does not affect subject-verb agreement.

	S V
Normal order:	Our old **friends are** here.
	V S
Inverted order:	Here **are** our old **friends.**
	V S
Inverted order:	**Are** our old **friends** here?

A. Copy the sentences, underlining the subject once and the verb twice.

Example: Where are you going in such a hurry?

Answer: Where <u>are</u> <u>you</u> <u>going</u> in such a hurry?

1. Were you late for your appointment?
2. Here is the shortcut to my house.
3. Where on earth did I leave my umbrella?
4. How do I get to the expressway from here?
5. There has been road construction everywhere this summer.
6. Do the downtown bus lines operate on weekends?
7. What is the best route to the airport?
8. Here are my suggestions for your visit.
9. What restaurants have you tried?
10. Did you see the entire city from the top of that building?

B. Copy each sentence, choosing the form of the verb in parentheses that agrees with the subject.

Example: There (is, are) miles of street beneath the sidewalks.

Answer: There are miles of street beneath the sidewalks.

11. Here (is, are) an underground city.
12. (Has, Have) you ever walked down there?
13. (Do, Does) stores have basement entrances to these streets?
14. (Is, Are) there traffic signals and crosswalks?
15. Where (do, does) that stairway lead?
16. Down the stairs (walk, walks) the girl.
17. There (was, were) many reasons for this lower level.

Subject-Verb Agreement: Indefinite Pronouns *pages 448–449*

When an indefinite pronoun is used as a subject, the verb in the sentence must agree with it.

Singular: **Each** of the car dealers **was** open Thursday evening.

Plural: **Some** of them **are** now **advertising** clearance sales.

A. Copy each sentence, choosing the form of the verb that agrees in number with the subject.

Example: All of the salesmen (was, were) busy.

Answer: All of the salesmen were busy.

1. Each of the new cars (looks, look) attractive.
2. Any of them (is, are) fine with me.
3. Most of the cars (has, have) air conditioning.
4. Several on the floor (has, have) "sold" stickers on them.
5. One of the sports-car models (is, are) turbo-charged.
6. Many of those (is, are) also available with fuel injection.
7. A few of the cars (has, have) sun roofs.
8. Some (is, are) very expensive.
9. Both of my parents (needs, need) new cars.
10. Neither of them (wants, want) unnecessary options.
11. No one except me (thinks, think) of a cassette player as a necessity.
12. Everyone (likes, like) the smell of a new car.

B. Follow the same directions as for Practice A.

13. Everyone in the terminal (has, have) waited a long time.
14. No one (has, have) arrived or departed since this morning.
15. Each of the airplanes (is, are) sitting near its gate.
16. Many of the passengers (has, have) been here all day.
17. Anyone with travel plans (worries, worry) about delays.
18. Nevertheless, nobody (complains, complain) much about it.
19. Several of the flights (was, were) canceled earlier.
20. Only one of them (has, have) boarded passengers.
21. Most of the crews (is, are) used to this.
22. Somebody (says, say) that the fog will lift soon.

Subject pronouns are used as subjects of sentences. Object pronouns can be used as direct objects, indirect objects, or objects of prepositions.

Subjects: **He** and **I** will play fullback, and **she** can be the goalie.

Objects: Give **her** back the ball, or kick **it** to **him** or **me.**

A. Copy the sentences, choosing the correct subject or object pronoun.

Example: Cindy and (I, me) went to the zoo Saturday afternoon.

Answer: Cindy and I went to the zoo Saturday afternoon.

1. (She, Her) and (I, me) brought her little brothers Justin and Timmy along.
2. Timmy asked (she, her) and (I, me) about the petting zoo.
3. It interested his brother and (he, him) more than anything else.
4. Justin wanted (we, us) to go there right away.
5. He nagged Cindy and (I, me) for an eternity.
6. Finally, (she, her) gave in to Timmy and (he, him) in desperation.
7. (She, Her) and (I, me) waited for (they, them) on a bench.
8. Justin begged (we, us) for some rabbit feed before they left.
9. A zookeeper let Timmy and (he, him) play with the animals.
10. After an hour, (he, him) and Timmy were ready for lunch.

B. Follow the same directions as for Practice A.

11. Cindy and (I, me) bought sandwiches and soft drinks for the boys and (we, us).
12. After lunch, (we, us) and her brothers saw the rest of the zoo.
13. Some playful seals amused both (we, us) and (they, them).
14. The seals almost drenched Cindy and (I, me) more than once.
15. Justin laughed at (we, us), but one almost splashed some other children and (he, him).
16. Next, Cindy and (I, me) took Timmy and (he, him) to see the African safari animals.
17. (He, Him) and Timmy liked the lions and the elephants, but the monkeys entertained Cindy and (I, me) the most.

Pronoun Agreement *pages 483–485*

A pronoun should agree with its antecedent.

> The delivery **man** parked **his** truck in the alley.
> Since **Lilian** answered the door, **she** signed **her** name.
> **Neither** of the boxes had a return address on **it.**

A. Write the sentences, using the correct pronoun in parentheses.

Example: Each of the contestants had (her, their) hopes of winning.

Answer: Each of the contestants had her hopes of winning.

1. The host of the show offered (his, their) best wishes to them.
2. Both of the women were given (her, their) first question.
3. The one who buzzed first was asked for (her, their) answer.
4. Everyone in the audience held (his, their) breath for a moment.
5. Since one of the women answered correctly, (she, they) was awarded the points.
6. Could either of the contestants answer (her, their) next question?
7. "What twentieth-century king gave up (his, their) kingdom for love?" asked the host.
8. Someone in the audience showed that (he, they) knew the answer.
9. Fortunately, this person did not open (his, their) mouth.
10. Each of the women thought that (she, they) had the answer.
11. Many in the audience showed (its, their) approval by cheering.
12. Suddenly the station broke for one of (its, their) commercials.

B. Follow the same directions as for Practice A.

13. When the show resumed, both of the women were about to give (her, their) answers.
14. "Wasn't it one of the Windsors who gave up (his, their) throne?" the first woman asked.
15. "I'm sorry, but you must tell me (his, their) first name," replied the host.
16. "Edward was (his, their) name, but which number?" said the other contestant.
17. Suddenly both gave (her, their) answers at the same moment.

64 **Using *who* and *whom*** *pages 486–487*

Who is generally used as a subject or a subject complement. *Whom* is used as a direct object or object of a preposition.

    Subject: **Who** knows a doctor for my dog? Ruth knows someone **who** is a veterinarian.

    Object: **Whom** should I call for an appointment? From **whom** did you get Dr. Edwards's name? I am the person **whom** Ruth sent.

A. Write the pronoun that belongs in the blank and whether it is a subject, direct object, or object of a preposition.

Example: Here comes a golfer _____ needs a golf cart.
Answer: who—Subject

1. _____ has ever caddied during the summer?
2. Caddies do more than carry the golf clubs of people _____ have hired them.
3. A caddie _____ is familiar with a course can be very helpful.
4. Someone _____ has never played the course will usually ask the caddie about it first.
5. Since caddies often work the same golf course, they are the people _____ best know its hazards and quirks.
6. Golfers seek advice on difficult shots from caddies _____ they trust.
7. The caddie is someone to _____ golfers turn for this information.
8. Phil has caddied for a professional golfer _____ everyone likes.
9. Though retired, he is the famous golfer _____ enormous crowds follow around the course.

B. Follow the same directions as for Practice A.

10. For _____ have you caddied recently?
11. Is she the golfer _____ won the tournament?
12. That is someone _____ my father once met.
13. _____ is the lucky golfer _____ shot a hole-in-one?
14. _____ else was in the foursome and witnessed it?
15. The caddies with _____ I work all enjoy playing golf.
16. _____ will sell me a set of left-handed golf clubs?
17. _____ should I thank for ending up in a sand trap?

This and *that* are singular. *These* and *those* are plural.

> **Incorrect:** **That here** road leads down to the beach.
> **Correct:** **That** road leads down to the beach.
> **Incorrect:** **These** sort of road are hard on the car.
> **Correct:** **This** sort of road is hard on the car.
> **Incorrect:** I don't like to drive on **them** roads.
> **Correct:** I don't like to drive on **those** roads.

A. Write the correct form of each adjective in parentheses.
Example: (This, This here) fire is about to go out.
Answer: This

1. Put (that, those) log on the fire.
2. Let's cook some of (them, those) steaks for supper.
3. We can broil them on (this, this here) grill.
4. (This, These) summer sunsets are really beautiful!
5. It's warm enough to sleep outside (this, these) evening.
6. Would you tell one of (them, those) scary ghost stories again?
7. What was (that, that there) sound?
8. It sounded like one of (them, those) banshees from the story.
9. I am not budging from (this, this here) campfire.
10. (That, Those) sort of noise can certainly fool you.
11. (This, These) kind of story is really frightening.
12. Did you see (them, those) meteors?

B. Follow the same directions as for Practice A.

13. (This, These) kinds of lakes are great for fishing.
14. (That, That there) island is where I caught so many last time.
15. Help me with (this, this here) boat.
16. You can put (those, them) fishing rods in the bow.
17. Be careful with (this, these) tackle box.
18. We can both pull on (these, these here) oars.
19. Would you hand me one of (those, them) fishhooks?
20. I will cast from (this, this here) side of the boat.
21. (This, These) sort of worm makes good bait.
22. (This, This here) cove is the place to try.

Tested Skills Practice

23. (This, These) fish are certainly biting today.

24. Let's make lunch on (that, that there) beach.

C. Follow the same directions as for Practice A.

25. Why are you wearing (that, those) crash helmet?

26. (This, These) sort of kayak is made of a new, hard plastic.

27. Kayakers prefer (this, these) kind of canoe.

28. A fiberglass kayak might split if it hits (them, those) rocks in the middle of the river.

29. (These, These here) boats can shoot white-water rapids at incredible speeds.

30. (That, That there) mountain river is so steep that strong, oceanlike waves actually develop in the middle.

31. Kayakers ride (them, those) waves all the way down the river.

32. (This, These) part of the sport is similar to surfing.

33. Some kayakers use (this, these) sort of double-sided paddle to steer and maneuver.

34. Watch (that, that there) kayaker in the river as she intentionally flips over.

35. (That, Those) sort of maneuver will be repeated several times during her ride.

36. I wonder if (this, this here) water is as cold as it looks.

37. Does (this, these) kind of sport interest you?

66 # Using Negative Words *pages 492–493*

Use only one negative word when you mean "no."

    Incorrect: I **never** listen to **nothing** but my portable radio.

      Correct: I **never** listen to **anything** but my portable radio.

    Incorrect: We **don't** have **no** batteries for the radio.

      Correct: We **don't** have **any** batteries for the radio.

    Incorrect: I **can't hardly** hear a thing with these earphones.

      Correct: I can **hardly** hear a thing with these earphones.

A. Copy the word that correctly completes each sentence.

Example: I haven't seen (any, none) of my classmates this summer.

Answer: I haven't seen any of my classmates this summer.

1. Haven't (either, neither) of you spoken to Pauline?
2. You can't leave (anything, nothing) in your locker over vacation.
3. Darrin couldn't find his skateboard (anywhere, nowhere).
4. I wouldn't want to be late for (any, none) of my classes.
5. We (could, couldn't) barely catch our breath.
6. I prefer pizza with hardly (any, no) seasonings.
7. Carol (has, hasn't) scarcely begun her social-studies report.
8. Wasn't there (anybody, nobody) in the home-arts room?
9. We (should, shouldn't) never have gone on that roller coaster.
10. I don't (ever, never) want to try one again.

B. Follow the same directions as for Practice A.

11. You shouldn't tell (anybody, nobody) about our big surprise.
12. Didn't (either, neither) team win yesterday?
13. Cecil wasn't (anywhere, nowhere) in the house.
14. Uncle Pete doesn't know (anything, nothing) about bridge.
15. The dog (has, hasn't) barely touched his food.
16. Wasn't (neither, either) of the cars in the driveway?
17. I don't work at the supermarket (no more, anymore).
18. The paint (has, hasn't) scarcely dried yet.
19. Haven't you (never, ever) tried water-skiing?
20. I (can, can't) see nothing through these field glasses.

C. Rewrite the sentences by eliminating unnecessary negatives. If you can, rewrite some sentences two ways.
Example: I don't have no paper.
Answer: I don't have any paper. I have no paper.

21. There wasn't nowhere to eat lunch.
22. Tom couldn't find no one with a key to the storeroom.
23. Our class wasn't hardly expecting another fire drill today.
24. The Taylors haven't never been to our new house.
25. Aren't there no bananas left for my cereal?
26. Nina hasn't never seen a Broadway show.
27. The bus driver won't wait no more than five minutes.
28. I couldn't hardly read the tiny print.
29. Those paintbrushes weren't nowhere in the basement.
30. Aren't there none in the garage?

A **diagram** is a picture of a sentence. It helps show the relationship of one part of a sentence to another. This Handbook will show you how to diagram the kinds of words, phrases, and clauses studied in this textbook. Sentences for you to diagram follow each example.

A **simple sentence** is diagramed on a horizontal line, called the **base line.** A vertical line separates the simple subject and the simple predicate.

Birds chirped.

1. We sing.
2. Lawanda is dancing.
3. Flowers are blooming.

Adjectives and adverbs are written on slanted lines below the words they modify. Notice how an adverb that modifies another modifier is diagramed.

The next boy answered somewhat hesitantly.

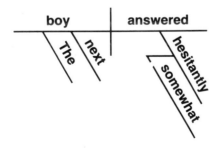

4. The heavy snow fell rapidly.
5. Our new car ran very smoothly.
6. The brass bell clanged harshly.

Prepositional phrases are diagramed below the words they modify. The preposition is placed on a slanting line, and its object is placed on a horizontal line. Any modifiers of the object are placed on slanting lines below the object.

The park in our area is across the street.

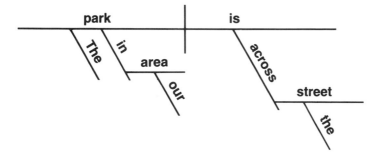

7. The illustrator in the museum drew with charcoal.
8. A picture of the President hung in the classroom.
9. Tom ran through the line with the ball.

Compound modifiers (words or phrases) are diagramed below the words they modify. The modifiers are joined by a broken line on which the conjunction is written.

The red and silver plane flew over the field and into the air.

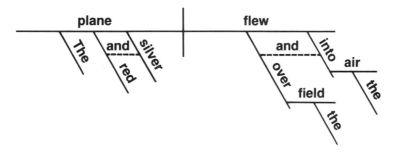

10. The red and green lights blinked cheerily.
11. Over the river and through the woods the sleigh went.
12. The basketball player, tall and lanky, strolled onto the court.

An **interrogative sentence** is easier to diagram if it is first reworded as a declarative sentence.

Were you in the classroom?   You were in the classroom.

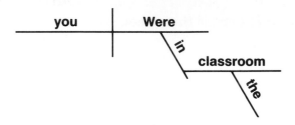

13. Did they arrive early?
14. Who is driving today?
15. Was she at the party?

An **imperative sentence** is diagramed with the understood subject *you* in parentheses.

Jump over the hurdles.

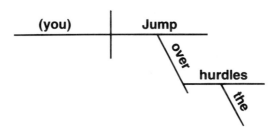

16. Walk slowly down the stairs.
17. Call loudly to the children.
18. Drive to the next corner.

Compound subjects and predicates are diagramed on parallel lines joined by a broken line on which the conjunction or conjunctions are placed.

Either Sam or Karen ran outside and jumped into the car.

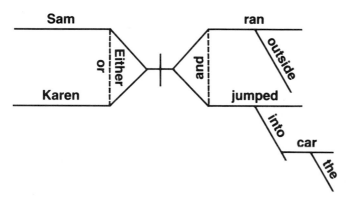

19. You and I are going to the movies.
20. Theresa looked out the window and smiled.
21. The children and their parents applauded and cheered.

A **compound sentence** is diagramed on parallel base lines, one line for each independent clause. A stepped broken line links the clauses. When the clauses are joined by a coordinating conjunction, it is written on the horizontal part of the broken line.

Juan spoke to Maria, and she smiled shyly.

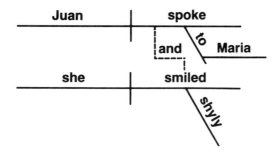

22. Casey struck out, and the fans groaned.
23. Was Jan talking to you, or was she talking to me?
24. Speak loudly, or you will not be heard.

A **direct object** is diagramed on the base line after the action verb. It is separated from the verb by a vertical line.

The scouts tracked the bear.

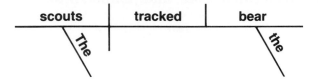

25. The orchestra played a waltz.
26. The Cougars won the championship.
27. Nancy answered the teacher's question.

The **subject complement** is diagramed on the base line after the linking verb. It is separated from the verb by a line that slants back toward the subject it identifies or describes.

Her profession is unusual.

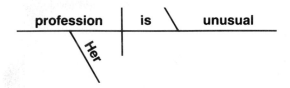

28. His disguise looks quite scary.
29. Her grandfather is an actor.
30. The slaw tasted bitter.

The **indirect object** is diagramed like an object of a preposition. However, there is no preposition on the slanted line. The indirect object is always placed below the verb.

They gave their parents a surprise party.

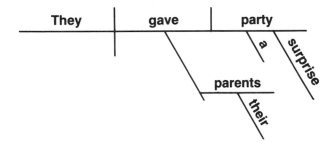

31. The judge gave Marva ten points.
32. The referee told them the rules.
33. Mrs. Pym sent the Ryans an invitation.

The **complex sentence** is diagramed on parallel base lines. The independent clause is diagramed first, and the dependent clause is joined by a broken line to the word that it modifies in the main clause. Example diagrams of adjective and adverb clauses follow.

Since an **adjective clause** is used as a modifier, it is diagramed below the independent clause. The adjective clause is joined to the independent clause by a broken line from the relative pronoun to its antecedent.

The story that we read was funny.

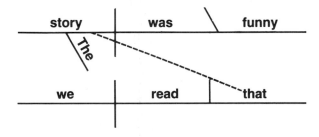

34. The people who lived across the street have moved to Arabia.
35. She is the friend who was in the accident.
36. The house, which looked spooky, frightened the children.

Because an **adverb clause** is used as a modifier, it is diagramed below the independent clause. It is joined to the independent clause by a broken line from the verb of the adverb clause to the verb of the independent clause. The subordinating conjunction is written on the broken line.

After Todd gathered wood, he started a fire.

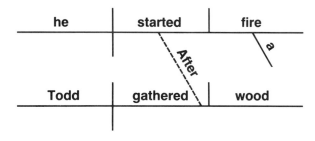

37. If Terry comes, Tom will leave.
38. The club canceled the picnic because it rained.
39. Although Lee campaigned hard, he lost the election.

An **appositive** is diagramed by placing it in parentheses after the word it identifies or explains. The modifiers in an appositive phrase are placed on slanted lines below the appositive.

Shawn, my younger brother, was at school.

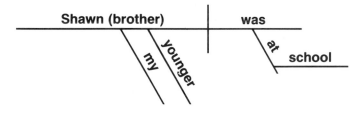

40. I made my favorite dessert, pecan pie.
41. Mr. Cruz, our gymnastics teacher, won a gold medal.
42. By noon we were in Chicago, the Windy City.

Words in a series that are parts of the basic sentence are diagramed on parallel lines. The lines are joined by a broken line on which the coordinating conjunction is written.

The colors of the flag were red, white, and blue.

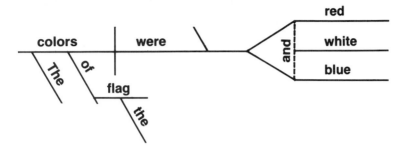

43. Marcos, Isabel, and Sean attended the fair.
44. They saw clowns, horses, and acrobats.
45. The three friends watched, laughed, and applauded.

This handbook is designed to help you write well. It answers the kinds of questions that you, the writer at work, might ask.

The handbook is divided into four sections. The first section is about **prewriting,** or how to get ready to write. The second section deals with **writing**—actually getting your ideas down on paper. The third section is about **revising,** or improving what you have written. The fourth section focuses on **presenting,** or sharing your writing with others.

Prewriting

1. I'm having a hard time thinking of a writing topic. Do you have any ideas?

Many writers have this problem. The more often you write, however, the easier it will become for you to think of writing topics. Here are some ways to help you choose suitable writing topics.

Read   The more you read, the more ideas you will come across that make good writing topics. Reading not only provides possible writing topics, but also gives you ideas and information to include in your own writing. Reading sparks the imagination.

Brainstorm   Work with a group of classmates to quickly call out as many ideas for writing, good or bad, as possible. Have someone lead the group while another person records all ideas on the board. After the brainstorming session, record some of the topics onto your own writing topics list. You can also brainstorm alone, although it is better to do this activity in a group.

Keep a Writer's Journal   Many writers carry a small notebook in which to record ideas for writing. They record snatches of conversations, ideas for story characters, titles for future magazine articles, and any interesting observations and ideas that occur to them. Keep your own writer's journal in which to record topics and other writing ideas. Look over your journal when you need an idea.

2. How can I narrow a topic that seems too broad?

When a topic is too broad you must narrow it so that you can cover the information on that topic adequately. Following are two ways to narrow a topic.

Asking Questions   Humorists say it is all right to talk to yourself as long as you don't answer yourself. Here is a case where you do both. Ask and answer your own questions to narrow a topic. For example, suppose your social studies teacher assigns a six- to nine-paragraph report on the American Civil War. Obviously, this topic is too broad for a brief report. How do you narrow the topic? Ask yourself questions. Here is an example.

Broad topic: The American Civil War
Question: What part of the Civil War interests me most?
Answer: Causes of the war, Generals Lee and Grant, Gettysburg
Question: Which of these subtopics do I know something about?
Answer: I know a little about each but most about Lee and Grant.
Question: Did Lee and Grant ever meet?
Answer: Yes, at a surrender ceremony at Appomattox.
Question: What happened there? Would it interest others?
Answer: Lee surrendered. There is a real human-interest story in this surrender. It would probably interest others.
Narrowed topic: When Lee Surrendered to Grant: Appomattox

Clustering   A cluster diagram is like a visual map showing how main topics, subtopics, and details are related to one another. To make a cluster diagram, first write a main topic in the center and circle it. Then write related subtopics around it. Circle them and draw lines to connect them to the main topic. Finally, list details related to subtopics. Notice in the cluster diagram below that *Reporters* is narrower than *Print* and much narrower than *Journalism.*

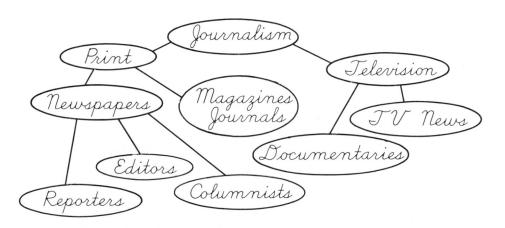

3. Does who I'm writing for make a difference in what I write?

Yes, your audience makes a big difference in what you say and how you say it. While it is true that your first audience is yourself, you are also writing for others: teachers, classmates, parents, and even other people you may not know.

You'll write much better if you think about your audience. For example, if you are applying for a job, your description of yourself and your qualifications must be accurate. The words you choose and ideas you include should be weighed carefully to convey a certain impression about yourself. On the other hand, a friendly letter to someone who has moved away might contain similar descriptions but be far less formal. In each case, a different audience requires a difference in what you say and how you say it.

Activity
Write a letter describing yourself to someone who is in a position to hire you as a salesperson. Then describe yourself in a letter to a friend who hasn't seen you for many years.

---

4. Where do I gather information on my writing topic?

Complete, accurate information is essential to all writing, including fiction. Here are some sources of information.

Library   Familiarize yourself with the facilities in your school and local libraries. Ask the reference librarian for help in using the card catalog, reference library, and computers to locate information in books, magazines, newspapers, journals, and reference materials.

Reference Books   Reference books include encyclopedias, almanacs, and atlases. Many libraries also have information stored on computer discs.

Magazines and Journals   Learn how to use *The Readers' Guide to Periodical Literature*. It lists topics covered in magazines and journals. For example, if you wanted current information on *Killer Bees,* this reference guide will tell you where to find it.

Interviews   If you want interesting, accurate information on, say *Diesel Engines,* ask an expert on the topic. For example, if you want to know about crime, ask a police officer. First, locate someone with the information you need. Then arrange an interview. Before the interview, read up on your topic and prepare a set of questions. Take notes or, when possible, record the interview.

> **Activity**
> List three reference sources for each of these topics: *Airplanes, Golf, American History, Stars, Plant Life, Jazz,* and *Forestry.*

5. What is the best way to organize information I have gathered?

How you organize depends on the kind of writing you are doing. For example, writing stories and poems may require different preparation than writing research reports and essays. Here are three steps that you might take when organizing materials for writing reports.

Take Notes   As you interview experts or read about your topic, write notes on 3 x 5 cards. A note card should tell the main topic, list important details, and give bibliographical information.

Organize Notes   After note taking, sort your cards into main topics. Reread each card as you sort it to be sure that the information fits into the group in which you put it.

Make an Outline   An outline is a verbal road map describing your plan for writing. An outline should have at least two or three main topics. Each main topic should have two or more subtopics. Subtopics usually have a number of related details.

> **Activity**
> Pretend you are going to write a research report entitled *What Newspaper Reporters Do.* What sources would you use to gather information? Once you have located sources, how would you go about organizing the information you have gathered?

Writing

PEANUTS By Charles Schulz

© 1985 United Feature Syndicate, Inc.

1. I'm having trouble getting started writing. What should I do?

First, check the information in this handbook listed under **Prewriting.** Remember that getting started is a problem for even the greatest of writers. Here are some ideas to get you going.

Review Your Notes   Go through your prewriting notes, looking for a single fact or idea that you can use to get your piece going. Suppose you're writing about *Whales*. You discover that a newborn whale weighs three tons. That's a whopper of a fact. Use it to grab your reader's attention: "Imagine a baby that weighs half as much as a full-grown elephant. That's the size of a baby whale!"

Just Start   Sometimes you just have to get black on white. Write anything that gets your pencil moving and your brain in gear. For example, you are writing about a book you've read and can't think of a good way to start. Maybe you just say, "For some reason, I can't think of a thing to say about this book. Maybe that's because the book didn't have much to say to me." Go on from there. Start somewhere and plunge in. Don't wait around until the perfect beginning occurs to you. That never happens!

> **Activity**
> If you were a professional writer, what kind of routine would you create to help you get started writing every day? When would you write? for how long? What sort of writing place would you want? What psyching-up routine would you perform?

2. I've gotten started all right, but now I've run out of things to say. What do I do now?

This is a common problem, but it can be overcome. Here are some ideas to help you get going again.

Reread What You Have Written   Rereading what you have written will often give you an idea for what to add. As you reread, try to think about your writing as though you were an "outsider." Ask questions such as: Does this make sense? What's missing here? Is this boring? What comes next? What am I trying to say?

Hold a Conference with a Classmate   Talk with a classmate or your teacher about your topic. Read your work aloud. Invite comments from your classmate or teacher.

Tune Out Distractions   Sometimes you have to tune out the outside world so that you can concentrate on what you are writing. At home this may mean no TV, radio, food, or friends while you are writing.

Take a Break   Sometimes you may need to get your mind off your writing for a while. Put your paper aside and do something else. When you return to your work, read through what you have written. You might note a word or idea that can get you back on track or start you in a new direction.

3. How good must my first draft be? Should I worry about mistakes in the first draft?

Sometimes a first draft turns out fine. Sometimes it is only a bare beginning. Most often it is somewhere in between these two extremes. Constant work to make your writing better is what is needed. Mistakes can be corrected later. First, get your ideas down as quickly as possible. If writers worried too much about mistakes, no writing of any consequence would ever get done.

Activity
Theodor S. Geisel (Dr. Seuss) once said, "To produce a sixty-page book, I may easily write one thousand pages before I'm satisfied." Why do you think Geisel writes so many drafts of his stories? What is the highest number of times you've rewritten a story, poem, or report?

---

4. How long should my first draft be?

Practical purposes, audience, and other such matters dictate length in many cases. Generally, a first draft will be slightly longer than your finished composition. In your initial attempt at writing, you want to get down as many ideas as possible. This gives you enough material to work with as you revise. As you rearrange your ideas, you will probably want to eliminate some of them.

5. Do I have to wait until I'm finished before I start revising?

Certainly not. Although you are trying to get your ideas on paper as quickly as possible, some changes will occur to you as you write. Go ahead and make them, but try not to get so involved in revising that you can't progress. You can simply circle a word that seems dull or inappropriate and then change it when you revise. Occasionally, you may cross out a word and replace it on the spot. Just remember that your main purpose is to finish your first draft.

PEANUTS By Charles Schulz

Revising

1. Why should I revise? Can't I make my work right the first time around?

In tennis, you have two opportunities to serve the ball into your opponent's court. If you fail, you lose the point. In writing, however, you can take as many serves as you wish. Seldom is anything done perfectly on the first attempt. Some writers admit they take a lot of serves. For instance, Roald Dahl, a well-known writer of children's books, said that he may rewrite the beginning of a story well over a hundred times.

Why should you revise? Revising gives writers a chance to rethink and re-see what they are saying. In fact, the word *revision* actually means to "see again." Re-seeing and rethinking your ideas gives you a better understanding of your topic than you can get from writing a single draft. In other words, revision develops writing power. It strengthens and stretches your "writing muscles."

2. What kinds of changes should I make when I revise?

There are four kinds of changes to make when you revise: adding, deleting, rearranging, and proofreading.

Adding Words and Ideas After drafting, reread your work to see if you have left out important information. For instance, suppose you had written a description of the Statue of Liberty. On rereading, you discover you forgot to mention the torch. Since the torch is an important part of the Statue of Liberty, you must go back and add some information about this detail. Revising helps you think of new information that needs to be added.

Deleting Unneeded Words, Sentences, or Paragraphs
Taking out material that is repetitive, doesn't fit, or is unnecessary to your topic makes your writing clearer. If you are writing about the migration of whales and find you have written a long section on the uses of whale oil, you have probably included unneeded information. Your report will be better simply because you deleted unrelated information.

Moving Words, Sentences, and Paragraphs Around Proper order and arrangement of words and ideas can improve your writing greatly. In writing a recipe, you may initially write the steps in the wrong order. If you are telling the plot of a story in a book review, you should give the events in the order they occurred. Revision gives you a chance to improve the sequence of your information. You may also improve the wording of sentences through the rearrangement of words. Sometimes you need to move only a word or two to improve a sentence. In other cases, you may want to move whole sentences to improve a paragraph or move entire paragraphs to improve a whole composition. You can indicate where a paragraph has to be moved by circling it and drawing an arrow to its proper location. You can also use your scissors and tape.

Proofreading and Editing   When you have improved the content and style of your writing, it is time to check spelling, punctuation, grammar, and capitalization. Use the proofreader's marks shown below to signal changes needed in your writing.

Proofreader's
Marks

≡
Make a capital.

/
Make a small letter.

⊙
Add a period.

⋏
Add a comma.

⋎
Add quotation
marks.

⋀
Add something.

ℯ
Take out something.

→
Move something.

¶
New paragraph.

ⓢⓟ
Correct spelling.

Activity
Copy the paragraph below. Correct the mistakes by following the proofreader's marks.

The largest animal that ever lived is the blue whale. Which can measure 100 feet long and weigh 150 tons! These mammals have fishlike bodies and fins. *tail fins called flukes.* Blue whales are an *endangered* indangered species. many countries forbid the hunting of whale meat and blubber.

3. Where can I get help when I revise?

Here are four kinds of conferences you might have with your classmates or teacher.

Content and Concepts Conference   This writing conference will focus on information and ideas. Questions arising in this conference might deal with accuracy, relevancy of your information, how clearly your ideas are explained, and how interesting your information and ideas seem to others.

Problem-solving Conference   In this conference, the focus is on a specific problem you may have with a piece of writing. For example, suppose you have written a report, but you are having trouble with the introduction. How do you solve this problem? One way is to talk about it with a group of your classmates or with your teacher.

Question-Suggestion Conference   Read your composition aloud to a small group of classmates. Then invite each conference partner to ask one question and make a suggestion. Make whatever changes you believe will improve your paper.

Teacher-Student Conference   Ask to have a conference with your teacher if you need help. Your teacher probably will ask you questions such as the following: What can you tell me about this piece? What are the main ideas you are trying to get across? What is the biggest problem you are facing? What parts do you think need changing?

Activity
Confer with your classmates about a piece of writing you have recently drafted. Afterwards, make necessary revisions.

---

4. Do I have to revise every piece of writing that I do?

No. The decision about whether to revise depends on your purpose and audience. For example, a research report requires greater accuracy and care than a friendly letter, and each will have a different audience. It is seldom necessary to revise a friendly letter, but it is always wise to revise a research report.

5. What guidelines should I follow when I revise?

In addition to the matters discussed in this handbook, you should make use of the following checklists to guide revision.

Content
- Did I say what I wanted to say?
- Is any information missing that should be added?
- Have I deleted any information that doesn't stick to the topic?
- Does my writing have a beginning, middle, and end?
- Are the steps or events in the right order?
- Should some sections be switched around?
- Does each paragraph have a clear main idea?
- Do all the sentences stick to the main idea?
- Have I replaced all vague, dull, and inaccurate words?
- Are all facts and figures accurate?

Mechanics
- Does each sentence have the correct end punctuation?
- Did I use correct punctuation in other places?
- Have I avoided fragments and run-on sentences?
- Did I capitalize the first word of each sentence?
- Did I capitalize all other words that should be capitalized?
- Did I check the spelling or meaning of words I was unsure of?
- Did I indent each paragraph?

Presenting

1. What are some ways I can share my writing?

There are many ways to share writing. Here are a few.

Read Your Writing Aloud   Read your final draft aloud to your classmates, parents, or a friend. Oral reading gives a sense of how writing *sounds* that silent reading cannot provide.

Give a Demonstration   Suppose you've written a how-to report. Make notes on the steps and turn them into a demonstration. Practice your talk as you actually perform the steps involved. Use a visual aid to help clarify the process.

Give an Oral Report   Written reports and essays lend themselves to oral reports. Focus on the main points of reports and essays to make an effective oral report (see pages 436–437).

2. How can I make bound books?

Below are two simple ways to make bound books. Check with your librarian to find other ways to make bound books.

Cardboard Book   Follow these steps.   **(1)** Cut two pieces of cardboard for the cover.   **(2)** Add a blank sheet of paper at the front and back of your final copy. Staple the pages together along the left edge.   **(3)** Glue the blank pages at front and back to the insides of the front and back cover. Now your book is bound.

Folded Paper   You can make a book by folding sheets of paper in half. Tuck these sheets inside one another. Add a cover sheet of construction paper. Then staple all the pages together along the fold. Add art and other features to decorate.

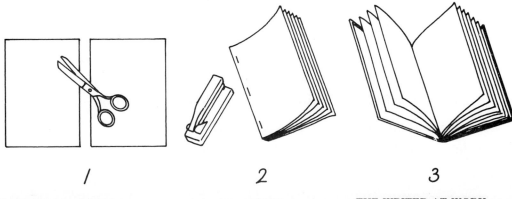

1   *2*   *3*

Spelling Rules

Spelling Plural Nouns

1. Most plural nouns are formed by adding *-s* or *-es*.

   cafeteria—**cafeterias**   campus—**campuses**   corduroy—**corduroys**
   climax—**climaxes**   roof—**roofs**   rodeo—**rodeos**
   tomato—**tomatoes**   great-grandmother—**great-grandmothers**

2. Sometimes letters in the singular form change when the word becomes plural.

   galaxy—**galaxies**   elf—**elves**   hypothesis—**hypotheses**

3. Some nouns don't change in the plural at all.

   sheep—**sheep**   forceps—**forceps**

Activity   Write the plural forms of the following words.

basis	armada	success	gentleman	hero
bluff	bookshelf	medley	leash	rendezvous
reflex	burrito	drive-in	comedy	vitamin

Spelling Verbs with *-ed* and *-ing*

4. Many verbs add *-ed* and *-ing* to the present tense of the verb with no spelling change.

   revolt—**revolted—revolting**   betray—**betrayed—betraying**

5. Verbs ending in **e** drop the **e** before *-ed* or *-ing* is added.

   file—**filed—filing**   pose—**posed—posing**

6. For one-syllable verbs ending in a consonant preceded by a single vowel, the final consonant is doubled before *-ed* or *-ing* is added.

   grin—**grinned—grinning**   lug—**lugged—lugging**

7. For words with more than one syllable ending in a consonant preceded by a single vowel, the final consonant is doubled only if the accent is on the last syllable.

   omit—**omitted—omitting**   occur—**occurred—occurring**

8. For verbs ending in a consonant plus **y,** the **y** is changed to **i** before *-ed* is added. The **y** is kept, however, when *-ing* is added.

   notify—**notified—notifying**   deny—**denied—denying**

Activity   Add *-ed* and *-ing* to each verb.

cycle	patrol	multiply	recede	permit	unify

Adding *-er* and *-est* to Adjectives and Adverbs

9. To make the comparative and superlative forms of many adjectives and adverbs, simply add *-er* or *-est*.

   odd—**odder**—**oddest**   soon—**sooner**—**soonest**

10. Words ending in **e** drop the **e** before *-er* or *-est* is added.

    noble—**nobler**—**noblest**   coarse—**coarser**—**coarsest**

11. For words ending in a consonant preceded by a single vowel, the final consonant is doubled before *-er* or *-est* is added.

    hot—**hotter**—**hottest**   thin—**thinner**—**thinnest**

12. For words ending in a consonant plus **y,** the **y** is changed to **i** before *-er* or *-est* is added.

    early—**earlier**—**earliest**   speedy—**speedier**—**speediest**

Activity   Add *-er* and *-est* to each word.

cheap   feeble   sleepy   flat   grave   sticky

Prefixes and Suffixes

13. Adding a prefix does not change the spelling of the basic word.

    able—**enable**   legal—**illegal**   regular—**irregular**

14. Often adding a suffix does not change the basic word.

    arrange—**arrangement**   collect—**collectible**   depend—**dependent**

15. When a suffix beginning with a vowel is added to a word ending in **e** (except *-ce* and *-ge*), the **e** is usually dropped.

    grieve—**grievous**   response—**responsible**   outrage—**outrageous**

16. When a suffix is added to a word ending with a consonant plus **y,** the **y** is usually changed to **i.**

    rely—**reliance**   penny—**penniless**   euphony—**euphonious**

Activity   Add the prefix *il-* or *im-* or the suffix *-ance, -ary, -ent, -ible, -ment,* or *-ous* to each word.

reverse   victory   mature   diction   ridicule   courage

Confusing Verb Pairs

17. Learn to use and spell confusing verb pairs.

    rise ("get up" or "go up"), raise ("lift something up")
    precede ("come before"), proceed ("carry on an activity")

Activity   Fill in each blank with either *rise, raise, precede, proceed,* or a form of these verbs.

I _____ to _____ the window to get some cool air. The opening of the window was _____ by my feeling the room's temperature _____.

Improving Your Spelling

Spelling Strategy: Spelling by Syllable

You probably never misspell words having just one or two letters. However, longer words may give you more trouble. In such cases, divide the word into its separate syllables before spelling it.

For example, the word *prescription* may seem difficult to spell. First, think of its three syllables: *pre scrip tion*. Then spell the entire word.

Activity   Write each word according to its syllables. Then write the entire word.

1. proclamation
2. commitment
3. respiration
4. bibliography
5. university

Spelling Strategy: Knowing Your Weaknesses

You can become a better speller by concentrating on the types of words that are hard for you. For example, you may have trouble spelling words that end with *-able* or *-ible*. There is no spelling rule that tells you when *-able* or *-ible* is correct. You will just have to memorize them. So, try thinking of words like *breakable, capable,* and *comfortable* as one group and *collectible, convertible,* and *responsible* as another group. It is easier to remember how *breakable* is spelled if you think of it in the group with *capable* and *comfortable*. Enlarge each group with other *-able* and *-ible* words you know. Get used to thinking of each word in its group.

Activity   Write each of the following words, supplying the missing letters. If you do not already know when an *a* or *i* is correct, use a dictionary.

1. pay_ble
2. incred_ble
3. remark_ble
4. syll_ble
5. elig_ble
6. divis_ble

Spelling Strategy: Checking Your Spelling

Sometimes you may have difficulty deciding if you have spelled a word correctly. Here are some ways to check:

- See if the word looks right to you.
- Say the word aloud. Listen for the sounds of the letters in your word and imagine how those sounds are spelled.
- Write the word again.
- Check a dictionary if necessary.

Activity   Choose the word in each group that is not spelled correctly. On your paper write the word correctly.

1. excellence   defendant   allowence
2. accomplish   iritate   community
3. eyelashs   receipt   collapse
4. formerely   omitted   multiplied
5. laser   athelete   parachute
6. shreik   panicked   rhythmic
7. maneuver   conscious   fossile
8. hybred   grammar   limousine

Spelling Strategy: Knowing How You Learn Best

There are several methods for learning how to spell words. You must find the method that works best for you. Read the following three strategies for learning a new or difficult word. Decide which strategy suits you best.

- Look at the letters in the word. Notice any special letter combinations or patterns.
- Say the word aloud. Listen to the sounds that the letters make. Note which letters, if any, are unsounded.
- Write the word. Practice making the letters.

Activity   Answer these questions about the four words in the following list.

illiterate   engage   inaccurate   diameter

1. Which words contain a double consonant or double vowel?
2. In which word is a repeated consonant given a different sound?
3. Which word contains the **ia** letter combination?

Spelling Strategy: Using the Dictionary

Sometimes there are words you can say but do not know how to spell well enough to even find in a dictionary. In such cases, use the special section in the front of most dictionaries titled "Spellings of English Sounds" or something similar. This section lists all possible spellings for each sound in a word. Here is an example of spellings of the sound /ā/.

Symbol	Spellings
ā	age, say, aid, vein, bouquet

Activity   Answer these questions about the words in the following list.

brain   tailor   beige   slay   gourmet

1. Which words have the sound /ā/ as spelled in *aid?*
2. Which word has the sound /ā/ as spelled in *vein?*
3. Which word has the sound /ā/ as spelled in *bouquet?*
4. Which word has the sound /ā/ as spelled in *say?*

Spelling Strategy: Taking Tests

Some spelling tests give you a sentence with a word missing. The missing word is then spelled four different ways. You must choose the correct spelling of the word.

Before making a decision, look at the four spellings offered under the incomplete sentence. Picture how you have seen the word in print before. Say the word and listen to its sounds. Then choose the spelling that looks right to you.

Activity   Read each sentence and decide how to spell the missing word. On your paper write the letter next to the correct answer.

1. The message is _____.
   a. ergent   c. urgant
   b. urgent   d. urjent
2. Don't be so _____.
   a. impachient   c. impatent
   b. impayient   d. impatient
3. He didn't mean to _____ you.
   a. decieve   c. deceive
   b. deseive   d. desieve
4. He _____ his mistake.
   a. admitted   c. addmitted
   b. admited   d. admetted

Confusing Homophones

Some words, called homophones, sound alike but have different meanings and usually different spellings. Pay attention to the meanings of the homophones in these sentences.

Patients are people treated by a doctor; *patience* is a willingness to endure something calmly.

Some doctors' *patients* have little *patience* when made to wait.

A *principal* is a director; a *principle* is a rule or law.

The *principal* discussed the *principle* with the school lawyer.

Threw is the past tense of *throw; through* means "from one end to another."

On a dare, he *threw* the ball *through* the kitchen.

A *capital* is the city where the government of a state is located; the *capitol* is the building in which the state legislature meets.

We sat in the *capitol* in Springfield, the *capital* of Illinois.

A *course* is an area marked out for a race or game; *coarse* means "made up of large parts or chunks; not fine."

The sand for the runners' *course* is very *coarse.*

To *slay* is to kill; a *sleigh* is a cart on runners for use on snow.

Don't *slay* that deer. The horses pulled the *sleigh* for hours.

Stationery is writing materials made of paper; *stationary* means "having a fixed position" or "not changing."

The price of envelopes at the *stationery* shop has stayed *stationary* for two years.

Activity   Write the word that fits each association.
Example: a tree is certainly this (stationery, stationary)
Answer: stationary

1. will have a population of tens of thousands (capitol, capital)
2. can be used to tell others your thoughts (stationery, stationary)
3. has the most famous office in a school (principal, principle)
4. can provide transportation (slay, sleigh)
5. often lost and often rewarded (patients, patience)
6. the same as *rough* (course, coarse)
7. how the pitcher warmed up yesterday (through, threw)

Studying

Plan your study time carefully. Keep a calendar in which you list your due dates. In this calendar, schedule the time for study, paper writing, and test preparation. Find a comfortable, quiet place to study at home, at school, or in a library. Keep study materials at hand—pencil, paper, and a dictionary. Use a colored marker or pencil to highlight important notes and material.

Examine your own study conditions. Copy the following chart. Place a check under *Yes*, *Usually*, or *No* for each condition listed.

Study Conditions	Yes	Usually	No
Do I always have . . .			
1. a quiet room?			
2. a comfortable temperature?			
3. adequate light?			
4. clean desk or table space?			
5. a straight, comfortable chair?			
6. materials such as pencils, paper, a ruler, a dictionary?			

If you checked *Yes* for all six items, you're fortunate to have ideal study conditions. But if you checked *Usually* or *No* a few times, it will help to figure out how to change those conditions.

For example, your home may be the scene of so much activity that it would be impossible to find a quiet, comfortable space whenever you needed to study. Have you ever considered what to do about that? If you can't find some space to be by yourself and concentrate, it might be a better use of your time to study in the library or during free time at school.

Activity Make a calendar for the week. Fill in your activities and assignments. Then schedule in time for study and test preparation.

Using Thinking Skills to Study Effectively

As you study, apply the thinking and study skills you have learned. Following are explanations of how some of these skills fit into the LEARNER Study System discussed in Warm-up Time.

Listening for Information   When you hear an assignment, listen for key words such as *write, prepare,* or *answer.* Ask questions about directions or information that you don't understand. If you are taking notes on a lecture, concentrate on the speaker and ignore distractions. Listen for words and phrases such as *for example* and *however* that signal important information.

Using Graphic Aids   As you examine a text, pay special attention to the graphic aids. Note the written information that surrounds a graphic aid, such as its title, key, or caption. The graphic aid will present you with facts. It is up to you to make inferences and draw conclusions from those facts.

Comparing and Contrasting   When you read, think of ways ideas, events, and people are like and unlike each other. Then ask questions or make charts that will help you understand comparisons.

Classifying   Sometimes as you read, you are bombarded with a lot of information. When you take notes, arrange this information in groups that make sense. For example, you could remember the fifty states by geographical area or by alphabetical order.

Evaluating Information   Be sure you recognize statements of fact, statements of opinion, and mixed statements. Keep on the lookout for bias in writing. Watch out for propaganda and errors in reasoning. Think about the cause-and-effect relationships.

Summarizing   One good way to review is to summarize what you have read. In a few sentences, write down the important information. Include only the main ideas.

Activity   Decide which thinking skill—classifying, comparing and contrasting, or evaluating information—could best be used to organize or judge information on the following topics.

1. The computer versus the human brain
2. Kinds of food that fit into the different food groups
3. Whether or not the claims in a TV commercial are valid

First, read each question or direction. Look for such key words as *describe, explain, tell why, compare,* or *identify*. These words tell you what to do.

Second, on scrap paper or in your mind, list facts that will answer the question or direction. Do not write sentences at this point. Just list information.

Third, get started as quickly as possible. One good way to get started is to turn the question or direction into a statement which will open your answer.

Read through the following items from an essay test and the possible beginnings for answers.

1. Why did the ancient Greeks invent gods?

   These are some major reasons that the ancient Greeks invented gods.

2. Each Greek god had at least one symbol. Describe the symbols of any four Greek gods and explain what each symbol stood for.

   Zeus, Hera, Poseidon, and Athena all had meaningful symbols.

How to Start an Essay Test
1. Be sure of what your answer must include—a description, explanation, or comparison, for example.
2. Turn the question or direction into a statement as a beginning for your answer.

Activity Each of the items below might appear on an essay test. Think of how you would begin an answer for each one.

1. Why was the invention of the automobile important?
2. In what ways are your eyes like a camera?
3. Explain the purpose of a nominating committee.
4. Compare the standard of living in the early 1900s to the standard of living today.
5. Describe the nests of chimney swifts.

Speaking

Preparing an Oral Presentation

Knowing what you are going to say and how you are going to say it will give you the confidence you need to communicate with your audience.

The first step is to choose a subject of interest to you and your audience. Then limit that subject to a specific topic. Keep in mind the amount of time you'll have for your speech.

After you gather the information you need, select the details that are most important to your talk. Organize the details and write the key words on note cards. Later, as you are speaking, you can glance at your notes to recall specific details.

If possible, prepare visual aids. You might sketch diagrams on the chalkboard, set up a display of photographs, show pictures from a large book, or have some charts ready to show. These will help your audience understand and enjoy your talk. They will also help you remember what you intend to say.

How to Plan a Speech

1. Choose a subject of interest to you and your audience.
2. Gather the information you need. Select the details important to your talk. Find interesting details and anecdotes.
3. Organize the details. Write the key words on note cards.
4. Prepare a visual aid or demonstration, if possible.

Activity   Select one topic from those listed below or choose one of your own. Think of four details you might include in a short speech on that topic. Write those details as notes you could use during a speech. Finally, describe a picture, diagram, or other visual aid that would help your audience understand and enjoy your talk.

An Old-fashioned Kitchen   Rules of Backgammon
Reading the Clouds   Buying Running Shoes

Speaking with Confidence

Successful speakers deliver talks with confidence. They know their subjects. They pronounce words clearly and speak with expression. They project their voices to all the audience. They use attention-getting devices. Most importantly, they make preparations so that they can speak with authority.

Speakers gain confidence by practicing their speeches. Practice in front of a mirror, with a tape recorder, or in front of a friend. Keep practicing until you can give your talk confidently and smoothly. You should be able to give a speech by glancing briefly at each note card.

To capture the attention of your audience, plan an interesting opening. Avoid starting out by saying, "My talk is going to be about. . . . " Instead, begin with an interesting or amazing fact or relate something light and humorous about the topic.

If you use a visual aid, be sure that you face your audience so that they can hear what you are saying. Also, be sure the visual is large enough for the audience to see clearly.

Try to think of an ending that your listeners will enjoy and remember. Tell a joke or give a final demonstration. Ask whether anyone has a question about your topic.

How to Deliver a Speech

1. Prepare an interesting, attention-getting opening.
2. Remain poised, not slouched. Look at your audience. Speak clearly.
3. Plan an ending that your audience will remember.
4. Use a visual aid such as a cartoon, map, or chart that will make your speech interesting.

Activity   Use the topic you chose for the Activity on page 581. Think of an opening and an ending that will capture the interest of your listeners. Consider using a quiz or telling a joke. Practice your speech until you are prepared to present it to the class.

Presenting Yourself Before an Audience

Whether you are giving a formal talk or just an announcement, demonstration, or introduction, you need to pay attention to how you look, act, and talk. The following guidelines can be applied to most speaking situations.

Appearance	Dress appropriately for the occasion. Always wear neat, clean clothes. Stand up straight, but try to appear relaxed. Always check your appearance in a mirror before you speak before an audience.
Eye Contact	Look straight ahead at your audience, or just above their heads. Do not stare at your notes or at the ground. Practice maintaining eye contact with an audience.
Voice	Speak loudly, but do not shout. Pronounce each word clearly. Vary your pitch, volume, and rate of speech, but do not speak too quickly. Match your tone to the content of your speech. If you are speaking about something sad, do not sound cheery, for example. Before you bring up important points, pause for emphasis.
Gestures and Expressions	Match your gestures and facial expressions to your speech. Smile when you tell a joke, and look serious when the content is serious.

Activity Say each of the following according to the directions given. Use appropriate gestures and facial expressions.

1. "Help me."

   First express this as someone might who is having trouble opening a present. Then act as if you were being chased by a threatening dog.
2. "It's raining."

   First express disappointment, then raise a question, and finally show happy surprise.
3. "I don't believe you."

   First express this to a friend who has told you a wonderful piece of news. Then say these words as if you were challenging someone who had told you something that was obviously untrue.

THESAURUS

A thesaurus can improve your writing by giving you more precise words to choose from. For a complete lesson on using a thesaurus, see page 138.

A

able   Look up *skillful.*

act (v)   *Act* means do something or cause something to happen. The firefighter *acted* quickly to put out the fire.
behave   *Behave* means act in a certain way. The class *behaved* well during the assembly.
perform   *Perform* means act or do something. It can also mean take part in a play or show. The plane *performed* perfectly. The dolphins will *perform* for the crowd.
function   *Function* can mean work properly or act as something else. This watch also *functions* as a calculator.

agree (v)   *Agree* means have the same opinion about something. My sister and I finally *agree* on a pet.
consent   *Consent* means agree to something that someone has asked for. I *consented* to go to the park with my little brother.
admit   When you *admit* to something, you accept or agree that it is either true or false, good or bad. Bev *admits* that our team is better.
approve   *Approve* means agree, but it also adds the meaning of having a good opinion of something. Mr. Zim *approved* of my topic for a report.
ANTONYMS: differ, disagree, disapprove, contradict, protest

aim   Look up *object.*

amusing   Look up *humorous.*

anger (n)   *Anger* is a strong feeling you have when something does not please you. Mom was *angry* with the dog. The chewed-up rug *angered* her.
irritation   *Irritation* is feeling disturbed about something that won't stop. Kim showed *irritation* whenever I tapped my pencil.
rage   *Rage* is a violent anger that may result in loss of self-control. In his *rage*, Terry threw his bat to the ground.
fury   *Fury* is anger so violent that self-control and reason are *lost. Fury* drove the man to burn a barn.
ANTONYMS: pleasure, self-control

answer (v)   *Answer* means say, write, or do something as a result of what someone asks or wants. Lois *answered* my question. Would you please *answer* the phone?
reply   *Reply* means answer. When he told me to return my library books, I *replied* that I would.
respond   *Respond* means react to something said or done. Many people *responded* to the advertisement.
solve   *Solve* is a good word to use when you mean explain something or find an answer to a problem. The detective *solved* the mystery.
ANTONYMS: ask, inquire, request

anxious   Look up *worried*.

argue (v)   *Argue* means give reasons for or against something. Tina and I *argued* about what movie to see.

disagree   You *disagree* with someone when you do not share the same opinion. Tom *disagreed* with the umpire's decision.

debate   You *debate* when you defend a position and attack your opponent's point of view. Both candidates will *debate* before the election.

quarrel   *Quarrel* means argue noisily. No one enjoys it when my sister and I *quarrel*.

ANTONYMS: agree, consent

arrange   Look up *put*.

assignment   Look up *task*.

B

beautiful (adj)   *Beautiful* is the opposite of ugly. Anything that you find very pleasing or attractive can be called *beautiful*. The sky looks *beautiful* at sunset.

pretty   *Pretty* may describe someone or something that is pleasing but not quite beautiful. Thank you for the *pretty* bouquet of daisies.

handsome   A *handsome* person is good-looking. Do you think Al is *handsome*? *Handsome* can also mean impressive. I ate a *handsome* serving of turkey.

lovely   *Lovely* means very beautiful and delightful. What a *lovely* day for a picnic!

graceful   *Graceful* means beautiful in form and movement. A good dancer must be *graceful*.

gorgeous   *Gorgeous* means very beautiful and colorful. A rainbow is a *gorgeous* sight.

ANTONYMS: ugly, homely, horrid, hideous, offensive

beginning (n)   The *beginning* is the point at which something comes into being. It can also mean the first step or part of something. Tell me the *beginning* of the story.

start   A *start* is the beginning or first part of an activity. We saw the race from *start* to finish.

origin   The *origin* is the beginning of something from which other things come about. What is the *origin* of the word sandwich?

source   A *source* is a place where something begins. The *source* of the river was in the mountains. Who was the *source* of the rumor?

ANTONYMS: end, finish, conclusion

behave   Look up *act*.

big   Look up *large*.

break (v)   *Break* means suddenly come apart or force something to separate. Those dishes may *break*.

shatter, smash   *Shatter* means break into many small pieces. *Smash* means break by force too, but not always into pieces. Glass might *smash* or *shatter* when struck.

split   *Split* means divide or separate into parts. You can *split* an orange with a friend.

fracture   If you break a bone, you *fracture* it. I *fractured* my arm.

ANTONYMS: mend, fix, repair, fasten

C

calm (adj) *Calm* means not excited or disturbed. *Calm* people are relaxed. The weather is *calm* today.

quiet, still *Quiet* and *still* can mean calm. A *quiet* street may have little traffic. The lake is quite *still* when there is no wind.

peaceful, tranquil *Peaceful* and *tranquil* describe something gentle or restful. I felt *peaceful* sitting by the fire. A *tranquil* person seldom gets upset.

ANTONYMS: excited, stormy, noisy, restless, disturbed

change (v) *Change* means make different. You *change* your clothes. The weather can *change* quickly.

alter, modify *Alter* and *modify* mean change only slightly. A tailor *alters* a coat. An adjective *modifies* a noun.

vary *Vary* means that something is not always the same. The driver *varied* his speed.

convert *Convert* means change something for a different use. The basement was *converted* into a workshop and studio.

switch, transfer *Switch* means change place, position, or direction. The train *switched* to another track. *Transfer* means change places. We can *transfer* to a southbound bus.

transform *Transform* means make a major change in something. The costume and make-up transformed Jim into a pirate.

ANTONYM: maintain

choose (v) *Choose* means make a decision to take or do something. Let's *choose* teams for football.

select *Select* means choose from many things. I *selected* a tie for Uncle George.

pick, prefer *Pick* and *prefer* mean choose something because you like it better. Why did you *pick* a red sweater? I *preferred* the olive one.

elect *Elect* means choose for an office or position. Mary was *elected* class president.

decide *Decide* means make up your mind from many possibilities. I can't *decide* which record I want.

ANTONYMS: reject, refuse

clear (adj) *Clear* means bright or easily seen. A *clear* day is not misty or hazy. Your directions to your house were *clear*.

plain *Plain* means not only easily seen, heard, or understood, but also simple. The point of the speech was *plain* to all. This room looks *plain* without my posters.

transparent You can see through something *transparent*. Window glass is *transparent*.

obvious *Obvious* means unmistakable. It was *obvious* someone had broken into the garage.

comical Look up *humorous*.

connect Look up *join*.

cut (v) *Cut* means open, divide, or take away with a sharp-edged tool. Nick has *cut* the pie into pieces.

clip *Clip* means cut or trim with

scissors or a similar tool. Lori is clipping the hedges.

carve, slice   *Carve* can mean cut carefully to form something. The artist *carved* a figure in a block of wood. You *slice* bread when you cut it into thin, flat pieces.

slit   *Slit* means cut lengthwise or in long, thin pieces. *Slit* the envelope along the fold at the edge.

chop   *Chop* means cut in pieces with short, hard blows. Cooks sometimes *chop* foods. I *chopped* some firewood.

D

damp   Look up *moist*.

danger (n)   *Danger* is any situation or thing that might cause serious harm or injury. Road signs warn drivers of *danger* ahead.

peril   *Peril* means the gravest kind of danger. It is usually hard to avoid. The mountain climbers faced the constant *peril* of avalanches.

hazard   A *hazard* is a great chance of injury or misfortune. Icy roads were a *hazard* to drivers.

menace   A *menace* is a danger that seems to hang over you. No harm may really come, but you feel that it might. The constant *menace* of drought worried the farmers.

threat   A *threat,* like a menace, is a warning of danger. Strong winds were a *threat* to boaters.
ANTONYMS: safety, security

decide (v)   *Decide* means make up your mind or come to a conclusion about something. We decided to stay home.

settle   *Settle* means make a final choice after you have cleared up any doubts. We *settled* on a day for the bake sale.

resolve   *Resolve* means decide on something once and for all. I *resolved* to get to school on time. Who will *resolve* our dispute?

difficult (adj)   Something *difficult* is not easy to do or understand. A *difficult* problem requires serious thought.

hard   Something *hard* requires a great deal of work, strength, or time. It's *hard* to move a piano.

complicated   *Complicated* means difficult because something is very involved. Jigsaw puzzles are often *complicated*.

puzzling   A *puzzling* problem is difficult to solve. The detective was famous for solving *puzzling* mysteries.
ANTONYMS: easy, simple, uncomplicated

discover   Look up *find*.

display   Look up *show*.

doubt (v)   *Doubt* means feel uncertain about something. I *doubt* that Lisa will keep her promise.

question   *Question* can mean feel a little bit uncertain. Len *questioned* our route because it wasn't on the map.

distrust   *Distrust* means doubt because you don't have confidence in someone or something. I *distrust* this leaky rowboat.

suspect   *Suspect* means doubt or distrust someone or something. We *suspected* that someone was eating cherries from our tree.
ANTONYMS: believe, trust

E

end (v)   *End* means stop doing something or come to the last part. This rain should *end* soon.

cease   *Cease* means stop or come to an end. I hope that barking *ceases* before I try to go to sleep.

halt   *Halt* means end suddenly for a certain period of time. The parade *halted* in front of city hall.

finish, complete   *Finish* and *complete* mean end naturally something that has been started. Bob *finished* shoveling the walk. Did you *complete* your homework?

conclude   *Conclude* means come to an end or finish something. Ellen *concluded* her speech just as time ran out.
ANTONYMS: begin, start, commence

example (n)   An *example* is something that describes or explains another thing or serves as a model. A bear is a good *example* of an animal that hibernates.

sample   A *sample* is an example taken from a group of things. The salesman showed us some paint and wallpaper *samples*.

illustration   An *illustration* is an example that explains or helps make something clear. The book included illustrations of experimental aircraft.

model, pattern   A *model* or *pattern* is something from which other things are copied. Many inventors first make a *model* of their inventions. I followed a *pattern* when I cut the material for this dress.

F

fake (adj)   *Fake* means not real. Some *fake* furs look almost real. Cotton makes a good *fake* beard.

imitation   *Imitation* means fake. Vinyl is used to make *imitation leather*.

counterfeit   *Counterfeit* means made to look exactly alike so that it passes for the real thing. The suitcase was filled with *counterfeit* money.

false, untrue   *False* and *untrue* mean incorrect. The rumor proved to be *untrue*. The spy carried *false* identification.
ANTONYMS: real, true, genuine

fast (adj)   *Fast* means moving, happening, or acting speedily. Hockey is a *fast* game.

rapid   *Rapid* means fast in movement. A *rapid* river has a fast current. Lynn walks at a *rapid* pace.

swift   *Swift* means moving or happening very fast. Cheetahs are *swift* animals.

quick   *Quick* means fast in doing something. Mom made a *quick* breakfast before leaving for work. The bus trip was *quick* for a change.
ANTONYMS: slow, sluggish, pokey

find (v)   *Find* means come upon something that is lost or learn something new. Bess *found* a set of keys. She will *find* out who they belong to.

discover   *Discover* means find something for the first time. Dad *discovered* a leak in the roof.

detect   *Detect* means find something hidden by searching carefully for it. Margot *detected* a mistake in my computer program.

learn   *Learn* means find out or come to know something. I am *learning* to speak French.

ANTONYMS: hide, forget, lose

finish   Look up *end*.

fix   Look up *repair*.

free (v)   *Free* means set loose. The lumberjacks *freed* the log jam in the river.

release   *Release* also means set loose, but without the promise of lasting freedom. Our guide *released* the undersized trout.

liberate   *Liberate* means free or set at liberty. The citizens *liberated* themselves from their cruel rulers.

funny   Look up *humorous*.

G

gloomy   Look up *sad*.

goal   Look up *object*.

great (adj)   *Great* can mean large, outstanding, well known, or important. Jane Addams was a *great* American social worker.

notable   *Notable* means worthy of respect and admiration. Many *notable* authors attended the reception.

superior   *Superior* means higher in position or greater in size or importance. A sergeant is *superior* in rank to a corporal.

supreme   Something that is *supreme* is unequaled. The *Supreme* Court is the highest court in the United States.

ANTONYMS: small, inferior, petty, trivial, unknown

group (n)   A number of people or objects gathered together or having something in common is a *group*. A *group* of musicians visited our school. I sorted the photographs into two *groups*.

kind, category   *Kind* and *category* are words for a group of animals, objects, or ideas with something in common. An apple is a *kind* of fruit. Fruits and vegetables are separate *categories*.

class   A *class* is a group sharing the same condition. Everyone in the *class* is the same age. Some people traveled in first *class*.

set   A *set* is a number of closely related things. That was our best *set* of china. Where is my chess *set?*

guard   Look up *protect*.

H

handsome   Look up *beautiful*.

happy (adj)   *Happy* means feeling well or being pleased or glad about something. We were *happy* to visit our cousins in Chicago.

cheerful   *Cheerful* means merry and full of good spirit. My sister is *cheerful* in the morning.

pleased   You are *pleased* with someone or something if you are happy with him or it. Hugh looked *pleased* with the applause he received.

contented, satisfied   *Contented* and *satisfied* are stronger than pleased. Everyone felt *contented* sitting by the fire. I was *satisfied* with my geography grade.

ANTONYMS: sad, unhappy, melancholy, gloomy, downcast, miserable

hard   Look up *difficult*.

help (v)   *Help* means do something for another person. Would you *help* me carry these packages?

aid   *Aid* means help by giving relief to someone. The Red Cross *aids* people in an emergency.

assist   *Assist* means help someone with what they are doing. The nurses *assisted* the doctor during the operation.

improve   *Improve* means help by making something better. Practice *improved* Ida's banjo playing.

ANTONYMS: hinder, obstruct

helpful   Look up *useful*.

huge   Look up *large*.

humid   Look up *moist*.

humorous (adj)   Something or someone that makes you laugh is *humorous*. Teddy told us a *humorous* story.

amusing   *Amusing* means humorous and entertaining. We saw an *amusing* movie about monkeys.

funny   *Funny* means causing laughter. We chuckled over the *funny* antics of the chimpanzees.

comical   *Comical* means funny or amusing. All of the clowns had *comical* expressions.

ANTONYMS: grave, serious

I

idea (n)   An *idea* can be a picture in your mind, a belief, or an opinion. We discussed our *ideas* for the science fair. I have a good *idea* of where you live.

notion   A *notion* is a vague idea about something. I have some *notion* of how to repair a bicycle tire.

thought   A *thought* can be an opinion or a belief. What is your *thought* about tonight's game?

concept   A *concept* is an idea about what something is really like or what something ought to be like. We all have our *concept* of happiness.

ideal   Look up *perfect*.

immediately   Look up *suddenly*.

important (adj)   *Important* means of great value or meaning. Our team won an *important* game. Sue told us some *important* news.

chief, principal   *Chief* and *principal* mean of the greatest importance. Speeding is the *chief* reason for traffic accidents. A famous actress played the *principal* character of the play.

major   *Major* describes something more important than others. Toronto is one of the *major* cities of Canada.

main   *Main* means the most important part of something. Can you find the *main* idea in this paragraph?

significant   *Significant* means important because of some special meaning or reason. A footprint proved to be the most *significant* clue in the case.

ANTONYMS: unimportant, trivial, minor, insignificant

information (n)   *Information* is what you learn about something from facts. I had no trouble finding *information* for my report.

news   *News* is information about recent events. Dad likes to watch the evening *news* on television.

intelligence   *Intelligence* can be secret information. The spies gathered *intelligence* for their governments.

data   *Data* are facts and information from which things can be learned. The scientists gained valuable *data* from their experiment.

knowledge   *Knowledge* is a general word meaning a body of information about a particular topic. My *knowledge* of history has grown.

J

job   Look up *task*.

join (v)   *Join* means put, bring, or fasten together. I *joined* the scouts. Jill completed the electric circuit by *joining* the wires together.

combine   *Combine* means join to make a new whole. The cook *combined* many unusual ingredients.

connect   *Connect* means join or fasten things together by putting something between them. The telephone company will *connect* the phone today.

link   *Link* means join or connect. The island was *linked* to the mainland by a bridge.

attach   *Attach* means join one thing to another. Lyle will *attach* the trailer to his car.

ANTONYMS: detach, divide, separate

K

keep   Look up *save*.

kind   Look up *group*.

know (v)   *Know* means have knowledge or information about something or someone. Betty *knows* a lot about sports.

understand, realize   *Understand* and *realize* mean know something well or have a clear idea about it. Ask questions if you don't *understand* something. I suddenly *realized* that I had lost my keys.

recognize   *Recognize* means be aware of, but it also can mean know again. Gil *recognizes* his mistake. Mia *recognized* me, even though I was wearing a disguise.

knowledge   Look up *information*.

L

large (adj) *Large* describes something that is bigger than usual in size or amount. These socks are too *large*.

huge, gigantic *Huge* and *gigantic* mean much larger than usual. The *huge* oak tree was hundreds of years old. The meteor left a *gigantic* crater.

vast *Vast* means stretching over a large area. A *vast* desert stretched for as far as the eye could see.

immense, enormous *Immense* and *enormous* mean so large the size can hardly be imagined. With no land in sight, the lake looked *immense* to us. An *enormous* mountain loomed above us.

ANTONYMS: little, minute, slight, small, tiny

learn Look up *find*.

link Look up *join*.

live (v) *Live* means exist or make a home in a certain place. Mark's grandmother *lived* to be one hundred. Our family *lives* in Denver.

dwell, reside *Dwell* and *reside* mean make a home in a certain place. An ancient people *dwelt* in these cliffs. The President *resides* in the White House.

inhabit Both people and animals can *inhabit* a place. Many unusual birds *inhabit* the Galapagos Islands. Will people ever *inhabit* the moon?

occupy *Occupy* means have possession of a place. Is this seat *occupied?*

ANTONYMS: die, vacate

look (v) *Look* means turn your eyes toward something. Ned *looked* at magazines in the reception room.

see *See* means identify something by sight. We couldn't *see* in the darkened theater.

glance *Glance* means look quickly, then look away. Mr. Shaul *glanced* at his watch.

gaze *Gaze* means look for a long time. Sometimes I daydream as I *gaze* at the sea.

stare, peer *Stare* and *peer* both mean look at or into with interest. The children *stared* at the strange-looking animals. Then they *peered* curiously into the huge fish tank.

lovely Look up *beautiful*.

M

main Look up *important*.

mend Look up *repair*.

modern Look up *new*.

moist (adj) *Moist* means slightly wet. Fresh bread sometimes feels *moist*.

damp *Damp* also means somewhat wet. I cleaned off my muddy shoes with a *damp* cloth.

humid *Humid* describes air that is moist or damp. A rain forest is hot and *humid*.

juicy, succulent *Juicy* and *succulent* mean full of moisture. The meat is very *juicy*. Plums are a particularly *succulent* fruit.

ANTONYMS: dry, arid

mournful Look up *sad*.

mystery (n)   A *mystery* is something that hasn't been explained or completely understood. Scientists have been solving the *mysteries* of space travel.

problem   A *problem* can be anything that you wonder about or have to solve. These math *problems* are hard.

puzzle   A *puzzle* is a problem you solve by putting pieces, words, or information together so that it all makes sense. Mom enjoys crossword *puzzles*.

N

need   Look up *want*.

nervous   Look up *worried*.

new (adj)   *New* means just created or never before used or known of. We live in a *new* house. Is that a *new* coat? Ron is *new* to our school.

recent   *Recent* means not long past. It describes something that has just happened or been made. Do you have a *recent* copy of this magazine?

current   *Current* means happening right now or very recently. Newscasters report on *current* events.

modern   *Modern* means up-to-date or of the latest design. There are many *modern* buildings in the city.

ANTONYMS: old, obsolete, ancient

O

object (n)   An *object* is anything you can see or touch. Many of the *objects* on the table were tools. An *object* can also be something toward which an action is directed. The *object* of the game is to get your marker home first.

thing, article   *Thing* and *article* are other words for object. It's hard to see *things* in the dark. We found several discarded *articles* on the island.

purpose, goal   *Purpose* and *goal* are objects to be reached or achieved. The *purpose* of many rules is safety. Dale's *goal* is to be a doctor.

aim, intent   *Aim* and *intent* mean what you have in mind to do. Admiral Perry's *aim* was to find the North Pole. My *intent* was to surprise you.

occupy   Look up *live*.

odd (adj)   *Odd* describes something out of the ordinary. We heard an *odd* noise coming from the yard.

unusual   *Unusual* means not common, ordinary, or usual. The platypus is an *unusual* animal.

curious   *Curious* can also mean unusual. The belt has a *curious* buckle made of brass.

strange   *Strange* means odd or hard to understand. The man spoke in a *strange* language.

peculiar   *Peculiar* means odd or something not shared by others. Mary has a *peculiar* way of snapping her fingers. The kangaroo is *peculiar* to Australia.

ANTONYMS: common, ordinary, usual, familiar, natural, normal, regular

origin   Look up *beginning*.

P

perfect (adj)   *Perfect* means free from faults, defects, or errors, but it can also mean the best of its kind. No one had a *perfect* score on the test. I found the *perfect* gift for Dad.

flawless   *Flawless* means free from faults or defects. The museum has a large, *flawless* diamond. The skater's performance was *flawless*.

pure   *Pure* means not mixed with anything else. *Pure* gold is too soft for making jewelry.

ideal   *Ideal* means absolutely the very best or that something suits a purpose perfectly. This is an *ideal* spot for a picnic.

ANTONYMS: defective, imperfect

perform   Look up *act*.

pick   Look up *choose*.

plain   Look up *clear*.

polite (adj)   *Polite* people show courtesy to others. It is difficult being *polite* to someone who is rude.

courteous   *Courteous* means having good manners and being considerate of others. A *courteous* man gave up his seat to an elderly woman.

well-mannered   *Well-mannered* means having or showing good manners. Tim is too *well-mannered* not to share his cake with me.

ANTONYMS: impolite, rude

pretty   Look up *beautiful*.

problem   Look up *mystery*.

protect (v)   *Protect* means keep from harm or injury. A heavy coat *protects* you from cold weather. Goggles protect the eyes.

guard   *Guard* means watch over something and protect it from danger. Two soldiers *guarded* the entrance to the post.

shield   *Shield* means protect by using a barrier. Sunglasses help *shield* your eyes from the sun.

shelter, harbor   *Shelter* and *harbor* mean protect by offering a covering or a safe place. Our tent *sheltered* us from the rain. It is against the law to *harbor* a fugitive.

ANTONYMS: endanger, expose

put (v)   *Put* usually means move something to a place, spot, or position. Dana *put* on her gloves. I *put* the dirty dishes in the sink.

place, set   *Place* and *set* mean put in a certain position or arrangement. The beautician *set* Lilian's hair. I *placed* my books on my desk.

lay   *Lay* means put something down in a horizontal position. The bat *lay* where I dropped it.

arrange   *Arrange* means put things in some kind of order. Joe *arranged* the clothes in his dresser. Let's *arrange* our chairs in a circle.

ANTONYM: remove

Q

quarrel (n)   A *quarrel* is a fight with words. If you have a *quarrel* with someone, you disagree, have harsh words, and end up not speaking.

argument   An *argument* can also be a fight with words. Usually both sides give their reasons why their views are right. The umpire settled the *argument* between the players.

disagreement   You have a *disagreement* with someone when you do not share the same views or opinions. There was some *disagreement* about where we should go for a vacation.

dispute   A *dispute* is an argument carried on for a long period of time. The farmers had a *dispute* for years over who could use the creek.

ANTONYM: agreement

quarrel (v)   Look up *argue*.

question   Look up *doubt*.

quick   Look up *fast*.

quiet   Look up *calm* and *silent*.

R

repair (v)   *Repair* means put in good condition again. The janitor *repaired* the broken window.

fix   *Fix* is the word most often used to mean repair. My sister helped *fix* the flat tire.

mend   *Mend* means put back into shape or back in working condition. Toni *mended* the hole in her pocket with a needle and thread.

restore   *Restore* means put something back in its original condition. Some cities have *restored* their historic buildings.

ANTONYMS: break, destroy, tear

rescue   Look up *save*.

result (n)   Something that happens because of an action is called a *result*. Many people were forced to leave their homes as a *result* of the flood.

outcome   *Outcome* is similar in meaning to result. We were surprised by the *outcome* of the bobsled race.

consequence   A *consequence* is the result of something that happens or exists. One *consequence* of installing new traffic lights was fewer accidents.

rough (adj)   *Rough* is the opposite of smooth. The truck bounced over the *rough*, gravel road. This sweater feels *rough* against my skin.

uneven   *Uneven* means not straight or level. The bookshelves are *uneven*.

stormy   *Stormy* is used to describe rough weather. A *stormy* sea has huge, crashing waves.

jagged   *Jagged* describes rough, uneven, hard surfaces. Finally we reached the *jagged* summit of the mountain.

rugged   *Rugged* describes a terrain with a rough surface. The path was *rugged* and hard to walk on.

ANTONYMS: smooth, even, level

S

sad (adj)   *Sad* means the opposite of happy, pleased, or glad. I was *sad* when my pet rabbit ran away.

unhappy   *Unhappy* means not pleased or cheerful. Al was *unhappy* that the baseball game was rained out. Dad was *unhappy* with my spelling test.

mournful Mournful means full of sadness or grief. The nation was *mournful* over the death of its leader.

downcast Downcast means sad and discouraged. The players were *downcast* about their loss in the playoffs.

gloomy Gloomy means low in spirits. This dark, rainy weather has put Ethan in a *gloomy* mood.

miserable Miserable means very sad or unhappy. A cold often makes people feel *miserable*.

ANTONYMS: happy, pleased, glad, cheerful, merry

save (v) Save means hold on to or keep in your possession. I have *saved* over one thousand baseball cards. *Save* also means protect or keep from harm or danger. Doctors *save* lives.

keep Keep is a good synonym for save. I *keep* my valuable coins in the bank vault. The crew *kept* the boat from capsizing.

accumulate Accumulate means save gradually. Look at the stack of newspapers that has *accumulated* in the basement!

store Store means save for later use. Mom *stores* canned goods in the pantry. We *stored* our old sofa.

rescue Rescue means save from danger or destruction. The Coast Guard *rescued* the crew and passengers of the sinking ship.

conserve Conserve means keep from using up. We must *conserve* our endangered natural areas.

ANTONYMS: *spend, discard, squander, destroy, throw away*

say (v) Say means express a thought by using spoken words. What did you *say* to Uncle Howie when you saw him?

state State means say formally. *State* your name and address, please.

declare Declare means say publicly or seriously. Donald Bloomfield *declared* his candidacy for the Senate. "I'm afraid of the water," *declared* Marilyn.

mention Mention means refer to or call attention to as you speak. Bob *mentioned* that it was getting late.

comment Comment means state your opinion. Lots of people *commented* on my oil paintings.

show (v) Show can mean cause something to be seen. Linda *showed* me her new watch. *Show* can also mean explain or make clear. *Show* me how to start the dishwasher.

display, exhibit Display and exhibit mean show things in a way that draws people's attention. This store *displays* its merchandise attractively. Sometimes artists *exhibit* their work at art fairs.

demonstrate Demonstrate means show how something is done. A salesperson *demonstrated* how the vacuum cleaner worked.

reveal Reveal means make known something that was hidden. The newspaper will *reveal* the solution to the puzzle in tomorrow's paper.

illustrate *Illustrate* means make clear by pictures or examples. The manual *illustrates* how the computer should be connected.
ANTONYMS: conceal, hide

silent (adj) *Silent* means without any sound or noise. The class was *silent* while Enrique spoke.
quiet *Quiet* means without much noise. You are asked to be *quiet* in the library so others may read.
still *Still* means silent and motionless. After the snowstorm, the forest was *still* and peaceful.
noiseless *Noiseless* means with little or no noise. Chess is a *noiseless* game.
ANTONYMS: boisterous, loud, noisy

skillful (adj) *Skillful* means able to do something well. Lauri is a *skillful* athlete.
able, capable *Able* and *capable* mean skillful at an activity. An *able* pilot could land a plane on a highway in an emergency. I am a *capable* baby-sitter.
clever *Clever* means skillful in a quick way. Don had a *clever* answer to the riddle.
dexterous, handy *Dexterous* and *handy* mean skillful in the use of the hands. Pianists must be *dexterous*. I am *handy* at fixing things around the house.
ANTONYMS: unskillful, awkward, clumsy

smash Look up *break*.

start Look up *beginning*.

strange Look up *odd*.

suddenly (adv) *Suddenly* means happening very quickly or unexpectedly. The roller coaster stopped *suddenly*.
unexpectedly *Unexpectedly* means happening suddenly or without any preparation or warning. The phone rang *unexpectedly* at 3:00 a.m.
abruptly *Abruptly* means both suddenly and unexpectedly. The meeting ended *abruptly* when the chairperson got up and left.
instantly, immediately *Instantly* and *immediately* mean happening very quickly or without delay. The room was *instantly* silent. Josh volunteered *immediately* to help us paint the mural.
ANTONYMS: gradually, deliberately, unhurriedly

T

task (n) A *task* is a certain amount of work that must be done. Pete was given the *task* of cleaning the car.
job A job can be any work you do. Painting the house was quite a *job*. Peg's older sister found a summer *job*.
chore A *chore* is a regular task or job. My *chores* include setting the table, washing the dishes, and taking out the garbage.
assignment An *assignment* is a task you are assigned or required to do. What is the homework *assignment* for tomorrow?

thing Look up *object*.

thought Look up *idea*.

threat   Look up *danger*.

throw (v)   *Throw* means use your hands and arms to make something move through the air. Who *threw* that snowball?

toss, cast   *Toss* and *cast* means throw lightly in a particular direction. Please *toss* me a pencil. We *cast* our fishing lines into the stream.

pitch   *Pitch* means throw something at a target. Our neighbors like to *pitch* horseshoes.

fling, hurl   *Fling* and *hurl* mean throw forcefully in a general direction. Lionel *flung* his jacket on the floor. The quarterback *hurled* the football fifty yards.

transform   Look up *change*.

transparent   Look up *clear*.

U

understand   Look up *know*.

uneven   Look up *rough*.

unhappy   Look up *sad*.

untrue   *Look up false*.

unusual   Look up *odd*.

useful (adj)   *Useful* means being of use. A road map is *useful* on a long car trip.

helpful   *Helpful* means being of help. Dad is *helpful* around the house. A flashlight is *helpful* in the dark.

handy   *Handy* can mean something that saves trouble and is easy to use. A can opener is a *handy* tool to have in the kitchen.

serviceable   *Serviceable* means useful because something does what is expected or gives good service. This car may be old, but it is still *serviceable*.
ANTONYMS: useless, helpless

V

vary   Look up *change*.

vast   Look up *large*.

visible (adj)   *Visible* means easily seen. The stars are *visible* on a clear night.

noticeable   *Noticeable* describes something that attracts attention. There is a *noticeable* crack in the living room wall.

conspicuous   *Conspicuous* describes something that stands out because it is different, very easily seen, or out of place. Do you think these red shoes are too *conspicuous*?

apparent   *Apparent* means clearly visible, easy to understand, or obvious. Toward the end of the game, it became *apparent* which team would win. Her surprise was *apparent*.
ANTONYMS: hidden, concealed, inconspicuous

W

walk (v)   *Walk* means move or go on foot. You *walk* when you raise one foot at a time and step forward.

stroll   *Stroll* means walk slowly or leisurely. The couple *strolled* along the beach.

prance   *Prance* means walk with a

springing motion. Horses often prance when they are in a parade.

march *March* means walk steadily with a certain rhythm, often in step with others. The band *marched* down the street.

strut, swagger *Strut* and *swagger* mean walk in a proud or boastful way. The drum major *struts* at the head of the band. The bully *swaggered* down the street.

shuffle *Shuffle* means walk without raising your feet very far off the ground. My little sister *shuffles* her feet when she is tired.

trudge *Trudge* means walk with a lot of effort. The children *trudged* home through the snow.

plod *Plod* means walk slowly and heavily. The old horse *plods* along the path.

want (v) If you *want* something, you would like to have or get or do it. Leo *wants* to go swimming with us. Peter *wanted* a microscope for his birthday.

wish *Wish* means want or hope for something. Arthur was *wishing* for a new bike. The fans *wished* for a miracle.

desire *Desire* means want very much, but it is used more formally. People everywhere *desire* peace.

crave *Crave* means want something badly. My cat *craves* a lot of attention.

need *Need* means not able to do without. Everyone *needs* plenty of sleep. I *need* this book to finish my report.

well-mannered Look up *polite*.

win (v) *Win* means gain victory or success. One contestant will *win* a trip to Hawaii. Which team *won?*

succeed You *succeed* when you accomplish what you set out to do. The runner *succeeded* in jumping all the hurdles. Marvin's new business is *succeeding* very well.

triumph *Triumph* means gain victory or rejoice after a victory. Our team *triumphed* in the playoffs.

prevail *Prevail* means win against great odds or because of greater strength. Jack *prevailed* against the giant.

ANTONYMS: lose, give

worried (adj) *Worried* means filled with doubt or fear about something. Elio was *worried* about making the swim team.

concerned *Concerned* means interested and worried about something. A group of *concerned* citizens met with the mayor.

troubled, disturbed *Troubled* and *disturbed* mean upset or uneasy. After seeing a horror movie, I had a *troubled* sleep. Fred is *disturbed* that he lost his notebook.

nervous *Nervous* means uneasy and even jumpy. I was so *nervous* about the test that I couldn't sit still.

anxious *Anxious* means extremely uneasy or fearful. The settlers became *anxious* about the coming bitter winter.

ANTONYMS: calm, easy, unconcerned

Index

Acknowledgments (cont.)

for Children. Used by permission of Highlights for Children, Inc., Columbus, Ohio; **p. 364**: Betsy Byars, *The Midnight Fox*. New York: The Viking Press, 1968, pp. 15–17; **pp. 376–378**: Joan W. Blos, adapted from *A Gathering of Days*. Copyright © 1979 Joan W. Blos. Reprinted with the permission of Charles Scribner's Sons, an imprint of Macmillan Publishing Company and Curtis Brown, Ltd. **pp. 408–411**: From "Dogging It Through the Wilderness" in *National Wildlife*, February–March 1986. Copyright © 1986 by the National Wildlife Federation. Reprinted by permission of National Wildlife; **p. 421**: From *Readers' Guide to Periodical Literature*. Copyright © 1986, 1987 by The H.W. Wilson Company. Material reproduced by permission of the publisher. **p. 425**: From "guide dog" in *Encyclopaedia Britannica*, 15th edition (1982), IV:784–785. Copyright © 1982 by Encyclopaedia Britannica, Inc. Reprinted by permission: **p. 425**: Carl Burger, *All About Dogs*. New York: Random House, Inc., 1962, pp. 42–43: **p. 458**: "The Fox and the Thrush" from *Three Rolls and One Doughnut* by Mirra Ginsburg. Text copyright © 1970 by Mirra Ginsburg. Reprinted by permission of the author; **p. 459**: Maude Barrows Dutton, *The Tortoise and the Geese and Other Fables of Bidpai*. Boston: 1908; **p. 459**: Thomas Bewick, *The Fables of Aesop with Designs on Wood*, 1818; **pp. 460–461**: "Far Looker" from *Hostiles and Friendlies* by Mari Sandoz. Copyright © 1959 by The University of Nebraska Press. Reprinted by permission of McIntosh and Otis, Inc.

Illustrations

Mike Carroll, Steven Clay, Communication Design Group Inc., Ralph Creasman, Mary Flock, Susan Friedman, Cary Lachman, Jim Lange, Lipman and Simon Inc., Bob Magheris, Cindy Maniates, Kurt Mitchell, Yoshi Miyake, Steve Musgrave, Eileen Mueller Neill, Kathy Petrauskas, Roger Schillerstrom, Tom Tomeck, Jack Wallen, John Walters and Associates, Don Wilson.

Photographs

All photographs not credited, and those taken expressly for Scott, Foresman, are the property of Scott, Foresman and Company. Dana Arnett: **pp. 133, 385**; Mark Battrell: **pp. 197, 216, 226, 230, 232, 233, 236–238, 384**; David Bentley: **pp. 23, 259, 263, 346**; Ellen Cocose: **pp. 71, 81, 311**; Ron Gordon: **pp. 138, 152, 183, 220, 368, 397, 448–449, 484, 489**; Allan Landau: **pp. 93, 102**; Michael Goss: **pp. 119, 299, 309**; Dewey Hentges: **pp. 266, 390**.
p. 13: Printed by permission of the Estate of Norman Rockwell; **p. 18**: Reprinted with permission from *The Saturday Evening Post Society*, A division of B.F.L. and M.S., Inc. © 1985; **p. 19 L**: Reprinted with permission from *The Saturday Evening Post Society*, A division of B.F.L. and M.S., Inc. © 1985; **p. 19 R**: Reprinted with permission from *The Saturday Evening Post Society*, A division of B.F.L. and M.S., Inc. © 1983; **p. 84**: H. Armstrong Roberts; **p. 89**: Art Wolfe/Aperture; **p. 111**: Mount Everest Foundation; **p. 124**: © Richard Howard; **p. 129**: D. Hallinan/FPG; **p. 134**: Jane Burton/Bruce Coleman Inc.; **p. 141**: Robert P. Carr; **p. 143**: (Claude Monet, On the Seine at Bennecourt, 1868, Potter Palmer Collection.) The Art Institute of Chicago; **p. 159**: D. Lyons/Bruce Coleman Inc.; **p. 171**: Ron Thomas/FPG; **p. 202**: © 1986 Mickey Pfeger; **p. 246 All**: © 1985 Dan Lamont; **p. 253**: Frank Müller-May/Woodfin Camp & Associates; **p. 263**: From the map of Illinois. Copyright © by Rand McNally & Co. Reprinted by permission; **p. 292**: Chicago Historical Society; **p. 294 All**: The Bettmann Archive; **p. 316**: Jim Brandenburg; **p. 321**: David Falconer/David R. Frazier Photolibrary; **p. 324**: David Black; **p. 358**: Mickey Palmer/DPI; **p. 363**: Don Landwehrle/The Image Bank; **p. 376**: Honi Werner, Jacket illustration from *A Gathering of Days* by Joan W. Blos. Copyright © 1979 Joan W. Blos. Reprinted with permission of Charles Scribner's Sons, an imprint of Macmillan Publishing Company; **p. 407**: Brett Froomer/The Image Bank; **pp. 408–409 All**: Kevin Horan; **p. 452**: U.S. Geological Survey; **p. 480**: National Portrait Gallery, Smithsonian Institution, Gift of the Morris and Gwendolyn Cafritz Foundation and the Regents Major Acquisition Fund; **p. 491**: Douglas Mazonowicz/Alpha; **p. 496**: THE PEACEABLE KINGDOM by Edward Hicks, ca. 1840–1845, The Brooklyn Museum, Dick S. Ramsay Fund.